A Diplomat in Japan

A Diplomat in Japan

The inner history of the critical years in the evolution of Japan when the ports were opened and the monarchy restored, recorded by a diplomatist who took an active part in the events of the time, with an account of his personal experiences during that period

Sir Ernest Satow

STONE BRIDGE CLASSICS
Stone Bridge Press
Berkeley, California

YOHAN
YOHAN CLASSICS
IBC Publishing
Tokyo, Japan

Originally published in 1921 by Seeley, Service, & Co. Limited, London.

Published simultaneously in the United States by Stone Bridge Press, P.O. Box 8208, Berkeley, California 94707, www.stonebridge.com, and in Japan by IBC Publishing, Akasaka Community Bldg 5F, 1-1-8 Moto- Akasaka, Minato-Ku, Tokyo 107-0051, www.ibcpub.co.jp.

Trade distribution in the United States and Canada by Consortium Book Sales and in Japan by Yohan, Inc.

For information on distribution and purchase worldwide contact Stone Bridge Press at sbp@stonebridge.com, 510-524-8732 (tel), or 510-524-8711 (fax).

Cover and book design by Robert Goodman, Silvercat™ San Diego, California.

Printed in the United States of America.

2011 2010 2009 2008 2007 2006   10 9 8 7 6 5 4 3 2 1

ISBN 978-1-933330-16-7 (USA)
ISBN 978-4-89684-289-0 (Japan)

Contents

Ernest Satow, c.1865-66.

INSIDE THE LOWER BATTERY AT SIMONOSAKI AFTER THE CONFLICT.
FROM *ILLUSTRATED LONDON NEWS*, DECEMBER 24, 1864.

CHAPTER I

Appointment As Student Interpreter At Yedo (1861)

My thoughts were first drawn to Japan by a mere accident. In my eighteenth year an elder brother brought home from Mudie's Library the interesting account of Lord Elgin's Mission to China and Japan by Lawrence Oliphant, and the book having fallen to me in turn, inflamed my imagination with pictures verbal and coloured of a country where the sky was always blue, where the sun shone perpetually, and where the whole duty of man seemed to consist in lying on a matted floor with the windows open to the ground towards a miniature rockwork garden, in the company of rosy-lipped black-eyed and attentive damsels — in short, a realised fairyland. But that I should ever have a chance of seeing these Isles of the Blest was beyond my wildest dreams. An account of Commodore Perry's expedition, which had preceded Lord Elgin's Mission, came in my way shortly afterwards, and though much more sober in its outward appearance and literary style, only served to confirm the previous impression. I thought of nothing else from that time onwards. One day, on entering the library of University College, London, where I was then studying, I found lying on the table a notice that three nominations to student-interpreterships in China and Japan had been placed at the disposition of the Dean. Here was the chance for which I had been longing. Permission to enter myself for the competition was obtained, not without difficulty, from my parents, and having gained the first place in the public examination, I chose Japan. To China I never wished or intended to go. My age was sufficient by a few hours to enable me to compete. I was formally appointed in August 1861, and quitted England full of joyful anticipation in November of that year.

Owing to the prevalence of a belief among those who then had the direction of our affairs in Japan that a knowledge of Chinese was a necessary preliminary to the study of Japanese, my fellow-student, R. A. Jamieson, and myself were at first stationed for a few months at Peking, where we were joined early in 1862 by Russell Robertson, who also belonged to the Japan establishment. I pass over our sojourn there, which, though not without its own interest, was not long enough for me to gain any useful knowledge of China. But I learnt a few hundred Chinese characters which were of great help to me afterwards, and I even began the study of Manchu.

Our stay at the Chinese capital was suddenly cut short by the arrival of a despatch from Yedo, containing the original text of a Note from the Japanese Ministers, which it was found no Chinaman could decipher, much less understand. This was decisive of the question whether the short cut to Japanese lay through the Chinese language. I thought then, and still think, that though an acquaintance with Chinese characters may be found useful by the student of Japanese, it is no more indispensable than that of Latin is to a person who wishes to acquire Italian or Spanish. We were consequently bundled off to Japan with the least possible delay.

Of the eight students belonging to the China establishment then at Peking, three only are still (1885) in the service — H. J. Allen, C. T. Gardner, and W. G. Stronach, each of whom attained the rank of consul in 1877. They had all passed the examination at the same time as myself. The man who came out second was "allowed to resign" in 1867, three are dead, and one, the best man of the whole set, and who oddly enough was last or last but one in the examination list, passed in 1872 into the Chinese Customs Service, in which he now holds one of the highest appointments.

So unequal are the results obtained by even limited competitive examination. When the competition was afterwards thrown open to the public, the results became even more uncertain, as later experience has shown, at least in Japan, and perhaps elsewhere.

The great fault of the system is that it takes no account of moral qualities. Whether a candidate has the manners or feelings of a gentleman cannot be ascertained from the way in which he will reproduce a proposition of Euclid or translate a passage from a Greek author. It does not test the intellectual powers, for a stupid young man who has been properly coached will almost always beat the real student who has not got the right "tips." Nowadays, every candidate for a public examination goes to a crammer, who trains him in a few months for the contest, and enables him to bring forth forced fruit for a moment. Show me a successful examinee, and I will show you a well-coached candidate. In the majority of cases the process disgusts the man who has undergone it, and takes away any inclination he may previously have had for study. And without serious study it is not possible to acquire such languages as Chinese, Siamese or Japanese. The scheme of examination is no test of the linguistic capabilities of the men, and sometimes sends into the service those who can no more learn to speak a foreign language than they can fly. My own success in the examination was due to my having left school more recently than any of the other competitors.

While I was at Peking the whole body of students was invited to dine one evening with the Bishop of Victoria, who was stopping at the Legation in the absence of Mr Bruce, the Minister. The conversation fell upon the effects of Chinese studies on the intellectual powers, and the Bishop inquired of us whether we did not find that the mind was weakened by close application to such a dry, unproductive form of learning. At least, his own experience had been to that effect. This was a curious admission to make, but the matter of his conversation certainly corroborated it. I do not think any of us was candid enough to confess to a similar result in his own case.

I should like to dwell longer on our life in Peking — the rides in the early morning over the plain on the north of the city, excursions to the ruins of the Summer Palace, beautiful still in its desolation, the monasteries among the blue mountains west of the city, the magnificent temples inside and outside the walls, the dirt and dust of the streets in wet or fine weather, the pink lotus blossoms on the lake of the marble bridge, the beggars with their cry of *K'olien, k'olien, shang i-ko ta,* the bazaar outside the Ch'ien Men Gate, with its attractive shops, the Temple of Heaven, the view of yellow, brown and green-tiled roofs embosomed in trees as one saw them from the city wall, the carts bumping over the stone pavements worn into deep ruts, the strange Eastern life that surrounded a band of boys fresh from school or college or their mothers' apron-strings, and the splendour of the newly restored buildings of the Liang Kung Fu, occupied by the British Legation — which will never be effaced from my memory: but there is no time. Mr, afterwards Sir Frederick, Bruce was then our Minister there, a tall man of about fifty, with a noble forehead and brown eyes, grey beard, whiskers and moustache; altogether a beautiful appearance. The Chinese Secretary was Mr, afterwards Sir Thomas, Wade, a great Chinese scholar, to whom we looked up with awe, and who was said to be of an irascible temper. A story was told of his visiting the Chinese Ministers with the chief, and waxing very warm in argument. The president of the Ts'ung-li Ya-mên remarked: "But, Mr Wade, I do not observe that Mr Bruce is so angry." "D'ye hear that, Mr Bruce, they say you're not angry." Whereupon Mr Bruce, with a benevolent smile and with the most good-tempered expression in the world, replied: "Oh, tell them I'm in a deuce of a rage."

We, that is to say Jamieson, Robertson and myself, got away early on the morning of August 6, arriving that evening at Ho-si-wu, a town on the way, and reached Tientsin next day. Thence we took boat to Taku, where we passed some days under the hospitable roof of the Vice-Consul Gibson. He was later on transferred to a post in Formosa, where he got into difficulties with the Chinese officials and called on the commander of a gunboat to bombard the Custom House, for which he was smartly reprimanded by the Foreign Office. Shortly afterwards he died, it was said, of a broken heart. This happened in the days when the so-called "gun-boat" policy was no longer in favour, and poor Gibson fell a victim to his excess of zeal.

At Shanghai Jamieson left us, to start a newspaper on terms which promised him a better future than the Consular service could offer. Robertson and I embarked in the steamer *Lancefield*, and started for Japan on September 2. The first land we sighted after leaving the coast of China was Iwô-Shima, a volcanic island to the south of Kiûshiû, and on the 7th we found ourselves close to Cape Idzu in a fog. Luckily it lifted for a moment, and the captain, who was new to the coast, ordered the ship to be put about, and we ran down among the islands. Next morning early we were steaming over the blue waves east of Vries Island, passed the serrated wooded range of Nokogiri-yama on our right and the tiny inlet of Uraga to our left, and stood across the broad bay towards Yokohama. It was one of those brilliant days that are so characteristic of Japan, and as we made our way up the bay of Yedo, I thought no scenery in the world could surpass it. Irregular-shaped hills, covered with dark-green trees, lined the whole southern coast, and above them rose into the air for 12,000 feet and more the magnificent cone of Fuji, with scarcely a patch of snow visible. The noble ranges of Oyama and others bounded the plain on its western side, while by way of contrast, a low-lying sandy coast trended rapidly away on our right, and speedily sank below the horizon in the direction of the capital.

Curious duck-shaped boats of pure unpainted wood, carrying a large four-square sail formed of narrow strips of canvas loosely tacked together, crowded the surface of the sparkling waters. Now and then we passed near enough to note the sunburnt, copper-coloured skins of the fishermen, naked, with the exception of a white cloth round the loins, and sometimes a blue rag tied across the nose, so that you could just see his eyes and chin. At last the white cliffs of Mississippi Bay became closer and more distinct:

we rounded Treaty Point and dropped anchor on the outer edge of the shipping. After the lapse of more than a year I had at last attained my cherished object.

CHAPTER II

Yokohama Society, Official and Unofficial (1862)

Three years had now elapsed since the opening of the country to foreign trade in consequence of the Treaties of 1858, and a considerable number of merchants had settled at the ports of Nagasaki and Yokohama. Hakodaté, however, offered then, as now, few attractions to mercantile enterprise, and being far removed from the political centre, shared very slightly in the uneasy feeling which prevailed elsewhere. At Nagasaki most of the territorial nobles of Western Japan had establishments whither they sent for sale the rice and other produce received in payment of tribute from the peasants, and their retainers came into frequent contact with foreigners, whose houses they visited for the purchase of arms, gunpowder and steamers. Some sort of friendly feeling thus sprang up, which was increased by the American missionaries who gave instruction in English to younger members of this class, and imparted to them liberal ideas which had no small influence on the subsequent course of events. At Yokohama, however, the foreign merchants had chiefly to do with a class of adventurers, destitute of capital and ignorant of commerce. Broken contracts and fraud were by no means uncommon. Foreigners made large advances to men of straw for the purchase of merchandise which was never delivered, or ordered manufactures from home on the account of men who, if the market fell, refused to accept the goods that would now bring them in only a loss. Raw silk was adulterated with sand or fastened with heavy paper ties, and every separate skein had to be carefully inspected before payment, while the tea could not be trusted to be as good as the sample. Now and then a Japanese dealer would get paid out in kind, but the balance of wrong-doing was greatly against the native aud the conviction that Japanese was a synonym for dishonest trader became so firmly seated in the minds of foreigners that it was impossible for any friendly feeling to exist.

The Custom House officials were in the highest degree corrupt, and demanded ever-increasing bribes from the foreigners who sought to elude the import duties. One of the worst abuses was the importation of large quantities of wines, beer, spirits and stores, for which exemption from the payment of duty was claimed as goods intended for "personal use."

The local administration was carried on by a large staff of officials established at the Custom House. There were two *Bugiô*, or Governors; two *Kumi-gashira*, or Vice-Governors; two *Metsuké*, whose function was that of keeping an eye on the doings of the others; a number of *Shirabé-yaku*, or Directors; and *Jô-yaku*, or chief clerks, besides a host of scribes, interpreters, tidewaiters and policemen, in black or green robes. Dutch was the common medium of communication both orally and in writing, for English was as yet scarcely studied by the natives, and the foreigners who could speak Japanese might be counted on the fingers of one hand. Yet all knew a little. A sort of bastard language had been invented for the uses of trade, in which the Malay words *peggi* and *sarampan* played a great part, and with the addition of *anata* and *arimasu* every one fancied himself competent to settle the terms of a complicated transaction. In this new tongue all the rich variety of Japanese speech, by which the relative social position of the speakers is indicated, and the intricate inflexion of the verbs, were conspicuous by their absence. Outside the settlements it was of course not understood, and its use by Europeans must have contributed not a little to the contempt for the "barbarian" which was characteristic of the native attitude towards foreigners.

By virtue of the treaties Kanagawa had been at first fixed upon for the residence of Europeans, but, lying on the Tôkaidô, or principal highway between Yedo and Kiôto it was only too well calculated to afford occasion for collision between the armed followers of the Japanese nobles and the foreign settlers. Early in the day the Tycoon's government sought to avoid this difficulty by erecting a Custom House and rows of wooden bungalows at the fishing village of Yokohama, across the shallow bay to the south. Some of the foreign representatives, more intent upon enforcing Treaty provisions than desirous of meeting the convenience of the native ofiicials and the European merchants, strongly opposed this arrangement, but the practical advantages of proximity to the anchorage and personal security won the favour of the merchants, and Yokohama became recognised as the port. Long after, and perhaps to this day, the foreign consuls continued to date their official reports from Kanagawa, though they were safely ensconced at the rival site, where a town of 100,000 inhabitants now exists, and curious stories are told of the difference in freight that used to be earned on goods shipped from Europe to Yokohama or Kanagawa as the case might be.

The foreign settlement, for greater security, was surrounded on the land side by wide canals, across which bridges were thrown, while ingress and egress were controlled by strong guards of soldiers placed there with the double object of excluding dangerous characters and levying a tax on the supplies introduced from the surrounding country. At first land was given away freely to all applicants, some of whom were employés of the different consulates. These latter afterwards sold their lots to new arrivals bent upon commercial pursuits, and thus pocketed gains to which they had no shadow of a right. When further additions were afterwards made to the "settlement," precautions were taken which effectually prevented any one, whether merchant or official, from obtaining land without paying an adequate price. Later on, title-deeds were made out, by which the ground was conveyed to the holders, their heirs, administrators, executors and assigns, thus creating a form of property new to English experience, which purported to be at once real and personal. Streets were laid out with but little thought of the general convenience, aud slight provision for the future. The day of wheeled carriages had not dawned upon Japan. It was sufficient if space were left for handcarts, and the most important Japanese commercial town of the future was thus condemned in perpetuity to inconveniences of traffic, the like of which can be best appreciated by those who knew the central parts of business London fifty years ago, or the successive capitals of the Italian kingdom when they were raised to that rank. Architectural ambition at first was contented with simple wooden bungalows, and in the latter part of 1862 there were not more than half a dozen two-storied buildings in the foreign portion of the town.

Behind the settlement lay a newly filled-in tract of ground known as the "swamp," still unoccupied except by a racecourse track, and in the rear of this again, across a foul marsh, were conspicuous the flimsy buildings of the Yoshiwara, euphemistically described by a noble Duke from his place in Parliament as an "establishment for the education of young ladies," and where a colonial bishop, to the intense amusement of the younger and more irreverent of the foreign community, had innocently left his visiting-card upon the elderly female who presided over the pleasures of the place. But in those days all the residents were young.

Two churches, however, had already been erected, by Catholics and Protestants respectively, and a foreign cemetery had been set apart on the outside of the settlement. The health enjoyed by the European and American inhabitants was such that the only occupants of the burial-ground were some Russian officers aud two Dutch merchant captains, who had fallen victims to the deadly and mistaken patriotism of Japanese *samurai* (two-sworded men). No one had yet succumbed to disease in that beautiful sunny climate.

The foreign community of Yokohama of that day was somewhat extravagantly described by an English diplomat as "the scum of Europe." No doubt there was a fair sprinkling of men who, suddenly relieved from the restraints which social opinion places upon their class at home, and exposed to the temptations of Eastern life, did not conduct themselves with the strict propriety of students at a theological college. That they were really worse than their coequals elsewhere is unlikely. But in a small community, where the actions of everyone are semi-public and concealment is not regarded as an object of first-rate importance, the vices that elsewhere pass unnoticed become prominent to the eyes of those who are not exposed to the same temptations. There were also not a few who came there without much capital to make a livelihood, or, if possible, something more, and hastened to the attainment of their object without being troubled with much scruple. And the difficulty which soon presented itself of obtaining a sufficiency of native coin in exchange for the silver dollar of Eastern commerce was the cause of extravagant demands being presented to the Japanese Treasury. But the compromise eventually arrived at, by which the merchant had to buy his *ichibus* in the open market, while the official obtained the equivalent of his salary, and often much more, in native coin nearly weight for weight of his "Mexicans," was to the minds of all unprejudiced persons a far greater scandal. Detractors said that the advantages thus given to Ministers, Consuls, sailors and soldiers was a bribe to induce their compliance with violation of treaty stipulations to the prejudice of their non-official countrymen; but this is unfair. It was the result of false theories as to the nature and function of money, and personal interest worked against a conversion to views more in accordance with the principles of political economy.

The fact, however, remains, that in September 1862 the current rate of exchange was 214 *ichibus* for 100 dollars, though the latter were really exchangeable for 311 *ichibus* according to the Treaty. Each diplomatic or consular establishment was allowed to exchange monthly a certain number of dollars, supposed to represent the total salaries of the staff, and other government charges, thirteen *ichibus* per $100 being deducted for coinage. An official whose salary was $100 received 298 *ichibus*, the surplus of which over his bazaar expenses he proceeded to change back into dol-

lars; but practically he received $139.25, or a profit of nearly 40 per
cent. The gains of a Minister whose salary was £3000 a year it
may easily be seen were very large. This was not all. The balance
of the monthly quota of *ichibus* was then reconverted into dollars,
the amount due to the official chest was deducted, and the profit
then divided among the staff in proportion to their salaries. On a
nominally small income it was consequently possible to live well,
keep a pony and drink champagne. As time went on, the number of
ichibus thus put into circulation increased, and the rate of exchange
eventually declined to par. Then and only then the system was
abandoned. Where the money came from that was thus transferred
to the pockets of officials can be best explained by those who are
versed in economical questions . For my own part, I cannot look
back on that period without shame, and my only excuse, which is
perhaps of little worth in the court of history, is that I was at the
bottom of the ladder, and received the proportion paid to me by
those who were in charge of the business.

A few words may be devoted to describing the Yokohama society
of those days. There were few ladies in the settlement. Japan was a
long way from Europe, with no regular steam communication, and
the lives of foreigners were supposed to be not very safe at the hands
of the arm-bearing classes. The two great China firms of Jardine,
Matheson & Co. and Dent & Co. were of course represented. The
latter came down with a crash a year or two after my arrival. Fletcher
& Co., another important Shanghai firm, had a branch, and so had
Barnet & Co., both now long forgotten. Most of the remainder were
Japan firms, amongst whom Aspinall, Cornes & Co., Macpherson,
Marshall & Co., were the foremost English, and Walsh, Hall &
Co., the leading American firms. Germans, French and Dutch were
considered of "no account." Money was abundant, or seemed to be,
every one kept a pony or two, and champagne flowed freely at frequent convivial entertainments. Races were held in the spring and
autumn, and "real" horses competed in some of the events. A favourite Sunday's excursion was the ride along the Tôkaidô to Kawasaki
for tiffin, and back again toward evening. Longer outings were to

Kanazawa, Kamakura and Enoshima; but anyone who had ventured as far as Hachiôji or Hakoné, which were beyond the Treaty limits, was regarded as a bold, adventurous spirit. The privilege of travelling beyond a distance of 25 miles from Yokohama was reserved to the diplomatic representatives of foreign powers, and Yedo could be visited only in the disguise of a member of one of the legations, with the permission of its head. Such favours were regarded with extreme jealousy by those who were debarred by circumstances from obtaining them, and loud murmurs were heard that it was the Ministers' duty to invite his countrymen to the capital, and give them board and lodging, irrespective of the shape which their private relations with him might have assumed. Then, and perhaps even yet, there existed a theory that public servants were practically the servants of the extremely small section of the public that inhabited Yokohama, and when the servants failed to comply with the wishes of their employers they were naturally and rightly abused — behind their backs.

So strong was the hostility excited in the breasts of the English-Scotch-Irish portion of the community by the unlucky phrase, "scum of Europe," that no member of either legation or consulate of their country was allowed admittance into the Yokohama Club, composed chiefly of British merchants; and this feeling lasted until the year 1865 brought about a permanent change in the representation of Great Britain. The excuse for such relations between the British residents and one who ought to have been the leader of the small society, is to be found in the comparative youthfulness and ignorance of the world which characterised the former. The experience of men and manners which saves the dwellers in Little Peddlington from believing that others are deliberately plotting to inflict insults on them is seldom attained before middle life, especially when Little Peddlington happens to be located in an Eastern land where the mind's growth comes to a standstill, and a man's age is virtually to be reckoned by the years actually spent in the mother country. For all purposes of mental and moral development the time passed on the opposite side of the world must be left out of the calculation.

It was agreed in the Treaties that Yedo should be the residence of the foreign diplomatic representatives, and four Buddhist mon-asteries had, in accordance with Japanese custom, been assigned to the representatives of the four chief powers — Great Britain, France, Holland and the United States. Sir R. Alcock* occupied Tô-zen-ji, in the suburb of Takanawa; M. de Graef van Polsbrock lived in Chô-ô-ji, a little nearer the city; then came Sai-kai-ji, the residence of M. Duchesne de Bellecourt; and Mr Harris had settled down at Zem-puku-ji in Azabu. But a series of alarming occurrences had caused the European portion of the diplomatic body to trans-fer their quarters to Yokohama, and the American Minister alone held out, declaring his confidence in the good faith of the Japanese Government and their ability to protect him. In September of 1862 he had already been replaced by General Pruyn, who followed the example of his predecessor, until eventually driven out of the capital by a fire which destroyed his house, whether purely accidental or maliciously contrived. The English legation in 1861 had been the object of a murderous attack in which the Secretary, Mr Laurence Oliphant, and Mr G. C. Morrison were wounded. The assailants were principally retainers of the *Daimiô* of Mito, but others belonging to various clans were concerned in the affair, and some of these are still living. Sir R. Alcock had consequently removed to Yokohama, where the strong guard placed by the Japanese government at the entrances to the town and the foreign men-of-war in the harbour offered sufficient guarantees for safety. On his quitting Japan for a term of leave early in 1862, his locum-tenens, Colonel Neale, not believing in a danger of which he had no experience, brought the legation back to Tô-zen-ji. But he had no sooner installed himself there than an event occurred which led him to change his opinion. This was nothing less than the murder of the sentry who stood at his

---

* It would be inconvenient to observe chronological exactness in matters of official rank or title, which in the case of most individuals are subject to progression. I shall speak therefore of persons by the titles they bore at the latest portion of the period covered by these reminiscences.

bedroom door and of a corporal on his rounds, at the hands of one of the Japanese guard, in revenge for an insult offered to him, it is said, by the youngest member of the staff, a heedless boy of fifteen or sixteen. So the British Legation packed up their archives and hastened back to Yokohama, where they installed themselves in a house that stood on the site of the present Grand Hotel. This building belonged to an Englishman named Hoey, who was murdered in his bed in 1870, apparently from motives of private revenge. The foreign consuls were all stationed at Yokohama with the exception of the American consul, Colonel Fisher, who remained at Kanagawa. Mr Harris, it is said, would never admit that Yokohama could be rightfully substituted for Kanagawa, the town mentioned in the Treaty, and would not permit his consul to reside there. He even carried his opposition so far as to declare that he never would countenance the change of settlement, and carried out his vow by leaving Japan without having set foot in Yokohama.

At the time of my arrival there, Colonel Neale, an old warrior who had seen service with the Spanish Legion commanded by Sir de Lacy Evans, and who, gossip said, regarded Sir R. Alcock, formerly attached to the Marine Brigade of Portugal in the quality of surgeon, with no friendly feelings, was Secretary of Legation, and consequently chargé d'affaires in the absence of his chief. He had great command of his pen, and composed most drastic Notes to the Japanese Government, some of which have been printed by my friend, Mr F. O. Adams in his *History of Japan*. He had previously been consul at Varna and Belgrade, and consequently had a sufficient experience of the system known as "extra-territoriality," which in most non-Christian countries of the East exempts Europeans from the operations of the local law. In stature considerably less than the average Englishman, he wore a heavy grey moustache, and thin wisps of grizzled hair wandered about his forehead. His temper was sour and suspicious. Of his political capacity there is not much to be said, except that he did not understand the circumstances amongst which he was thrown, as his despatches sufficiently indicate, well-written and incisive as they are. But this is only an example of the fact that power of speech with tongue or pen is not a measure of a man's fitness for the conduct of affairs. In his jovial moments he easily unbent, and would entertain his companions with snatches of operas of which he carried a large assortment in his memory.

At this period he was about fifty-five, and probably already affected with the beginnings of the disease which carried him off a few years later at Quito.

The second in rank was the so-called Japanese Secretary. He was neither a native of Japan nor had he any knowledge of the language, so that the title must be understood as signifying "secretary in charge of correspondence with the Japanese Government." At our mission in China there is always an official who bears the corresponding title of Chinese Secretary, but there the post has always been held by a scholar. Dutch was the only European language of which the Japanese knew anything, and therefore when the Foreign Office came to provide a staff of officials for the consular establishment, they sought high and low for Englishmen acquainted with that recondite tongue. Four were at last discovered, one of whom was first appointed interpreter to the legation and afterwards accorded the higher title. Part of his salary was expressly granted by way of remuneration for instructing the student-interpreters in the language of the country, and consequently could not be said to be earned. He retained his office for eight years, when a consulate became vacant, and the opportunity was at once seized of "kicking him up the ladder." All the domestic virtues were his, and of actively bad qualities he showed no trace.

Next to this gentleman came a First Assistant, sociable and accomplished, musical, artistic and speaking many languages beside his own, but no lover of hard work. In his hands the accounts fell eighteen months in arrear, and the registers of correspondence were a couple of years behind hand. It was his function to preside over the chancery, and he left it to his successor in a condition which the latter aptly compared to that of an "Aegean stable." He was the sort of man who is always known among his friends by his Christian name, and no higher tribute to personal qualities is possible. In the course of time he became a consul, and retired from the service at an early age, carrying with him the regrets and good wishes of everybody who knew him.

In the legation staff there were also included two doctors, who at the same time discharged the functions of Assistants in the chancery. One of them shortly quitted the service, and set up in Yokohama as a general practitioner, to retire with a competent fortune after but a few years. The other merits more extended notice, on account both of his character and public services of every kind. I mean my life-long friend, William Willis. Perhaps no other man ever exhibited in a greater measure the quality which we are wont to call conscientiousness, whether in his private relations or in the discharge of his duties. Those who have had the fortune to profit by his medical or surgical aid, feel that no man could be more tender or sympathetic towards a patient. He was devoted to his profession, and lost no opportunity of extending his experience. In those days a doctor had frequently to encounter personal risks such as fall to the lot of few civilians; he exposed himself freely, in order to succour the wounded. In the chancery his services were indispensable. He it was who "swept the 'Aegean stable,'" arranged the archives in order, and brought the register up to date. Always on the spot when he was wanted, an indefatigable worker, and unswervingly loyal to his chief. After nine years service he was promoted to be a vice-consul, but by this time the Japanese had become so impressed with his value as a surgeon and physician that they begged him to accept a salary more than four times what he received from the Foreign Office, and he went where his great qualities were likely to be of more use than in trying petty police cases and drawing up trade reports of a city which never had any foreign commerce. His gigantic stature made him conspicuous among all the Europeans who have resided in Japan since the ports were opened, and when I first knew him he was hardly five and twenty years of age. A man endowed with an untiring power of application, accurate memory for words and things, and brimful of good stories from the three kingdoms. Big men are big-hearted, and he was no exception.

We shall come across him again repeatedly in the course of these reminiscences, and for the present these few words must suffice.

Besides these, the legation staff included Russell Brooke Robertson and myself, as student-interpreters.

Last, but not least, were the officers of the mounted escort and infantry guard. The latter was commanded by Lieut. Price of the 67th Regiment, and was soon replaced by fifty marines under the command of a man widely known in the service to which he belonged as "Public-spirited" Smith. I shall say more of him later on. The cavalry escort consisted of a dozen men from the Military Train, a corps which went by the honorary title of "Pig-drivers," and at their head was a lieutenant, a good, harmless sort of fellow, whose only weakness was for fine uniforms and showy horses. Not being learned in the extremely complicated subject of military costume, full dress, half dress, and undress, I cannot say what it was that he had adopted for himself, but it was whispered about that he had been audacious enough to assume the insignia of a field-officer, which is undoubtedly a serious offence against discipline. However that may be, the blaze of gold which decorated his person was wonderful to behold, and on at least one occasion, when we were going in solemn procession to an audience of the Tycoon, caused him to be mistaken for the Envoy by the Japanese officials, who gave him the salutes that rightfully belonged to his less conspicuously adorned diplomatic chief. To determine whether the pleasure derived from this confusion of persons by the one outweighed the mortification which might not unnaturally have been felt by the other would have required a delicate moral balance, which was not available at the moment; but judging from the relative scale of the two men in other points of character, I am inclined to infer that the good preponderated largely over the evil, and that applying consequently the criterion so unfairly attributed to the utilitarians by their opponents, we must arrive at the provisional conclusion that the lieutenant's uniform was highly virtuous and worthy of the applause of mankind.

But it is time to quit this gossiping tone and speak of more serious matters.

CHAPTER III

Political Conditions in Japan

At this period the movement had already commenced that finally culminated in what may fitly be called the Revolution of 1868, by which the feudal system was destroyed and the old monarchical government revived. The tendency of the times was as yet scarcely perceived by foreigners, with but one or two exceptions. They generally supposed that political strife had broken out between the sovereign and a few unruly vassals dissatisfied with the treaties that permitted the sacred soil of Japan to be defiled by the footsteps of "barbarians," and secured all the profits of trade to the head of the State, the vassals being enabled to defy their suzerain owing to his own feebleness and the incapacity of his Ministers. It was still believed that the potentate in whose name the Treaties had been concluded was the Temporal Sovereign, and that the Mikado was little more than the head of the priesthood, or Spiritual Emperor. This theory of the Japanese Constitution was almost as old as the earliest knowledge of the country possessed by Europeans. Marco Polo, indeed, says nothing of its system of government in the two short chapters which he devotes to Zipangu, but the Jesuit missionaries who laboured in Japan during the 16th and 17th centuries uniformly held the Mikado to be a spiritual dignitary, and spoke of the Shôgun as the real ruler of the country, the temporal king, and even Emperor. Kaempfer, the best known and most often quoted of the authorities on Japan, writing at the beginning of the 18th century, calls the two potentates Ecclesiastical and Secular Emperors, and his example had, up to the time I am writing of, been followed by all his successors without exception. The truth is that the polity of the Japanese State had assumed already in the 12th century the form which it was still displaying at the beginning of the latter half of the 19th, and institutions which could boast of such a highly respectable antiquity might well be supposed to have taken a deep enough hold to be part and parcel of the national life.

The history of Japan has still to be written. Native chronicles of the Mikados and annals of leading families exist in abundance, but the Japanese mind is only just now beginning to emancipate itself from the thraldom of Chinese literary forms, while no European has yet attempted a task which requires a training different from that of most men who pursue an Eastern career. Until within the last two decades, the literature of Japan was almost entirely unknown to Europeans, and the existing keys to the language were ridiculously inadequate. The only historical works accessible to foreigners were the scanty *Annales des Dairi*, translated by Titsingh with the aid of native Dutch interpreters and edited by Klaproth with a degree of bold confidence that nothing but the position of a one-eyed man amongst the blind can give; and a set of chronological tables, translated by Hoffman for Siebold's *Nippon*. It is no wonder, therefore, if at the outset of Treaty relations, the foreign representatives were at a loss to appreciate the exact nature of the political questions that confronted them, and were unable to diagnose the condition of the patient whose previous history was unknown to them.

To trace in detail the development of the Japanese monarchy, from its beginnings as a pure theocracy of foreign invaders, attracting to itself the allegiance of a number of small tribal chieftains, the fusion of these tribes with their conquerors into one seemingly homogeneous race, the remodelling of the administration which followed upon the introduction of Chinese laws and philosophy, the supplanting of the native hero and native worship by the creed of Gautama, the rise of a military caste brought about by the constant warfare with the barbarous tribes in the east and north of the country, the rivalry of the Taira and Minamoto clans, both sprung from base-born younger sons of the Mikados, and the final suppression of the civil administration in the provinces by the distribution of the country amongst the followers of the Minamoto and their allies, would require a profound study of documents which no one has yet undertaken. With the appointment of Yoritomo to be Commander-in-Chief the feudal system was fully established. The ancient official hierarchy still existed at Kiôto, but in name only, exercising no influence whatever over the conduct of affairs, and in the 14th century its functions were already so far forgotten as to become the subject of antiquarian research. The civil and penal codes borrowed from the great Empire of Eastern Asia fell into disuse, and in part even the very traces of them perished. Martial law reigned throughout the land, half the people were converted into a huge garrison, which the other half toiled to feed and clothe. Reading and writing were the exclusive accomplishments of the Buddhist priesthood and of the impoverished nobles who formed the court of a Mikado shorn of all the usual attributes of a sovereign, and a deep sleep fell upon the literary genius of the nation. The absence of danger from foreign invasion rendered the necessity of a strong central administration unfelt, and Japan under the Shôguns assumed the aspect of Germany in the middle ages, the soil being divided between a multitude of petty potentates, independent in all but name, while their nominal head was little better than a puppet.

This state of things lasted till the second quarter of the 14th century, when an attempt was made under the Mikado Go-Daigo to re-establish the pristine rule of the legitimate sovereigns. A civil war ensured that lasted for over fifty years, until the Ashikaga family finally established themselves in the office of hereditary Shôguns. Before long they split up into two branches which quarrelled among themselves and gave opportunity for local chiefs to re-establish their independence. In the middle of the 16th century a soldier of fortune, Ota Nobunaga by name, profited by the central position of the provinces he had acquired with his sword to arrogate to himself the right of arbitrating between the warlike leaders who had risen in every direction. After his assassination a still greater warrior, known most commonly by the title of Taicosama, carried on the work of pacification: every princelet who opposed his authority was in turn subdued, and he might bave become the founder of a new line of "*maires du palais*." He died, however, before time had sufficiently consolidated his position, leaving an inexperienced youth heir to his power, under the tutelage of guardians who speedily quarrelled. The most distinguished of these was Iyéyasu, who, besides the vast domains which he had acquired in the neighbourhood of Yedo, the modern Tôkiô, possessed all the qualities which fit a man to lead armies and rule kingdoms. He had been Taicosama's sole remaining competitor for power, and at the death of the latter naturally assumed the most prominent position in the country. A couple of years sufficed for the transference to him of all, and more than all, the authority wielded by his two predecessors. No combination against him had any chance of success. The decisive battle of Sékigahara in 1600 brought the whole nation to his feet, and he made full use of this opportunity to create checks upon the *Daimiôs* of whose fidelity he was not sufficiently assured, by grants of territories to his own friends and followers, a few of the older families alone being allowed to retain their ancient fiefs. Among these were Shimadzu in the south of Kiûshiû, Môri in the extreme west, and Daté, Nambu and Tsugaru in the northern provinces of the main island. His own sons received portions in Owari, Kishiû, Mito and elsewhere. In 1616 at Iyéyasu's death 19-20ths of the whole country was held by his adherents. Thus there arose five or six classes of barons, as they may best be called, to render their position intelligible to the English reader. Firstly, there were the Three Families descended from his most favoured sons, from whom according to the constitution established by him in case of a default of direct heirs, the successor to the Shôgunate was to be chosen (as a matter of fact resort was had only to Kishiû when a break in the line occurred). Next came the Related Families (*Kamon*) sprung from his younger sons, and in the third place were ranked the Lords of Provinces (*Koku-shi*). The members of these three classes enjoyed the revenue of fiefs comprising one or more provinces, or lands of equivalent extent. Below them in importance were the Hereditary Servants (*fu-dai*) and Banner-men (*hatamoto*) composed as has been said before of the immediate retainers of the Tokugawa family, and the Stranger Lords (*tozama*), relics of the former barons, who had submitted to his supremacy and followed his banner in his last wars. The qualification of a *daimiô* was the possession of lands assessed at a production of l0,000 *koku* (=about 5 bushels) of rice and upwards. The *hatamotos* were retainers of the Tokugawa family whose assessment was below 10,000 *koku* and above 1,000. Below them came the ordinary vassals (*go-ke-nin*).

The fiefs of all classes of the *daimiôs* were in their turn at first partitioned out among their retainers, and called *Ke-rai* in their relation to their immediate lords, and *bai-shin* (arrière vassals) as being vassals of those who acknowledged the suzerainty of the *Shôgun*. *Samurai* and *ashigaru* denoted the two ranks of sword-bearing gentlemen and common soldiers among the retainers of the *daimiôs*. In the end every retainer, except the *samurai* of Satsuma, received an annual allowance of so much rice, in return for which he was bound to perform military service and appear in the field or discharge the ordinary military duties required in time of peace, accompanied by followers proportioned in number to his income. In Satsuma the feudal sub-division of the land was carried out to the fullest extent, so that the vassal of lowest rank held the sword in one hand and the hoe in the other. No taxes were paid by any feudal proprietor. The *koku-shi* and other barons of equal rank ruled their provinces absolutely, levying land-tax on the farmers and imposts on internal trade as they chose. They had further the power of life and death, subject only to the nominal condition of reporting once a year the capital sentences inflicted by their officers. The other nobles were less independent. Every *daimiô* had to maintain an establishment at the capital, where his wife and children resided permanently, while the lord passed alternate years in Yedo and in his territories.

On his journeys to and fro he was accompanied by a little army of retainers, for whose accommodation inns were built at every town on the main roads throughout the country, and the expense involved was a heavy tax on his resources. A strict system of etiquette regulated the audiences with which the *daimiôs* were favoured on their arrival and departure, and prescribed the presents they were to offer as a symbol of their inferiority. There was little social intercourse among them, and they lived for the most part a life of extreme seclusion surrounded by vast numbers of women and servants. A fixed number of hereditary councillors (*karô* and *yônin*) checked all initiative in the administration of their fiefs. They were brought up in complete ignorance of the outer world, and the strings of government were pulled by the unseen hands of obscure functionaries who obtained their appointments by force of their personal qualities. After a few generations had passed the descendants of the active warriors and statesmen of Iyéyasu's time were reduced to the state of imbecile puppets, while the hereditary principle produced a similar effect on their councillors. Thus arose in each daimiate a condition of things which may be compared to that of a Highland clan, where the ultimate power was based upon the feelings and opinions of a poor but aristocratic oligarchy. This led to the surprising results of the revolution of 1868, when the power nominally exercised by the chief *daimiôs* came to be wielded by the more energetic and intelligent of their retainers, most of whom were *samurai* of no rank or position. These men it was who really ruled the clan, determined the policy of its head and dictated to him the language he should use on public occasions. The *daimiô*, it cannot be too often repeated, was a nobody; he possessed not even as much power as a constitutional sovereign of the modern type, and his intellect, owing to his education, was nearly always far below par. This strange political system was enabled to hold together solely by the isolation of the country from the outer world. As soon as the fresh air of European thought impinged upon this framework it crumbled to ashes like an Egyptian mummy brought out of its sarcophagus.

The decline of the Mikado's power dates from the middle of the 9th century, when for the first time a boy of nine years ascended the throne of his ancestors. During his minority the country was governed by his father-in-law, the chief of the ancient Fujiwara family, who contrived for a long period to secure to themselves the power of setting up and removing their own nominees just as suited their convenience. A similar fate befel the institution of the Shôgunate. After the murder of Yoritomo's last surviving son, the country was nominally ruled by a succession of young princes, none of whom had emerged from the stage of boyhood when appointed, and who were deposed in turn after a few years of complete nullity, while the real heads of the government were the descendants of Hôjô Tokimasa, Yoritomo's father-in-law. The vices of the hereditary principle in their case had again full sway, and the later Hôjô were mere puppets in the hands of their principal advisers. A revolution in favour of the Mikado overthrew this system for a short interval, until the Shôgunate was restored for a time to reality by the founder of the Ashikaga family. But after the lapse of a few years its power was divided between Kiôto and Kamakura, and the two heads of the family fell under the dominating influence of their agents the *Kwan-rei* Uyésugi and Hosokawa.

Towards the end of the Ashikaga period the Shôgun had become as much an empty name as the Mikado himself, and the country was split up among the local chieftains. The bad condition of the internal communications between the provinces and the capital probably contributed to this state of things. Iyéyasu was the first to render consolidation possible by the construction of good military roads. The governmental system erected by him seemed calculated to ensure the lasting tranquillity of the country. But the hereditary principle again reasserted its influence. The third Shôgun, Iyémitsu, was a real man. Born four years after the battle of Sekigahara and already twelve years of age when his grandfather died in the year succeeding his final appearance in the battlefield, he had the education of a soldier, and to his energy was owing the final establishment of the Tokugawa supremacy on a solid basis. Iyéyasu and his successor had always been in the habit of meeting the *daimiôs* on their visits to Yedo outside the city. Iyémitsu received them in his palace. He gave those who would not submit to their changed position the option of returning home, and offered them three years for preparation to try the ordeal of war. Not a single one ventured to resist. But he was succeeded by his son Iyétsuna, a boy of ten. During Iyétsuna's minority the government was carried on in his name by his Council of State, composed of Hereditary Servants (*fu-dai daimiôs*), and the personal authority of the head of the Tokugawa family thus received its first serious blow. But worse than that, the office of chief councillor was from the first confined to four baronial families, Ii, Honda, Sakakibara and Sakai, and the *rôjiû* or ordinary councillors were likewise *daimiôs*.

On them the hereditary principle had, in the interval between the close of the civil wars and the accession of the fourth Shôgun, produced its usual result. Nominally the heads of the administration they were without any will of their own, and were guided by their own hereditary councillors, whose strings were pulled by someone else. The real power then fell into the hands of ministers or *bu-giô*, chosen from the *hatamoto* or lesser vassals, and many of these were men of influence and real weight. Still with them the habit of delegating authority into the hands of anyone of sufficient industry and energy to prefer work to idleness, was invincible, and in the end the dominions of the Tokugawa family came to be ruled by the *Oku go-yû-hitsu* or private secretaries. The machine in fact had been so skilfully constructed that a child could keep it turning. Political stagnation was mistaken for stability.

Apart from one or two unsuccessful conspiracies against the government, Japan experienced during 238 years the profoundest tranquillity. She resembled the sleeping beauty in the wood, and the guardians of the public safety had a task not more onerous than that of waving a fan to keep the flies from disturbing the princess's slumbers. When her dreams were interrupted by the eager and vigorous West the ancient, decrepit and wrinkled watchers were found unfit for their posts, and had to give way to men more fit to cope with the altered circumstances which surrounded them.

Socially the nation was divided into two sections by a wide gulf which it was impossible to pass. On the one hand the sword-bearing families or gentry, whose frequent poverty was compensated for by their privileges of rank, on the other the agricultural, labouring and commercial classes; intermarriage was forbidden between the orders. The former were ruled by the code of honour, offences against which were permitted to be expiated by self-destruction, the famous *harakiri* or disembowelment, while the latter were subject to a severe unwritten law enforced by cruel and frequent capital punishment. They were the obedient humble servants of the two-sworded class.

Japan had already made the experiment of free intercourse with European states in the middle of the 16th century, when the merchants and missionaries of Portugal were welcomed in the chief ports of Kiûshiû, and Christianity bade fair to replace the ancient native religions. They were succeeded by the Spaniards, Dutch and English, the two latter nations confining themselves however to commerce. The gigantic missionary undertakings of the two great English-speaking communities of the far West were the creation of a much later time. It will be recollected that in 1580 Spain for a time absorbed Portugal. The Roman Catholics began before long to excite the enmity of the Buddhist and Shintô priesthood, whose temples they had caused to be pulled down and whose revenues they seemed on the point of usurping. Nobunaga had favoured them, but in the civil wars that raged at that period the principal patrons of the Jesuits were overthrown, and the new ruler Taicosama soon proclaimed his hostility to the strangers. Their worst offence was the refusal of a Christian girl to become his concubine. Iyéyasu, a devout Buddhist, pursued the same religious policy as his predecessor in possession of the ruling power. His dislike to Christianity was stimulated by the fact that some of Hidéyori's adherents were Christians, and the young prince Hidéyori was himself known to be on friendly terms with the missionaries. The flame was fanned by the Dutch and English, now become the hereditary political foes of Spain, and the persecution was renewed with greater vigour than ever. Missionaries were sought out with eager keenness, and in the company of their disciples subjected to cruel tortures and the most horrible deaths. The fury of persecution did not relax with Iyéyasu's disappearance from the scene, and the final act of the drama was played out in the time of his grandson.

An insurrection provoked by the oppression of the local *daimiôs* broke out in the island of Amakusa, where thousands of Christians joined the rebel flag. After a furious struggle the revolt was put an end to on the 24th February, 1638, by the assault and capture of the castle of Shimabara, when 37,000 people, two-thirds of whom were women and children, were put to the sword. It is hardly possible to read the native accounts of this business without a feeling of choking indignation at the ruthless sacrifice of so many unfortunate creatures who were incapable of defence, and whose only crime was their wish to serve the religion which they had chosen for their rule of life. The Portuguese were forbidden ever to set foot again in Japan. The English had previously retired from a commercial contest in which they found their rivals too fortunate and too skilful, and the edict went forth that the Dutch, who now alone remained, should thenceforth be confined to the small artificial island of Déshima, off the town of Nagasaki, where for the next 2 1/4centuries they and the Chinese were permitted to carry on a restricted and constantly diminishing trade. Attempts were made once or twice by the English, and early in the present century by the Russians, to induce the government of Japan to relax their rule, but in vain. The only profit the world has derived from these abortive essays is the entrancing narrative of Golownin, who was taken prisoner in Yezo in connection with a descent made by Russian naval officers in revenge for the rejection of the overtures made by the Russian envoy Resanoff, perhaps the most lifelike picture of Japanese official manners that is anywhere to be met with. No further approaches were made by any Western Government until the United States took the matter in hand in 1852.

CHAPTER IV

Treaties—Anti-Foreign Spirit— Murder of Foreigners

The expedition of Commodore Perry to Loochoo and Japan was not the first enterprise of its kind that had been undertaken by the Americans. Having accomplished their own independence as the result of a contest in which a few millions of half-united colonists had successfully withstood the well-trained legions of Great Britain and her German mercenaries (though not, it may be fairly said, without in a great measure owing their success to the very efficient assistance of French armies and fleets), they added to this memory of ancient wrongs a natural fellow-feeling for other nations who were less able to resist the might of the greatest commercial and maritime Power the world has yet seen. While sympathising with Eastern peoples in the defence of their independent rights, they believed that a conciliatory mode of treating them was at least equally well fitted to ensure the concession of those trading privileges to which the Americans are not less indifferent than the English.

In 1836 they had despatched an envoy to Siam and Cochin-China, who was successful in negotiating by peaceful methods a treaty of commerce with the former state. In China, Iike the other western states, they had profited by the negotiations which were the outcome of the Opium War, without having to incur the odium of using force or the humiliation of finding their softer methods prove a failure in dealing with the obstinate conservatism of Chinese mandarins. For many years their eyes had been bent upon Japan, which lay on the opposite side of the Pacific fronting their own state of California, then rising into fame as one of the great gold-producing regions of the globe. Warned by the fate of all previous attempts to break down the wall of seclusion that hemmed in the 'country of the gods,' they resolved to make such a show of force that with reasonable people, unfamiliar with modern artillery, might prove as powerful an argument as theories of universal brotherhood and the obligations imposed by the comity of nations. They appointed to the chief command a naval officer possessed of both tact and determination, whose judicious use of the former qualification rendered the employ of the second unnecessary. Probably no one was more agreeably surprised than Commodore Perry at the comparative ease with which, on his second visit to the Bay of Yedo, he obtained a Treaty, satisfactory enough as a beginning. No doubt the counsels of the Dutch agent at Nagasaki were not without their effect, and we may also conjecture that the desire which had already begun to manifest itself among some of the lower *Samurai* for a wider acquaintance with the mysterious outer world was secretly shared by men in high positions. Fear alone would not have induced a haughty government like that of the Shôguns to acquiesce in breaking through a law of restriction that had such a highly creditable antiquity to boast of.

Most men's motives are mixed, and there was on the Japanese side no very decided unwillingness to yield to a show of force, which the pretext of prudence would enable them to justify. England and Russia, then or shortly afterwards at war, followed in the wake of the United States. Next an American Consul-General took up his residence at Shimoda, to look after the interests of whaling vessels, and skilfully made use of the recent events in China to induce the Shôgun's government to extend the concessions already granted. In 1858 the China War having been apparently brought to a successful conclusion, Lord Elgin and the French Ambassador, Baron Gros, ran across to Japan and concluded treaties on the same basis as Mr Harris, and before long similar privileges were accorded to Holland and Russia. In 1859 the ports of Nagasaki, Hakodaté and Yokohama were thrown open to the trade of the Five Powers, and a new age was inaugurated in Japan.

It was not without opposition that the Shôgun's government had entered into its first engagements with the United States, Great Britain and Russia. An agitation arose when the first American ships anchored in the Bay of Yedo, and there were not wanting bold and rash men ready to undertake any desperate enterprise against the foreign invaders of the sacred soil of Japan. But at this time there was no leader to whom the malcontents could turn for guidance. The Mikado was closely watched by the Shôgun's resident at Kiôto, and the *daimiôs* were divided among themselves. The principal opponent was the ex-Prince of Mito, whose constitutional duty was to support the Shôgun and aid him with his counsels in all great national crises.

During the presence of Commodore Perry the reigning Shôgun Iyéyoshi had fallen ill, and he died not long after the squadron had sailed. He was succeeded by his son Iyésada, a man of 28, who does not seem to have been endowed with either force of character or knowledge of the world. Such qualities are not to be expected from the kind of education which fell to the lot of Japanese princes in those days.

In view of the expected return of the American ships in the following year, forts were constructed to guard the sea-front of the capital, and the ex-Prince of Mito was summoned from his retirement to take the lead in preparing to resist the encroachments of foreign powers. By a curious coincidence, this nobleman, then forty-nine years of age, was the representative of a family which for years had maintained the theoretical right of the Mikado to exercise the supreme government, and was at the same time strongly opposed to any extension of the limited intercourse with foreign countries then permitted. Nor can it be wondered that Japan, who had so successfully protected herself from foreign aggression by a policy of rigid exclusion, and which had seen the humiliation of China consequent upon disputes with a Western Power arising out of trade questions at the very moment when she was being torn by a civil war which owed its origin to the introduction of new religious beliefs from the West, should have believed that the best means of maintaining peace at home and avoiding an unequal contest with Europe, was to adhere strictly to the traditions of the past two centuries. But when the intrusive foreigners returned in the beginning of the following year, Japan found herself still unprepared to repel them by force. The treaty was therefore signed, interdicting trade, but permitting whalers to obtain supplies in the three harbours of Nagasaki, Hakodaté and Shimoda, and promising friendly treatment to shipwrecked sailors.

While making these unavoidable concessions, the Japanese buoyed themselves up with the belief that their innate superiority could enable them easily to overcome the better equipped forces of foreign countries, when once they had acquired the modern arts of warfare and provided themselves with a sufficient proportion of the ships and weapons of the nineteenth century. From that time onwards this was the central idea of Japan's foreign policy for many years, as the sequel will show. Even at this period there were a few who would have willingly started off on this new quest, and two Japanese actually asked Commodore Perry to give them a passage in his flagship. They were refused, and their zeal was punished by their own government with imprisonment. The residence of Mr Harris at Shimoda and the visit which he insisted on paying to the capital created fresh difficulties for the advisers of the Shôgun. Written protests were delivered by non-official members of his council, and he was obliged at last to ask the Mikado's sanction to the treaties, in order to strengthen his own position. This invocation of the Mikado's authority may fairly be called an innovation upon ancient custom. Neither Nobunaga, Hidéyoshi nor Iyéyasu had thought it necessary to get their acts approved by him, and Iyéyasu granted trade privileges entirely on his own responsibility, without his right to do so ever being questioned. This reference to Kiôto is the first sign of the decadence of the Shôgun's power.

The supremacy of the Mikado having been once admitted, his right to a voice in the affairs of the country could no longer be disputed. His nobles seized the opportunity, and assumed the attitude of obstruction, which has always been a powerful weapon in the hands of individuals and parties. One man out of a dozen, of sufficient determination, can always force the others to yield, when his position is legal, and cannot be disturbed by the use of force. On the one hand, Mr Harris pressed for a revision of the treaty and the concession of open ports at Kanagawa and Ozaka; on the other was the Court, turning an obstinately deaf ear to all proposals. In its desperation the Shôgun's government appointed to be Prime Minister, or Regent as he was called by foreigners, the descendant of Iyéyasu's most trusted retainer, the *daimiô* Ii Kamon no Kami of Hikoné, and Mr Harris, as has already been said, skilfully turning to account the recent exploits of the combined English and French squadrons in the Chinese seas, obtained his treaty, achieving a diplomatic triumph of the greatest value purely by the use of "moral" pressure. The English, French, Russian and Dutch treaties followed. The Shôgun stood committed to a policy from which his new allies were not likely to allow of his receding, while to the anti-foreign party was imparted a consistency that there had previously been little chance of its acquiring.

Scarcely was the ink of these engagements dry, when the Shôgun, who had been indisposed for some weeks past, was gathered to his fathers, leaving no heir. According to the custom which had been observed on two previous occasions when there had been a break in the direct line, a prince was chosen from the house of Kishiû to be his successor. The ex-Prince of Mito, and several of his sympathisers among the leading nobles, namely, Hizen, Owari, Tosa, Satsuma and the Daté of Uwajima, a man of abilities superior to the size of his tiny fief in Shikoku, had desired to choose a younger son of Mito, who had been adopted into the family of Hitotsubashi. But the Prime Minister was too strong for them. He insisted on the election of his own nominee, and forced his opponents to retire into private life. Thus to their disapproval of the political course adopted by the Shôgunate, was added a personal resentment against its chief minister, and this feeling was shared in a remarkable degree by the retainers of the disgraced nobles. A bloody revenge was taken two years later on the individual, but the hostility to the system only increased with time, and in the end brought about its complete ruin.

Mito was the ringleader of the opposition, and began actively to intrigue with the Mikado's party against the head of his own family. The foreigners arrived in numbers at Kanagawa and Yokohama, and affronted the feelings of the haughty *samurai* by their independent demeanour, so different from the cringing subservience to which the rules of Japanese etiquette condemned the native merchant. It was not long before blood was shed. On the evening of the 26th August, six weeks after the establishment at Yedo of the British and American Representatives, an officer and a seaman belonging to a Russian man-of-war were cut to pieces in the streets of Yokohama, where they had landed to buy provisions. In November, a Chinese servant belonging to the French vice-consul was attacked and killed in the foreign settlement at Yokohama. Two months later, Sir R. Alcock's native linguist of the British Legation was stabbed from behind as he was standing at the gateway of the British Legation in Yedo, and within a month more two Dutch merchant captains were slaughtered in the high street at Yokohama. Then there was a lull for eight or nine months, till the French Minister's servant was cut at and badly wounded as he was standing at the gate of the Legation in Yedo. On the 14th January, 1861, Heusken, the Secretary of the American Mission, was attacked and murdered as he was riding home after a dinner-party at the Prussian Legation. And on the night of July 5 occurred the boldest attempt yet made on the life of foreigners, when the British Legation was attacked by a band of armed men and as stoutly defended by the native guard. This was a considerable catalogue for a period of no more than two

years since the opening of the ports to commerce. In every case
the attack was premeditated and unprovoked, and the perpetrators on every occasion belonged to the swordbearing class. No
offence had been given by the victims to those who had thus
ruthlessly cut them down; they were assassinated from motives
of a political character, and their murderers went unpunished in
every instance. Japan became to be known as a country where the
foreigner carried his life in his hand, and the dread of incurring
the fate of which so many examples had already occurred became
general among the residents. Even in England before I left to
take up my appointment, we felt that apart from the chances of
climate, the risk of coming to an untimely end at the hands of an
expert swordsman must be taken into account. Consequently, I
bought a revolver, with a due supply of powder, bullets and caps.
The trade to Japan in these weapons must have been very great in
those days, as everyone wore a pistol whenever he ventured beyond
the limits of the foreign settlement, and constantly slept with one
under his pillow. It was a busy time for Colt and Adams. But in
all the years of my experience in Japan I never heard of more than
one life being taken by a revolver, and that was when a Frenchman
shot a carpenter who demanded payment for his labour in a somewhat too demonstrative manner. In Yedo I think we finally gave
up wearing revolvers in 1869, chiefly because the few of us who
resided there had come to the conclusion that the weight of the
weapon was inconvenient, and also that if any bloodthirsty two-
sworded gentleman intended to take our lives, he would choose his
time and opportunity so as to leave us no chance of anticipating
his purpose with a bullet.

In the spring of 1862 Sir Rutherford Alcock returned to England
on leave of absence, and Colonel Neale was left in charge. As I
have said before, disbelieving in the validity of the reasons which
had led the Minister to remove his official residence to Yokohama,
the Chargé d'Affaires re-established himself at the temple formerly
occupied as the British Legation. On the anniversary, according
to the Japanese calendar, of the attack referred to on a previous

page, some Commissioners for Foreign Affairs in calling upon Colonel Neale, congratulated him and themselves on the fact that a whole year had elapsed since any fresh attempt had been made on the life of a foreigner. It was not unnatural, therefore, that in the first impulse of indignation at the savage and bloody slaughter of the sentry and corporal almost at his bedroom door, he should have conceived the suspicion that the visit of the Commissioners and their language in the morning, had been intended to put him off his guard, and that consequently the Japanese government, or rather the Shôgun's ministers, were implicated in what looked like a barbarous act of treachery that deprived the Japanese nation of all right to be regarded as a civilized community; more especially as the native watch had been recently changed, and fresh men substituted for those who had fought so well in defence of Sir Rutherford Alcock the year before. But on reflection it will easily be seen that there was no real justification for such a belief. The assassin was one of the guard. After the murder of the two Englishmen he returned to his quarters and there committed suicide by ripping himself up in the approved Japanese fashion. We may be sure that if his act had been the result of a conspiracy, he would not have been alone. Ignorant as the Shôgun's ministers may have been, and probably were, of the sacred character of an envoy, it was not their interest to bring upon themselves the armed vengeance of foreign powers at a moment when they were confronted with the active enmity of the principal clans of the west. I think they may be entirely absolved from all share in this attempt to massacre the inmates of the English Legation. But on the other hand it seems highly probable that the man's comrades were aware of his intention, and that after his partial success they connived at his escape. But he had been wounded by a bullet discharged from the pistol of the second man whom he attacked, and drops of blood on the ground showed the route by which he had made his way out of the garden. As his identity could not be concealed, he had to commit suicide in order to anticipate the penalty of death which the Shôgun's government could not have avoided inflicting on him. The apparent cognisance of the other men on guard (who were what our law would call accessories before the fact), and the fact that nevertheless they took no share in his act, is consonant with the statement that he was merely accomplishing an act of private revenge. His selection of the darkness of night seems to indicate that he hoped to escape the consequences. Willis said that when he arose and looked out, the night was pitch dark. It was the night before full moon, and in the very middle of what is called in Japan the rainy season. He informed me that there was a high wind and that heavy black clouds were drifting over the sky. The stormy weather and the lateness of the hour (11 to 12 o'clock) might perhaps account for the native lanterns which were hung about the grounds having ceased to give any light, but even under those circumstances it is a little suspicious that the guard should have neglected to replace the burnt out candles.

It was at Taku on our way down from Peking that Robertson, Jamieson and I heard of this new attack on the legation. I believe our feeling was rather one of regret that we had lost the opportunity of experiencing one of the stirring events which we had already learnt to regard as normally characteristic of life in Japan. It certainly did not take us by surprise, and in no way rendered the service less attractive. But Jamieson had found a better opening in Shanghai, and the remaining two went on to Yokohama as soon as they could get a passage.

CHAPTER V

Richardson's Murder— Japanese Studies

The day after my arrival at Yokohama I was taken over to Kanagawa and introduced to the Rev. S. R. Brown, an American Missionary, who was then engaged in printing a work on colloquial Japanese, and to Dr J. C. Hepburn, M.D., who was employed on a dictionary of the language. The former died some years ago, but the latter is at this moment (1886) still in Japan,* bringing out the third edition of his invaluable lexicon and completing the translation of the Bible on which he has been occupied for many years. In those days we had either to take a native sculling boat for an ichibu across the bay to Kanagawa or ride round by the causeway, the land along which the railway now runs not having been filled in at that time. Natives used to cross by a public ferry boat, paying a tempô (16-1/2 to the ichibu) a-piece, but no foreigner was ever allowed to make use of the cheaper conveyance. If he was quick enough to catch the ferryboat before it had pushed off, and so seize a place for himself, the boatmen simply refused to stir. They remained immovable, until the intruder was tired of waiting, and abandoned the game. It was only after a residence of some years, when I had become pretty fluent in the language and could argue the point with the certainty of having the public

---

* Dr Hepburn died in 1911.

on my side, that I at last succeeded in overcoming the obstinacy of the people at the boathouse who had the monopoly of carrying foreigners. There was in those days a fixed price for the foreigner wherever he went, arbitrarily determined without reference to the native tariff. At the theatre a foreigner had to pay an ichibu for admittance, and was then thrust into the "deaf-box," as the gallery seats are called, which are so far from the stage that the actors' speeches are quite indistinguishable. The best place for both seeing and hearing is the doma, on the area of the theatre, close in front of the stage. On one occasion I walked into the theatre, and took my place in one of the divisions of the doma, offering to pay the regular price. No, they would not take it. I must pay my ichibu and go to the foreigner's box. I held out, insisting on my right as one of the public. Did I not squat on the floor with my boots off, just like themselves? Well then, if I would not come out of that, the curtain would not rise. I rejoined that they might please themselves about that. In order to annoy a single foreigner, they would deprive the rest of the spectators of the pleasure they had paid to enjoy. So I obstinately kept my place, and in the end the manager gave way. The "house" was amused at the foreigner speaking their language and getting the best of the argument, and for the rest of my time in Yokohama I had no more difficulty in obtaining accommodation in any part of the theatre that I preferred.

In those days the Yokohama theatre used to begin about eleven o'clock in the morning and keep open for twelve hours. A favourite play was the Chiû-Shin-Gura, or Treasury of Faithful Retainers, and the Sara-Yashiki, or the Broken Plate Mansion. The arrangement of the interior, the fashion of dress and acting, the primitive character of the scenery and lights, the literary style of the plays have not undergone any changes, and are very unlikely to be modified in any marked degree by contact with European ideas. There is some talk now and then of elevating the character of the stage and making the theatre a school of morals and manners for the young, but the good people who advocate these theories in the press have not, as far as I know, ventured to put them to practical proof, and the shibai will, I hope, always continue to be what it always has been in Japan, a place of amusement and distraction, where people of all ages and sizes go to enjoy themselves without caring one atom whether the incidents are probable or proper, so long as there is enough of the tragic to call forth the tears which every natural man sheds with satisfaction on proper occasions, and of the comic by-turns to give the facial muscles a stretch in the other direction.

On the 14th September a most barbarous murder was committed on a Shanghai merchant named Richardson. He, in company with a Mrs Borradaile of Hongkong, and Woodthorpe C. Clarke and Wm. Marshall both of Yokohama, were riding along the high road between Kanagawa and Kawasaki, when they met with a train of daimiô's retainers, who bid them stand aside. They passed on at the edge of the road, until they came in sight of a palanquin, occupied by Shimadzu Saburô, father of the Prince of Satsuma. They were now ordered to turn back, and as they were wheeling their horses in obedience, were suddenly set upon by several armed men belonging to the train, who hacked at them with their sharp-edged heavy swords. Richardson fell from his horse in a dying state, and the other two men were so severely wounded that they called out to the lady: "Ride on, we can do nothing for you." She got safely back to Yokohama and gave the alarm. Everybody in the settlement who possessed a pony and a revolver at once armed himself and galloped off towards the scene of slaughter.

Lieut.-Colonel Vyse, the British Consul, led off the Legation mounted escort in spite of Colonel Neale's order that they should not move until he or their own commander gave the word. M. de Bellecourt, the French Minister, sent out his escort, consisting of a half-dozen French troopers; Lieut. Price of the 67th Regiment marched off part of the Legation guard, accompanied by some French infantry. But amongst the first, perhaps the very first of all, was Dr Willis, whose high sense of the duty cast on him by his profession rendered him absolutely fearless. Passing for a mile along the ranks of the men whose swords were reeking with

the blood of Englishmen, he rode along the high road through
Kanagawa, where he was joined by some three or four more
Englishmen. He proceeded onwards to Namamugi, where poor
Richardson's corpse was found under the shade of a tree by the
roadside. His throat had been cut as he was lying there wounded
and helpless. The body was covered with sword cuts, any one of
which was sufficient to cause death. It was carried thence to the
American Consulate in Kanagawa, where Clarke and Marshall
had found refuge and surgical aid at the hands of Dr Hepburn
and later on of Dr Jenkins, our other doctor. There was only one
British man-of-war lying in the harbour, but in the course of the
evening Admiral Küper arrived in his flagship, the Euryalus,
with the gun-vessel Ringdove. The excitement among the foreign
mercantile community was intense, for this was the first occasion
on which one of their own number had been struck down. The
Japanese sword is as sharp as a razor, and inflicts fearful gashes.
The Japanese had a way of cutting a man to pieces rather than leave
any life in him. This had a most powerful effect on the minds of
Europeans, who came to look on every two-sworded man as a
probable assassin, and if they met one in the street thanked God
as soon as they had passed him and found themselves in safety.

It was known that Shimadzu Saburô was to lie that night at
Hodogaya, a post-town scarcely two miles from Yokohama. To
surround and seize him with the united forces of all the foreign
vessels in port would, in their opinion, have been both easy and
justifiable, and viewed by the light of our later knowledge, not only
of Japanese politics but also of Japanese ideas with regard to the
right of taking redress, they were not far wrong. In the absence of
any organised police or military force able to keep order among the
turbulent two-sworded class it cannot be doubted that this course
would have been adopted by any Japanese clan against whom such
an offence had been committed, and the foreign nationalities in
Japan were in the same position as a native clan. They were subject
to the authorities of their own country, who had jurisdiction over
them both in criminal and civil matters, and were responsible for

keeping them within the bounds of law and for their protection against attack. A meeting was called at Hooper's (W. C. Clarke's partner) house under the presidency of Colonel F. Howard Vyse, the British Consul, when, after an earnest discussion and the rejection of a motion to request the foreign naval authorities to land 1,000 men in order to arrest the guilty parties, a deputation consisting of some of the leading residents was appointed to wait on the commanding officers of the Dutch, French and English naval forces and lay before them the conclusions of the meeting. The British admiral, however, declined to act upon their suggestion, but consented to attend another meeting which was to be held at the residence of the French Minister at 6 a.m. on the following morning. The deputation then went to Colonel Neale, who with great magnanimity waived all personal considerations and promised to be present also. The idea had got abroad amongst the foreign community that Colonel Neale could not be trusted to take the energetic measures which they considered necessary under the circumstances. In fact, they found fault with him for preserving the cool bearing which might be expected from a man who had seen actual service in the field and which especially became a man in his responsible situation, and they thought that pressure could be put upon him through his colleagues and the general opinion of the other foreign representatives. But in this expectation they were disappointed. At the meeting Colonel Neale altogether declined to authorise the adoption of measures, which, if the Tycoon's government were to be regarded as the government of the country, would have amounted virtually to making war upon Japan, and the French Minister expressed an opinion entirely coinciding with that of his colleague. Calmer counsels prevailed, and Diplomacy was left to its own resources, arrangements, however, being made by the naval commanders-in-chief to patrol the settlement during the night and to station guard-boats along the sea-front to communicate with the ships in case of an alarm.

Looking back now after the lapse of nearly a quarter of a century, I am strongly disposed to the belief that Colonel Neale took the best course. The plan of the mercantile community was bold, attractive and almost romantic. It would probably have been successful for the moment, in spite of the well-known bravery of the Satsuma samurai. But such an event as the capture of a leading Japanese nobleman by foreign sailors in the dominions of the Tycoon would have been a patent demonstration of his incapacity to defend the nation against the "outer barbarian," and would have precipitated his downfall long before it actually took place, and before there was anything in the shape of a league among the clans ready to establish a new government. In all probability the country would have become a prey to ruinous anarchy, and collisions with foreign powers would have been frequent and serious. Probably the slaughter of the foreign community at Nagasaki would have been the immediate answer to the blow struck at Hodogaya, a joint expedition would have been sent out by England, France and Holland to fight many a bloody battle and perhaps dismember the realm of the Mikados. In the meantime the commerce for whose sake we had come to Japan would have been killed. And how many lives of Europeans and Japanese would have been sacrificed in return for that of Shimadzu Saburô?

I was standing outside the hotel that afternoon, and on seeing the bustle of men riding past, inquired what was the cause. The reply, "A couple of Englishmen have been cut down in Kanagawa," did not shock me in the least. The accounts of such occurrences that had appeared in the English press and the recent attack on the Legation of which I had heard on my way from Peking had prepared me to look on the murder of a foreigner as an ordinary, every-day affair, and the horror of bleeding wounds was not sufficiently familiar to me to excite the feelings of indignation that seemed to animate every one else. I was secretly ashamed of my want of sympathy. And yet, if it had been otherwise, such a sudden introduction to the danger of a horrid death might have rendered me quite unfit for the career I had adopted. This habit of looking upon assassination as part of the day's work enabled me later on to face with equanimity what most men whose sensations had not been deadened by a moral anæsthetic would perhaps have considered serious dangers. And while everyone in my immediate surroundings was in a state of excitement, defending Vyse or abusing Colonel Neale, I quietly settled down to my studies.

In those days the helps to the acquisition of the Japanese language were very few. A thin pamphlet by the Rev. J. Liggins, containing a few phrases in the Nagasaki dialect, a vocabulary compiled by Wm. Medhurst, senior, and published at Batavia many years before; Rodriguez' Japanese Grammar, by Landresse; a grammar by MM. Donker Curtius and Hoffmann in Dutch, and a French translation of it by Léon Pagè's; a translation by the latter of part of the Japanese-Portuguese Dictionary of 1603; Hoffmann's dialogues in Japanese, Dutch and English; Rosny's Introduction à la langue Japonaise, were about all. And but few of these were procurable in Japan. I had left London without any books on the language. Luckily for me, Dr S. R. Brown was just then printing his Colloquial Japanese, and generously allowed me to have the first few sheets as they came over at intervals from the printing office in Shanghai. A Japanese reprint of Medhurst's vocabulary, which could be bought in a Japanese bookshop that stood at the corner of Benten-Dôri and Honchô Itchôme, speedily proved useless. But I had a slight acquaintance with the Chinese written characters and was the fortunate possessor of Medhurst's Chinese-English Dictiohary, by whose help I could manage to come at the meaning of a Japanese word if I got it written down. It was very uphill work at first, for I had no teacher, and living in a single room at the hotel, abutting too on the bowling alley, could not secure quiet. The colonel ordered us, Robertson and myself, to attend every day at the "office" (we did not call it the chancery then) to ask if our services were required, and what work we had consisted chiefly of copying despatches and interminable accounts. My handwriting was, unfortunately for me, considered to be rather better than the average, and I began to foresee that a larger share of clerical work would be given to me than I liked. My theory of the duty of a student-interpreter was then, and still is, to learn the language first of all. I considered that this order would be a great iuterruption to serious work if he insisted upon it, and would take away all chances of our learning the language thoroughly. At last I summoned up courage to protest, and I rather think my friend Willis encouraged me to do this; but I did not gain anything by remonstrating. The colonel evidently thought I was frightfully lazy, for when I said that the office work would interfere with my studies, he replied that it would be much worse for both to be neglected than for one to be hindered. At first there was some idea of renting a house for Robertson and myself, but finally the Colonel decided to give us rooms at one end of the rambling two-storied building that was then occupied as a Legation. It stood at the corner of the bund and the creek, where the Grand Hotel now is, and belonged to a man named Hoey, who took advantage of my inexperience and the love of books he had discovered to be one of my weaknesses to sell me an imperfect copy of the Penny Cyclopædia for more than a complete one would have cost at home. I used to play bowls sometimes with Albert Markham (of Arctic fame), who was then a lieutenant on board H.M.S. Centaur, and Charles Wirgman, the artist-correspondent of the Illustrated London News. Towards the end of October we induced the colonel to consent to our getting two lessons a week from the Rev. S. R. Brown, and to allow us to engage a native "teacher," at the public expense. So we had to get a second, and pay for him out of our own pockets. He also agreed to leave us the mornings free for study up to one o'clock. A "teacher," it must be understood, does not mean a man who can "teach." In those days, at Peking and in Japan also, we worked with natives who did not understand a word of English, and the process by which one made out the meaning of a sentence was closely akin to that which Poe describes in the Gold Beetle for the decyphering of a cryptograph. Through my "boy," who was equally ignorant of English, I got hold of a man who explained that he had once been a doctor, and having nothing to do at the moment would teach me Japanese without any pay. We used to communicate at first by writing down Chinese characters. One of his first sentences was literally "Prince loves men, I also venerate the prince as a master"; prince, as I afterwards divined, being merely a polite way of saying you. He said he had lots of dollars and ichibus and would take nothing for his services, so I agreed with him that he should come to my room every day from ten to one. However, he never presented himself again after the first interview.

My "boy" turned out to be what I considered a great villain. I had at an early date wanted one of the native dictionaries of Chinese characters with the Japanese equivalents in Katakana. I sent him out to buy one, but he shortly returned and said that there were none in the place, and he must go over to Kanagawa, where he would be sure to find what I wanted. After being out the whole day, he brought me a copy which he said was the only one to be found and for which he charged me four ichibus, or nearly two dollars. This was just after my arrival, when I was new to the place and ignorant of prices. Six weeks afterwards, being in the bookseller's shop, I asked him what was the price of the book, when he replied that he had asked only 1-1/2 ichibu. My boy had taken it away and returned next day to say that I had refused to give more than one, which he consequently accepted. Unconscionable rascal this, not content with less than 300 per cent. of a squeeze! I found out also that he had kept back a large slice out of money I had paid to a carpenter for some chairs and a table. He had to refund his illicit gains, or else to find another place.

After a time I got my rooms at the Legation and was able to study to my heart's content. The lessons which Mr Brown gave me were of the greatest value. Besides hearing us repeat the sentences out of his book of Colloquial Japanese and explaining the grammar, he also read with us part of the first sermon in the collection entitled Kiu-ô Dôwa, so that I began to get some insight into the construction of the written language. Our two teachers were Takaoka Kanamé, a physician from Wakayama in Kishiû, and another man, whose name I forget. He was stupid and of little assistance. Early in 1863 Robertson went home on sick leave, and I had Takaoka Kanamé to myself. In those days the correspondence with the

Japanese Government was carried on by means of Dutch, the only European tongue of which anything was known. An absurd idea existed at one time that Dutch was the Court language of Japan. Nothing was farther from the truth. It was studied solely by a corps of interpreters attached to the Dutch settlement at Nagasaki, and when Kanagawa and Hakodaté were opened to foreign trade, some of these interpreters were transferred to those ports. On our side we had collected with some difficulty a body of Dutch interpreters. They included three Englishmen, one Cape Dutchman, one Swiss, and one real Dutchman from Holland, and they received very good pay. Of course it was my ambition to learn to read, write, and speak Japanese, and so to displace these middlemen.

So Takaoka began to give me lessons in the epistolary style. He used to write a short letter in the running-hand, and after copying it out in square character, explain to me its meaning. Then I made a translation and put it away for a few days. Meanwhile I exercised myself in reading, now one and now the other copy of the original. Afterwards I took out my translation and tried to put it back into Japanese from memory. The plan is one recommended by Roger Ascham and by the late George Long in a preface to his edition of the de Senectute, etc., which had been one of my school books. Before long I had got a thorough hold of a certain number of phrases, which I could piece together in the form of a letter, and this was all the easier, as the epistolary style of that time demanded the employment of a vast collection of merely complimentary phrases. I also took writing lessons from an old writing-master, whom I engaged to come to me at fixed hours. He was afflicted with a watery eye, and nothing but a firm resolve to learn would ever have enabled me to endure the constant drip from the diseased orbit, which fell now on the copy-book, now on the paper I was writing on, as he leant over it to correct a bad stroke, now on the table.

There are innumerable styles of caligraphy in Japan, and at that date the on-ye-riû was in fashion. I had unluckily taken up with the mercantile form of this. Several years afterwards I changed to a teacher who wrote a very beautiful hand, but still it was on-ye-riû. After the revolution of 1868 the kara-yô, which is more picturesque and self-willed, became the mode, and I put myself under the tuition of Takasai Tanzan, who was the teacher of several nobles, and one of the half dozen best in Tôkiô. But owing to this triple change of style, and also perhaps for want of real perseverance, I never came to have a good handwriting, nor to be able to write like a Japanese; nor did I ever acquire the power of composing in Japanese without making mistakes, though I had almost daily practice for seven or eight years in the translation of official documents. Perhaps that kind of work is of itself not calculated to ensure correctness, as the translator's attention is more bent on giving a faithful rendering of the original than on writing good Japanese. I shall have more to say at a later period as to the change which the Japanese written language has undergone in consequence of the imitation of European modes of expression.

The first occasion on which my knowledge of the epistolary style was put into requisition was in June 1863, when there came a note from one of the Shôgun's ministers, the exact wording of which was a matter of importance. It was therefore translated three times, once from the Dutch by Eusden, by Siebold with the aid of his teacher from the original Japanese, and by myself. I shall never forget the sympathetic joy of my dear Willis when I produced mine. There was no one who could say which of the three was the most faithful rendering, but in his mind and my own there was, of course, no doubt. I think I had sometime previously translated a private letter from a Japanese to one of our colleagues who had left Yokohama; it must have been done with great literalness, for I recollect that sessha was rendered "I, the shabby one." But it could not be made use of officially to testify to my progress in the language.

After the Richardson affair the Tycoon's government erected guardhouses all along the Tôkaidô within Treaty limits, and even proposed to divert the trains of the daimiôs to another route which ran through the town of Atsugi, but this project fell through.

Foreigners were in the habit of using it for their excursions, but Robertson and I had to pass along it twice a week on our way to and from our Japanese lesson at Mr Brown's, and though determined not to show the white feather, I always felt in passing one of these trains that my life was in peril. On one occasion as I was riding on the Tôkaidô for my pleasure, I met a tall fellow armed with the usual two swords, who made a step towards me in what I thought was a threatening manner, and having no pistol with me, I was rather alarmed, but he passed on, content probably with having frightened a foreigner. That is the only instance I can recollect of even seeming intention on the part of a samurai to do me harm on a chance meeting in the street, and the general belief in the bloodthirsty character of that class, in my opinion, was to a very great extent without foundation. But it must be admitted that whenever a Japanese made up his mind to shed the blood of a foreigner, he took care to do his business pretty effectually.

My first experience of an earthquake was on the 2nd November of this year. It was said by the foreign residents to have been a rather severe one. The house shook considerably, as if some very heavy person were walking in list slippers along the verandah and passages. It lasted several seconds, dying away gradually, and gave me a slight sensation of sickness, insomuch that I was beginning to fancy that a shaking which lasted so long must arise from within myself. I believe the sensations of most persons on experiencing a slight shock of earthquake for the first time are very similar. It is usually held that familiarity with these phenomena does not breed contempt for them, but on the contrary persons who have resided longest in Japan are the most nervous about the danger. And there is a reason for this. We know that in not very recent times extremely violent shocks have occurred, throwing down houses, splitting the earth, and causing death to thousands of people in a few moments. The longer the interval that has elapsed since the last, the sooner may its re-occurrence be looked for. We have escaped many times, but the next will be perhaps our last. So we feel on each occasion, and the anticipation of harm becomes stronger and stronger, and where we at first used to sit calmly through a somewhat prolonged vibration, the wooden joints of the house harshly creaking and the crockery rattling merrily on the shelves, we now spring from our chairs and rush for the door at the slightest movement.

My experiences in Japan of an exciting kind were pretty numerous, but, I regret to say, never included a really serious earthquake, and those who care to read more about the insignificant specimens that the country produces now-a-days must be referred to the pages of the Seismological Society's Journal and other publications of the distinguished geologist, my friend Professor John Milne, who has not only recorded observations on a large number of natural earthquakes, but has even succeeded in producing artificial ones so closely resembling the real thing as almost to defy detection.

CHAPTER VI

Official Visit to Yedo

During the later months of 1862 a good deal of correspondence went forward about the Itô Gumpei (murderer of the sentry and of the corporal) affair and the Richardson murder, and Colonel Neale held various conferences with the Shôgun's ministers. The diplomatic history of these proceedings has been already recounted by Sir Francis Adams, and as for the most part I knew little of what was going on, it need not be repeated here. The meeting-place for the more important discussions was Yedo, whither the Colonel used to proceed with his escort and the larger portion of the Legation staff. Some went by a gunboat, others rode up to the capital along the Tôkaidô. At that period and for several years after, the privilege of visiting Yedo was by Treaty restricted to the foreign diplomatic representatives, and non-official foreigners could not cross the Rokugô ferry, half way between Kanagawa and Yedo, except as the invited guest of one of the legations. And now all the foreign ministers had transferred their residences to Yokohama in consequence of the danger which menaced them at Yedo. We younger members, therefore, appreciated highly our opportunities, and it was with intense delight that I found myself ordered to accompany the chief early in December on one of his periodical expeditions thither. We started on horseback about one o'clock in the afternoon in solemn procession, the party consisting of Colonel Neale, A. von Siebold, Russell Robertson, and myself, with Lieutenant Applin commanding the mounted escort.

It was a miserably cold day, but R. and I combated the tempera-
ture by dropping behind to visit Mr Brown on our way through
Kanagawa, and then galloping on after the others. They had evidently been going at a foot's pace during the interval. At Kawasaki
we encountered an obstruction in the shape of an obstinate head
ferryman, who did not recognize the British Chargé d'Affaires,
and refused to pass us over. The men on guard at the watch-house
commanding the ferry, on seeing some of us approach to demand
their assistance, ran away. The Colonel fumed with wrath, but
fortunately at this moment there arrived in breathless haste a
mounted officer from Kanagawa, who had followed us of his own
accord on hearing that the English Chargé d'Affaires had passed
without a Japanese escort. So the ferryman collected his men, and
we got over without further trouble. A couple of miles beyond
the river we came to the well-known gardens called *Mmé Yashiki*,
the plum-orchard, where we were waited on by some very pretty
girls. Everybody who travelled along the Tôkaidô in those days,
who had any respect for himself, used to stop here, in season or
out of season, to drink a cup of straw-coloured tea, smoke a pipe
and chaff the waiting-maids. Fish cooked in various ways and
warm *saké* (rice beer) were also procurable, and red-faced native
gentlemen might often be seen folding themselves up into their
palanquins after a mild daylight debauch. Europeans usually
brought picnic baskets and lunched there, but even if they started
late were glad of any excuse for turning in to this charmingly
picturesque tea-garden. Everyone now-a-days is familiar with
the Japanese plum-tree as it is represented in the myriad works
of art of these ingenious people, but you must see the thing itself
to understand what a joyful surprise it is to enter the black-paled
enclosure crowded with the oddly angular trees, utterly leafless
but covered with delicate pink or white blossoms which emit a
faint fragrance, and cover the ground with the snow of their fallen
petals. It is early in February that they are in their glory, on a calm
day when the sun shines with its usual brilliance at that season,
while in every shady corner you may find the ground frozen as

hard as a stone. But to my taste the plum-blossom looks better on a cloudy day against a dull background of cryptomeria when you sit by a warm fire and gaze on it out of window. In December, however, only the swelling buds are to be seen stretching along the slender shoots of last spring. We proceeded on our way without any special incident until we reached the notorious suburb of Shinagawa, half consisting of houses, or rather palaces, of ill-fame, where a drunken fellow who stood in the middle of the road and shouted at us got a fall from one of the troopers, and so we reached the Legation about sunset. The rest of the staff and the infantry guard, who had come by sea, landed about an hour later.

The building occupied as the legation was part of a Buddhist temple, Tô-zen-ji, behind which lay a large cemetery. But our part of it had never been devoted to purposes of worship. Every large temple in Japan has attached to it a suite of what we might call state apartments, which are used only on ceremonial occasions once or twice in the year, but from time immemorial it has been the custom to accommodate foreign embassies in these buildings. A suitable residence for a foreign representative could not otherwise have been found in Yedo. As a general rule every Japanese, with the exception of the working classes, lives in his own house, instead of renting it as do most residents in an European capital. The only purely secular buildings large enough to lodge the British Minister and his staff were the *Yashiki* or "hotels" of *Daimiôs*, but the idea of expropriating one of these nobles in order to accommodate a foreign official was probably never mooted. There remained, therefore, only the "state apartments" of some large monastery as a temporary residence until a site could be obtained and the necessary buildings constructed. Consequently there was no ground for the reproach which one writer at least has urged against the foreign ministers, that by turning sacred edifices into dwelling-houses they had insulted the religious feelings of the Japanese people. In the early years of our intercourse with Japan it is true that we were regarded as unwelcome "intruders," but in native opinion we "polluted" the temples by our presence no more than we should have "polluted" any other residence that might have been assigned to us. Tô-zen-ji lay in the suburb of Takanawa fronting the seashore, and was therefore conveniently situated for communication with our ships, the smallest of which could anchor just inside the forts, at a distance of perhaps a mile and a half. Owing, however, to the shallowness of the bay, boats were unable to get up to the landing place at low tide, and the assistance which could have been rendered by a gunboat in the event of a sudden attack, such as had been experienced in 1861, was absolutely *nil*. There remained, however, the comfort derived from knowing that a refuge lay at no great distance, and no doubt the appearance of a gunboat within the line of forts that had been built to keep out foreign fleets produced a considerable moral effect upon the general population, though desperadoes of the sort that assaulted the guard in July 1861 would certainly have been no whit deterred by any number of threatening men-of-war which could not reach them. Behind the house there was a small ornamental garden with an artificial pond for gold fish, on the opposite side of which rose a hill covered with pine-trees. A good way off from the quarters of the minister, and at the back of the cemetery belonging to the temple, there was a small house named Jô-tô-an, which was occupied by the senior chancery assistant. A tall bamboo fence cut us off entirely from this part of the grounds, and joined the house at either end. The rooms were not spacious, and very little attempt had been made to convert them into comfortable apart-ments. I think there was an iron stove or two in the principal rooms, but elsewhere the only means of warming was a Japanese brasier piled up with red hot charcoal, the exhalations from which were very disagreeable to a novice. The native who wraps himself up in thick wadded clothes and squats on the floor has no difficulty in keeping himself warm with the aid of this arrangement, over which he holds the tips of his fingers. His legs being crumpled up under him, the superficies he presents to the cold air is much less than it would be if he sat in a chair with outstretched limbs in European fashion. To protect himself against draughts he has a screen standing behind him, and squats on a warm cushion stuffed with silk wool. These arrangements enable him even in winter to sit with the window open, so long as it has a southern aspect, and foreigners who adopt the same system have made shift to get on. But if you are going to live in Japan in European style, you must, in order to be moderately warm during the winter months, replace the paper of the outer wooden slides with glass, stop up the openwork above the grooves in which the slides work that divide the rooms, and either build a fireplace or put up an American stove. But even all this will not make you thoroughly comfortable. Underneath you there are thick straw mats laid upon thin and badly jointed boarding, through which the cutting north-west wind rises all over the floor, while the keen draughts pierce through between the uprights and the shrunken lath-and-plaster walls. The unsuitability of such a building as a residence for the minister and his staff had been perceived from the outset, and long negotiations, having for their object the erection of a permanent legation, had by this time resulted in the assignment of an excellent site, on which a complete series of buildings was being constructed from English designs, but at the expense of the Shôgun's government. Other sites in the immediate vicinity had been given to the French, Dutch and Americans for the same purpose. All these were carved out of what had been once a favourite pleasure resort of the people of Yedo, whither in the spring all classes flocked to picnic under the blossoms of the cherry-trees in sight of the blue waters of the bay. Gotenyama was indeed a famous spot in the history of the Shôgunate. In its early days the head of the State was wont to go forth thither to meet the great *daimiôs* on their annual entry into Yedo, until Iyémitsu, the third of the line, to mark still more strongly the supremacy to which he felt he could safely lay claim, resolved that henceforward he would receive them in his castle, just like the rest of his vassals. From that time the gardens had been dedicated to the public use. But already before the foreign diplomats took up their abode in Yedo, Gotenyama had been partially diverted from its original purpose, and vast masses of earth had been carried off to form part of the line of forts from Shinagawa to the other side of the junk channel that leads into the river. The British minister's residence, a large two-storied house, which from a distance seemed to be two, stood on an eminence fronting the sea. Magnificent timbers had been employed in its construction, and the rooms were of palatial dimensions. The floors were lacquered, and the walls covered with a tastefully designed Japanese paper. Behind and below it a bungalow had been erected for the Japanese secretary, and a site had been chosen for a second, destined for the assistants and students. On the southern side of the compound was an immense range of stables containing stalls for 40 horses, and on the second storey quarters for a portion of the European guard. Some slight progress had been made with the buildings for the French and Dutch legations. But we knew that the people disliked our presence there. The official and military class objected to the foreigner being permitted to occupy such a commanding position overlooking the rear of the forts, and the populace resented the conversion of their former pleasure-ground into a home for the "outer barbarians." To press on the completion of the houses and to take possession was rightly considered an important matter of policy. A deep trench was being dug round the enclosure, and a lofty wooden palisade was built on the inner margin, which, it was expected, would afford sufficient protection against a repetition of such attacks as that of the 5th July 1861, and the British ensign was to be hoisted again in Yedo as soon as the buildings should be ready for occupation. We all looked forward to that event with the liveliest feelings of anticipation, and for myself I anxiously expected its arrival because Yokohama was a hybrid sort of town, that by no means fulfilled my expectations, and I hoped before long to become a resident of the famous city to which I had looked with longing eyes from the other side of Europe.

We rode daily in the environs of Yedo, to the pretty tea-house at Oji, which is depicted with such bright colours in Laurence Oliphant's book, to the pond of Jiû-ni-sô on the road to Kôshiû, to the other pond called Senzoku half way to Mariko, and to the temple of Fudô at Meguro, where the pretty damsels at the tea-houses formed more than half the attraction. Within the city we made excursions to the temple of Kwannon at Asakusa, then and for long afterwards the principal sight of interest to the foreign visitor, to Atagoyama, where other pretty damsels served a decoction of salted cherry-blossoms, and to the temple of Kanda Miôjin for the view over the city. But the gorgeous mausoleums of the Shôguns at Shiba and Uyéno were closed to the foreigner, and remained so up to the revolution of 1868. We were allowed in riding back from Asakusa to catch a passing glimpse of the lotus pond Shinobazu-no-iké, which is now surrounded by a racecourse after the European manner, but the Fukiagé Park, since known as the Mikado's garden, and the short cut through the castle from the Sakurada Gate to the Wadagura Gate of the inner circle were shut to us in common with the Japanese public. A large portion of the city in the immediate neighbourhood of the castle, and large areas in every quarter were occupied by the *Yashiki* of *Daimiôs* and *Hatamotos*, of which little could be seen but long two-storied rows of stern barrack-buildings surrounding the residence of the owner. From the top of Atagoyama alone was it possible to get a view of the interior of such enclosures, and it must be admitted that the knowledge thus gained completely upset the idea that the nobles lived in palaces. Irregular masses of low brown roofs and black weather-boarded walls alone were visible. The use of telescopes was strictly forbidden on Atagoyama, lest the people should pry into the domestic doings of their masters. Wherever we went a band of mounted guards surrounded us, ostensibly for our protection, but also for the purpose of preventing free communication with the people. These men belonged to a force raised by the Shôgun's ministers from the younger sons of the *hatamotos*, and numbered 1,000 or 1,200. They wore the customary pair of swords (*i.e.* a long and short sabre thrust through the belt on the left side), a round flat hat woven from the tendrils of the wistaria, for the rank and file, and a mound-shaped lacquered wooden hat for the officers, a mantle or *haori*, and the wide petticoat-shaped trousers called *hakama*. Between them and the members of the foreign legations there existed no tie of any kind, for they were changed every fifteen days just like so many policemen, and mounted guard indifferently at all the legations. It was not until

1867 that I managed to break through this rule and get a special body of men attached to myself. Small guard-houses were dotted about the legation grounds for their accommodation. As soon as it became known that a foreigner was about to go out on foot or on horseback, half a dozen were detailed to follow him at all hazards. It was impossible to escape their vigilance. They were to prevent our speaking to any person above the rank of a common citizen or to enter a private house. On one occasion two members of our legation managed a visit to the father of a young *samurai* named Kotarô, who lived with us to study English. The fact was reported, and when the visitors went a second time they found the occupants of the house had removed to another part of the city. We were allowed to sit down in shops, and even to bargain for articles that took our fancy; but two kind of purchases were strictly prohibited, maps and the official list of *daimiôs* and government officials. Anything we bought had to be sent afterwards to the legation, and delivered to the officials of the foreign department who lived within our gates, and payment was made to them. On one occasion the Prussian representative, Herr Max von Brandt, made a determined stand against this prohibition. Entering the shop of the bookseller Okada-ya in Shimmei-maye, where we foreigners were in the habit of buying books, he inquired for the List of Daimiôs. The bookseller replied that he had it not in stock. Herr von Brandt knew that he had, and announced his intention of remaining there until he was furnished with what he required. He sent a member of his party home to the Legation to bring out the materials for luncheon, and sat determinedly down in the shop. The guards were at their wits' end. At last they dispatched a messenger to the castle to represent the impossibility of inducing him to give way, and at last towards evening there came an order to say that for this once the foreigner was to have the book. So the day was won. As a matter of fact, however, it was never necessary to proceed to this extremity, as we could easily procure what we wanted in the way of maps and printed books through our Japanese teachers. MSS. were always a difficulty. As nothing could be published without permission, any book that touched upon governmental matters had from of old to be circulated in MS. Amongst such works were the so-called *Hundred Laws of Iyéyasu*, which were supposed to embody the constitution of the Japanese government. The book contains references to offices of state that were instituted after his time, and the utmost that can be alleged in its favour is that it perhaps contains a few maxims from his lips and certain rules as to the appointment of high political functionaries that were observed in actual practice. There was another book, of undoubted authenticity, containing a vast mass of administrative regulations, of which I never obtained a copy until after the revolution, when it was no longer of practical value. That MS. is now in the British Museum. Another expedient for eluding the censorate was printing forbidden books with moveable types. It was frequently resorted to during the last years of the Shôgunate and at the beginning of the new rule of the Mikado, especially for narratives of political events during that period and for one or two important treatises on politics. Shimmei-maye was one of our favourite resorts in those days; here were to be had cheap swords, porcelain, coloured prints, picture-books and novels. I much regret that I did not then begin to collect, when the blocks were comparatively fresh; a complete set of Hokusai's Mangwa, in perfect condition, could be had for a couple of dollars, and his Hundred Views of Fuji for about a couple of shillings. But I had little spare cash for such luxuries, and all my money went in necessaries.

Two days after our arrival in Yedo we paid a visit to the *Gorôjiû*, or Shôgun's Council. The word means "August Elders." It was somewhat *infra dig.* for a foreign representative to use the prefix *go* in speaking of them, but the phrase had been caught up from the Japanese who surrounded the minister, and for a long time I believe it was thought that *go* meant five. I unveiled the mistake, and when I afterwards became interpreter to the Legation we adopted the practice of giving them the bare *rôjiû*, except in addressing them direct, when etiquette demanded the honorific. I was unprovided with anything in the shape of uniform, and had to borrow a gold-laced forage cap from Applin. We came afterwards to look with much contempt on these gauds, and to speak derisively, of "brass caps," but in 1862 I was young enough to take considerable pride in a distinctive mark of rank, and after this occasion lost no time in buying a bit of broad gold lace to wear like my fellow officers. It was an imposing procession, consisting as it did of half-a-dozen "brass caps," the military train escort of twelve men under their gorgeous lieutenant, and a flock of about forty Japanese guards hovering about us before, behind, and on either flank. In these days a foreign representative may often be detected approaching the office of the minister for foreign affairs without any suite, and in the humble *jinrikisha* drawn by one scantily clad coolie. The interview took place in a long room in the house of one of the *rôjiû*. A row of small black-lacquered tables extended down each side, and chairs were set for the Japanese as well as the foreigners. On each table stood an earthen brasier, a black-lacquered smoking-stand, with brass fire-pot and ash-pit, and two long pipes, with a supply of finely cut tobacco in a neat black box. Three of the ministers sat on the right side of the room, and with them an *ometsuké*, whose title was explained to me to mean spy. I suppose "censor" or "reporter" would be nearer. Below them sat eight *gai-koku bu-giô*, or commissioners for foreign affairs. We used to call them governors of foreign affairs, probably because the governor of Kanagawa was also a *bu-giô*. In the centre of the room sat a "governor" on a stool, while two interpreters (one of whom was Moriyama Takichirô) squatted on the floor. The four higher Japanese officers alone were provided with tables and chairs, the "governors" sitting on square stools, with their hands in the plackets of their trousers. After some complimentary talk about the weather and health, which are *dc rigueur* in Japan, a double row of attendants in light blue hempen robes (we used to term the upper part "wings") came in bearing aloft black lacquer boxes full of slices of sponge cake and *yôkan* (a sweetened bean paste), and afterwards oranges and persimmons. Then tea was served in two manners, simply infused, and also the powdered leaf mixed up with hot water and frothed. The conversation proceeded at a very slow pace, as it had to be transmitted through two interpreters, ours who spoke Dutch and English, and theirs who spoke Japanese and Dutch. This gave rise to misunderstandings, and the Japanese ministers seemed every now and then to profit by this double obstruction to answer very much from the purpose, so that Colonel Neale's observations had to be repeated all over again, interpreted and re-interpreted. Often the ministers would seem at a loss, whereupon one of the "governors" would leave his stool and glide up to whisper something in his ear. This proceeding reminded one of the flappers in Laputa. The principal topic was the murder of the sentry and corporal at Tô-zen-ji which has already been related. To all the demands made by Colonel Neale, in accordance with the instructions he had received from Lord Russell, the *rôjiû* objected, and when he informed them that the British Government required the payment of £10,000 in gold as an indemnity to the families of the two murdered men, they opened their eyes very wide indeed. They offered $3000. Colonel Neale at last lost all patience, which no doubt was what they were aiming at. He gave them a piece of his mind in pretty strong language, and the interview came to an end, after, I suppose, a sitting of about three hours length, without, anything having been settled. I forget whether it was on this occasion that Siebold literally translated the epithet "son of a gun" by *teppô no musuko*; the adjective that preceded it he did not attempt to translate, as it has not even a literal equivalent in Japanese. The way in which the ministers contradicted themselves from time to time was something wonderful, and the application of the good unmistakeable Anglo-Saxon word for him who "says the thing that is not," was almost venial.

Of course Colonel Neale did not omit to complain of the ferryman and the guards at Kawasaki, who had run away instead of putting us over the river, and Eusden in translating used the words *zij sloopen alle weg*, which excited my risible muscles kept at too great a stretch through these tedious hours. I whispered to my neighbour, "they all sloped away"; a terrible frown from the old gentleman rebuked my indecorous behaviour, and I was afterwards informed that I should never be allowed thenceforth to be present on one of these solemn occasions. That was a relief to me, but I confess I ought to have felt more contrite than I did. At the age of nineteen and a half a boy is still a boy, but I ought to have manifested more respect for my elders.

Early in February we received news that the legation buildings in Gotenyama had been destroyed by fire on the night of the 1st. Many years afterwards I learnt on the best possible authority that the incendiaries were chiefly Chôshiû men belonging to the anti-foreign party; three at least afterwards rose to high position in the state. These were Count Itô, Minister President of State (1886); Count Inouyé Kaoru; who the third was I forget. It need scarcely be said that they long ago abandoned their views of the necessity of putting an end to the intercourse of their country with the outside world, and they are now the leaders of the movement in favour of the introduction into Japan of whatever western institutions are adapted to the wants and wishes of the people.

Willis and I were now living together in a wing of the legation house at No. 20 on the Bund, and a young Japanese *samurai* named Kobayashi Kotarô messed with us. He had been placed under Willis' charge by the Japanese Government in order to acquire the English language, and was a nice boy, though perhaps not endowed with more than average abilities. He disappeared to his home about the time that the ultimatum of the British Government was presented to the Council of the Tycoon in the spring of 1863, and we never heard of him again. I had the teacher Takaoka Kanamé now all to myself, and was beginning to read Japanese documents. Across the hills south of the settlement lived a priest who knew something of the Sanskrit alphabet as used in Japan, and I used to go once or twice a week to him for instruction, but these studies were interrupted by the rumours of war that began soon to prevail; and the lessons from the American missionary, Mr Brown, also came to an end, as I was now able to get on alone.

CHAPTER VII

Demands for Reparation—Japanese Proposal to Close the Ports—Payment of the Indemnity (1863)

A very complete account of the murder of Richardson, and the failure of the Japanese Government to afford satisfactory redress either for that injury or for the attack on the Legation in June, had been sent home to the Foreign Office, and in March 1863 Colonel Neale received instructions to demand ample reparation from both the Tycoon and the Prince of Satsuma. On the 6th April he sent Eusden up to Yedo on board the gunboat "Havoc" to deliver a Note, demanding the payment of £10,000 in gold for the wives and families of Sweet and Crimp, an ample apology for the other affair, and the payment of £100,000 as a penalty on the Tycoon for allowing an Englishman to be murdered in his territory in open daylight without making any effort to arrest the murderers. He warned the Council that refusal would be attended with very deplorable consequences to their country, and gave them twenty days to consider their reply. This lengthened period was allowed on account of the absence of the Tycoon and his chief advisers, who had left for Kiôto on the 3rd. If at the conclusion of the term allotted no answer was returned, or an unsatisfactory one was given, coercive measures would immediately be taken. It was also intended that on the return of the "Havoc" from Yedo, the "Pearl" should be despatched to Kagoshima to demand of the Prince of Satsuma the trial and execution of the murderers of Richardson in the presence of one or more English officers, and the payment of £25,000 to be distributed to the relatives of Richardson, to Marshall, Clarke and Mrs Borradaile.

On the 10th Eusden came back from Yedo, bringing a receipt for the note and a refusal on the part of the Council to send an officer down to Kagoshima to advise the Prince of Satsuma to admit the demands to be made upon him. So the idea of despatching the "Pearl" was abandoned for the moment, as it was impossible to foretell whether the Council would give in. If they were obstinate, reprisals would at once, it was thought, be commenced, and all our available force would be required to coerce the Tycoon's people. Satsuma must be left to be dealt with afterwards. So the Colonel waited until the 26th. By the 24th April we had in the harbour the "Euryalus," 35 guns, bearing the flag of Admiral Küper, the "Pearl," 21 guns, "Encounter," 14 (commanded by the brave Roderick Dew), "Rattler," 17, "Argus," 6, "Centaur," 6, and 3 gunboats. The despatch boats "Racehorse" and "Ringdove" were employed in travelling backwards and forwards between Yokohama and Shanghai with the mails, and the "Coquette" was daily expected from Hongkong.

But as was to be anticipated, the Council begged for further delay. They asked for thirty days, and Colonel Neale gave them fifteen.

My teacher Takaoka, who had private relations with the *yashiki* of the Prince of Kishiû, said they had never expected to get more than a fortnight, and as they felt certain the English Chargé d'Affaires would cut down their demands, they asked for double. He believed that the only motive for the delay was to gain time for preparation, and that war was certain. In the native quarter it was rumoured that the English had asked for the delay, which had been graciously granted by the Council; otherwise we should have been attacked the very day after the term elapsed. The inhabitants of Yedo expected war, and began to remove their valuables into the country. Young Kotarô had been carried off by his mama about the 20th. At Uraga, the little junk-port just outside the entrance to the bay of Yedo, there was a panic, and the people were said to have decamped with all their movable property to Hodogaya on the Tôkaidô. On the other hand, there was some alarm felt in the foreign settlement. Meetings were held at which resolutions were passed to the effect that it was the duty of the executive to provide for the safety of the European residents. At the same time the merchants declared their intention of not leaving the settlement unless specially called on to do so by Colonel Neale, as they believed that if they deserted their property without such an order, they would not be able to recover its value afterwards in the event of its being destroyed. The precedent of the opium surrendered to Captain Elliot, the British Superintendent of Trade at Canton in 1839, was of course in their minds, and they acted prudently in throwing the responsibility on the authorities.

On the 1st May the Council asked for another delay of fifteen days. Eusden was sent up to Yedo with a message to the Council that before the Colonel could grant their request they must send down to Yokohama one of their number to receive an important communication which he had to make to them. The native population now began to be seriously alarmed, and the shopkeepers of Kanagawa removed their effects to Hodogaya so as to be out of reach of a bombardment, and to secure a further retreat into the interior, if necessary, by the cross-country paths. The 2nd of May was the last day on which the Yokohama people were permitted by the native authorities to send away their property to Yedo. The government circulated a sensible proclamation from door to door telling them not to be alarmed as there would be no war. At the same time notice was served on the peasants within two miles of Yokohama to be prepared to give up their houses to the troops, but as yet no soldiers had appeared on the scene.

On the 4th and 5th May long conferences took place between the English and French representatives and Admirals and two Commissioners for Foreign Affairs, Takémoto Kai no Kami and Takémoto Hayato no Shô, who had been deputed by the Council to explain the reasons why a further delay was necessary. They probably represented that the difficulty in acceding to the English demands arose from the opposition of the *daimiôs*, for it seems that an offer was made to them that the English and French forces should assist the Tycoon to quell the resistance of the anti-foreign party, in order to enable him to carry out the promises to which he was bound by treaty. They offered, it was reported, to pay the money indemnity, disguising it under the ingenious fiction of payment for a man-of-war ordered in England, and wrecked on its way out. Finally an extension of time was accorded until the 23rd of May, in order that the personal consent of the Tycoon, who was expected to return by that date, might be obtained to the English ultimatum.

I rode out to Hodogaya on the afternoon of the 5th and met the train of the wife of a *daimiô* going westwards, but saw very few armed men other than those who accompanied her. A rumour had got about that 10,000 men were in the village and its neighbourhood, but the report was obviously without foundation.

During the night of the 5th May there was a general exodus of all the native servants employed in the foreign settlement. Many of them took advantage of the occasion to "spoil the Egyptians." When Willis and I rose in the morning and called for "boy" to bring breakfast, there was a dead silence. I descended to the pantry and found it empty. Servants and cook had gone off, carrying with them a revolver, a Japanese sword, several spoons and forks which they doubtless imagined to be silver, and the remains of last night's dinner wrapped in a table-cloth. This theft was the more curious, as I had the day before entrusted my servant with a considerable sum of native money to change into Mexican dollars, which he had faithfully delivered to me. But we ought to have suspected their intentions, as they had asked for an advance of half a month's wages, and had contentedly received wages up to date. Takaoka and my groom were faithful, so was also the messenger who went off into fits of congratulation on learning that the petty cash-box, of which I had charge, had not disappeared. It is much to the credit of the latter class that they have often stuck by their masters on occasions of trouble and even danger, when every one else has deserted the foreigner.

With some difficulty we procured some eggs and sponge cake, and I went off to the customhouse to report the robbery. The officials, of course, promised to find the thieves, but we never heard anything more of them or of our property. All day long the townspeople continued to depart at a great rate. I went down to the native town, where I found many of the houses shut up, and at others everything ready packed for removal. Among the rest my friend the bookseller, at the corner of Benten-dôri, had taken to his heels. But during the afternoon a proclamation was issued by the customhouse to tell the people that there would be no fighting, and many of them returned. The excitement was great throughout the town, both among foreigners and natives, and a lamentable instance of hastiness occurred on the part of a Frenchman. A native merchant, accompanied by two others, went to ask payment of a small debt that he claimed, and on its being refused, tried to obtain the money by force. Thereupon the Frenchman shot him, and two others, including the vice-consul, also fired their revolvers. Four bullets passed through the body of the unfortunate man, but without killing him. The French Admiral was excessively angry. He at once arrested the merchant and had him conveyed on board the flagship. Two Americans were likewise attacked, and one of them was carried off halfway across the swamp by eight men, who frightened him with a spear and an iron hook which they held over his head. He was rescued by the tall sergeant of our legation guard, or else he would probably have been severely beaten, if not killed, for the Japanese were unable to distinguish between foreigners of different nationalities.

On the 11th my teacher told me that a messenger had come to him from Yedo, sent by a personage of high rank, who desired to learn confidentially the intentions of the English Chargé d'Affaires, and whether he was disposed to await the return of the Tycoon, which would not be for three or four months, before taking hostile measures. In that case the high personage, who was superior in rank to the Council, would agree to issue a proclamation that a delay of a thousand days had been agreed upon, which would have the effect of restoring tranquillity at Yokohama. That if Colonel Neale, getting tired of these repeated delays, should change the seat of the negotiations to Ozaka, the high personage would have to perform *harakiri*, which he rather wished to avoid, as a penalty for failing to induce the foreigner to listen to his representations. I communicated this to Colonel Neale, and the reply sent was that he could not consent to wait so long as three months.

The Council had announced the return of the Tycoon for the 24th May, and Colonel Neale had replied that under the circumstances he would give time for "His Majesty's" settling down again at home, but on the 16th a note was received from them stating that circumstances had arisen which prevented their fixing any date whatever for his arrival at Yedo. This seemed to point to an indefinite postponement of a settlement, but the Colonel's patience was not even yet exhausted. This accorded with what my teacher had told me. The high personage turned out to be the Prince of Owari. Takaoka now said that having transmitted Colonel Neale's answer to Kiôto, he would no longer be under the necessity of committing suicide, as he had been able to show that he was not responsible for the foreigner's obstinacy.

Up to the 16th the general feeling was that the Council would give way, but the demand for a further postponement of the Japanese answer did not tend to encourage the hope of a peaceful settlement. A Japanese friend told me that the Tycoon could not by any means accept the assistance of foreign powers against the *daimiôs*, and that the abolition of the Mikado's dignity was impracticable. If we attacked Satsuma the Tycoon and *daimiôs* would be bound to make common cause with him. I suppose the idea of the foreign diplomatic representatives at that time was to support the Tycoon, whose claim to be considered the sovereign of Japan had already been called in question by Rudolph Lindau in his "Open Letter" of 1862, against the anti-foreign party consisting of the Mikado and *daimiôs*, and if necessary to convert him into something more than a mere feudal ruler. For we had as yet no idea of the immense potency that lay in the mere name of the sovereign *de jure*, and our studies in Japanese history had not yet enabled us to realize the truth that in the civil wars of Japan the victory had as a rule rested with the party that had managed to obtain possession of the person of the Mikado and the regalia. There has probably never been any sovereign in the world whose title has rested upon so secure a basis as that of the ancient emperors of Japan.

On the 25th another conference took place between the English and French diplomatic and naval authorities on the one side, and Takémoto Kai no Kami and a new man named Shibata Sadatarô on the other. The latter began by thanking the foreign representatives in the name of the Tycoon for their offer of material assistance, which he was, however, compelled to decline, as he must endeavour to settle the differences between the *daimiôs* and himself by his own unaided forces and authority. As to the indemnity, the Tycoon's government recognized that the demand was just, but they were afraid to pay immediately, as their yielding would bring the *daimiôs* down upon them. But they offered to pay the money by instalments in such a manner as not to attract public notice, and the further discussion of the details was put off to a future occasion. Probably Colonel Neale did not care very much how the matter was arranged, provided he could show to Her Majesty's Government that he had carried out his instructions. So the basis of an understanding was arrived at, and it was further conceded that the foreign representatives, that is those of England and France, should take measures to defend Yokohama from attack by the anti-foreign party.

Colonel Neale had written to Major-General Brown, who was in command at Shanghai, applying for a force of two thousand men, but a despatch now arrived from the general stating his inability and objections to furnishing any troops. It was said that he had ridiculed the idea of a military expedition against Japan long before Colonel Neale proposed it to him. Nevertheless the establishment of a garrison of English troops at Yokohama was merely delayed by this refusal, and after Sir Rutherford Alcock's return to Japan in the spring of 1864 good reasons were given to the same general why he should change his mind.

All this time there existed considerable alarm with respect to the aims and intentions of a somewhat mysterious class of Japanese called *rônin*. These were men of the two-sworded class, who had thrown up the service of their *daimiôs*, and plunged into the political agitations of the time, which had a two-fold object, firstly, to restore the Mikado to his ancient position, or rather to pull down the Tycoon to the same level as the great *daimiôs*, and secondly, the expulsion of "the barbarians" from the sacred soil of Japan. They came principally from the south and west of the country, but there were many from Mito in the east, and a splinkling from all the other clans. About the end of May there was a rumour that they designed to attack Kanagawa, and the Americans still living there were compelled to transfer their residence to Yokohama, not, however, without "compensation for disturbance."

The Tycoon's people were naturally desirous of doing all that was practicable to conciliate their domestic enemies, and turned such rumours to account in the hope of being able to confine the foreigners at Yokohama within a limited space, such as had formed the prison-residence of the Dutch at Nagasaki in former times. Incidents, too, were not wanting of a character to enforce their arguments. One of the assistants of the English consulate was threatened with personal violence by a couple of two-sworded men as he was entering a tea-house on the hill at Kanagawa. He pulled out his pistol, and pointed it at them, on which they drew back. Taking advantage of the opportunity he ran down to the landing-place, where he got a boat and so returned in safety to Yokohama. It was reported that the officials at the guard-house tried to prevent the boatmen from taking him across the bay, but however this may be, they pacified his assailants, one of whom had half-drawn his sword; and in those days we were always told that a *samurai* might not return his sword to the scabbard without shedding blood, so that the affair was entitled to be ranked as very alarming.

At the beginning of June, in consequence of a report that half-a-dozen *rônins* were concealed in the place, the *betté-gumi* (a body from which the legation guards at Yedo were supplied), together with some drilled troops, came down to Yokohama, and took up their quarters at some newly erected buildings under Nogé hill, and from that date until long after the revolution of 1868 we had constantly a native garrison. I recognized among the former several men with whom I had become friends during the visit to Yedo already narrated. Fresh additions were made to the British squadron in the shape of two sloops, the "Leopard" and the "Perseus." The rumours of warlike operations had died away, and it was given out that the intention of directly enforcing our demands on Satsuma had been abandoned, as the Tycoon had undertaken to see to that part of the business, and it was believed also that to insist upon them at present would give rise to a civil war.

On the 14th June there arrived at the legation in Yokohama Kikuchi Iyo no Kami and Shibata Sadatarô, Commissioners for Foreign Affairs, to complete arrangements for paying $440,000 (representing £110,000) in seven instalments extending over six weeks, the first to be delivered on the 18th. But on that day came a note of excuse from one of the Council stating that unavoidable circumstances had arisen which prevented the agreement being carried out, and that he himself would in a day or two arrive at Yokohama to discuss matters with the English Chargé d'Affaires. Colonel Neale very properly refused to hold any more communications with the Tycoon's ministers, and after a couple of days' consideration, finally placed the solution in the hands of Admiral Küper. The latter, it was said, did not know what to do. He had never seen a gun fired in action, and hardly appreciated the Colonel's suggestion that he should at once proceed to seize the steamers lately purchased in such numbers by the Japanese.

The Council at Yedo now became thoroughly frightened; they had temporized as long as possible, and had worn out the patience of the English authorities. But they left no stone unturned to avoid openly giving way, and Ogasawara himself came down to Yokohama to bring the French Chargé d'Affaires and Admiral to intercede. The latter, however, refused; insisted on the demands of Great Britain being satisfied, and claimed that the defence of Yokohama should be entrusted to them. Ogasawara had just returned from Kiôto with an order from the Tycoon, dictated to him by the Mikado and the anti-foreign element in the ancient capital, to make arrangements with the foreign representatives for closing all the ports! For himself he seemed to dislike his instructions, and even gave hints to the French Chargé d'Affaires as to the nature of the reply which had best be given. A pageful of notes of exclamation would not be sufficient to express the astonishment of the foreign public of Yokohama when this extraordinary announcement was made, but the presence of the combined squadrons in the harbour relieved them from any anxiety as to the manner in which the diplomatic representatives would reply to it.

The Japanese Government, having completely failed to persuade the French authorities to intervene on their behalf, which would have indeed been impossible when the request was accompanied by the preposterous demand that foreigners should forthwith clear out of Yokohama, sent a message to Colonel Neale at one a.m. on the morning of the 24th June to say that the money should be paid, and requesting to be informed at what hour he would receive it. The reply was that the original agreement to pay in instalments, having been broken by the Japanese Government, was now null and void, and that the whole must be delivered in the course of the day. This was accordingly done; at an early hour carts laden with boxes containing each a couple of thousand dollars began to arrive at the legation. All the Chinese shroffs (men employed by merchants and bankers in the Far East to examine coin to see whether it is genuine) were borrowed to do the shroffing and counting. The chancery was crowded with the intelligent Chinamen busily employed in clinking one coin against another, and putting them up into parcels, to be replaced in the boxes and carried off on board the squadron. The process occupied three days. But already on the 24th Colonel Neale had addressed a letter to the Admiral relieving him of the unwelcome task of undertaking coercive operations.

The note, dated on the very day on which the indemnity was paid, in which Ogasawara Dzusho no Kami (to give him his full title) had conveyed to Colonel Neale the orders of the Tycoon to close the ports and expel all foreigners from the country, was the first on which I was called to exercise my capacity as a translator. Of course I had to get the help of my teacher to read it, but my previous practice in the epistolary style enabled me to understand the construction, and to give a closer version perhaps than either of the others which were prepared in the legation. This, to me supremely important, document ran as follows: —

I communicate with you by a despatch.

The orders of the Tycoon, received from Kiôto, are to the effect that the ports are to be closed and the foreigners driven out, because the people of the country do not desire intercourse with foreign countries. The discussion of this has been entirely entrusted to me by His Majesty. I therefore send you this communication first, before holding a Conference as to the details.

Respectful and humble communication.

It is perhaps a little too literal. The opening phrase is simply equivalent to the "Monsieur le Chargé d'Affaires," and the sentence with which the note concludes is about the same thing as the "assurance of high consideration," which we have borrowed from the French. But the rest of it is accurate, and the allusion to the Mikado which appears in the version made from the Dutch translation furnished by the Japanese (*vide* the *Bluebook*) had nothing to support it in the original text. I cannot forbear from quoting the reply of Colonel Neale, though as far as possible I intend in these "Reminiscences" not to rely on published sources of information. It ran thus: —

Lieutenant-Colonel Neale to the Japanese Minister for Foreign Affairs.
Yokohama, June 24, 1863.

The undersigned, Her Britannic Majesty's Chargé d'Affaires, has received, in common with his colleagues, and with extreme amazement, the extraordinary announcement which, under instructions from the Tycoon, His Excellency has addressed to him.

Apart from the audacious nature of this announcement, which is unaccompanied by any explanations whatever, the Undersigned is bound to believe that both the Spiritual and Temporal sovereigns of this country are totally of the disastrous consequences which must arise to Japan by their determinations thus conveyed through you to close the opened ports, and to remove therefrom the subjects of the Treaty Powers.

For himself, as Representative of Her Britannic Majesty, the Undersigned has to observe, in the first instance, that the Rulers of this country may perhaps still have it in their power to modify and soften the severe and irresistible measures which will, without the least doubt, be adopted by Great Britain most effectually to maintain and enforce its Treaty obligations with this country, and, more than this, to place them on a far more satisfactory and solid footing than heretofore, by speedily making known and developing any rational and acceptable plans directed to this end, which may be at present concealed by His Majesty the Tycoon or the Mikado, or by both, to the great and imminent peril of Japan.

It is therefore the duty of the Undersigned solemnly to warn the Rulers of this country that when the decision of Her

Majesty's Government, consequent upon the receipt of Your Excellency's announcement, shall have in due course been taken, the development of all ulterior determinations now kept back will be of no avail.

The Undersigned has in the meantime to inform Your Excellency, with a view that you may bring the same to the knowledge of His Majesty the Tycoon, who will doubtless make the same known to the Mikado, that the indiscreet communication now made through Your Excellency is unparalleled in the history of all nations, civilized or uncivilized; that it is, in fact, a declaration of war by Japan itself against the whole of the Treaty Powers, and the consequences of which, if not at once arrested, it will have to expiate by the severest and most merited chastisement.

With Respect and Consideration.

EDWD. ST. JOHN NEALE.

With the exception of the lapse from the third person to the second, in the second, third and fourth paragraphs, this note is well constructed, and its periods nicely balanced. The language is perhaps rather stronger than more modern taste would approve, but with a powerful, almost overwhelming squadron of men-of-war at one's back, the temptation to express one's feelings with frankness is not easy to resist.

What the writer meant by "rational and acceptable means" directed to the end of placing the treaty obligations of Great Britain with Japan on a more "satisfactory and solid footing than heretofore" can only be conjectured. I think it is an allusion to the plan that had been mooted of our affording material assistance to the Tycoon in suppressing the opposition of the *daimiôs* of the west and south to the pro-foreign policy of the Japanese Government, and perhaps to a formal agreement between the Tycoon and the Mikado that the latter should ratify the treaties. Certainly the successful execution of such a plan would have placed the Tycoon

firmly in the seat of his ancestors, and have forestalled the revolution of 1868 by which his successor was upset, but it would not
have been effected without enormous bloodshed, and the Japanese
people would have hated the ruler who had called in foreign aid
to strengthen his position. He could then only have maintained
himself there by the adoption of the severest measures of repres-
sion, and the nation would have been subjected to a terrible and
lasting despotism. It is certainly a thing to rejoice at that the
Tycoon's council had sufficient patriotism to reject such an offer.
The Japanese were left to work out their own salvation, and when
the revolution did at last break out, the loss of life and property
was restricted within narrow limits, while the resulting benefits
to the Japanese nation in the establishment of civilized and comparatively free institutions have been such as would have been for
ever precluded had the suggestions of certain Europeans been
listened to.

CHAPTER VIII

Bombardment of Kagoshima

Thus one portion of the instructions sent out from home had been carried into effect, and there now remained only the exaction of reparation from the Prince of Satsuma. The demands to be made included, it will be remembered, the trial and execution in the presence of English officers of the murderers of Richardson, and the payment by the Prince of an indemnity of £25,000 as compensation to Richardson's relatives and to the three other members of the party who had been attacked. Marshall and Clarke had recovered from their wounds, which in the case of the latter were serious enough, as he had received a dangerous sword cut in the shoulder, and Mrs Borradaile, who was not wounded, had returned to China. The Tycoon's people were naturally desirous of having the settlement with Satsuma left in their hands, but I suppose Ogasawara, when pressed on the point by Colonel Neale, acknowledged that the government were impotent in the matter, and the British Chargé d'Affaires consequently assumed the responsibility of requesting the Admiral to convey him and his staff to Kagoshima, in order to present the demands he had been instructed to formulate.

The Admiral had at first been unwilling to send more than a couple of ships, but it was finally determined that the squadron should consist of H.M.S. "Euryalus," "Pearl," "Perseus," "Argus," "Coquette," "Racehorse," and the gunboat "Havoc." The whole staff of the legation, from Colonel Neale down to myself, embarked on board the various ships, Willis and myself being in the paddle-sloop "Argus," Commander Lewis Moore. The weather on the voyage down was remarkably fine, and the squadron arrived at the mouth of the Bay of Kagoshima, where it anchored for the night, on the afternoon of the 11th August. Early on the following morning we proceeded up the bay, and came to an anchor off the town.

A letter had been prepared beforehand stating the demands, which had somehow or other been translated into Japanese by Siebold and his teacher; it was a difficult document, and I fancy the Japanese version did not read very well. A boat at once came off from the shore with two officers, to whom the letter was delivered. In the afternoon of the following day some other officials visited the flagship, and stated that it was quite impossible to say when the answer would be given. The name of the principal official who visited Colonel Neale on this occasion was Ijichi Shôji. I knew him very well afterwards in Yedo. He and his retinue of forty men came on board, after having exchanged a parting cup of *saké* with their prince, with the full design of making a sudden onslaught upon the British officers, and killing at any rate the principal ones among them; they intended in this way to make themselves masters of the flagship. It was a bold conception, and might have been successful but for the precautions taken on our side. Only two or three were admitted into the Admiral's cabin, while the marines kept a vigilant eye upon the retinue who remained on the quarter deck. While they were still on board another boat arrived, whether with reinforcements or orders to countermand the intended slaughter I do not know, but Ijichi, after communicating with the men who came in her, said he must return to the shore. In the evening a written reply was received, the bearer of which was told to return on the following morning to learn whether it was considered of a satisfactory character.

The letter on examination proved to contain a *fin de non recevoir*; it said that the murderers could not be found, blamed the Tycoon for having made treaties without inserting a clause to prevent foreigners from impeding the passage of the prince along the highroads; spoke of delay until the criminals could be arrested, captured, and punished, after which the question of an indemnity could be discussed, and practically referred the British Chargé d'Affaires back to the Yedo Government. When the messenger arrived on the morning of the 14th, he was informed that the reply was considered unsatisfactory, and that no further communication would be held with the Japanese except under a flag of truce. The Admiral then made a little trip up the bay to reconnoitre some foreign-built steamers lying at anchor off Wilmot Point in the plan, and take some soundings at the head of the bay beyond. On his return in the afternoon the commanders of the various ships were summoned on board the flagship to receive their instructions from the Admiral. There was no intention on our part of immediately attacking the batteries, but the Admiral probably supposed that by adopting reprisals, that is taking possession of the steamers, he would induce the Satsuma men to give some more satisfactory reply than that already received.

In pursuance of this plan, Captain Borlase in the "Pearl," with the "Coquette," "Argus," and "Racehorse," proceeded to seize the steamers at dawn of the 15th. We were, of course, very excited, and busily engaged, as we approached, in estimating the probability of their offering resistance; but as the "Argus" was laid alongside the "Sir George Grey," we saw the crew rapidly disappearing over the other side into shore boats with which they had already provided themselves. No attempt was made by us to take any prisoners, but two remained on board the "Sir George Grey," who gave their names to me as Godai and Matsugi Kôwan. On being transferred to the flagship they adopted the aliases of Otani and Kashiwa. The fomer was a remarkably handsome man, with a noble countenance, and was, I believe, the captain of the steamer. The profession of the second was that of a physician; he had been to Europe with the first Japanese embassy in 1862, and had in fact only just returned. Both of them were afterwards well known, the first as a rather speculative man of business who established indigo works at Ozaka with capital borrowed from the Mikado's government, the second was for a short time prefect of Yokohama in 1868, and afterwards Minister for Foreign Affairs under the name of Terashima Munénori, and he still (in 1887) holds office at Tôkiô.

We returned, with our prizes lashed alongside, to the anchorage under the island of Sakura-jima, whither the squadron had removed on the afternoon of the 12th in order to be out of range of the guns in the forts before the town, the "Euryalus" and "Pearl" lying about mid channel, between us and the forts. Here we awaited the development of events, which came sooner than was expected. The Japanese made no sign, and we could not divine their intentions from the slight glimpses obtainable of the movements on shore. But at noon the report of a gun was suddenly heard, and immediately all the batteries opened fire upon the squadron. Although it was raining and blowing like a typhoon, the Admiral at once gave orders to engage, and made a signal to us and the "Racehorse" and the "Coquette" to burn the prizes. On this we all rushed on board our prize and began to plunder. I secured a Japanese matchlock and a conical black war-hat (*jin-gasa*), but some of the officers found money, silver *ichibus* and gilt *nibus*. The sailors seized hold of everything portable, such as looking glasses, decanters, benches and even old pieces of matting. After about an hour of this disorder the steamer was scuttled and set on fire, and we went to take up our order in the line of battle. The plan shows how the line was formed.

Some time elapsed before we returned the fire of the Japanese, and it was said that the tardiness of the flagship in replying to the first shot of the Japanese (two hours) was due to the fact that the door of the ammunition magazine was obstructed by piles of boxes of dollars, the money paid for the indemnity being still on board. The "Perseus," which was lying close under fort No. 9, had to slip her cable, and the anchor was months afterwards recovered by the Satsuma people aud returned to us. Owing to this delay she had to take the last position in the line. It was a novel sensation to be exposed to cannon shot, and the boisterous weather did not add at all to one's equanimity. The whole line went a little way up the bay, and then curving round to the left returned along the northern shore at a distance of about 400 yards, each vessel as she passed pouring her broadside into the successive forts. About three quarters of an hour after the engagement commenced we saw the flagship hauling off, and next the "Pearl" (which had rather lagged behind) swerved out of the line. The cause of this was the death of Captain Josling and Commander Wilmot of the "Euryalus" from a roundshot fired from fort No. 7. Unwittingly she had been steered between the fort and a target at which the Japanese gunners were in the habit of practising, and they had her range to a nicety. A 10-inch shell exploded on her main-deck about the same time, killing seven men and wounding an officer, and altogether the gallant ship had got into a hot corner; under the fire of 37 guns at once, from 10-inch down to 18 pounders. The "Racehorse" having got ashore opposite fort No. 8, the "Coquette" and "Argus" went back to tow her off, which we succeeded in doing after about an hour's work. During this time she kept up a constant cannonade, and the gunners in the fort were unable to do her any mischief. But at one moment it was feared that she would have to be abandoned and set on fire. I shall never forget the interest and excitement of the whole affair, from the bursting of the shells high in the air against the grey sky all round the flagship as she lay at anchor before we weighed, till we came into action ourselves and could see first the belching forth of flame from the middle of a puff of smoke, and then, strange to say, a round black thing coming straight at us. This black thing, however, suddenly rose high into the air just as it seemed about to strike us, and passed overhead. The "Argus" was struck only three times, first in the starboard gangway, then by a shot which went right through the mainmast, but left it standing, and thirdly by a round shot near the water line which penetrated about three inches, and then fell off into the sea. By five o'clock we were all safely anchored again under Josling point, except the "Havoc," which went off to set fire to five Loochooan junks that were lying off the factories. Probably

KAGOSHIMA HARBOUR

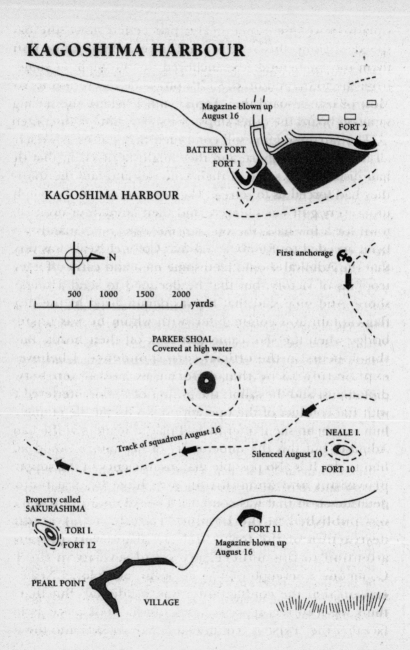

Magazine blown up
August 16

FORT 2

BATTERY PORT
FORT 1

KAGOSHIMA HARBOUR

N

First anchorage

500   1000   1500   2000
yards

PARKER SHOAL
Covered at high water

Track of squadron August 16

NEALE I.

Silenced August 10

FORT 10

Property called
SAKURASHIMA

TORI I.
FORT 12

FORT 11

Magazine blown up
August 16

PEARL POINT

VILLAGE

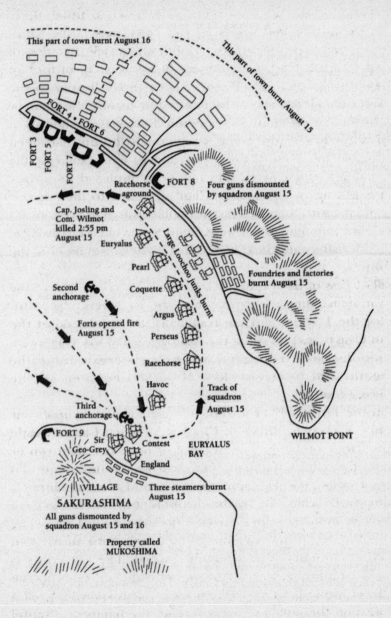

This part of town burnt August 16

This part of town burnt August 15

FORT 4 • FORT 6

FORT 3

FORT 5

FORT 7

Racehorse aground

FORT 8

Four guns dismounted by squadron August 15

Cap. Josling and Com. Wilmot killed 2:55 pm August 15

Euryalus

Pearl

Coquette

Argus

Perseus

Racehorse

Havoc

Large Loochoo junks burnt

Foundries and factories burnt August 15

Second anchorage

Forts opened fire August 15

Track of squadron August 15

Third anchorage

FORT 9

Sir Geo-Grey

Contest

England

EURYALUS BAY

WILMOT POINT

VILLAGE

SAKURASHIMA

Three steamers burnt August 15

All guns dismounted by squadron August 15 and 16

Property called MUKOSHIMA

the latter were set on fire by sparks from the junks, but credit was taken for their wilful destruction. Under the impression that a large white building in the rear of the town was the prince's palace, every effort was made to destroy it, but it turned out afterwards to be a temple, and we learnt that during the engagement the prince and his father had not been within range. Rockets were also fired with the object of burning the town, in which we were only too successiul. The gale had increased to such a height that all efforts on the part of the towns-people to extinguish the flames must have been unavailing. It was an awful and magnificent sight, the sky all filled with a cloud of smoke lit up from below by the pointed masses of pale fire.

Our prize was still burning when we came back to our former anchorage, and as she had 140 tons of coal on board she made a good bonfire. At last she gave a lurch and went to the bottom. It was no doubt a great disappointment to the sailors, for the steamers alone were worth $300,000, and everyone would have had a good share of prize money if we had been able to carry them off. It was rumoured that the prizes were burnt at Colonel Neale's instance, who was very anxious, like the old warrior that he was, that every ship should go into action unhampered. It was also said that poor Captain Josling urged the Admiral against his better judgment to fight that day, in spite of the adverse weather.

On Sunday morning the 16th August the bodies of Captain Josling, Commander Wilmot and of the nine men who had lost their lives in the action were buried in the sea. In the afternoon the squadron weighed anchor and proceeded down the bay at slow speed, shelling the batteries and town at long range until we left them too far behind. We anchored for the night at some distance from the town, and on the 17th proceeded to return to Yokohama. Most of us on board the "Argus," and I believe the feeling was the same on board the other ships, came away bitterly discontented.

The Japanese guns still continued firing at us as we left, though all their shot fell short, and they might fairly claim that though we had dismounted some of their batteries and laid the town in ruins, they had forced us to retreat. Had we maintained the bombardment until every gun was silenced, and then landed, or even lain off the town for a few days, the opinion was that the demands would have been acceded to. Rumour said that Colonel Neale was very anxious that the Admiral should land some men and carry off a few guns as trophies of victory, but that he declined to send a single man on shore. And men said that he was demoralized by the death of his flag-captain and commander, with whom he was talking on the bridge when the shot came that took off their heads. But none of this appears in the official correspondence. I believe the real explanation to be that differences had arisen between the diplomatist and the sailor, the former of whom interfered too much with the conduct of the operations. No doubt the etiquette was for him to remain silent after he had placed matters in the hands of the Admiral, but this the impetuosity of his nature would not permit him to do. It is also possible that insufficiency of the supply of coals, provisions and ammunition may have been a factor in the determination that was come to. The Admiral in his report, which was published in the London *Gazette*, took credit for the destruction of the town, and Mr Bright very properly called attention to this unnecessary act of severity in the House of Commons; whereupon he wrote again, or Colonel Neale wrote, to explain that the conflagration was accidental. But that I cannot think was a correct representation of what took place, in face of the fact that the "Perseus" continued to fire rockets into the town after the engagement with the batteries was at an end, and it is also inconsistent with the air of satisfaction which marks the despatch reporting that £1,000,000 worth of property had been destroyed during the bombardment.

After the return of the squadron to Yokohama we settled down quietly again, and the trade went on pretty much as usual; there were some complaints that the Tycoon's council were laying hands on all the raw silk destined for exportation, with a view doubtless of forcing up the price and so recouping themselves out of foreign pockets for the indemnities they had been forced to pay to the

British Government. But on a strong protest being made to them by Colonel Neale, the embargo was removed. Rumours reached us of disturbances at Kiôto, where the retainers of Chôshiû had been plotting to take possession of the palace, and seize the person of the Mikado. Failing in their plans, they had been dismissed from their share in guarding the palace, and had departed to their native province, taking with them seven court nobles who had been mixed up in the plot. Amongst them were Sanjô Sanéyoshi, Higashi-Kuzé and Sawa, who afterwards held high office in the government of the restoration.

The ill-success of the Chôshiû clan, which had been one of the foremost in demanding the expulsion of the foreigners, was a turn of luck for the Tycoon, and the result was the withdrawal of the circular of Ogasawara proposing the closing of the ports. Ogasawara himself was disgraced. Foreigners at Yokohama began to breathe freely again, and to renew their former excursions in the neighbouring country.

But on the 14th October a fresh outrage completely upset our tranquillity. A French officer of Chasseurs named Camus, while taking his afternoon's ride at a distance of not more than two or three miles from the settlement, and far from the high road, was attacked and murdered. His right arm was found at a little distance from his body, still clutching the bridle of his pony. There was a cut down one side of the face, one through the nose, a third across the chin, the right jugular vein was severed by a slash in the throat, and the vertebral column was completely divided. The left arm was hanging on by a piece of skin and the left side laid open to the heart. All the wounds were perfectly clean, thus showing what a terrible weapon the Japanese *katana* was in the hands of a skilful swordsman. No clue to the identity of the perpetrators of this horrible assassination was ever discovered, but it made a profound impression upon the foreign community, who after that were careful not to ride out unarmed or in parties of less than three or four. Not that we were able to place much confidence in our revolvers, for it was pretty certain that the *samurai* who was lying in wait to kill a foreigner would not carry out his purpose unless he could take his victim at a disadvantage, and cases of chance encounters with peaceably inclined Japanese were not known to have occurred. Excepting perhaps the Richardson affair, from the very first all these murders were premeditated, and the perpetrators took care to secure their own safety beforehand.

It was an agreeable surprise to us a month later, when there appeared at the legation two high officers of Satsuma, who undertook to pay the indemnity of £25,000 and gave an engagement to make diligent search for Richardson's murderers, who upon their arrest were to be punished with death in the presence of British officers, in accordance with the original demand. We may give Colonel Neale credit for knowing that there was no genuine intention on the part of Satsuma to carry out this promise, but on the other hand there was strong reason to suppose that Shimadzu Saburô himself had actually given the order to cut down the foreigners, and it could hardly be expected that the Satsuma men would ever consent to do punishment upon him. The actual doers of the deed were merely subordinate agents. We could not with justice have insisted on their lives being taken, and at the same time suffer the principal culprit to go scot-free. In order to succeed therefore in enforcing the whole of the demands made by Her Majesty's Government, it would have been necessary to invade Satsuma with an overwhelming force and exterminate the greater part of the clan before we could get at their chief; and we may be sure that he would never have fallen alive into our hands. We had bombarded and destroyed the greater part of the forts and town, probably killed a good many persons who were innocent of Richardson's murder, and had thereby elevated what was in the beginning a crime against public order into a *casus belli*. There would indeed, it seems to me, have been no justification after that for taking more lives by way of expiation. The Satsuma envoys, however, formally acknowledged that their countrymen had been in the wrong, and they paid the fine demanded by the British Government. No one therefore can blame the British Chargé d'Affaires for having made peace on these terms. It should be mentioned, however, that the Satsuma men borrowed the money from the Tycoon's treasury, and I have never heard that it was repaid.

CHAPTER IX

Shimonoseki; Preliminary Measures

Sir Rutherford Alcock returned from Europe early in March 1864, and Colonel Neale took his departure. The members of the legation gave him a farewell dinner, at which he delivered himself of prognostications as to the future of those who had served under him. For me he prophesied a professorship of Japanese at an English University, but so far his words have not come true. The new chief was liked by everyone, and he was particularly gracious to myself, relieving me from all chancery work, so that I could devote the whole of my time to my Japanese studies. Willis and I occupied a wooden house in a back street between the native town and the foreign settlement, and there I worked industriously with my three teachers. Sir Rutherford had brought with him very ample powers, which he determined to make use of to chastise the Chôshiû clan for its hostile attitude. We had, it might be said, conquered the goodwill of Satsuma, and a similar process applied to the other principal head of the anti-foreign party might well be expected to produce an equally wholesome effect. In the summer of the previous year the Chôshiû people, acting upon the orders which they had extorted from the Mikado for the "expulsion of the barbarians," had fired upon an American merchant vessel, a Dutch corvette and a French despatch-boat as they passed through the straits of Shimonoséki. The corvette had returned the fire, and in the other two cases satisfaction of an incomplete kind had been obtained by the United States sloop "Wyoming" and the French squadron under Admiral Jaurès respectively. The batteries had been destroyed, but as soon as the foreign men-of-war quitted the scene, the Chôshiû men set to work to rebuild the forts, to construct others, and to mount all the guns they could bring together. So the hornet's nest was after no long interval in good repair again, and more formidable for attack and defence than before. That no foreign vessels could take their way through the straits of Shimonoséki, which they had been in the habit of passing from time to time after touching at Nagasaki in order to make a pleasant and easy passage to Yokohama, instead of encountering the stormy Cape Chichakoff, was felt to involve a diminution of western prestige. Nothing but the complete subjugation of this warlike clan, and the permanent destruction of its means of offence, would suffice to convince the Japanese nation that we were determined to enforce the treaties, and to carry on our trade without molestation from anybody, irrespective of internal dissensions.

Sir Rutherford Alcock therefore lost no time in diligently setting to work in order to bring about a coalition with the representatives of France, Holland and the United States. In this he completely succeeded. The Tycoon's government were warned that if they did not within twenty days give a satisfactory undertaking to re-open the straits, the foreign squadrons would be despatched thither to bring the Prince of Chôshiû to reason. By a curious coincidence there had just returned to Japan two out of a band of five young samurai of Chôshiû, who the year before had been smuggled away to England to see the world, and learn something of the resources of foreign powers. Their names were Itô Shunsuké and Inouyé Bunda. The other three who remained in England while their companions, armed with the new knowledge, set forth on their journey to warn their fellow clansmen that it was no use trying to run their heads against a brick wall, were Endo Kinsuké, Inouyé Masaru and Yamao Yôzo. They made themselves and the object of their return known to Sir Rutherford, who promptly seized the opportunity thus offered of entering into direct communication with the *daimiô* of Chôshiû, and while delivering a sort of ultimatum, of affording him the chance of abandoning his hostile attitude for one more in accordance with the treaties. He obtained the consent of his colleagues to the despatch of two men-of-war to the neighbourhood of Shimonoséki in order to land the two young men at a convenient spot, and delivered to them a long memorandum for presentation to their prince.

A French officer (Commandant Layrle) and a Dutch naval officer, besides Major Wray, R.E., were sent at the same time to gain what information might be obtainable as to the present condition of the batteries, and to my great joy I was lent as interpreter, along with my colleague, Mr J. J. Enslie. On the 21st July we left in the corvette "Barrosa," Captain W. M. Dowell, and the gun vessel "Cormorant," Commander Buckle, and passing up the Bungo channel, anchored off Himéshima Island after dark on the 26th. We ran ashore, but managed to get off again, smashing the jib-boom of the "Cormorant" as we did so. Early on the following morning we landed our two Japanese friends Itô and Inouyé (who at that time went by the name of Shiji), after promising to call for them on the 7th August at the island of Kasato, off the coast of Suwô. On the way down I had talked a good deal with them, and between us, with the aid of my teacher, Nakazawa Kensaku (a retainer of Ogasawara, who had to seek his livelihood in consequence of his master's disgrace), we had managed to put Sir Rutherford's memorandum into Japanese. They were to cross over in an open boat and land at Tonomi in Suwô. At eight o'clock we saw them leave the shore. In Nakazawa's opinion the chances were six or seven out of ten that their heads would be cut off, and that we should never see them again.

We landed later on in the day at Himéshima and found the people very friendly. They sold to us a plentiful supply of fish, but there were no vegetables, beef or chickens to be had. Cattle were pretty plentiful and fat, but the people looked poor and half starved. The population was about 2,000. The island was not fertile. I tried to buy some beef, but the pretext that it was wanted as medicine for sick sailors (a Japanese idea) was useless. Half the population was engaged in salt-burning; 1/2d and 1d banknotes were current, and very little coin was to be seen. At one place we gave a man an *ichibu*, worth say 10d. He pretended to turn it over and look at it carefully, and then said "these are very rare things here."

Next day we went round to the north side of the island and anchored there. Here we again landed to visit the salt pans, and met with the same friendly reception as before. On the 29th we crossed in one of the ship's boats to Imi in Iyo, where the villagers refused to have anything to do with us, but at Takeda-tsu, a mile or two further west, they made no difficulties, and we were able to lay in a supply of pumpkins and brinjalls. On the 1st August we weighed anchor before sunrise, and stood away towards the straits. The "Barrosa" anchored about ten miles on this side of Shimonoséki, and we went on in the "Cormorant," steaming towards the coast of Buzen and then up to Isaki Point. When half-way across the mouth of the straits we saw signal guns fired all along the north coast from Chôfu to Saho. After going nearly up to Tanoura, keeping carefully out of the range of the batteries, and cruising backwards and forwards for a while, in order that the situation of the batteries and the number of guns might be accurately noted, we finally returned to Himéshima. We used to go on shore there for a walk every day, and found the people inquisitive but friendly. On one occasion, however, as we were returning through the village to our boats, we met a party of four *samurai*, who appeared to form part of a detachment sent over from Kitsuki in Buzen to protect the island against a possible attack from us. I spoke civilly to them, and asked where they had come from, but they answered in a surly manner, "from a distance." They looked as villainous a set as one could wish to see, and remained at the water's edge watching our movements until we got on board.

On the 6th August we made another trip to Shimonoséki in the "Cormorant" to reconnoitre, going in a little further than before in the direction of Tanoura. On this occasion, in addition to the signal guns, the batteries fired a round shot and a shell as a warning, which fell in the sea about a mile ahead. When we got

back to the "Barrosa" at half-past ten in the evening we found Itô
and Shiji had already returned. After dinner we had a long talk,
and received the prince's answer. They brought with them a single
retainer, but said they had been accompanied down to the coast by
a guard of soldiers given them by their prince. They commenced
the delivery of the communication with which they were charged
by saying that they had found him at Yamaguchi, and had handed
over the letters of the four foreign representatives to him in person.
He had then consulted with his chief retainers and come to the following conclusion: that he entirely acknowledged the truth of what
was stated in the letters, and was conscious of his own inability to
cope with the forces of western nations. But he was acting under
orders which he had received, once from the Tycoon, and oftener
from the Mikado, and not on his own responsibility, and it was
out of his power to reply to the foreign representatives without first
receiving permission. It was his intention, therefore, to proceed to
Kiôto in order to impress his own views on the Mikado, which he
calculated would take about three months. He begged therefore
that the powers would postpone operations for that period.

They brought no written documents with them, not even a letter
to certify that they were the accredited agents of their prince, but
told us they could procure one if the vessels were delayed for two
or three days. They were informed that a mere verbal reply such
as they had brought could not be expected to satisfy the foreign
representatives. They then inquired whether they should send a
written reply to Yokohama with copies of the orders of the Tycoon
and Mikado, but Captain Dowell replied that their prince might
do as he liked about that. His instructions did not go so far as to
enable him to express an opinion.

In private conversation they afterwards told me that their prince
had originally been favourable to foreigners, but had gone too
far now in the opposite direction to be able to retract, and they
did not believe that the matters at issue could be settled without
fighting. They suggested that it would be a good measure for the
foreign representatives to throw over the Tycoon, and proceeding

to Ozaka, demand an interview with the Mikado's ministers in order to conclude a direct treaty with him. They spoke with great bitterness of the Tycoon's dynasty, accused them of keeping all the trade, both foreign and native, in their own hands, by taking possession of every place where trade was likely to develope, such as Nagasaki and Niigata, and they said these feelings were shared by most of the people. The way in which they delivered their message made me suspect that it was couched in far more uncompromising terms than those which they made use of in communicating it. This was the first occasion on which I had been in full and frank communication with men belonging to the anti-Tycoon party. Their proposal that we should at once try to enter into negotiations with the Mikado was a bold one, and calculated, if it had been adopted, rather to injure than help their cause. The time was not yet ripe, for the Shôgun's authority, though much weakened, was still admitted and obeyed by a large majority of the *daimiôs*. His troops had not as yet exhibited their inferiority in arms, and as a matter of fact almost at this very moment the forces of the Prince of Chôshiû were suffering an overwhelming defeat in their attack upon Kiôto, which was defended in the Tycoon's interest by Aidzu and Satsuma. By the time we returned to Yokohama, and before the idea could have been even considered by the foreign representatives, Chôshiû's principal men were either fugitives or dead, and the Tycoon was temporarily master of the field.

Itô and his companion left again during the night. I could not help feeling sorry for their failure to impress on their prince the warning which they had come all the way from Europe to impart. But there was no help for it. We weighed anchor early on the following morning and arrived at Yokohama on the 10th.

As soon as it became known that Chôshiû would not give way preparations were actively made for carrying out the resolutions previously agreed upon by the representatives of the four Powers. They held a conference with the ministers of the Shôgun, in order to impress on them that the moment had now come when the naval forces must be charged with the duty of opening the straits, but before the meeting had separated there came like a thunderbolt on their deliberations an announcement of the return from Europe of a mission that had been despatched in the month of January to treat with Great Britain and France. They brought with them a convention concluded with the latter Power which provided for an indemnity in respect of the attack on the French gunboat, for the removal by the Shôgun's government within three months of the impediments to the navigation of the straits of Shimonoséki, for a modification of the import tariff in favour of French manufactures, and for the payment of an indemnity of $35,000 to the relatives of Lieutenant Camus. This news seemed to Sir Rutherford Alcock to threaten an utter collapse of his plans, for if the convention were ratified, the French at least would be compelled to withdraw from the coalition. But it was of course clear to those on the spot that the second article could not be possibly carried out by the Tycoon's government, and never could have been seriously intended, at least on the Japanese side. Pressure was therefore put on the council to make them declare that they would not ratify the convention, and a note from them to this effect reached the foreign representatives on the 25th August. On the same day they signed a memorandum declaring the necessity of a resort to force, which was then communicated to the naval commanders-in-chief, and four days later the allied squadrons put to sea to carry into execution the plans decided on before the return of the envoys had for a moment seemed to threaten the disruption of the diplomatic union so strenuously worked for by our chief. It was an immense responsibility that he had assumed. There was no telegraph in those days to any point nearer than Ceylon, but a despatch dated 26th July was already on its way to him positively prohibiting the adoption of military measures in the interior of Japan, and limiting naval operations against the Japanese Government or princes to defensive measures for the protection of the life and property of British subjects. By the time it reached his hands, his schemes had already been accomplished with the happiest possible results, and he was able to console himself with the conviction that he had done the right thing, even though he might be censured for acting contrary to the wishes of Lord John Russell, and have incurred the penalty of a recall from his post.

The United States steamer "Monitor" had been fred at as she lay at anchor in a bay on the north coast of Nagato on July 11. This afforded fresh justification of the action adopted by the foreign representatives.

CHAPTER X

Shimonoseki—Naval Operations

To my great satisfaction I was appointed interpreter to Admiral Küper, and, packing up a few necessaries, embarked on board the "Euryalus." I was messed in the ward room, and as there was no cabin available, slept on a sofa. The officers were a very pleasant set of fellows; among them I especially remember Tracey and Maclear, both of them now post-captains. The former is a very distinguished officer, but what particularly attracted me towards him was his love of books, and his wide knowledge of modern languages, acquired by dint of sheer perseverance amid all the noisy distractions of life on board ship.

The "Coquette" was sent off to Nagasaki to bring up Sir Rutherford's stepson, Fred. Lowder, to be additional interpreter. The only other civilian on board the flagship was Felix Beato, the well-known photographer, who, making his first start in life with a camera in the Crimean war, had also accompanied the Anglo-French expedition to North China in 1859, and had subsequently settled in Japan, where his social qualities had gained him many friends. My teacher Nakazawa had been secretly taken away from me by the Tycoon's government as a punishment for having accompanied me on the visit to Himéshima; many years afterwards I was made acquainted with the treachery of the foreigner who had denounced him to the Commissioners for Foreign Affairs. But Willis lent me his Japanese instructor and pupil in medicine,

Hayashi Bokuan, and I was able to make shift with this faithful man, though as a scholar he was greatly inferior to Nakazawa.

The English squadron consisted of the flagship "Euryalus," 35, commanded by Captain Alexander; the corvettes "Tartar," 21, Captain Hayes; "Barrosa," 21, Captain W. M. Dowell; the two-decker "Conqueror," 48, Captain Luard; the paddle-sloop "Leopard," 18, Captain Leckie; the paddle-sloop "Argus," 6, Commander Moresby; the "Coquette," 14, Commander Roe; and gunboat "Bouncer," 2, Lieutenant Holder. The French frigate "Sémiramis," 35, bearing the broad pennon of Admiral Jaurès, and the American chartered steamer "Takiang," carrying a Parrot gun and its crew from the United States corvette "Jamestown," under the command of Lieutenant Pearson, accompanied us. The French corvette "Dupleix," 10, and despatch boat "Tancrède," 4, with the Dutch corvettes "Metalen Kruis," 16, Captain de Man; "Djambi," 16, Captain van Rees; "Amsterdam," 8; and "Medusa," 16, Captain de Casembroot, left the bay of Kanagawa on the 28th August, and the remainder of the ships on the following day. We had calm weather and a smooth sea on the way down, sighting the south-west corner of Shikoku on the 1st September. About 5 p.m. we fell in with the "Perseus," 17, Commander Kingston, towing a collier, and bringing the Admiral's mail. The "Perseus" had met Commander Buckle in the "Cormorant" on his way to Shanghai for the mail, who, having started from Yokohama about the time of the return of the Japanese embassy, reported that the expedition was indefinitely postponed; she had therefore cast off the collier and steamed away at full speed for Yokohama, but falling a little later in with the "Coquette" on her way to Nagasaki, learnt a very different tale, and turning round, had picked up the collier again and brought her on. On the following day we reached Himéshima and anchored a little after noon; here we found the "Djambi" and "Metalen Kruis." Shortly afterwards the "Medusa" and the three French ships appeared, and by midnight every ship of the allied squadron had arrived. We had still to wait for the "Coquette," and either the "Cormorant" or "Osprey."

In the afternoon the Admiral, Captain Alexander, with other officers, went ashore for a walk, and I acted as their guide. The poor village mayor made his appearance in a great state of alarm. He was indeed in an uncomfortable position, uncertain of the disposition of the strangers, and sure of punishment from his own countrymen if he manifested too great friendliness towards us. He promised, however, to send us off some fish, "quite privately," but was positive that he could sell no bullocks. He had despatched a messenger to Kitsuki to inquire whether the islanders might hold intercourse with the squadron and furnish us with what supplies they had.

During the night we took in 150 tons of coal, and the 3rd of September was spent by the rest of our squadron in replenishing their bunkers. In the afternoon I went ashore to the mayor's house, where I found three of the garrison from Kitsuki. They were very reticent, not to say sulky, and only one of them, who was evidently afraid of his companions, could be induced to open his mouth. It was a grand sight to see the master of the collier and his wife parading along the beach with a couple of dirty little village urchins running ahead of them. The common people were friendly enough, except when the eyes of the two-sworded men were upon them.

On the 4th September we weighed anchor at nine o'clock and proceeded towards the straits of Shimonoséki, the eight British ships in the centre, with "Euryalus" leading, the French squadron and the "Takiang" in a line on the left, and the four Dutch vessels on the right. It was a beautiful show as the allied squadrons steamed in the consciousness of irresistible strength calmly across the unruffled surface of this inland sea, which lay before us like a glassy mirror in its framework of blue hills. Towards half past three we anchored at a distance of about two miles from the mouth of the straits, and prepared for action. Everything was in readiness by the time we had got half-way through our dinner, but to the disappointment of the more eager spirits, we remained where we were without firing a shot. Every one was naturally very anxious

THE STRAITS OF SHIMONOSEKI

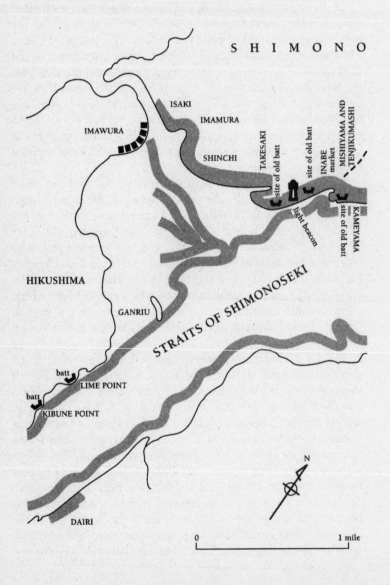

SHIMONO

ISAKI

IMAMURA

IMAWURA

SHINCHI

TAKESAKI

site of old batt

site of old batt

INABE market

MISHIYAMA AND ATENJIKUMASHI

light beacon

KAMEYAMA

site of old batt

HIKUSHIMA

GANRIU

STRAITS OF SHIMONOSEKI

batt

LIME POINT

batt

KIBUNE POINT

N

DAIRI

0   1 mile

SEKI

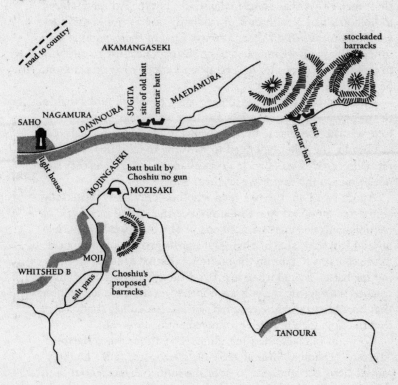

road to country

AKAMANGASEKI

stockaded
barracks

SUGITA

site of old batt

mortar batt

MAEDAMURA

NAGAMURA

DANNOURA

SAHO

light house

batt

mortar batt

MOJINGASEKI

batt built by
Choshiu no gun

MOZISAKI

MOJI

WHITSHED B

salt pans

Choshiu's
proposed
barracks

TANOURA

that no new complication should arise to delay the longed-for encounter with the enemy. Early on the following morning two Chôshiû men, common soldiers, came on board to inquire why all these men-of-war had come to the straits, but the Admiral refused to hold any parley with men of evidently inferior rank, and they were told to return on shore at once. One of them told me very innocently that if we intended to go through he must go on shore to make preparations for us, and when I asked what preparation, he said "for fighting."

I was then sent in a boat to overhaul a couple of junks that in the meanwhile had been stopped as they were entering the straits. One was the "Isé-maru," of Matsuyama in Iyo, going to load coals at Hirado, the other belonged to Kurumé in Chikugo, and was returning from Ozaka with a miscellaneous cargo. As they did not belong to the enemy we let them go.

About two p.m. the two men who had previously visited the ship came on board again to announce the arrival of a *bugiô* or commissioner of some sort, accompanied by Inouyé Bunda (he had now laid aside his alias of Shiji). But signals had already been made to the captains to take up the positions allotted to them for shelling the batteries, and when my friend Inouyé and his companion reached the flagship the only answer they received to their request that hostilities might be deferred with a view to negotiation was that the time for a peaceable arrangement had passed.

We went into action at ten minutes past four. The "Barrosa," "Tartar," "Djambi," "Metalen Kruis," "Leopard," and "Dupleix" moved along the southern coast of the funnel-shaped entrance to the strait, and took up their station in front of Tanoura, as shown in the annexed plan, while a light squadron consisting of the "Perseus," "Medusa," "Tancrède," "Coquette," and "Bouncer" passed along the northern shore, the "Amsterdam" and "Argus" being held in reserve. The "Euryalus," "Sémiramis," "Conqueror," and "Takiang" anchored out of range of the enemy's batteries, at a distance of about 2,500 yards from the central cluster at Maeda-mura, and consequently near enough to reach them with our 110-pounder breech-loading

Armstrong gun on the forecastle. The first shot was fired from the "Euryalus," and the whole of the Tanoura squadron then followed her example. The light squadron speedily silenced the three-gun battery on Kushi Saki Point, but not before it had managed to pitch a shot pretty near the British flagship. Then the "Sémiramis," which had been occupied in getting springs on her cable, opened fire from her quarter-deck guns with terrible effect, scarcely a shot falling short. The "Takiang" did her best with her single gun, and the "Conqueror" fired three shells, one of which burst beautifully among the great cluster of batteries. The "Euryalus" fired only sixteen rounds between 4.10 and 5.10 p.m. from her 110-pounder, which was pretty good work, considering that the vent piece got jammed once and a considerable time was lost in digging it out with handspikes. Another time the vent piece was blown up into the fore-top owing to its not having been screwed in tightly enough. The six vessels anchored south were soon engaged in a sharp conflict with the batteries opposite, while the light squadron, having silenced the batteries on the north, came to their aid, enfilading the 4, 7, and 9-gun batteries. The furthest shot fired from the "Euryalus" was at 4,800 yards, and it went plump into a battery.

By 5.10 the principal batteries had been silenced, and a signal was made to discontinue firing. A fire now burst out among the buildings in the Maeda-mura batteries and a magazine exploded, making the third "blow-up" during the afternoon. We continued firing a shot now and then up to six o'clock. The quarter-deck 40-pounder Armstrongs were fired once only, as their range proved to be too short, and none of the smooth-bore guns on the main deck were brought into action, to the great disappointment of the bluejackets, who had probably not forgotten the slaughter made amongst their comrades at Kagoshima, and burned to avenge it. It must be admitted that the Japanese fought well and with great persistence, for I attach no value to the story that was told that the gunners were only allowed to fire once, and were then replaced by fresh men. At first many of our shot fell short, but when the range was found, they struck the batteries every moment, as we could see by the clouds of dust that were knocked up. After the signal to discontinue firing had been made, Kingston of the "Perseus" and De Casembroot of the "Medusa" landed and spiked fourteen guns in the Maeda mura batteries. At the small battery on Kushi Saki Point two out of the three guns had been dismounted by our fire. The entire casualties on our side this first day were six men wounded in the "Tartar," which bore the brunt of the fire.

Early on the following morning one of the Maeda-mura batteries re-opened fire on the squadron anchored off Tanoura, but was replied to with such effect that it was speedily silenced, and the barrack behind was set on fire. The "Dupleix" lost two killed and two wounded, while the first lieutenant of the "Tartar" was struck by a round shot on the posteriors and severely wounded. He recovered, however, contrary to the expectations of the surgeons. I slept through the noise, but was woke by somebody with a message that I had to land with Captain Alexander, who was to command the small-arms party of the "Euryalus," 200 strong. From the "Conqueror" there landed the battalion of 450 marines under Colonel Suther, besides her own complement of 100, and some bluejackets, small detachments of marines being added from the other ships of our squadron. The French landed 350, and the Dutch 200. Another calculation showed that 1,900 men were put ashore, of whom we furnished 1,400.

We rowed straight for the nearest land, followed by a string of cutters and pinnaces so full of men that there was only just room to work the oars, and got on shore at nine o'clock exactly. The task assigned to Captain Alexander's party was to scale a bluff immediately to the east of the Maeda-mura batteries, and take a one-gun battery. It was a stiff pull up the steep grassy hill, but up went the bluejackets pell-mell, as if they were out on a picnic, every man for himself. On climbing over the earthwork we found that the gun had been either carried off or concealed. There were a score or so of the enemy on the platform, who retreated as soon as the first of our people showed his nose above the parapet, but they kept up a dropping fire from the other side of the hill. Here one of our men received a bullet wound in the leg, and a second was accidentally shot through the body by the sailor immediately behind him. Passing through the battery, we clambered up the hill behind, through a tangled brake of ferns and creepers. The heat was intense. It was a difficult job to keep one's footing on the narrow path cut through the slippery grass. Our bluejackets were very eager to get at the enemy, but not a single one was to be seen. Descending the other side of the hill, we at last found ourselves in a sort of covered way, which ran along the side of a narrow valley. It was reported that the enemy were posted further up the valley in considerable numbers, but instead of pursuing them we turned to the left along the covered way, which brought us down past a magazine into the central battery of the principal group. It turned out afterwards to be a fortunate counter-march, for if we had proceeded in the other direction we should have stumbled on a stockade defended by three field guns, which would have played "Old Harry" with our small force.

The first battery we entered was already in the possession of the French landing party and some of our marines, who, having disembarked below the bluff, had marched along the beach, meeting with no opposition. This work was of earth, having a parapet about twenty feet wide, armed along the edge with a chevaux-de-frise of pointed bamboo stakes. In battery No. 7 the guns were mounted en barbette, on carriages with enormous wheels, and worked on pivots. They were of bronze, very long, and threw a 32-pound shot, though marked as 24's. They bore a Japanese date corresponding to 1854, and had evidently been cast in Yedo. Besides these, there was a short 32-pounder, and on the other side of a traverse, containing a small magazine, was a single 10-inch gun, also of bronze. We upset them all, broke up the carriages, threw the shot and shell into the sea, burned the powder, and even dragged a couple of guns down on to the beach. This occupied us till three or four o'clock in the afternoon. During this time our men were perpetually firing musketry at the enemy on the hill, who every now and then showed themselves to give us a shot or two. In the 9-gun battery were a couple of heavy 11-inch bronze guns. Afterwards we proceeded to the next battery, which was almost *à fleur d'eau*. It was divided into two by a traverse containing a magazine, on one side of which were one 10-inch howitzer, two 32-pounders, and one 24-pounder; on the other side were the same number, with the addition of single 24-pounder. These likewise were overturned, and the carriages and ammunition disposed of as before. The Japanese field battery up the valley, which had been advanced some little way from the stockade along a path leading towards Maeda-mura, Dannoura and Shimonoséki annoyed us considerably during this operation, firing shells over us and at long ranges into the sea, while their musketeers kept up a pretty constant fire, though no one was touched on our side. Part of our men were told off to keep them in check, but our aim was not much better than that of the enemy. The great thing in war, until you come to close quarters, seems to be to make as much noise as you can to put your foes in a funk, or in other words to demoralize them. You can't do much harm, and it was laughable to see how many of our men ducked to avoid the shot, and I confess I followed their example until reason came to my aid.

The "Medusa" moved up and threw a few shells in among them, while the "Perseus," "Amsterdam," and "Argus" fired over the hill from their station before Tanoura. This quieted the zeal of our warrior foes for a while, and we returned to the first battery we had dismantled, for the men to have their dinners. Crowdy of the Engineers, McBean the assistant-surgeon of the flagship and I divided a loaf of bread and a tin of sardines, which we opened with Crowdy's sword. There were no knives or forks handy, but that did not hinder us from satisfying our well-earned appetite as we sat on the steps of the magazine in the traverse. After dinner we helped the French to overturn the guns in their battery, which were four in number, very long 32-pounders, mounted on field carriages. The enemy still continued annoying us from their position up the valley, while some of our men kept up a fitful musketry fire in reply, without much damage on either side.

The afternoon being already far advanced, the signal to re-embark was made from the "Euryalus," and the French and Dutch detachments, some of the marine detachment, and the "Conqueror's" small-arms men, were already in their boats, when about six o'clock we saw Colonel Suther's battalion of marines returning from the Maeda-mura 15-gun battery through a heavy fire from the Japanese. The Japanese on perceiving them threw a round shot in among them, but without doing any harm; our men replied, and for fifteen minutes there was nothing but ping, ping, ping on both sides. At last the Colonel came up to Captain Alexander and said: — "Where are these men who are annoying us. I've enough men to take any battery." "All right," replied Alexander, "I'll take the left side of the valley and you the right." So the marines clambered up into the French battery (the eastern-most one) and proceeded up the covered way, while the "Conqueror's" men disembarked again, and the advance commenced. Beato and I stuck close to Alexander, and followed the bluejackets across the paddyfields by the narrow "bunds," and then along the path on the western side of the valley. How the bluejackets shouted and cheered, each man running on by himself, now stopping to take aim at an enemy from behind one of the pine trees that lined the edge of the road, and then on again. There was no order or discipline. Some of them wasted their ammunition on imaginary foes on the hillsides. I passed several wounded men as I went up, some seriously hurt, and the corpse of a sailor who had been killed by an arrow.

At last we reached the battery, whence the gunners had been driven by our fire, dismounted the guns and threw them into the paddyfield close by, after destroying the carriages. Here Alexander was wounded by a ball which passed through the ankle-joint of his right foot, and he had to be carried to the rear on a stretcher. From this point the valley contracted rapidly, while immediately in front of us was a stockaded barrack into which most of the Japanese retreated, turning back repeatedly to fire. But I saw others in black armour and white surcoats retreating with great rapidity

along the road to the left. Lieutenant Edwards and Crowdy of
the Engineers were ahead with a middy named D. G. Boyes, who
carried the colours most gallantly; he afterwards received the V.C.
for conduct very plucky in one so young. When I got up to the
front of the stockade there were three or four dead Japanese lying
about and one of our men, shot through the heart. He presented
a most ghastly sight as he lay there, getting visibly bluer and bluer,
without any exterior signs of blood to show how he had come by
his death. Having directed some of the men to put his corpse into
a huge oblong basket which was on the ground close by and carry
him off, I passed on into the stockade whence the Japanese had
already fled. In retiring they had set fire to some houses close to
the magazine, with the amiable intention of blowing us up, but
the train was discovered and the explosion prevented.

After ranging over the whole place and removing whatever was
worth carrying off as trophies, such as armour, bows and arrows,
spears and swords, and bayonets bearing a foreign maker's name,
we set fire to the buildings and retired in good order. The loss
of the enemy was about twenty killed, but they had carried off
all their wounded. We had five killed and thirteen or fourteen
wounded, two mortally. What the marine battalion was doing all
this time I cannot say, for the excitement about what was going on
ahead left me no disposition to look elsewhere, but I rather think
that having marched along the covered way with great steadiness
they managed to arrive just as the more active and impetuous
"jacks" had finished the business. And no blame to them either
for going about their work in a business-like manner. If we had
met with a check in our heedless, headlong advance, the marines
would have saved us from destruction. It was lucky for us that
the skirmish terminated as it did, for our loss in small-arms' men
would have been much greater if the Japanese had been strong
enough to stand to their guns, or had posted marksmen on the
hills to take us in flank as we hurried up the valley. They had the
advantage in position, besides possessing seven small field pieces,
while on the other hand we had at least a couple of hundred men

in excess of their number, which it was supposed was 600. But I fancy I remember having heard since from a Chôshiû man who was present that their force was only one half of that. The blue-jackets bore the brunt of the business, as they had to cross the line of fire and to advance along the outer edge of the horn-shaped valley, which curved away to the east out of sight of the shipping. The Japanese could not stand our advance, the sharp musketry fire threw them into disorder, and they had to run for it. In only one case was an attempt made to come to close quarters. One fellow had concealed himself behind a door with uplifted sword in both hands, ready to cut down a man just about to enter. But contrary to his expectation, his intended victim gave him a prod in the belly which laid him on his back and spoilt his little game. Our French companions in arms were disgusted at not having been present at the affair, and turned up their noses at it, as *pas grand chose après tout*. It was the fortune of war, and we commiserated them sincerely.

The marines who in the first instance marched on Maeda-mura had one man killed and two wounded. They dismantled fifteen guns in the battery there.

During the day a boat belonging to one of the Dutch men-of-war, with two men in her, got loose and drifted down with the tide towards the town. They were immediately shot, though quite defenceless. Fred. Lowder and his brother George, who had come up with him from Nagasaki "to see the fun," had a narrow escape as they were paddling about in a Japanese boat, which became unmanageable and was drifting off in the same direction; they jumped into the water and swam ashore, or they would probably have encountered the same fate.

The eastern end of the town of Shimonoséki (more properly speaking, I believe, Akamagaséki) was set on fire, but the number of houses burnt was extremely small. It was alleged that this was done by the French because some Japanese soldiers had fired thence on their men, but I do not know whether this is a fact. The "Perseus" ran ashore opposite the nearest batteries, and as the tide ebbed her bow was high out of the water, nor did she get off again until the following day.

I found myself on board again at half-past seven o'clock, very dirty, very tired, very hungry and very thirsty.

On the 7th September working parties of bluejackets landed under the protection of some marines to take possession of the guns, ten of which they got into the boats. Others went up to the stockade and found some field pieces, which they destroyed, hove down wells, or brought away. We got together sixty, all but one of bronze, with two mortars and six cohorns. We blew up all the powder and threw the shot and shell into the sea. There was not a single hostile Japanese to be seen. The "Perseus" had to be lightened by discharging all her guns and coals, and so managed to get afloat by noon.

Our list of casualties during the two days' operation was eight killed and thirty wounded, of whom one or two were not expected to live. We landed at half-past one on the Tanoura side to bury our dead, the French having already buried two in the forenoon. In digging the graves our men found particles of a glittering sub-stance which was at first taken to be gold dust, but turned out to be mica. I met a party of Ogasawara's two-sworded men, who asked how many dead we had, and how we had fared on the pre-vious day. On learning what a complete thrashing we had given the enemy at the stockade, they expressed great satisfaction, and recounted how the Chôshiû people had crossed over the straits in the previous year, cut down their crops, carried off their live stock, and driven the peasants away, after which they held pos-session of Tanoura for some time, until public opinion and the necessity of providing for the defence of Chôshiû's own territories had compelled them to withdraw. Ogasawara's men feared that when Chôshiû came to find out that communication had taken place between us and the Buzen folk, he would visit them again after the withdrawal of the squadron, but I boldly assured them that they need not alarm themselves, as we intended to destroy the batteries, and deprive Chôshiû of his territory. For I knew that part of the plan entertained by Sir Rutherford and his colleagues was the seizure of a sufficient piece of territory near Shimonoséki as material guarantee for the payment of an adequate indemnity, and to hold it until it could be conveniently handed over to the Tycoon's government.

Sir Rutherford contemplated nothing less than the complete subjugation of the Chôshiû clan, and he had enjoined upon the Admiral the necessity of attacking Hagi, which was supposed to be the stronghold of the *daimiô*. The Admiral, however, who was a prudent commander, and by no means disposed to take orders from the civil representatives of Her Majesty further than he was obliged, came to the conclusion that the resources at his disposal did not permit of a permanent occupation of any portion of Chôshiû's territory, and considered that as soon as the forts were destroyed and the straits opened, his task was accomplished. Fear had made the Ogasawara *samurai* wondrously polite. The villagers were also friendly enough, and I made them laugh good-humouredly with some commonplace jokes, but did not succeed in inducing them to sell any supplies. The officials, after hunting all through the village, as they assured us, produced eight or ten eggs, which they said was all they could find. Our bluejackets brought me some papers which they had picked up in the stockade, and which appeared to contain evidences of plots by Chôshiû against the Mikado, also quantities of pills made, or said to be made, from bear's gall, and banknotes for small sums, such as were commonly used in the territories of all the *daimiôs*. I believe that silver coin was current at that time in the dominions of the Tycoon alone.

On the 8th, fatigue parties landed again to bring off more guns; we got all but two from the group of batteries, which made nineteen, besides fifteen from Maeda mura and an equal number from the batteries on Hikushima, the large island in the western entrance of the straits. I went on shore to Maeda-mura, and found a well built battery, with a parapet twenty feet wide cased with stone towards the sea, and divided into four sections by traverses, between which the guns were planted in unequal numbers. In the rear stood a stone-built magazine, the roof of which had been smashed by a round shot that went right through it. The powder magazine, also of stone, which stood on one side of the valley behind, had been blown up the previous day. Further up was a stockaded barrack, which the French had burned. I went towards the advanced guard near the town, but as the enemy began to show themselves and fire at us, I made a prudent retreat.

CHAPTER XI

Shimonoseki; Peace Concluded with Choshiu

Returning to the ship at noon, I found there my acquaintance Itô Shunsuké, who had come to say that Chôshiû desired peace, and that a *karô* or hereditary councillor, provided with full powers, was coming off to treat. A boat was accordingly despatched to meet the great man, who shortly afterwards stood on the quarter-deck of the flagship. He was dressed in a robe called the *daimon*, which was covered with large light blue crests (the paulownia leaf and flower) on a yellow ground, and wore on his head a black silk cap, which he took off on passing the gangway. His queue was then seen to be loose, hanging over the back of his head like a tassel, and his white silk underclothing was a marvel of purity. His two companions, who bore a rank next only to his own, wore their hair in the same fashion, but were without mantles. They were conducted into the cabin, and presented to the Admirals, the Abbé Girard, Lowder and myself acting as interpreters. They began by stating that the Prince of Chôshiû acknowledged his defeat, and desired to make peace with a view to the establishment of friendly relations. The Admiral thereupon asked to see their credentials, and finding they had none, intimated that he would give them forty-eight hours to provide themselves with a letter from their *daimiô*. They were told that the letter must contain the substance of what they had said, acknowledging that he had committed a grievous wrong in firing upon foreign ships, and begging for peace, that it must be signed with his own hand and sealed with his seal, and that a copy must be addressed to each of the four senior naval officers in command.

The conditions imposed were — first, that we should continue to remove the guns and destroy the forts; second, that we would discontinue hostilities, they on their side doing the same, but that if they fired another shot we should burn everything we could lay our hands on in Chôshiû's territories; third, they must deliver up intact the Dutch sailors and boat which had fallen into their hands on the 6th; and fourth, that they should endeavour to induce the villagers to bring off poultry and fresh vegetables for sale. In order that they might have a token of a peaceable disposition on our part, a white flag should be hoisted at the main until the expiration of the time fixed for their return. They gave as their names Shishido Giôma, adopted son of Shishido Bizen, minister of Nagato; Sugi Tokusuké and Watanabé Kurata, councillors. They then returned on shore, leaving communications addressed to each of the commanders of the allied squadron, which they had been charged to deliver at Himéshima before the bombardment. They handed these over at the Admiral's desire, remarking that we should perceive from the contents that the documents were useless now.

Itô gave me also transcripts of the orders received from the Mikado and the Tycoon to expel foreigners from Japan, which Shishido certified with his own hand to be true copies. The translations made of these papers were afterwards published in the bluebook on Japan, where the curious can consult them. There is no doubt that they were perfectly authentic. It was amusing to observe the change which manifested itself gradually in the demeanour of the envoy, who was as proud as Lucifer when he stepped on board, but gradually toned down, and agreed to every proposal without making any objections. Itô seemed to exercise great influence over him. After the truce was agreed to, the country people ventured freely along the road near the batteries, and passed on into the town, no doubt heartily pleased at the termination of hostilities. It must be said to their credit that the terms were faithfully adhered to by the Chôshiû people, none of whom, except Itô and Inouyé, had supposed Europeans to be any better than mere barbarians.

On the 9th September the "Coquette" took the two Admirals through the straits to visit the batteries on Hikushima, and as usual I accompanied them to interpret. From the eastern side the strait contracts rapidly, between lofty well-wooded hills, to a width of no more than six cables' lengths, and then as quickly opens out again, with the long line of houses forming the town of Shimonoséki on the northern shore, while to the left the coast trends away southwards past the village of Moji and the town of Kokura. In front lay the broad undulating Hikushima. Passing right out through the strait till we reached the north-west corner of the island, we turned back again and came along its coast, passing a little cove crowded with junks, till we came to Lime Point. Here we disembarked to inspect the site of the batteries, from which the guns had already been removed by our people. One of the batteries, which originally had six guns mounted, was cut out of the cliff, and there had evidently not been time to complete it. Immediately below the parapet was a single gun in a pit. A little further east was a battery of eight guns mounted *à fleur d'eau*, and close by was a smaller battery with four embrasures which had never been armed. The only other sign of a battery on this island was an old earthwork to the west of Lime Point, also without guns. Kokura appeared to be strongly fortified, and it was reported that the Chôshiû people had demanded, but unsuccessfully, to be allowed to work the batteries against us. The "Tartar," "Dupleix," "Djambi," and "Metalen Kruis " had been stationed here since the 7th, chiefly for the purpose of dismantling the batteries.

Leaving them we steamed up to Kushi saki Point, where three brass and four *wooden* guns had been taken. The latter were about four feet long, and were constructed of single logs with a bore about eight inches in diameter, having a chamber behind capable of holding about a pound and a half of powder. Bamboo hoops surrounded the gun from breech to muzzle, then came a layer of boards, and then more bamboo hoops; the wood itself was only about 3 1/2 in. thick. The shot consisted of a small bag of pebbles fastened to a wooden disk, and was intended to act like grape at close quarters against a landing party. These curious weapons were simply laid on the earthen parapet, and were not calculated to be used more than once.

The Japanese had shown themselves very friendly to the working party, and had themselves carried down the guns for delivery. They were not improbably glad to get rid of the toys that had brought them into so much trouble. On returning to the flagship we found a couple of boats laden with fowls and vegetables which Shiji Bunda had sent on board as a present. There was a note from him saying that the common people were much too frightened to come near us to sell supplies, and complaining that one of the ships had been firing again, an action which, he said, would tend to endanger the friendly relations so recently established. But this was a mistake on his part, for no incident of the kind had occurred. The bumboatmen were shown over the ship, and expressed themselves much delighted with the novel and wonderful sight. We sent half of Shiji's present to the French Admiral, and our share was divided among the officers and men of the flagship.

On the following day the envoys of the Prince of Chôshiû arrived punctually on board the "Euryalus." Shishido and Sugi, however, did not make their appearance, their absence being explained to be caused by illness from want of sleep and the hot weather in combination. Admiral Küper observed that it was singular how often this sort of thing happened, and ironically begged that if the negotiations were not concluded in one sitting, the delegates would take care of their health until everything was settled. Their names were Môri Idzumo, Minister (*Karô*) Yamada Uyémon, Hadano Kingo (Hadano was afterwards better known as Hirozawa Hiôsuké) and Watanabé Kurata, councillors (*sansei*), and Isota Kenzô and Harata Junji of Chôfu, councillors, with

Shiji Bunda. We had looked up the Japanese "blue-book" in the meantime, and fancied we had reason to suppose the previous envoy had given an incorrect account of his position, but they were able to clear up the discrepancy in a satisfactory manner. The officer there called Shishido Mino had recently changed his name to Shishido Bizen, and retired from public life in favour of Giôma, who now represented the family. They produced a letter from their prince which, on being read, was found to declare in satisfactory terms that he sued for peace. The Admiral then said: "We quite agree with your prince in desiring peace. It was never our intention to fight your countrymen. We solely desire to cement amicable relations between Japan and foreign countries, and to carry on trade."

Môri replied that these were entirely the views held by the prince.

> *Ad. Küper* — "Do you wish us distinctly to understand that you will offer no further opposition to the free passage of the straits?"
> *Môri* — "We do."
> *Ad. Küper* — "We should like very much to have an interview with the prince, for we could concede much to him that we could not perhaps concede to you. We are ourselves of high rank in our own country, but will come on shore to meet him at Shimonoséki."

After consulting among themselves they named the 14th September as the date on which he should come down from his capital to receive the two Admirals in the town.

> *Ad. Küper* — "We will first state our demands, which can be ratified by the prince when he comes. We shall then be able to explain to him many matters connected with the customs of foreign countries which will prevent mistakes arising in future. In any case the transaction of business will be facilitated and

time will be saved by the prince's coming, as in any case his ratification has to be obtained to the terms agreed on."

"In the first place, no batteries must be constructed in the straits until all questions between foreigners and Japanese have been settled by the Tycoon's government and the foreign ministers at Yedo."

"Secondly, according to the custom of foreign nations in time of war, a ransom for the town of Shimonoséki must be paid, because we spared it when we had a perfect right to set it on fire, for our people had been fired on from the houses. The amount shall be communicated to the prince himself at the conference which is to take place."

"Thirdly, when foreign vessels passing through the straits are in need of coals, provisions, or water, they shall be permitted to purchase what they want."

These conditions were readily accepted by the envoy, who said that as the tides were very strong in the straits, and both wind and waves sometimes violent, persons in distress should be permitted to land.

The Admiral then informed him that during our stay we should go on shore at Shimonoséki to buy whatever we required, and requested him to tell the townspeople to bring together for sale what they could, in fact to start a market for the fleet. To this they at first objected, on the ground that the town had been completely abandoned by its inhabitants, but eventually agreed to do what was desired. Then Môri got up, and leaning over to me said confidentially that there was one thing about which he was very anxious. The peace they had obtained was a most precious and valuable thing, and they would greatly regret if any untoward event were to injure our present friendly relations. It might happen that an ill-disposed person would lie in wait to attack foreigners, and, to prevent anything of this kind occurring, he begged that those who went ashore would be on their guard. This was interpreted to Admiral Küper, who at once replied that we had no fear of any such evilly disposed persons, but that if a single European were hurt, the whole town should be burnt to the ground. The Japanese authorities, he added, were in the habit of saying this sort of thing, solely to prevent our landing, and it looked to him a little suspicious.

Môri answered that he feared the purity of his intentions in giving this warning was not understood. He was sure the Japanese authorities would on their part take every precaution to prevent mishaps, and he had only mentioned this to prevent mistakes.

Ad. Küper — "Very well. We shall not go into the country at all. No doubt there is a governor in the town. You can give orders to him to keep out the ill-disposed, and if he cannot defend the place, we will land and do it for him."

Môri — "We will give orders to the governor."

This finished the business part of the conference, but the Admiral was curious to know the details of what had recently taken place at Kiôto, where it was reported there had been fighting between the Chôshiû and Aidzu men. Thereupon Shiji told us a long story, the gist of which was that after Chôshiû had received the orders of both the Mikado and Tycoon for "the expulsion of the foreigners," and had acted upon them to the best of his ability, he got a great deal of abuse for having done so. Being both surprised and hurt at this treatment, he sent several times to Kiôto to inquire the reason, but his people were driven out of the capital, and he was forbidden to present himself there again. He became indignant at this injustice, and his retainers sympathized with him very strongly. At last a band of them, who could bear it no longer, set out for Kiôto to demand an explanation from the Mikado's ministers. They took swords, spears, and other warlike weapons in their hands. For why? On a former occasion, nay twice, Aidzu had put to death every Chôshiû man to be found in Kiôto. So, said they, "Aidzu may attack us also, and then we must defend ourselves; we will not be killed for nothing." The prince, happening to hear of their departure, sent three of his ministers (*karô*) to recall them, but they refused to return. Then the governor of Kiôto summoned Chôshiû's agent at the capital to send the men home again, "for if you don't," said he, "I shall attack them." However, the agent refused, and a battle ensued. When the "Barrosa" came the first time to Himéshima with the letters of the foreign representatives, the prince despatched his son to communicate with the Mikado, but owing to the disturbed state of affairs he was unable to effect anything. Shiji hoped we would not believe that the Chôshiû clan harboured any treasonable intentions towards the Mikado, and the whole truth was that they had simply tried to get an explanation of the manner in which they had been treated. He added that we ought not to put any trust in what was told us by the Kokura people or the junk sailors, who came from Yedo and Hizen and all parts of the country, and were enemies of Chôshiû.

Our visitors were then conducted over the ship, and after being entertained with some music by the band they went over the side, and we parted on very friendly terms.

A comparison of dates with the account given in Adams, chapters 25 and 26, of what had passed at Kiôto during the summer, shows that the Chôshiû clansmen were marching from Ozaka to Kiôto at the very time that Ito and Shiji landed from the "Barrosa" and reached Yamaguchi to convey the messages of the foreign representatives to the princes. From time to time other bodies of Chôshiû men reached the capital, and the accumulated elements of civil war finally exploded on the 20th August, before the younger prince of Chôshiû, who seems to have really started from home to calm the excited spirits of the clansmen with news of a new enemy in their rear, had time to arrive. The best fighting men were consequently absent when the allied squadron appeared at the straits, and our victory was therefore a much easier affair than it would otherwise have been. I doubt whether any of the fugitives from Kiôto got home in time to take part in the defence of the place.

Next day Captain Hayes of the "Tartar," Major Wray, R.E., and I went ashore for a walk through Shimonoséki. The eastern end of the town had received a good many round shot on the 6th September, and some of the houses were almost knocked to pieces. I believe the Chôshiû men had brought out a field piece or two and fired from that point against the squadron lying in front of Tanoura. This had drawn on them our heavy artillery. The townspeople were flocking back, and had commenced to settle down again, but very few shops were open. The common people followed us in crowds, and appeared very friendly, but the prices asked by the shopkeepers were exorbitant. We were somewhat surprised, though of course without reason, to find that the proportion of *curio* shops was very small as compared with Yokohama. We saw several soldiers, some armed with rifles, others carrying swords and spears; they of course could not be expected to look very amicably at their late foes.

On the 12th, Hadano and the two governors of the town came off to tell the Admiral that a market would be opened at a wharf called Nabéhama from ten to twelve in the forenoon for the sale of fresh provisions. We of course suspected them of having made this arrangement in order to have everything under their own control, and to keep the prices as high as possible. The Admiral demanded a market from six to eight o'clock, to which after much discussion they agreed. I learnt through my teacher that the people were told to sell dearly to us, in spite of the promise given to us by the officials that they would not interfere. The latter had begged that our men might be ordered not to purchase anything in the shops, on the ground that we should buy up all the provisions intended for the townsfolk.

On the 13th, Captain Dowell transferred to the "Euryalus" as flag-captain, vice captain Alexander invalided. Next day I accompanied the two Admirals on shore to the clean little village of Moji. On asking some Kokura men whom we met to show us the way up to the battery on the point where the strait sweeps round, they inquired whether we had permission from the guard established at a temple close by. The answer to this astounding query was that we were not in the habit of asking leave. "Was that the path?" "Yes, that's the path." So we toiled up a hill through the pine trees, turned to the left, and descended into the battery, which was constructed for three guns. It commanded a view right up and down the straits, from Manshiû to Hikushima. It was a splendid position for guns, though a shell pitched in the line of the work would of necessity have fallen into it, unless passing very high, as it was cut out of the hillside. All about it there were places cleared for guns which would have a powerful effect against ships. The thick brushwood would prevent any attempt at escalade, and a single gun is not easily hit. I do not know what might be done with modern artillery, but it was the opinion of all our engineer officers that if the Japanese of that day had known the advantages of the position, they could easily have rendered it impregnable.

At two o'clock in the afternoon arrived the Chôshiû delegates, who by agreement made earlier in the day were to represent the prince. The story they told us was that he had voluntarily shut himself up in order to await the will of the Mikado, or as they phrased it, he had placed himself in an attitude of respectful attention (*tsutsushindé oru*). Lest it should be supposed that this is merely a joke, I must explain that in the old times, whenever a member of the *samurai* class had committed an act in person or vicariously which might be expected to bring down upon him the wrath of his political superiors, he at once assumed a submissive posture, and as it were delivered himself up, tied hands and feet, to the pleasure of his lord. It was a sort of voluntary self-imprisonment as a first-class misdemeanant. We did not accept the excuse, which it was natural to suppose had been invented to save him the trouble of travelling to Shimonoséki, but I now incline to think that horrorstruck at the violent proceedings of his followers who had dared to fight against the defenders of the palace (and also repenting of their failure), the old prince had hastened to atone for the crime of treason, as far as lay in his power, by declaring his readiness to undergo any penalty that might be decreed by the sovereign — if his retainers would let him, being understood.

Their names were Shishido Bizen, Môri Idzumo, Shishido Giôma and Ibara Kazuyé, ministers; and Nawozaki Yahichirô (*metsuké*, a secretary), Ito Shunsuké, Hadano Kingo and another whose name I did not note down. Bizen, it appeared, had after all not completely retired from public affairs. Both the Admirals were present. As soon as the conference was formed, Admiral Küper asked why they had not let him know earlier that the prince was in seclusion, as the truce had been granted solely that there might be time for him to reach Shimonoséki. They answered that the boat was slow, and they had only arrived late on the previous day. They had spent a long time arguing with the prince and using their best efforts to persuade him to come, but he always answered that it was an old custom from which he could not depart. He was in disgrace with the Mikado, and was not able to see even his own confidential retainers, much less could he see the Admirals. They regretted it very much, but it could not be helped. The prince would have greatly liked to meet the Admirals.

After this question had been so thoroughly thrashed out that the Japanese could not but suppose that great importance was attached to a direct undertaking on the part of the prince, the Admirals' demands were announced, as follows: —

> *Firstly.* Foreign vessels passing through the straits to be treated in a friendly manner; to be permitted to purchase coals, provisions, water and other necessaries. If driven in through stress of weather, the crews to be permitted to land.
> *Secondly.* Henceforth no new batteries to be constructed, the old ones not to be repaired, and no guns to be mounted in them.

This article caused some discussion, for as now put it deprived them of a loophole that had been left open on the previous occasion. But when they were asked for what purpose the batteries had been erected, they had but one answer — "for making war on foreigners." "Well then, those foreigners having destroyed the batteries, and taken the guns, will not permit any more to be put in the same place. The article is indispensable, and must stand as it is." So they agreed to it.

> *Thirdly.* The town of Shimonoséki might justly have been destroyed, because it fired on our ships. But it was left unhurt, and therefore a ransom must be paid. Furthermore, the prince must defray the cost of the expedition. The whole amount will be determined by the foreign representatives at Yedo.

To this our friends offered strenuous opposition. Chôshiû and Bôshiû were two very small provinces, and possessed a revenue of scarcely 360,000 *koku* of rice. Of this, 200,000 went to support the retainers, the balance having been spent in batteries, guns, and all other manner of warlike equipments. If the sum demanded were beyond their resources, they could not pay it. There were plenty of men in the province who cared nothing for their lives in comparison with the fulfilment of their duty towards the prince. It is he who wishes to make peace, and he has much difficulty in repressing their zeal. The Admiral replied that they should have calculated the price beforehand. They had chosen to make war, and now that the bill was being presented to them, they must pay it. Finally they agreed to this article, but it struck me that their object was solely to let us know that their spirit was not entirely broken, and that if our demands were too exorbitant they would fight rather than yield.

Last of all we inserted in the draft a declaration that this was merely a treaty for the temporary cessation of hostilities, and was entirely independent of any questions connected with Chôshiû which might have to be settled later on between the foreign representatives and the Japanese Government. I imagine that this clause had reference to the indemnities which might be demanded on the part of France, Holland and the United States. At any rate, it was agreed to without any discussion. A fair copy was written out, to which two of the *karôs* affixed their signatures, and a couple of days were given to them to go to Yamaguchi in order to obtain the prince's signature. Those who had not previously seen the ship were taken the usual round through the lower deck and engine room, and they left in a body.

On the 15th things seemed quiet enough for a little private exploration on my own account in company with my teacher. We went first to call on Ibara Kazuyé, one of the envoys who had negotiated the agreement of the day before, and asked him to come on board to be photographed by Beato. Then while Hayashi, whose crown was by this time black with a fortnight's bristly growth, went to a barber's shop to get himself clean shaved, I strolled about the streets alone, and turned into an eating-house where we had agreed to meet. The people received me civilly, and showed me upstairs to a room, one side of which was entirely open to the air, and overlooked a small courtyard. In the next apartment were some Chôshiû two-sworded men leaning over the wooden balcony, who waved their hands to me to go away, but I called out, "What do you want!" in a fierce tone, and they collapsed immediately, so great was the prestige of our victory. When Hayashi joined me, we ordered an *awabi* to be got ready, and while it was being cooked, devoured nearly the whole of a ripe water melon. The *awabi* (rocksucker) was cooked with sugar and proved terribly tough. Two sorts of *saké* were served, and the waiting maid smoked all the while to perfume the room. We wound up with terrapin soup and rice. During the rest of my stay at Shimonoséki, which lasted nearly a month, I was constantly on shore, and never had any trouble with the townspeople, who were always civil and friendly.

The treaty was brought down on the 16th, and found to be duly signed and sealed. At the same time the Japanese produced a paper which they wanted the Admirals to sign, undertaking that the officers and crews should keep within certain limits, and above all, should not land at night. There was a good deal of misunderstanding about this document. The Abbé Girard's teacher maintained that it was a memorandum or note-verbale from the Chôshiû authorities, and as I was younger and had not the prestige of the Abbé as a Japanese scholar, I had to give way. So we concocted a letter in reply, which I wrote out, and took on shore to the governor. Our letter said that the principal restrictions which the Japanese asked us to agree to had been granted already, and that as for the rest, the governor had on the occasion of his last visit said there were no complaints to make of our people trespassing on either guardhouses or temples, and therefore it was unnecessary for them to make such demands. In future, if they had anything to communicate, it must be done by letter, signed and sealed by Ibara Kazuyé. On reading this, the governor to my delight said, "Here's a mistake. What I brought to you was a draft of a letter for the naval commanders to write to us."

The object of the naval operations in the straits having been completely attained by the destruction of the batteries and the establishment of a good understanding with the Prince of Chôshiû, preparations were now made to withdraw the major portion of the allied squadrons, leaving only three ships to prevent the possibility of the passage being again fortified. I received orders to remain behind on board the "Barrosa." A day before the Admiral sailed a letter came from the governor asking him to give a passage as far as Yokohama to a *karô* and two officers. The request was at once granted, but the three passengers not arriving in time, word was left that they might apply to the French Admiral, who was to leave a day later. But this they declined to do, having been instructed to ask for a passage in an English ship, and they would go by no other. Eventually the "Barrosa" took them.

On the 20th accordingly, all the British ships except the "Barrosa," and all the Dutch ships but the "Djambi," sailed away up the inland sea towards Ozaka, the French, however, remaining. I went ashore afterwards with some officers of the "Barrosa" for a walk, and as we passed the guardhouse, its occupants called out, "Take off your hats." I replied, "What do you say." The man on guard, "Take off your hats.

This is the honourable guardhouse of Shimonoséki." Answer from our side, "What folly do you talk! If you repeat it, the governor shall be informed." So we passed on into the town to the governor's house and laid a complaint in due form against the over-zealous guardhouse keeper. The governor promised to administer a reprimand, and was as good as his word, so that when some other officers came ashore and passed the same spot, the Japanese officers rushed out into the road to tell them that they need not uncap.

I found the townspeople very communicative about the exploits of the Americans and French in 1863, and from their relation it was easy to see that while Captain M'Dougall of the "Wyoming" had given a very modest account of his achievements in the way of sinking ships and firing houses, the French had greatly exaggerated their own deeds of valour. The "Wyoming" ran the gauntlet of all the batteries and sank the "Lancefield" and the brig right in front of the town, whereas the "Sémiramis" never ventured further than Tanoura. The common folk were all entirely convinced that the Tycoon had given orders for the expulsion of the foreigners, and I overheard a man in the market say "the *Baku-fu* is playing a double game." *Baku-fu* was the most common term by which the Tycoon's government was then designated. I was asked whether the Tycoon had asked us to come down and destroy the batteries, to which I answered "No; but he said he could not open the straits." Then I gave them our view of the case, which was that the Tycoon, finding himself in a tight place between the *daimiôs* and the foreigners, had to give assurances to both which were inconsistent with each other, whereupon they all cried out with one voice: "*Homma da*, it is true." That evening there arrived from Nagasaki the steamer "Victoria" with the vice-governor of that port and an interpreter. Passing in front of the town they paid the French Admiral a call, and then anchored near us in Tanoura Bay. Coming on board to make inquiries, they asked whether Chôshiû had been beaten, and on our replying in the affirmative, they produced a copy of the prince's first letter begging for peace addressed to the *Americans*, which they said had been furnished to them by the Kokura people.

That I told them bluntly must be a lie, but they would not confess the source from which they had obtained the document. They said their instructions were to ask the Admiral not to believe the lies Chôshiû was telling about orders received from the Tycoon to expel foreigners, and also that having heard the fleet was going to Ozaka, the governor of Nagasaki, who was afraid that the appearance of so large a force before the city, fresh from the destruction of the batteries of Shimonoséki, might cause a panic, had sent them to prevent any difficulties between the Admiral and the governor of Ozaka. They were very anxious lest a treaty had been concluded with Chôshiû for the opening of Shimonoséki to foreign trade, which would have caused the commercial ruin of Nagasaki; but we declined to give them any information. Having beaten the Chôshiû people, we had come to like and respect them, while a feeling of dislike began to arise in our minds for the Tycoon's people on account of their weakness and double-dealing, and from this time onwards I sympathized more and more with the *daimiô* party, from whom the Tycoon's government had always tried to keep us apart.

On the 21st the "Sémiramis" and "Dupleix" quitted the straits, leaving behind them the "Tancrède." Some of us went ashore to the *honjin* to inquire whether we could obtain a supply of bullocks for the ship. The officials promised to do all they could, but said it would be difficult, as they killed none for themselves. We also asked them to change some Mexican dollars into Japanese money, which they promised to do at the Nagasaki market rate, but it was finally arranged that if we found ourselves in actual need of coin, they should lend us a thousand *ichibus*, to be returned to their agent at Yokohama. They proved so obliging that we could not help regretting that in order to gain their friendship it had been necessary to come to blows with them. And it is not a little remarkable that neither the Satsuma nor the Chôshiû men ever seemed to cherish any resentment against us for what we had done, and during the years of disturbance and revolution that followed they were always our most intimate allies.

That day we walked the whole length of the town unattended by any guard, and got a glimpse of the China sea beyond the straits. We met, however, with a little show of insolence from a couple of two-sworded men, who motioned us back to our boats, but I discoursed to them in their own tongue, and they were speedily reduced to silence: the exhibition of a revolver had something to do with the production of this effect.

Itô came on board one day with a couple of men who, he said, were merchants, but it was evident from the respect he paid to one of them, who wore two swords, that they belonged to the high official class. They were conducted round the ship and entertained with various liquors. He declared that in all the fighting they had only seven or eight men killed, and about twice that number wounded, but one of his companions told me that the number killed was nearly twenty. Itô said that trade could be done at Shimonoséki in cotton, wax and silk produced in Chôshiû, as well as in all the productions of the northern provinces and Ozaka. Probably they might manufacture paper for the English market. The prince, he added, was very desirous of opening the port to foreign commerce, but just at present they expected an invasion of the combined forces of the Tycoon and all the *daimiôs*, and all their attention was directed to their own defence. The two vessels sunk by the "Wyoming" in 1863 had been raised, and sent round to Hagi. I was surprised to learn that the batteries at Maeda-mura, as well as those at Kushi saki Point, were within the territory of the *daimiô* of Chôfu, who was however not in so far independent that he could stand aside when the head of the family went to war. Last year, at the time when the Dutch corvette "Medusa" was fired on as she passed the straits, batteries had existed on the low hills behind the town, and at two points on the sea front, but the guns had subsequently been removed thence to Dannoura and Maeda-mura; their fate was to fall into our hands. The small three-gun battery on Moji Point within the Kokura territory was also the work of the Chôshiû men, who had levelled land and commenced the construction of barracks, which were however destroyed by the Kokura people when the failure of the prince's Kiôto schemes drove him to withdraw within his own boundaries for self-protection.

We went one day in our boats down to Kokura with the intention of landing there to walk through the town, but after keeping us waiting an hour and a half, and repeatedly promising to open the gate, they finally refused to admit us. They did indeed open it, but only to let out a couple of fellows, who told us in the lowest of low voices that Kokura not being a treaty port, we could not be allowed to enter. I took care to inform them of our opinion that it was a great piece of ingratitude on their part to treat us in so inhospitable a manner after we had thrashed their enemy for them. Crowds of people had collected to look at us, and doubtless we should have been mobbed if we had landed. There was no idea on our part of forcing our way in.

Towards the end of the month smallpox broke out on board, and W. H. Cummings, who had succeeded to the temporary command on Captain Dowell's transfer to the flagship, determined to leave for Yokohama as soon as the necessary arrangements could be made. On the 27th we applied therefore to the authorities for a pilot to take the ship through the inland sea, and gave notice that the commanders of the three ships would pay a visit to Ibara on the morrow in order to settle about the passage up to Yokohama which had been promised to him and two other officers. I took the message on shore, and stopped to have a meal with Itô, who good-naturedly had made great efforts to get up a dinner in European style. He had built a table seven feet long by half that width, covered with a short cloth of some coarse foreign material. Four plates were laid, flanked by long knives, villainously sharp, attenuated brass spoons with flat bowls, and a pair of chopsticks. The first dish consisted of a boiled rockfish, which I found great difficulty in cutting, but accomplished the task at last by inserting a sharpened chopstick into the head, and using a spoon to remove the flesh. Soy, a large bowl of rice, and a small saucer full of coarse salt, were also placed on the table. The second course was broiled eels, and then came a stewed terrapin, both of which were very good, but the boiled *awabi* and boiled chicken which followed were quite out of the question. It was a problem how to cut up a fowl with a knife that had no point, and whose blade threatened at every moment to part company with its handle. I abandoned the attempt, and served my companions with slices from the breast. Unripe persimmons, peeled and cut in four, with sweet rice beer (*mirin*) were now produced, and this was excellent. This was certainly the earliest attempt ever made in that part of Japan at giving a dinner in European style, perhaps the first in Japan.

It was finally determined that the party that was to visit Yokohama should consist of Ibara, a councillor named Sugi Tokusuké, a secretary, and Itô, with four servants, who were to be accommodated on board the "Barrosa" and "Djambi." The "Tancrède," which was to leave before us, could not find room for more than half the party, and as they did not wish to be separated longer than they could help, they elected to come with us. On the 4th October the "Racehorse," Commander Boxer, arrived to relieve us. Ibara and his secretary, Yamagata Keizô, and we sailed the following morning.

News of our successful result of the naval operations and of the conclusion of a convention with the Prince of Chôshiû was at once conveyed to the foreign representatives at Yokohama, who lost no time in calling the Tycoon's government to account for their apparent complicity with Chôshiû, as evidenced by the copies of orders from Kiôto which Itô had given us. The explanation was feeble, and the representatives found no difficulty in obtaining from the ministers their consent to pay whatever war indemnity might be due from Chôshiû, or else to throw open to trade a port in the inland sea. Although in the sequel the receipt of the indemnity money by us actually took place, it was in a manner forced upon the four Powers and their diplomatic agents, and certainly as far as Sir R. Alcock is concerned, he may be entirely exonerated from the accusation of a desire to exact an indemnity from either the defeated *daimiô* or the government which assumed responsibility for him. The principal object he sought was to obtain the sanction of the Mikado to the treaties, so as to put an end to the agitation against foreign commerce which had been carried on by hostile *daimiôs* in the Mikado's name ever since the opening of the ports. Now that Satsuma and Chôshiû, the two ringleaders of the opposition, had been brought to their senses, it ought to have been, he thought, an easy matter for the Tycoon's government, if they sincerely desired to carry out their treaty obligations, to assert their authority and compel the whole country to accept the new policy of foreign intercourse. The fixing of an indemnity was intended only to provide a means of pressure upon the Tycoon's government in order to procure the Mikado's ratification of the treaties, and the consequent extension of commercial relations.

Ibara and his companions reached Yokohama on the 10th October, and obtained an interview the same day with Sir Rutherford Alcock and Mr Pruyn, the United States minister. The reception accorded to them was of such a nature as to convince them that the foreign powers were not hostilely disposed towards the *daimiô* of Chôshiû, and it was no doubt with a sense of relief that they learnt the intention of the foreign representatives to claim the payment of the indemnity from the Tycoon. At the same time it was clearly understood by both parties that the other engagements entered into by Chôshiû respecting the permanent disarmament of the straits of Shimonoséki and the hospitable treatment of foreign vessels were to be faithfully adhered to, and on these heads his subsequent conduct gave no ground for complaint. It was somewhat a curious position for the retainers of a prince, who had been declared a rebel against the Mikado and enemy of the Tycoon, to land at Yokohama, a port belonging to the latter, but as far as I remember, they confined their visit to the foreign settlement, where they were safe from interference, and on the 14th the "Tartar" left with them on board to return to their native province.

CHAPTER XII

The Murder of Bird and Baldwin

It was about this time that Sir Rutherford Alcock received Lord Russell's despatches recalling him to England. Ostensibly for the purpose of consulting with him on the situation of affairs, this summons to London was accompanied by the expression of an opinion that the passage of the inland sea was not necessary to foreign commerce, which amounted to a censure upon his conduct. It is seldom that an agent of the Foreign Office is told in so many words that he is recalled because his conduct of affairs has not given satisfaction, but inasmuch as leave of absence is usually granted upon the application of the ambassador, envoy, or whatever the title of the head of a mission may be, an invitation to return home is equivalent to the removal of a diplomatic officer from his employment. But arriving just at the moment when his policy had been successful in every direction, and when all the foreigners in the country were united in a chorus of gratitude to him for his energetic action, he and all the members of his legation felt that the displeasure of Lord John Russell was not a matter of much moment. The crushing defeat of Chôshiû by the foreign squadrons coming so immediately after the repulse of his troops from the gates of the palace at Kiôto restored confidence to the Tycoon's government, and enabled them to declare firmly to the Mikado that the idea of expelling foreigners from the country and putting an end to trade was utterly and entirely impracticable, while on the other hand the demonstrated superiority of European methods of warfare had converted our bitterest and most determined foes into fast friends. The vindication of his proceedings was no difficult task, and the despatch in which he justified the course he had taken was conceived in a style at once calm and convincing. It is only fair to Lord Russell to say that he lost no time in acknowledging that his agent had been in the right, and in conveying to him the Queen's full approbation of his conduct. But this solatium to his feelings did not reach Yokohama until he was already on his way to England.

The Shôgun's government voluntarily undertook to be responsible for whatever sum might be fixed upon as the indemnity to be paid by the Prince of Chôshiû. On the 22nd October a convention was signed by a member of the Shôgun's second council and the four foreign representatives by which three millions of dollars were to be paid in satisfaction of all claims, or as an alternative the opening of Shimonoséki or some other port in the inland sea, if the Tycoon preferred to offer it and the Powers were willing to accept. The division of this sum of money among the different Powers was reserved for adjustment between the four governments. Advantage was also taken of the desire to conciliate foreign Powers now manifested by the Tycoon's ministers to obtain the promise of various improvements at Yokohama calculated to add to the comfort and well-being of the foreign residents, and Sir Rutherford, having thus reaped all the fruits of his courage and perseverance was preparing to quit Japan in obedience to the instructions of Lord Russell, when a fresh and totally unforeseen event occurred which for a time delayed his departure.

After our successes at Shimonoséki, and the frank admission by the Tycoon's government of the necessity of maintaining the treaties, the confidence of foreign residents in the safety of the neighbourhood had so completely revived that they no longer feared to make excursions within the limits marked out by the treaties. But they received a rude shock on the night of the 20th November when the governor of Kanagawa came to Mr Winchester, the British Consul, and informed him that Major

Baldwin and Lieutenant Bird of the xxth regiment had been barbarously murdered at Kamakura, a well-known resort some twelve miles from Yokohama. Baldwin was killed on the spot, but aocording to the testimony of the inhabitants, Bird had lived for some hours after he was disabled. The two officers had visited the famous colossal Buddha, and riding along the road towards the temple of Hachiman, were just about to turn the corner into the avenue when a couple of men sprang out upon them with their keen-edged swords and inflicted such ghastly wounds as brought them to the ground almost unresistingly. The horror of the foreign community can be more easily imagined than described, and it was further deepened when as the result of the inquest it came to be suspected that the mortal wound to which Bird had succumbed had been inflicted some hours after the assassins had left the spot. This, in the opinion of the surgeons, was a wound in the neck completely dividing the spinal cord between the second and third cervical vertebrae, which clearly must have been followed by instant death. Now all the evidence went to show that the younger victim had lived until ten o'clock in the evening. If so, by whom was this wound given, and with what motive? Those who implicitly relied upon the report of the regimental surgeons jumped to the conclusion that it was the act of one of the officials despatched to the scene of the murder by the governor as soon as the news was brought to him, which was no doubt some three or four hours before he himself went to communicate it to Mr Winchester, and the motive was suggested to be a desire to prevent the wounded man from giving such information to his countrymen as might have led to the identification of the murderers. But I cannot believe that any Japanese, official or not, could ever have compassed such a treacherous deed. I believe on the contrary that the surgeons who dissected out the wound, not using sufficient care, themselves divided the spinal cord with a probe or some other instrument, and that Bird's death was caused in reality by the loss of blood from his numerous wounds. And this was the view taken by Dr Willis of our legation and Dr Jenkins, then established as a general practitioner in Yokohama, neither of whom was invited to assist at the *post mortem*.

The two surgeons having made a hurried examination and enunciated certain views as to the nature of Bird's wounds, without foreseeing the inferences that might be drawn, would naturally, and probably with entire good faith, adhere to those views afterwards, especially as it would not appear to them at all incredible *à priori* that the countrymen of the men who had committed such a foul assassination should be capable of a deed, dastardly enough in itself, but no doubt justifiable in the opinion of any foreigner-hating Japanese official. There are many additional considerations suggested by the reports contained in the Parliamentary papers which would corroborate the view here put forth, if I had space to discuss them. But as this book is intended to be a record of my own experiences and memories, and not a compilation from published materials, it is not the place to go into all these particulars at length.

The Tycoon's government made all the exertions in their power to trace the assassins, and before a month was over they had arrested one of the guilty persons, named Shimidzu Seiji. Already on the 16th two of his associates named Gamaiké and Inaba, accused of combining with him in a plot to murder foreigners, and of extorting money from a rich farmer, had been executed, though they were not actual accomplices in the Kamakura crime.

I was present at the execution of these two men, which took place in an enclosure outside the Japanese gaol in the afternoon of the 16th December 1864. There was a large concourse of spectators, both foreign and native. A little after three o'clock a whisper ran round that the condemned were being brought out. A door opened, and a man blindfolded and bound with cords was led through the crowd. He was made to kneel down on a rough mat placed in front of a hole dug in the ground to receive his blood. The attendants drew his clothes downwards so as to lay the neck bare, and with the hand brushed his hair upwards, so as to give full play to the sword. The executioner secured a piece of cotton

cloth round the handle of his weapon, and having carefully whetted the blade, took up a position to the left of his victim, then
raising the sword high above his head with both hands, let it fall
with a swoop that severed the neck completely. The head was
held up for the inspection of the chief officer present, who simply
remarked: "I have seen it," and it was thrown into the hole. The
second man being then carried in, the attendants seemed to have
a little trouble in getting him to kneel in the proper position, but
at last the arrangements were completed to their satisfaction. The
neck having been bared as before, a fresh executioner advanced,
took his place at the prisoner's left side, and raising the sword with
a flourish, let it descend with the same skill as his predecessor.
It was a horrible sight to see the attendants holding the headless
corpse down to the hole, and kneading it so as to make the blood
flow more readily into the hole, and I left the spot in all haste,
vowing that mere curiosity should never induce me to witness
another execution.

Capital punishment was much commoner in Japan in those
days than it has been since the promulgation of the present
humane penal code, and included transfixing with spears. Many
of the foreign residents must have been present at such sanguinary
spectacles, merely impelled by curiosity, and without the natural
excuse of desiring to see the sentence of the law fulfilled upon an
offender against their own blood.

The night before Sir Rutherford embarked for England news
was brought to him of the arrest of Shimidzu Seiji, one of the
actual murderers of Baldwin and Bird. Owing to the reputed
excellence of the native detective police, which under a despotic
government is usually efficient, it was believed by us that the
Japanese Government could always have procured the arrest of
the assailants of foreigners, if they had been determined to do so.
The names, *e.g.*, of many of those who were engaged in the attack
on our legation in 1861 were, as I learnt some years afterwards,
matter of common notoriety, but in the difficult political position
that the Tycoon's advisers had created for themselves, they did not

dare to convict the murderer of a foreigner. This then was the first instance of such a crime being brought home to its perpetrators. The British minister had good reason to feel gratified at this proof that his policy had beeh the right one, and it was a very natural movement that induced him to take off his watch and chain and throw them over the neck of the messenger of good tidings.

Shimidzu Seiji was executed on the 28th December at ten o'clock in the morning, in the presence of a detachment of the English garrison. Whatever doubts may have existed as to the complicity of Gamaiké and Inaba in his designs against the lives of the foreign residents, there is none as to the fact that this man was one of the actual murderers of Baldwin and Bird. I was instructed to accompany Mr M. O. Flowers, the acting consul, to the prison on the preceding day to hear the sentence pronounced. We waited some hours till he arrived from Yedo in custody of a strong guard, and he was at once confronted with the witnesses, who examined his features in silence. They were then separately interrogated, and one and all recognized him, the most important witness being the boy who had seen the attack. Afterwards we proceeded to another room and questioned the prisoner, who acknowledged his guilt in the clearest manner possible. He was proceeding to say something more, but was ordered by the Japanese officers to be silent. But the best evidence of his identity was obtained by another member of the consular service, who after the murderer had been paraded round the town preceded by a banner on which his sentence was inscribed (this was part of his punishment), accompanied the procession back to the execution ground. Here Mr Fletcher overheard him say: "When I killed the foreigners, I expected one of them might be a consul," and every one who knew our colleague will acknowledge that he was a man of the most exact truthfulness, who was not in the least degree likely to make a mistake in such a matter, or over anxious to believe that the Japanese Government were in this instance departing from the bad faith which is the usual refuge of Asiatics in a difficult position.

On the morning of the 28th the garrison was marched over to the execution ground, and drawn up on one side. The prisoner was brought out about ten o'clock. The first words he uttered were a request for some *saké*. Being again questioned, he frankly acknowledged his guilt. I asked him what it was that he had been prevented from saying to us on the previous day, to which he answered that if Bird and Baldwin had got out of his way he would not have attacked them. Whether this was true or not I have no means of judging, but it does not accord with his written deposition. That, it must be recollected, is not in Japan a simple record of everything a prisoner says, but is a reduction in writing by an officer of the court of the final result of all the statements made by him on the different occasions when he was examined, and resembles much more the summing up of the evidence on a criminal trial in England by the presiding judge. He begged the Japanese officials not to bandage his eyes, and began to chant a verse which might be thus translated:

"I do not regret being taken and put to death,
For to kill barbarians is the true spirit of a Japanese"

As the attendants were drawing back the clothes from his neck to prepare it for the executioner's stroke, he bade them loosen his cords so that they might do it with greater ease, adding: "In after ages they will say, what a fine fellow was Shimidzu Seiji." He also remarked, "I don't think the sword that cut off Gempachi's head will do for me," alluding probably to the thickness of his own neck, and begged that the blade might be well whetted. Then saying, "Cut neatly if you please," he stretched out his neck for the stroke. These were the last words he spoke, but just as the sword began to descend he turned his head to the left as if to address some further observation to the officials, so that the cut partly missed its purpose, and the executioner had to hack the head off — a most horrible sight. Simultaneously with the delivery of the first blow, a gun fired by the battery of Royal Artillery announced to all that the assassin had received the punishment of his crime, and we dispersed as quickly as possible. The head was taken to the bridge at the northern entrance of Yokohama and there exposed on a gibbet for three days. Copies of the sentence were posted up at Totsuka and at the scene of the murder, and a few days later I accompanied the Legation mounted guard to see that this part of the undertaking given by the Japanese authorities had been duly performed. We found that they had fulfilled their promises to the letter, and thus ended one of the most dramatic incidents in the whole of my experience in the country.

It was impossible not to hate the assassin, but nevertheless, looking at the matter from a Japanese point of view, I confess that I could not help regretting that a man who was evidently of such heroic mould, should have been misguided enough to believe that his country could be helped by such means. But the blood of the foreigners who fell under the swords of Japanese murderers, and the lives which were sacrificed to avenge it bore fruit in later days, and fertilised the ground from which sprang the tree of the national regeneration.

CHAPTER XIII

Ratification of the Treaties by the Mikado

Sir Rutherford having quitted Japan, the conduct of affairs was assumed by Mr Winchester as Chargé d'Affaires. Before long despatches reached us from Lord Russell expressing the entire satisfaction of the British Government with the policy pursued by our late chief, and we heard that he had been rewarded by promotion to the more important post of minister at Peking. He was succeeded by Sir Harry Parkes, who came to us invested with the prestige of a man who had looked death in the face with no ordinary heroism, and in the eyes of all European residents in the far east held a higher position thau any officer of the crown in those countries. And whatever may have been his faults and shortcomings, especially towards the latter part of his career, it must be acknowledged that England never was represented by a more devoted public servant, and that Japan herself owes to his exertions a debt which she can never repay and has never fully acknowledged. If he had taken a different side in the revolution of 1868, if he had simply acted with the majority of his colleagues, almost iusurmountable difficulties would have been placed in the way of the Mikado's restoration, and the civil war could never have been brought to so speedy a termination. He was an indefatigable worker, entirely absorbed in the duties of his post, untiring in his endeavours to obtain a correct view of his surroundings, never sparing himself, and requiring from his subordinates the same zealous assiduity. Of his personal courage I had the opportunity afterwards of witnessing one strking example, and brilliant as have been the achievements of many of our Indian civilians, I do not think that his coolness and fortitude in the moment of peril have ever been surpassed by any man not bred to war. He was strict and severe in service matters, but in his private relations gracious to all those who had occasion to seek his help, and a faithful friend to all who won his goodwill. Unfortunately I was not one of these, and the result was that from the beginning we were never friends, down to the very last, though he never had reason to complain of sloth or unreadiness to take my share of the work, and so it came about that before long I became one of his assistants, and in the end of 1866 was finally transferred from the Yokohama Consulate (where I had been appointed interpreter early in 1865) to the Legation.

The accomplice of Shimidzu Seiji in the murder of Bird and Baldwin, named Mamiya Hajimé, was executed on the 30th October 1865. I went out early with Flowers in pouring rain to question the prisoner on some points which had to be cleared up in connection with the crime. He was condemned to the same punishment as his confederate, and we went out again at one o'clock to be present at his decapitation. It was a pouring wet day, and the dull leaden sky overhead was in keeping with the melancholy occasion. Mamiya was a young fellow, and endowed with far less fortitude than Shimidzu, and in order to enable him to face the executioner he had been allowed to stupify himself with drink. His head was taken off at a single blow. The usual doubts as to his identity were expressed by the local foreign press, but for myself I was convinced that he was one of the assassins. If the Tycoon's government had substituted any other criminal for a man whom they had not succeeded in capturing, the truth would have surely leaked out, and by this time we had sources of information which would have enabled us speedily to detect any trick.

Sir Harry Parkes reached Yokohama early in July, and Mr Winchester took his departure for Shanghai, where he had been appointed to be consul. F. S. Myburgh was transferred at the same time from Nagasaki to the Yokohama consulate. In passing through Nagasaki Sir Harry had already learnt from the agents of some of the *daimiôs* that a civil war was expected at no distant date, the object of which would be the overthrow of the Tycoon. He already in September began to speak to the Tycoon's council of the desirability of obtaining the Mikado's ratification of the treaties, but the credit of the idea is in reality due to Mr Winchester, who (I did not know it at the time) as early as April had suggested to the British Government that the written adhesion of the Mikado to the treaties, and the reduction of the import duties to a uniform tariff of 5 per cent *ad valorem* might be obtained in return for the partial abandonment of the Shimonoséki indemnity, the Tycoon's ministers having stated they could not continue to make the quarterly payments of $500,000 at a time, as had been stipulated in the convention. In fact Sir Rutherford Alcock had begun to lay stress on the necessity of the Mikado's ratification of the treaties almost immediately after the bombardment of Shimonoséki. This suggestion was approved by Lord Russell, who at once communicated it to the governments of Holland, France, and the United States, and sent despatches to Japan to the same effect which reached Sir Harry Parkes towards the end of October. He lost no time in consulting with his colleagues, and in proposing that they should proceed in a body to Ozaka, supported by a considerable squadron of men-of-war, to negotiate direct with the main body of the Tycoon's ministers. I should have mentioned before that the Tycoon was at Kiôto, having proceeded thither in the month of June, ostensibly for the purpose of taking command of the army which was to chastise the presumptuous rebel, the Prince of Chôshiû, and was still detained there by various intrigues and the insufficiency of his military means.

The French minister, who was at first strongly opposed to the abandonment of the indemnity in exchange for the opening of a port, had received instructions from his government which had induced him to come over to the views of the British rep-

resentative, who found the United States Chargé d'Affaires and
Netherlands Political Agent equally willing to follow his lead.
As to the latter, we were accustomed to believe that Sir Harry
had him "in his pocket," as the phrase goes, and the Americans
had at that time partially abandoned the affectation of acting on
different lines from the "effete monarchies of Europe." Unity of
action being thus secured, the word was passed to the naval commanders to get ready for sea, and the legations having packed up
a sufficient quantity of foolscap paper, silk tape, quill pens and
bottles of ink, embarked on board the next day but one after the
signature of a protocol in which the four diplomatic representatives
had recorded their views and projects. Sir Harry took with him
John Macdonald, Alexander von Siebold and myself.

The squadron was an imposing one, though not so over-
whelmingly strong as that which had destroyed the batteries at
Shimonoséki in the previous year. Of British ships there were the
"Princess Royal," 73, flying the broad pennant of Admiral St George
Vincent King; the "Leopard," 18; "Pelorus," 22; and "Bouncer," 1;
of French, the "Guerrière," 36; "Dupleix," 12; and "Kienchang," 4;
while the Netherlands contributed the corvette "Zoutman." Our
Admiral was extremely good-natured, and had fitted up private
cabins for us three civilians on the main deck. I was delighted to
find myself on board with my friend A. G. S. Hawes, a marine
officer recently transferred to the flagship from the "Severn."

The foreign representatives, it was rumoured, proposed, in addition to the Mikado's ratification of the treaties and the reduction
of the tariff, to ask for the opening of Ozaka and Hiôgo to foreign
trade on the 1st January 1866. By the Treaty of 1858 these places were
to have been opened on the 1st January 1863, but the powers had in
1862 agreed to a postponement of five years, in order to give time
for things to settle down. In return, the four powers were ready to
forgo two-thirds of the Shimonoséki indemnity, and the option
of deciding was to be left to the Tycoon. This much was bruited
about among the members of the foreign legations. Outsiders said
that we were about to present an *ultimatum*, and that the creation

of two new centres of foreign trade was to be demanded without alternative. The men in the service who expected appointments would of course have been eager to believe this version but for the glorious uncertainty which surrounds all diplomatic projects.

The Yedo government were alarmed at the energetic step on which the representatives had resolved, and Midzuno Idzumi no Kami, the only member of the first council who had remained behind in Yedo when the Tycoon went up to Kiôto, came down in the company of Sakai Hida no Kami, one of the second council, to exert all his powers of dissuasion with Sir Harry. It was the first time that a functionary of so high a rank had ever visited a foreign legation, and the evidence of anxiety thus afforded simply confirmed the resolution that had been taken to bring matters to a crisis. That Midzuno and his subordinate hoped their efforts would be successful there is no reason to suppose, and in fact they contented themselves mainly with offering some advice as to the best method of proceeding on the arrival of the representatives at Hiôgo.

We left on the 1st November, and proceeding in a leisurely manner along the coast, passed the Idzumi Straits at 8 a.m. on the 4th. The guns were loaded and the men beat to quarters, but the garrison of the forts at Yura showed no signs of molesting us, and everybody soon quieted down again. At half-past eleven we came in sight of Ozaka, lying on the low land at the mouth of the Yodo river. The mountains which enclose the bay on either side here appear to retire far into the interior, until they disappear in the haze. The Tycoon's castle was easily distinguished by its innumerable many-storied white towers, rising at the back of the city. But of the town very little was visible owing to the slight elevation of the houses and the distance from the deep water outside where we were passing. The allied squadron formed in one line, headed by the "Princess Royal," and gradually rounded off in the direction of Hiôgo, where we anchored at half-past one. One by one the other ships came in and took up the positions indicated to them.

The bay was crowded with junks of all sizes, and we counted seven Japanese steamers lying at anchor. From one of these, belonging to the Tycoon's War Department, a couple of officers came on board to make the usual inquiries, and shortly afterwards some very inquisitive shore-going officials came off, who put a great many questions about the object of our visit and where we had come from. They got very little information in reply, but were told that some officers would be going by sea to Ozaka on the following day, and that notice should be sent to the governor of the city in order that he might despatch somebody down to the landing-place to meet them. They were also requested to provide pilots for the two vessels to be despatched to Ozaka, but they declared themselves unable to promise anything we asked. However, as by their own rules they were under an obligation to send information to the governor, this refusal was not of any great consequence.

The Abbé Girard, who had acted as interpreter to Admiral Jaurès the previous year at Shimonoséki, was on this occasion replaced by M. Mermet de Cachon, a Jesuit attached to the French legation. He, with Messrs Macdonald and von Siebold of our legation, and Mr Hegt, the clerk of the Netherlands Political Agent, were despatched on the following day in the "Kienchang" to Ozaka bearing letters from the foreign representatives. The "Bouncer" was to have taken our people, but her commander was not able to get up steam in time, so that the French flag alone made its appearance at the bar of Ozaka. First point scored by the French. M. Mermet had ingeniously prepared the French's minister's letter in Japanese, inserting at the end a long peragraph, which did not appear in the other three letters, empowering himself to state in outline to the Tycoon's council the objects of the foreign representatives, hoping thus to become the spokesman for all four.

On arriving at the mouth of the river, they were met by the two governors of the city (all officials were kept in duplicate in those days), who conducted them to a building close at hand, evidently prepared beforehand for their reception. On learning that M. Mermet and his companions desired to have a personal interview with one of the council, the governors started off immediately to fetch him, as they said, promising that he should be down by four o'clock. In the meantime Macdonald, Siebold and Hegt started off to walk to Ozaka, intending to seek out the ministers there, but after wandering a long distance, they found themselves at three o'clock only just in sight of the city, and had to hurry back in a boat. The governors, however, did more than keep their promise, and instead of one, produced two of the council, namely Ogasawara Iki no Kami and Abé Bungo no Kami. The letters were delivered to them, and they listened civilly and even affably to the messages which Mermet aud Macdonald delivered, but were unprepared of course to give any answer. It was agreed, however, that Abé should proceed to Hiôgo on the 9th to meet the four representatives on board the "Princess Royal," as sole negotiator on behalf of the Tycoon, who, it was stated, had gone up to Kiôto. For me had been reserved the less glorious task of opening up communications with the local officials, and in company with Captain W. G. Jones I went ashore to talk about beef, water, coals, and other ship's requirements. We also informed them that the officers would land, and requested that the townspeople might be ordered to treat them with civility. This they promised to do, but added that their duty to their chiefs, the governors of Ozaka, would oblige them to detail one or two constables to watch over the safety of each party. After we had conversed awhile with the head constable, a young man of 19 or 20, some higher officials made their appearance and assumed the power. They promised to do everything we asked, and to help their memories made very full notes. In the afternoon accordingly, leave to go ashore was given to all the ships, ahd many of the officers availed themselves of the opportunify of visiting what was then a *terra incognita* to most Europeans. The Admiral, Sir Harry and myself walked from one end of the town to the other, and found the inhabitants well-disposed, though they followed us in crowds.

This was a very different reception from what the Tycoon's officers had warned us to expect. They always talked to us of the hostility of the *daimiôs* and the dislike and fear of us entertained by the common people, but we met with nothing but indications of goodwill from all classes. It became clearer to us every day that the Shôgunate feared lest free communication between foreigners and those sections of the Japanese people who were outside its direct control would impair the authority of the institutions that had now lasted, with no small benefit to the Tokugawa family, for the last 260 years, and that consequently it could not be a desirable policy for Great Britain to endeavour to bolster up a decaying power. As an instance of the manner in which the Tycoon's officials endeavoured to obstruct intercourse, it may be mentioned that they published a notification in Ozaka forbidding the townspeople to visit the ships, knowing full well that a closer acquaintance would make their subjects and foreigners better friends.

The next few days were spent in exploring the neighbourhood with a view to selecting a site for a foreign settlement, and there was a good deal of running up and down to Ozaka by sea with messages for the council. Abé was not able to come on Thursday, and at first it was held out that another member of the council would replace him, but when the day arrived, the two governors of Ozaka made their appearance with other excuses. Sir Harry spoke very strongly to them, and insisted on seeing some one on Saturday at the latest. But as he did not expect that his request would be complied with, he despatched Siebold, Hegt and myself early in the morning to Ozaka. On approaching the anchorage, however, we saw a Japanese steamer coming from the opposite direction, and lowering a boat we went on board. We found that she was conveying Abé Bungo no Kami to Hiôgo to see the foreign ministers. It was arranged therefore that Siebold should return with him, while Hegt and I went on with a couple of officials lent to us by Abé. But as soon as we anchored these men began to be obstructive, refusing to accompany us on shore until the port officers had first visited the ship. Seeing, however, that we were determined to go, without them if necessary, they at last stepped over the side into the boat with a very bad grace indeed. We rowed in safely in the ship's gig, with four bluejackets well-armed, over the bar, which a few days before had been rendered impassable by a strong west wind, and landed in a small creek behind the battery at Tempôzan Point. We at once took possession of a house where Macdonald and Siebold had lodged on their last visit, disregarding the excuses of the officials, who said it was occupied by a sick person, but we were used to such subterfuges, and of course there was no sick man there at all. After a while we returned to the gig, and rowing up the river in half-an-hour, reached the outskirts of the city, where we landed to inspect a house that had been assigned for the accommodation of the foreign representatives. The latter intended to negotiate in Ozaka itself, but this idea was subsequently abandoned. As this one house was evidently not large enough for the representatives and their suites, I said I would go to the governor and ask him to provide other accommodation. The officials became alarmed at this, and at once offered to show us another house, to which they would take us in a boat. As we wished to see something of the city, I declined this proposal, and to their horror we proceeded to walk along the bank. A dense crowd of people gathered round us, but they were very quiet, and after passing the Ajikawa-bashi, the first of the series of bridges that span the river right up to the castle, we were shown a temple which, however, proved to be again insufficient for our needs. It being clear that our guides were not animated by goodwill, I again menaced them with a visit to the governor, but here they became utterly obstinate, and I had to give way. So we returned to our gig, and resolving to have a good look at the city, got on board and started to row up stream.

Before long we reached a barrier composed of native boats moored right across from bank to bank, with the evident intention of impeding our further progress. Some officials in a guardhouse on the bank shouted to us to go back, but we pushed straight ashore, and I ascended the steps to demand the reason of this obstruction. Orders from the governor was the reply. A somewhat heated altercation ensued, and I demanded that either we should be allowed to pass or that I should at once be conducted to the governor's house. At last they gave way and removed one or two of the junks, leaving just enough space for our gig. Taking one of the guardhouse officials on board, we proceeded up the river, not a little proud of our victory over the bumbledom of a city of 400,000 people, and fully determined to go right up to the castle. Dense crowds of people collected on the bridges, sometimes yelling and abusing us, now and then throwing stones. Hegt began to lose his temper, and drawing his revolver, threatened to fire, but I made him put it back in his pouch. We were in no danger, and could not afford to commit murder for such a trifling reason.

At last, after grounding once or twice on the sandbanks, we reached the Kiô-bashi just below the castle. On our left was a small boat full of officials who called to us to come and report ourselves, while on the right extended a grassy bank crowded with soldiers dressed in semi-European costume, among whom were a few men in plain dress, apparently noblemen's retainers. One of these came down to tbe water's edge, close to which we had approached, and shouted out to the Japanese who was with us for his name and office. Our man replied: "Who are you?" and they wrangled for about five minutes, while we kept a watchful eye on the straggling soldiery. But it was clearly unadvisable to land in the midst of a hostile armed crowd, and we reluctantly turned the boat's head down stream, which now carried us swiftly along. The same crowds still occupied the bridges, and shouted abusive epithets as we passed, to the great alarm of the Japanese official, who had not got over Hegt's fierce demeanour on the way up, and trembled for fear lest there should be a row. Landing the poor fellow, whose tone had become remarkably fainter and humbler since he first made our acquaintance in the morning, we pulled out across the bar to the "Bouncer," and in a few minutes more were on our way back to Hiôgo, having seen a good deal more of Ozaka than any one else, and braved the wrath of multitudinous *yakunins*. I began to feel contempt for the weak-kneed officials who so easily allowed themselves to be browbeaten by a few Europeans.

A curious rencontre took place during our stay at Hiôgo. A Satsuma steamer was lying in the port, and one day the captain, Arigawa Yakurô, came on board the flagship with some of his officers. One of them remembered having seen me at Kagoshima, and we immediately fraternized very heartily. After drinking and smoking a good deal they took leave, promising to send a boat for me next day to accompany them ashore to a Japanese dinner. But they forgot their promise. The day after my expedition to Ozaka, Siebold and I went on board Arigawa's ship to find him on the point of weighing anchor. He was very glad to see us, abounded in apologies for being unable to fulfil his engagement to give an *onna gochisô*, and showed us the cabin that had been fitted up for the entertainment. This gentleman was too civil by half, but still the contrast to the "offishness" of the Tycoon's officials was very agreeable. If I would like to visit Kagoshima and Loochoo he would be glad to give me a passage. We passed some time on board eating raw eggs and drinking *saké*. I rather think I here met Kawamura for the first time. A few days later when the steamer returned I again went on board and made an even more interesting acquaintance. This was a big burly man, with small, sparkling black eyes, who was lying down in one of the berths. His name, they said, was Shimadzu Sachiû, and I noticed that he had the scar of a sword cut on one of his arms. Many months afterwards I met him again, this time under his real name of Saigô Kichinosuké. I shall have more to say of him hereafter.

Abé Bungo no Kami had a *five hours'* interview with Sir Harry on the 10th, after which he went on board the "Guerrière" to see Mr Roches, the Frehch envoy. I learnt from Siebold that the conversation had not been of a satisfactory character. His answer to the three propositions of the representatives amounted to a *non possumus*. The Tycoon would pay up the second instalment of the indemnity rather than run the risk of incurring unpopularity by giving way to our demands. *Jin-shin fu-ori-ai*, the popular mind very unsettled, was the excuse then, and for many a day after. Sir Harry had given Abé a piece of his mind, and said he had better return to his colleagues and get them to reconsider their answer.

On the 13th he was to have come down again, but feigning indisposition as an excuse (this is well-known in Japan under the neme of *yaku-biô*, official sickness), he sent a member of the second council, Tachibana Idzumo no Kami, to inform the representatives that the Tycoon had hitherto never spoken to the Mikado about acknowledging the treaties, but that now he had made up his mind to do so. But he required a delay of fifteen days for this purpose. The ministers up to this moment had believed, on the faith of assurances given by the Tycoon's council in 1864 after the Shimonoséki business, that the Mikado had long ago been approached on this subject, and that Abé himself had been entrusted with a mission to Kiôto to that effect. They were therefore naturally both surprised and incensed, but consented to a delay of ten days. The prospects of the negotiation looked very dark indeed. The Tycoon seemed either unable or unwilling to obtain the Mikado's sanction to the treaties, and it began to be thought that we should have to throw him over entirely. If the Tycoon was controlled by a superior authority, he was clearly not the proper person for foreign Powers to deal with, who must insist upon direct communication with the authority. For the present, however, it was too early to talk of going to see the Mikado against his will. We had not sufficient men in the allied squadrons to force a way up to Kiôto, and even if we had, Sir Harry's instructions would not have enabled him to take such a step. So there was nothing for it but to wait.

An interesting visit was that of some retainers of Aidzu and Hosokawa, who came on board privately to talk politics and to pick up what information they could for their own princes. The former was the commander of the Tycoon's garrison in Kiôto, the latter one of the more important *daimiôs* in the island of Kiûshiû, nominally a partizan of the Tycoon, but already beginning to consider whether it would not suit him better to go over to the other party. For by this time a definite issue had been raised between the Tycoon and the court of the Mikado. The former being the friend of foreigners and an usurping vassal, the war cry of the latter was "serve the sovereign and expel the barbarians." My visitors talked a great deal about the "unsettled state of popular feeling." They said the Mikado had already given his sanction to the treaties in

a general sort of way, and had consented to Nagasaki, Hakodaté
and Shimoda being opened to foreign trade. But Kanagawa had
been substituted for the latter port without his approval. They felt
quite certain that the Mikado would not agree at present to the
establishment of foreign merchants at Hiôgo. They maintained
that the anti-foreign feeling was pretty general among the people,
but admitted that Chôshiû made use of it as a mere party cry with
the object of dispossessing the Tycoon of his power.

After an interval of five days Tachibana paid Sir Harry another
visit. He reported that the Tycoon had not yet started for Kiôto
to obtain the Mikado's ratification of the treaties, being detained
at Ozaka by a headache! Abé and Ogasawara were afflicted with
indisposition which prevented their having the pleasure of coming
down to call on the British minister. Sir Harry administered some
home-truths to the unfortunate prevaricator, and demonstrated
very clearly to him that as the council acknowledged the inability
of the Tycoon to carry out the treaty stipulations in respect of the
opening of new ports without the Mikado's consent, which they
had little hope of obtaining and still less desire to get, they must
eventually go to the wall, and the foreign Powers would be compelled to make a demand for the ratification direct on the Mikado.
It was pitiable to see the shifts that the Tycoon's officials were put
to in face of his merciless logic; they were perpetually being driven
into a corner and left without a leg to stand on.

The demands presented by the foreign representatives had created a considerable movement at Kiôto, and dissension followed
among the advisers of the Tycoon. In a few days we heard that
Abé and Matsumai Idzu no Kami had been dismissed from office.
They were believed to be in favour of accepting our demandes, and
their disgrace seemed to threaten the failure of the negotiations.
The representatives thereupon resolved on the important step of
addressing a *note identique* to the Tycoon himself, containing a
repetition of the demands already made and warning him that if
an answer were not made within the period of ten days originally
fixed, it would be assumed by them that their propositions were

refused. M. Mermet and I went ashore together to deliver the letters of our respective chiefs, and I learnt that the indefatigable little man had translated the French copy into Japanese and induced his minister to sign the translation. He had also addressed it to the council, instead of to the Tycoon, though he told me otherwise. On our arrival at the governor's house, he wrapped it in a sheet of Japanese paper, in order that I might not see the address, but the officials who received the Notes, of whom I afterwards inquired, voluntarily assured me that it was addressed to the council at Ozaka. What Mermet's object can have been I was not able to conjecture, and it is probable that he did it merely to keep his hand in. It is a dangerous thing for an habitual intriguer to get out of practice by acting straightforwardly, even in unimportant matters. We learnt that the Tycoon had presented a memorial to the Mikado urging him to ratify the treaties as well for his own sake as for that of the nation in general. That on its being refused, he had resolved to return to Yedo, but was stopped by an order from the court before he had got half-way to Ozaka.

The dismissal of the pro-foreign members of the council seemed to forebode resistance and the probable outbreak of hostilities. Japanese steamers lying at Ozaka got up steam and went off in every direction, some passing through Hiôgo on their way. Siebold and I pulled on board one of these which belonged to Satsuma, and learnt that she was going off to Yura in Kishiû in order to be out of the way in case the Mikado should issue such orders to the Tycoon as might result in war-like measures being taken by the allied squadron. On the 24th, the last day, notice was given to the governor of Hiôgo that the ships would move on the morrow to Ozaka to await there the answer of the Tycoon's government. From him we learnt that Ogasawara would surely be down next day with the reply, but as had already happened so often in the course of these negotiations, he was ill, and Matsudaira Hôki no Kami took his place. The interview with the foreign representatives lasted several hours, but the gist of it was that the Tycoon had at last obtained the Mikado's consent to the treaties, by his own urgent representations, backed by those of his cousin Shitotsubashi, who declared (so it was said) that he would perform disembowelment unless the Mikado yielded. At last the latter gave way, saying "Well, speak to the nobles of my court about it." The opening of Hiôgo was, however, to be still deferred until January 1, 1868, but the tariff would be revised, and the remaining instalments of the indemnity paid punctually. Thus the foreign representatives had obtained two out of the three conditions, and those the most important, while giving up nothing iu return. It must, however, be acknowledged that the payment of the indemnity was never completed by the Tycoon, and survived the revolution to be a constant source of irritation and ill-feeling between the Mikado's government and the British minister.

Hôki no Kami, on leaving the "Princess Royal," promised that a note embodying these arrangements should be sent off in the course of the evening. But as it had to be sent up to Ozaka to receive the signatures of his two remaining colleagues, the document did not reach us before half-past two in the morning. I sat up till that hour in expectation of its arrival, and was called into the cabin to read it to Sir Harry and M. Roches, and then make a translation. The Mikado's decree to his vizier the *Kwambaku* delegating the conduct of foreign affairs to the Tycoon, a short document of only three lines, was enclosed in it. At Sir Harry's request Hôki no Kami added an engagement to promulgate the decree throughout the country. It was a proud night for me when I displayed my knowledge of written Japanese in the presence of the French minister, whose interpreter, M. Mermet, even could not read a document without the assistance of his teacher.

Thus successfully ended the negotiations which up to the day before showed no signs of fruit. The foreign representatives had to congratulate themselves on having secured the means of tranquillizing the country, while at the same time consolidating the relations between the Japanese people and foreign nations. The opening of Hiôgo on the 1st January 1866 was a concession which few people had been sanguine enough to expect, but something had been secured which was of more immediate value, namely the solemn reiterated promise of the council to adhere to the London agreement of 1862. It was hoped also on good grounds that Sir Rutherford's convention of the previous October would also be carried out in its entirety. At dinner the following evening the Admiral made a speech, proposing Sir Harry's health and giving to him the whole credit of the success achieved. He replied by disclaiming any merit, and attributing a far greater share of the achievement to M. Roches; "but after all," he added, "it was you who did it, Admiral, for without you and your magnificent ship, we should not have made the slightest impression."

On our return to Yokohama we found that the wildest rumours had been flying about. The United States Chargé d'Affaires, Portman, was said to have been killed, and Sir Harry taken prisoner, while Siebold and myself were also reported to have fallen martyrs to the cause. The *Japan Times*, a newspaper conducted by Charles Rickerby, affected to pooh-pooh the whole affair, and denied the authenticity of the Mikado's decree, which, he said, ought to have been covered with seals. I wrote a letter to his paper, controverting his arguments, but without convincing him. There was one point about it, however, that escaped notice at the time, namely that the existing treaties were not explicitly sanctioned. All that the Mikado had given was a general authority to conclude treaties with foreign countries, and he had added a rider enjoining on the Tycoon the cancellation of the undertaking to open Hiôgo and Ozaka to trade. This, however, was carefully concealed from the foreign representatives, and we only came to know of it later. But without seeing it, no one could have guessed that the document represented to the foreign ministers to be the Mikado's sanction to the existing treaties had not that meaning, because of the absence of the definite article in Japanese. In English it makes a great deal of difference whether you say "the treaties are sanctioned," or simply "treaties are sanctioned," but in Japanese the same form of expression does for both, and we had no ground for suspecting the Tycoon's ministers of taking refuge in an ambiguity in order to play a trick on us and to gain time.

CHAPTER XIV

Great Fire at Yokohama

In pursuance of instructions from the chief, I proceeded to Yedo the day after my return to find out if possible what had been the popular feeling about our doings at Hiôgo, but did not succeed in discovering anything of importance. A general curiosity prevailed, and the result of the negotiations was yet unknown. A meeting of the *daimiôs'* agents had been held on the receipt of the news that two of the council had been dismissed, and it was rumoured that the Tycoon had asked to be allowed to retire, but that his petition had been rejected. I stopped at the monastery of Dai-chiû-ji, which had been temporarily lent to Sir Harry for a residence. It was in a convenient position, nearer to the centre of the city than our former location at Tô-zen-ji, but the rooms were dark and scarcely numerous enough for the accommodation of the staff in addition to the minister and his family. A new building had therefore been already commenced in front of Sen-gaku-ji, about half-way between the two, and, instead of being called the British Legation, was to be named the *setsugu-jo* or "place for meeting (sc. foreigners)," in order to avoid the risk of its being burnt down by the anti-foreign party. Report said that the Prince of Sendai, offended at not having been consulted on this matter, had retired to his castle in great dudgeon. Sen-gaku-ji is a well-known monastery containing the tombs and effigies of the celebrated "Forty-seven faithful retainers." After a couple of days' stay at the capital, I returned to my duties at the consulate in Yokohama, where I now held the post of interpreter.

I was beginning to become known among the Japanese as a foreigner who could speak their language correctly, and my circle of acquaintance rapidly extended. Men used to come down from Yedo on purpose to talk to me, moved as much by mere curiosity as by a desire to find out what foreign policy towards their country was likely to be. Owing to my name being a common Japanese surname, it was easily passed on from one to another, and I was talked about by people whom I had never met. The two-sworded men were always happy to get a glass of wine or liqueur and a foreign cigar, and they were fond of discussion. They would sit for hours if the subject interested them. Politics afforded the principal material of our debates, which sometimes became rather warm. I used to attack the abuses of the existing régime, and then explain that I liked them very much, but hated despotic institutions. Many of the men who visited me were retainers of *daimiôs*, from whom I gained every day a firmer conviction that the Tycoon ought not to be regarded by foreigners as the sovereign of the country, and that sooner or later we must enter into direct relations with the Mikado. And the state papers, of which copies came into my hands through these men, proved that the Tycoon regarded himself as nothing more than the Mikado's principal vassal. At the same time the Tycoon's ministers still persevered in their endeavour to keep the conduct of foreign affairs in their own hands, and had succeeded in persuading Mr Winchester this was an ancient and indefeasible prerogative of the Tokugawa family. Sir Harry Parkes, however, from the first, with clearer insight, held that this was untenable, and resolved to press matters to a definite solution, which should bring the sovereign face to face with foreign Powers.

Sir Harry had gone over to Shanghai to meet Lady Parkes and his children, and immediately after his return set to work at the revision of the tariff on the basis agreed to at Hiôgo. The negotiations, which began about January 1866, took much less time than is usual in these days, and the new convention was signed in June. I had little to do with it beyond assisting in its translation into Japanese. In February he began to make use of me as a translator, in addition to my work at the consulate.

My salary as interpreter at the Yokohama consulate, which I had joined in April 1865, was only £400 a year, and after the Hiôgo business, where I had demonstrated my knowledge of the Japanese language, I began to think my services worth quite as much as those of the Dutch interpreters, who received £500. At an interview with the Japanese ministers they used to translate into Dutch what the minister said, and the native Dutch interpreters translated this again into Japanese. The reply had in the same way to go through two men. But when Siebold or I interpreted, the work was performed much more quickly and accurately, because we translated direct into Japanese. It was the same with the official correspondence, for I was able, with the assistance of a native writer, and sometimes without, to put an official note directly into Japanese. Then I was able to read and translate into English all sorts of confidential political papers, which the Dutch interpreters could make nothing of. We took a bold resolution, and in August 1866, Sir Harry having given me a quantity of political documents to translate, we addressed letters to him asking that he would recommend us to the Foreign Office for an additional £100 a year. This brought down his wrath upon our heads, and I became convinced that my application would be refused. Under these circumstances I wrote to my father that the service was not worth remaining in. At that time the telegraph reached only to Ceylon, but in as short a time as possible I received a telegram from him telling me to come home at once, and that I should have an allowance sufficient to enable me to go to the university and afterwards to the bar. Armed with this, I approached Sir Harry again, and asked him to accept my resignation. I had received a telegram from home which necessitated my immediate return to England. After a little humming and hawing, he finally produced from a drawer a despatch from Lord Clarendon, which had been lying there for several days, granting the applications of both Siebold and myself, and I consequently abandoned my intention of quitting the service.

About March 6, 1866, a review and sham fight were held of the English garrison in combination with the Japanese drilled troops commanded by Kubota Sentarô on the dry rice fields between Jiû-ni-ten and Hommoku. The enemy was entirely imaginary, his place being taken by a crowd of spectators. The marching of the Japanese was very good, and received all the greater praise because they had received no practical instruction. Their officers had got it up from books, the difficult passages being explained to them by ours. The English soldiers looked magnificent by the side of the rather dwarfish Japanese. The bluejackets from the fleet were very amusing; one or two got drunk and danced a hornpipe in the face of the supposed enemy, to the great wrath and disgust of their commander, a young lieutenant. There was the usual amount of firing with blank cartridge, which, when it comes from one side only, renders every one so plucky and desirous of charging the foe. It was a wonder that no ramrods were fired away, nor was any one hit by a wad. The day was universally voted a great success.

The 2/xx regiment was despatched to Hongkong about March 20, and replaced by the 2/ix.

The danger to foreigners had so much abated since the execution of the murderers of Bird and Baldwin, and the ratification of the treaties by the Mikado that we began freely to make excursions into the surrounding country.

On one occasion I went away for a few days with Charles Rickerby of the *Japan Times*, and having thus become intimate with him, was permitted to try my inexperienced pen in the columns of his paper. My first attempt was au article upon travelling in Japan, but before long an incident occurred which tempted me to write on politics. It was doubtless very irregular, very wrong, and altogether contrary to the rules of the service, but I thought little of that. A Satsuma trading steamer had come into the bay, and was ordered by the authorities to anchor far away on the Kanagawa side, so that there might be no communication between the foreign community and the people on board. Taking this for my text, I descanted on the insufficiency of the treaties concluded with the Tycoon, which confined us to commercial intercourse with the inhabitants of his dominions, and thus cut us off from relations with a good half of the country. I called therefore for a revision of the treaties, and for a remodelling of the constitution of the Japanese government. My proposal was that the Tycoon should descend to his proper position as a great territorial noble, and that a confederation of *daimiôs* under the headship of the Mikado should take his place as the ruling power. And then I proceeded to make various suggestions for the improvement and modification of the existing treaties. With the aid of my teacher, Numata Torasaburô, a retainer of the Prince of Awa, who knew some English, I put them into Japanese in the form of a pamphlet for the perusal of his prince, but copies got into circulation, and in the following year I found myself to be favourably known through this means to all the *daimiô's* retainers whom I met in the course of my journeys. In the end the translation was printed and sold in all the bookshops at Ozaka and Kiôto under the title of "Ei-koku Saku-ron," English policy, by the Englishman Satow, and was assumed by both parties to represent the views of the British Legation. With this of course I had nothing to do. As far as I know it never came to the ears of my chief, but it may fairly be supposed to have been not without its influence upon the relations between the English Legation and the new government afterwards established in the beginning of 1868. At the same time, it doubtless rendered us more or less "suspect" to the Tycoon's government while the latter lasted.

During Sir Harry's absence in July on a visit to the *daimiôs* of Satsuma and Uwajima after the signature of the tariff convention, some of us at the legation made up a party with three or four officers of the ix regiment, and went for a trip to Hachiôji and Atsugi. In those days all the high roads were intersected at certain points by strictly guarded barriers, where all travellers had to show their passports. Beyond Hachiôji a few miles to the west was one of these, just at the foot of a hill known as Takao-zan, about 1,600 feet high, with a good road to the top. Up this we rode on our sure-footed ponies, and after lunching under the shade of the lofty cryptomerias, descended to the high road again, but unintentionally reached it beyond the barrier. The guards, who were inclined to interpret their duties rather too strictly than otherwise, shut the gates and refused to let us pass. It was in vain that we explained our mistake; they had orders not to let foreigners through. One would have thought that as we were on the side where we had no business to be, and were desirous of getting back to the right side, the officers in command would have facilitated our wishes to repair our error. But nothing would move them. At last Willis, who stood 6 feet 3 inches in his stockings and weighed then about 20 stone, made as if he would charge the gate on his pony, and seriously alarmed lest he should batter the whole thing down in a rush, they prudently flung it open, and we rode through triumphantly.

A similar incident occurred on another occasion when I was out with Francis Myburgh, Captain W. G. Jones, R.N., of the flagship, and Charles Wirgman. The limit of excursions from Yokohama in the direction of the capital was formed by the Tama-gawa, which in the treaties is called the Logo river (a corruption of Rokugô). We had slept at Mizoguchi, and ascended the right bank on horseback to Sekido, where without difficulty we induced the ferryman to put us across, and rode into the town of Fuchiû to visit a well-known Shintô temple. We were bound for a monastery on the other side of the river, where we had planned to spend the night, and to do this it was necessary to recross further up to the Buddhist monastery of Ren-kô-ji. But on arriving there, and shouting to the ferryman, we got a blank refusal, accompanied by the information that we had no business to be where we were. "We know that we are, and want to get back where we ought to be." *Ferryman*: "Can't help that. Our orders are not to ferry any foreigner over." It was impossible to convince him that though he would be right in refusing to facilitate a breach of the law, he was bound to assist the repentant and contrite offenders in repairing such a breach, and we saw ourselves menaced with separation from our baggage and perhaps a cold night on the stones. Just above the ferry was a shallower spot, too deep to cross on ponies without getting rather wet. Charles Wirgman and I therefore took off our trousers, and tucking our shirts up as high as possible waded to the other bank, walked down to the ferry house, jumped into the boat before the ferrymen had time to recover from their surprise at our audacity, poled it across to our friends amid cries of

Koré wa rambô-rôzeki (about equivalent to "Robbery and murder") from the guardians of the posts, and so got the whole party across.

On the 26th of November occurred one of the most destructive fires with which Yokohama has ever been visited. One fourth of the foreign settlement and one-third of the native town were laid in ashes. The fire-bell began to ring about nine o'clock in the morning. Willis and I ascended to the look-out on the roof of our house and saw the flames mounting to the sky exactly to windward of us, maybe half a mile away. I rushed into a pair of boots (unluckily my oldest), and putting on my hat, hastened forth to find out the location of the fire. My servants said it was only a few doors off, but when I got that distance it proved to be further away, and I pursued my course for a quarter of an hour before arriving on the scene. From the lower end of a narrow street, usually well crowded but now absolutely crammed with people, there surged along an agitated multitude carrying such of their goods as they had been able to snatch from the devouring element that closely pursued them. I approached as near as I could to the burning houses, but finding that the conflagration was rapidly advancing, beat a hasty retreat and made my way to the open space at the back of the settlement, where a terrible spectacle of confusion presented itself to my eyes. The portion of the native town where the fire was raging most violently was on a small island surrounded by a muddy swamp and connected with the rest of Yokohama by a wooden bridge, already crowded with fugitives; to wade or swim across to the firm ground was impossible. There were one or two boats available, but they were already overcrowded, and their occupants were so paralysed by fear that they never thought of landing and sending back the boats to take off others. Most of the inhabitants of the quarter were women. I saw a few poor wretches plunge into the water in order to escape, but they failed to reach the nearer bank. It was a fearful sight to see the flames darting among the roofs of the houses on the causeway, and sending forth jets here and there where the fire had not yet attained full mastery, when suddenly one half of the street nearest blazed up with a tremendous flash, and a volume of black smoke arose which obscured the sky. This was an oil merchant's shop that had caught fire. I turned and fled homewards, for there was no time to lose. I knew my own house was doomed, as it lay directly to leeward, and a violent wind was blowing from the north-west. As I passed through the little garden I shouted to Willis to bestir himself, and called my servants to assist in packing up my movables. My first thought was for my MS. dictionary; if that went I lost the results of two years' labour. So I put it into a light chest of drawers, and huddled some clothes in from the wardrobe. To get our things out we had to break down the high wooden fence round the garden. At this moment up came some friends, who plunged into the house and reappeared, some with books, others with half a chest of drawers, and we worked with a will until the building was cleared of everything but carpets, curtains, and the heavier furniture. My harmonium, a massive article, was also got into the street, and some men from the garrison carried it away to a place of safety.

By the time we had removed the salvage to what we thought was a respectable distance, the fire had reached the house, which five minutes later was a heap of glowing embers. It now became evident that the houses in the rear of the settlement had caught fire, and as my property was lying on the open space between the foreign and native towns, it had to be transported further. Here occurred a serious loss. Most of my books were in boxes which had been carried out bodily, but the rest, hastily wrapped up in blankets, had to be left. There were plenty of pilferers about, who, under the pretence of helping, carried off chests full of clothing that I never saw again. I lost a good many European volumes and a large number of Japanese books, besides some notes on Manchu and Chinese which were irreplaceable.

After we had deposited our property where we thought it would be in safety, it was threatened by the progress of the flames, and was therefore removed to a godown belonging to our friends Wilkin and Robison at No. 3 in the settlement. By this time the area of destruction had extended to the main street of the native town, and the houses where A. B. Mitford, A. von Siebold, Walsh and

Vidal lived, as well as our own, had already gone. A Japanese house lightly built of wood, with paper instead of glass, takes little time to burn. Next the fire spread to the nearest houses in the foreign settlement. Huge sparks and pieces of red hot wood flew across the intervening space, set the American consulate alight, ignited the roof of Jardine, Matheson & Co., and began to spread along both streets of the settlement. The supposed "fireproof" godown where most of our things were deposited caught fire, and nearly everything we had saved was destroyed. It was a scene of the wildest confusion. Bluejackets were landed from the ships, and soldiers came down from the camp to work at the fire engines. There was no discipline among the men, and no organization existed for dealing with the disaster. After the final destruction of my own property I went about helping others to save theirs or to fight the flames, handing buckets, fetching water, pouring it on whatever seemed most inflammable. Some of the redcoats behaved disgracefully. They had managed to get hold of liquor, and stood by drinking and jeering, while we civilians did the work they had been brought there to perform. At the close of the day there remained to me only the clothes I had on my back, and I was hatless. But the excitement had been so lively that I felt rather pleased at the idea of beginning the world afresh. I had saved the manuscript of the English-Japanese dictionary on which Ishibashi and I were then engaged, as well as that of an annotated edition of Sir R. Alcock's *Colloquial Japanese*, which was then in the press, though destined never to see the light. My loss came to between £300 and £400, a portion of which was afterwards made good to me by Her Majesty's Government. The losses of the insurance offices amounted to $2,800,000, or about £700,000. The value of what was not insured was not great.

The conflagration raged so fiercely among the foreign warehouses and residences that before four o'clock in the afternoon it had made its way half down the bund, leaving only the club-house standing, and at one period it was thought that the whole settlement would be in a blaze before night. If that had happened the European community would have had to seek an asylum on board ship, but fortunately our fears were not realized. The flames seemed invincible by the side of our puny efforts.

The expedient was resorted to of blowing up houses in the line of fire, but not with great success, for some of those so destroyed were never touched by it at all, while in other instances the *débris* could not be cleared away, and only helped it to spread to the buildings beyond. One hundred and seven Europeans and Americans were rendered homeless, and many of those who had trusted in their so-called fireproof godowns were left without anything in the world but the clothes they stood in. Merchants whose goods were uninsured were devoured by a terrible anxiety, for the most solidly-constructed stone godowns seemed to offer little more resistance than the wooden houses of the Japanese.

Although the wind had fallen, much apprehension was entertained for the safety of what still remained unburnt, for owing to the damaged condition of the hose, all the fire engines had become useless, and nothing could be done to extinguish the smouldering embers. The fire was therefore left to burn itself out, and four days elapsed before the flames entirely died down. The price of clothing rose incredibly, as also did house rent. Yokohama was not as well supplied with hatters, tailors and bootmakers as it is in these days, and most men were in the habit of supplying themselves from home. For the next two years, consequently, I was reduced to a very moderate wardrobe. I had, for example, to pay $4, or 18 shillings, for five pocket handkerchiefs.

After the fire I took up my abode with my friend Tom Foster, then the manager of Gilman & Co.'s Yokohama branch, until the 9th or 10th of December, when I migrated to the Legation at Yedo. The new buildings in front of Sen-gaku-ji were now completed, and enclosed by a lofty black wooden fence which imparted to the establishment somewhat of the aspect of a jail. There were two long wooden buildings, one of which was the minister's residence, the other being occupied by the members of the chancery. Eusden had gone to Hakodaté as acting consul, and the staff consisted of Mitford as second secretary, Willis as assistant accountant and medical officer, Siebold and myself as interpreters, and Vidal as student interpreter. The infantry guard was commanded by Lieutenant Bradshaw. Sidney Locock, the first secretary, a married man with a family, lived at Yokohama, as did also H. S. Wilkinson, still a student. They were "ramshackle" buildings, all windows and doors, terribly cold from want of proper fireplaces and bad construction, which admitted draughts on every side. But I did not live there long.

After my transfer from the Yokohama consulate to the Legation in the autumn of 1866, one of the first matters in which I was able to be of use to our new chief was connected with the wording of the treaty. In the English text the Tycoon was spoken of as "His Majesty," and thus placed on a level with the Queen. In the Japanese version, however, this epithet was rendered by the equivalent of "Highness," and it was thus to be inferred that our sovereign was of lower rank than the Mikado. Moreover, the word "queen" had been translated by a title which was borne by great-grand-daughters of a Mikado. I recommended that a new Japanese version should be made, in which "Majesty" should be rendered by its proper Japanese equivalent, and "Queen" by the word *Kôtei* (Hwang-ti), usually translated by "Emperor" in all the Chinese-English dictionaries, but really meaning "supreme sovereign," and applicable to both sexes. The preparation of the new version was entrusted to my hands, and with the aid of my teacher I managed in about a month's time to complete an accurate translation, which was adopted as official. It was the keynote of a new policy which recognized the Mikado as the sovereign of Japan and the Tycoon as his lieutenant. We gave up the use of "Tycoon," which my reading had taught me was properly a synonym for the Mikado, in our communications with the Japanese government, though retaining it in correspondence with the Foreign Office, in order not to create confusion, but the most important result was to set in a clearer light than before the political theory that the Mikado was the treaty-making power. As long as his consent had not been obtained to the existing treaties we had no *locus standi*, while after he had been induced to ratify them, the opposition of the *daimiôs* ceased to have any logical basis.

DAIMIŌ OF CHŌSIŪ AND HIS HEIR

Mōri Daizen and Mōri Nagato

CHŌSIŪ COUNCILLORS

Katsura Kogerō and Kikkawa Remmotsu

CHAPTER XV

Visit to Kagoshima and Uwajima

A few days after I had assumed my new duties, and had settled down, as I thought, for a period of uninterrupted study, Sir Harry informed me that he contemplated sending me down to Nagasaki in the "Princess Royal," which was about to proceed thither through the inland sea, to collect political information at Hiôgo and elsewhere. I was to return in the "Argus" by way of Kagoshima and Uwajima. The Tycoon had recently died, and had been succeeded by his cousin Shitotsubashi, whose position, however, was not very clearly defined. Before his elevation to the headship of the Tokugawa family he had been regarded as a partisan of the "return to the ancient régime," now so much in men's mouths, and it was desirable to learn as much as possible of his probable line of policy. In Yedo we were too far away from the political centre to learn much. I was greatly pleased at the prospect of visiting Nagasaki, but took care not to seem too desirous of being sent on the proposed mission, lest over-eagerness should defeat itself. Next day I got a note from Sir Harry, who resided chiefly at Yokohama, telling me that he had not yet seen the Admiral, but that he still thought I should have to go. So I packed up some clothes in a wicker basket such as the Japanese use when travelling, and went down to Yokohama in the gunboat which was our principal means of conveyance between the two places. In the evening I learnt that the matter had been arranged, and that the "Princess Royal" would sail the next day but one.

I wrote to Willis for his teacher Hayashi, whom I intended to put ashore at Hiôgo to collect news, and for a tin box containing some stationery, and a little money, but neither arrived in time. In despair I borrowed a few hundred *ichibus* from Foster, bought a box of cheroots, wrapped a few sheets of foolscap in a newspaper, and got on board on the 12th December just in time.

We had fine weather for our start, but encountered a strong westerly wind outside, which prevented our passing between Vries Island and the mainland. For four days I lay in my cot, utterly unable to eat, but consoling myself with reference to previous experiences of the same kind. At last I was revived by a plateful of greasy beefsteak pudding that Admiral King sent me, and a glass of champagne. The gale had not abated, and the huge two decker rolled terribly. At one time the betting was strong on Hongkong as our first port of anchorage, and Hiôgo was given up as quite unattainable. Hakodaté, Yokohama and Nagasaki rose by turns to the position of favourite. We were blown right out of the chart of Japan, and at last, after many days of tossing to and fro, tacking and wearing, we sighted the Linschoten Islands, where we turned to the north, and steaming as fast as 400 horse power will carry a vessel of 3500 tons, got into Nagasaki on the evening of the 23rd.

The appearance of the town and foreign settlement, lighted up by innumerable lamps dotted all over the hillsides, reminded me of Gibraltar as I had seen it from the deck of the "Indus" a little more than five years previously.

At Nagasaki I made the acquaintance of some retainers of Uwajima, the most important of whom was Iséki Sayémon, afterwards prefect of Yokohama in the first years of the Mikado's rule. He came to call on me, and said that the proposed assemblage of a council of *daimiôs* at Kiôto had been put off for the present. But it was sure to take place eventually, and one of the first topics of discussion would be the position of Chôshiû. About half of Shikoku was in favour of Hiôgo being opened to foreign trade, but the Kiûshiû people opposed it, on account of the anticipated decline of Nagasaki. He thought that the visit of the Admiral and Sir Harry

Parkes in the "Princess Royal" to Uwajima had done immense good, by familiarizing the common people with the appearance of foreigners, and their ingenuity in the construction of ships and warlike appliances. The *daimiô* of Uwajima and his brother the ex-*daimiô* (who was the leading spirit of the clan) had excused themselves on the ground of sickness from attending the council at Kiôto. Shitotsubashi had not yet been invested with the office of Shôgun and its attendant court titles, and the probability was that they would be withheld until he had settled the Chôshiû difficulty, which would doubtless give him a good deal of trouble. When I met him again on the following day the conversation turned upon our relations with Chôshiû. I told him that the British Government had stationed a man-of-war at Shimonoséki to prevent merchant vessels frequenting the straits during the continuance of hostilities between Chôshiû and the Tycoon; we did not wish to interfere in any of the civil quarrels of the Japanese. We were at peace with Chôshiû, who had agreed to let foreign vessels pass without molestation, and had undertaken to let them purchase wood, water, and other necessaries, while promising to build no more batteries.

The Tycoon's government had undertaken to pay the indemnity imposed upon the Prince of Chôshiû. The powers, however, did not care for the money, and would be willing at any time to abandon the indemnity if their doing so would tend to the improvement of relations with Japan. The Tycoon's people had asked for delay in making payment of the remaining instalments, and in consenting to this, the foreign ministers had obtained in return the concession of permission for Japanese to travel in foreign countries. It was to be supposed, however, that the nation was desirous of having the ancient prohibition removed, and the government would have had, therefore, no excuse for maintaining it. Hiôgo would certainly be opened on the 1st of January 1868 in accordance with the undertaking entered into by the Tycoon; the intention of the Powers was to uphold the treaties in their entirety and get them carried out. We could not ask for the opening of Shimonoséki under the present treaties, as the Tycoon's authority did not extend so far. It would require a separate treaty with Chôshiû. As long as the present treaties remained unchanged, no ports could be opened in *daimiôs'* territories.

At Hiôgo we had discussed matters with the Tycoon's Council, who, we now learnt, had deceived us by concealing the Mikado's injunction to them to negotiate for the abandonment of Ozaka and Hiôgo as seats of foreign commerce. It was a pity we had not thrown them over, and negotiated direct with the Mikado's court, from which we heard that a noble had been deputed to visit the foreign representatives.

During my stay at Nagasaki I made the acquaintance of officers from Tosa and Higo. One of the latter said that there never would be another Shôgun, but that the Mikado would be restored to the throne. Here was a clear glimpse into the future. My instructions from Sir Harry were to proceed from Nagasaki to Kagoshima and Uwajima, and call in at Hiôgo on my way back. I embarked, therefore, on the 1st January 1867 in the "Argus," Commander Round, with my two servants, Noguchi Tomizô and Yasu. The former was a young *samurai* of Aidzu, who had left his home and attached himself to Vyse, our consul at Hakodaté, in order to study English. In the autumn of 1865 he came to live with me, to carry on his studies, and on the present occasion he had accompanied me to Nagasaki, whence he was to have gone to England as cabin-servant to Alexander Buller, the Commander of the flagship. But whether it was the tossing about on the way down, or the disagreeable servant's position, he now changed his mind, and begged me to take him back to Yedo. Buller expressed himself as somewhat annoyed, but I could not help it. Noguchi eventually went with me in 1869 to England, where I paid for his schooling during a couple of years. After my return to Japan he stayed on awhile in London at the expense of the Japanese government, and eventually came back to Tôkiô, where he obtained a minor appointment in a public office. In spite of his then comparatively elevated position, he never gave himself airs, or forgot that I had befriended him, and it was with great regret that I heard of his death about the beginning of 1885. He was honest and faithful to the end. Yasu was a young monkey belonging to the lower classes, and I don't remember that he had any virtues.

Round did not treat me very well, and made me sleep in the cockpit, a sort of common den in the bottom of the ship, where the midshipmen keep their chests and sling their hammocks. There was no privacy, and we were crowded together in a most uncomfortable manner. I got a cot to sleep in, but no mattress or pillow, and was forced to borrow a cushion off a bunk in the captain's cabin and roll up my greatcoat for a pillow.

We reached Kagoshima next day early in the afternoon. As soon as we dropped our anchor, some officers pulled off from the shore, bringing a flag for us to hoist while firing the salute in answer to theirs. Matsuoka Jiûdaiyu came on board to explain that the prince and his father were in retirement owing to the recent death of the latter's mother. As neither was able to receive visitors, the duty of receiving the Admiral's letter, of which we were the bearers, would be performed by the prince's second brother and two councillors. This was a letter thanking him for kindness shown to shipwrecked sailors. Sir Harry and the Admiral on their visit in the previous summer had seen and conversed with both the prince and his father Shimadzu Saburô, but I do not suppose that my being unable to meet them made much difference to the result of my visit, as the conduct of affairs was to a great extent in the hands of the principal retainers. I went ashore to stay at the factory with three Englishmen named Sutcliffe, Harrison and Shillingford. The last of these, an engineer by profession, had been engaged by the *daimiô* in connection with some cotton mills which he was erecting, the other two had come to Kagoshima in search of employment.

On the 3rd, Round came on shore with a party of officers to deliver the Admiral's letter, and I accompanied him to interpret. We were met at the landing-place by some high officials, who conducted us through the town for half a mile to the house, where we were received by Shimadzu Dzusho, a handsome youth, the second son of Shimadzu Saburô, Niiro Giôbu, a councillor who had been in England, and Shimadzu Isé, also a councillor. It was a house set apart for the reception of visitors. The prince's brother, 29 years of age, seemed a perfect child as far as intelligence went. All the talking was done by the high officials who sat on his right hand. I interpreted the contents of the letter, which was then handed to Shimadzu Dzusho, the whole ceremony not occupying more than five minutes. We then sat down to an entertainment, which opened with a few courses of Japanese cookery with *saké*, but consisted in the main of an interminable succession of European dishes, moistened with sherry, champagne and brandy. I took my revenge upon Round by keeping up a lively conversation in Japanese, and translating none of it, so the poor man was driven to count the oranges in a dish which stood near, in order to keep off *ennui*. After the banquet, the officers dispersed themselves through the town, while I remained behind to assist in making a translation of the Admiral's letter. Niiro also stopped. We talked about the proposed meeting of *daimiôs*, which had been postponed *sine die*. Then I praised the composition of a letter which had been addressed to the Mikado in the name of the Prince of Satsuma some months back.

"Did you see it? What a stupid document it was," said Niiro.

"Not at all," I replied. "I thought it excellent, and the style was worthy of all praise."

"Had it not reference to Hiôgo?"

"No. I mean the memorial objecting to sending Satsuma troops to co-operate with those of the Tycoon against Chôshiû."

"Oh, yes. Shimadzu Ise, who sat next to me to-day, was the writer of that letter. He was in Kiôto at the time."

"How is the Chôshiû business getting on," I asked. "I hear the Tycoon has withdrawn the greater part of his troops."

"Chôshiû is very strong," he replied, "and he has right on his side. None of the *daimiôs* will support the Tycoon, and the latter has now no chance of beating him."

"Well, I think that if he had put his best troops into the field, and attacked Chôshiû energetically at first, he must have conquered him."

"No, never. He had not right on his side."

"You appear to be very friendly with Chôshiû," I remarked.

"No," said he, "not friendly, but we have a natural fellow-feeling for one of our own class."

Niiro's reference to the letter of the Prince of Satsuma, which he supposed I had seen, revealed the important fact that the Satsuma clan were opposed to the opening of Hiôgo, and in fact it was the presentation of this letter or memorial to the Mikado during the visit of the foreign representatives in November 1865 which had encouraged the Mikado to make it a condition of giving his sanction to the treaties that the Tycoon should arrange for that port being given up. It was necessary, therefore, to impress on Niiro's mind, for the benefit of his fellow clansmen, that the foreign Powers would not for a moment entertain the idea of giving up Hiôgo or any other part of the treaties.

At this moment there was lying in the bay a little steamer named the "Otentosama," belonging to Chôshiû. She had brought down the leading man of that clan, Katsura Kogorô, afterwards known during the year of the revolution as Kido Junichirô. I said to Niiro that I should like to call on him to inquire after some of my Shimonoséki friends. Niiro replied that Katsura was to have an interview with Shimadzu Saburô at ten o'clock the same evening, and a meeting afterwards with some of the Satsuma councillors at three in the morning. If I wished particularly to see him, I might go and sleep at his lodgings, and wait till he turned up. I declined the invitation, preferring a European bed, for at that time I was not so accustomed to Japanese ways as I afterwards became. It was weak on my part. But what Niiro said rendered it perfectly clear that an understanding was being negotiated between the two most powerful of the western clans, and that they would henceforth be united against the Tycoon. Fortunate for us that they were on friendly terms with us, and fortunate also for the general interest of foreign Powers, between whom and the revolutionary government of 1868 the British Legation acted as mediators. The French Legation on the other hand supported the Tycoon. M. Roches was projecting the foundation of the arsenal at Yokosuka, which would place the military organization of the Tokugawa family on a new and superior footing, and he had procured a distinguished staff of French officers to drill the Tycoon's troops. It was even rumoured that he had made, or was contemplating making, offers of material assistance to Shitotsubashi. And this policy he pursued until the logic of facts at last demonstrated its folly, being followed by the North German Chargé d'Affaires, Herr von Brandt, and the Italian Minister, Count La Tour. The Netherlands Political Agent, however, adhered to Sir Harry, while the new American Minister, General van Valkenburg, was neutral.

We had felt the pulse of the Japanese people more carefully and diagnosed the political condition better than our rivals, so that the prestige of the British Minister in the years 1868 and 1869 was completely in the ascendant.

On the 4th January the prince's reply was to have been delivered on board the "Argus," but at noon Niiro presented himself to say that it was not yet ready. We therefore landed and inspected the glass factory, shot and shell foundry, gun foundry and pot and kettle foundry near the prince's garden at Iso. The letter now arrived in charge of Matsuoka, and after its formal delivery, we sat down once more to a banquet in European style. It was shorter than that of the previous day, and the dishes better cooked, but it was politeness rather than gastronomic satisfaction that caused us to praise it. For in truth the dinner was bad and ill-arranged.

About five o'clock I started off with Sutcliffe to call on Niiro, who had not been seen since the morning. After an hour's walking, we arrived at his house, darkness having already set in. Niiro received us very cordially, and entertained us with tea, oranges, beer, cakes and conversation for an hour and a half. He told me that in passing through Hiôgo lately he had heard that the French Minister was shortly expected there with a letter from the Emperor Napoleon III, and that there was to be a general gathering of foreign representatives. Shitotsubashi had disappointed his friends by accepting the succession to the headship of the Tokugawa family, and was suspected of wishing to establish his power as Tycoon with the aid of foreigners.

He gave me to understand that they regarded the French with dislike and distrust, and seemed to be all the more friendly with us because they had learnt to appreciate the value of our enmity. The Satsuma people seemed to be making great progress in the civilized arts, and gave me the impression of great courage and straightforwardness. I thought they would soon be far ahead of the rest of Japan.

Tycoon, as I have said before, was the title given in the treaties to the temporal sovereign. The Japanese, however, never used it. *Sei-i-tai Shôgun*, or "Generalissimo for the subjugation of barbarians," was his official designation, which delicacy prevented his ministers from employing in their official communications with the foreign representatives, while the common people spoke of him as *Kubô sama*. The "opposition" *daimiôs*, however, had adopted the term *Baku-fu*, which most closely might be rendered by "military establishment," and it was this term that my friends and I used in conversation. In like manner, for the honorific designation *Gorôjiû* (noble old men) applied in the east of Japan to the Tycoon's council of ministers, the expression *Kaku-rô* (old ones) was substituted. The opposition refused to recognize that the government which they wished to upset was entitled to any mark of respect.

On the 5th January we left Kagoshima and anchored in Uwajima Bay at eleven o'clock on the following day.

The beautiful bay is completely landlocked, and surrounded by hills of varying height up to 2,000 feet. Close behind the town, on its east side, rises a high peak known as Oni-ga-jô, the "demon's castle." The prince's fortress was a conspicuous object to the right of the town; it stood on a low, wooded hill, close to the seashore, and consisted of a three-storied keep, surrounded by a double wall of stonework surmounted by white plastered walls, almost hidden by the trees. South of this lay the official quarter, the citizens' quarter being to the east and north, stretching for some distance along the shore, as the hills behind leave the town no room to expand. Close in shore the water is very shallow, and advantage had been taken of this to construct salterns and reclaim rice fields by building a dyke. There was a small battery on each side of the bay, more for show than for defensive use.

About an hour and a half after we anchored, a boat was noticed hovering about the stern, with a person in the stern-sheets busily engaged in examining the ship through an opera glass. Finding out that it was the prince, Commander Round sent a gig at once to invite him on board. He explained his curious behaviour by saying that he had wished to remain *incognito*. The Admiral's letter wishing him a happy new year was produced, and after I had translated its contents, he took possession of it. He was aged 32, of about middle height, and had an aristocratic cast of countenance, with a slightly aquiline nose, on the whole a handsome man. As a matter of course he was shown over the ship. In the meantime I had some conversation with a gentleman-like young man of about twenty years of age named Matsuné Kura, son of the principal *karô*. He said that Satsuma and Uwajima were on very friendly terms, which was natural, as the ex-*daimiô* and Shimadzu Saburô had been amongst the little band of princes who were disgraced for their opposition to the elevation of the lately deceased Tycoon. Shitotsubashi had not been appointed Shôgun, and perhaps never would be.

When the prince returned on shore I accompanied him in the gig, and found a number of his women waiting for him on the bank with his children, the eldest of whom was a little boy of seven years of age. The others were mostly babies in arms, and each was attended by an undernurse bearing a small sword wrapped in gold brocade. The Japanese *samurai* was accustomed to the companionship of his weapon from his very infancy. The prince was extremely affable, and promised to repeat his visit on the following day, and to bring the *in-kio* or ex-*daimiô* with him. I said good-bye, and went into the town, where I met three officers from the ship engaged in "curio" hunting. An immense crowd followed us everywhere, examining our clothes and asking all manner of questions, but behaving with the utmost civility. I felt my heart warm more and more to the Japanese.

On the 7th January it rained violently and blew hard all day, but the weather did not prevent the *daimiô* and the *in-kio* from coming on board. The latter was a tall man with strongly marked features and a big nose, and reputed to be one of the most intelligent of his class, imperious in manner, and 49 years of age. He was not a born Daté (that was the surname of the Uwajima *daimiôs*), but had been adopted from a *hatamoto* family in Yedo. After his adoption the present *daimiô* was born, and the relationship between them was that of brothers by adoption. But still the adopted son could not be set aside, and he eventually succeeded to the title and fief, but by way of compensation to the younger brother who had lost his birthright, he adopted him as his son. Consequently, when the prince was disgraced in 1858 the real heir succeeded. *In-kio* (living retired) is a common term for the head of a family, whether noble or commoner, who has given up the active headship and the management of the estate to his son, a not unusual thing in "Old Japan" for a father who had reached the sixties. Here the *in-kio* was manifestly the ruling spirit, and it was touching to observe the immense respect paid to him by the titular prince, who always addressed him as father, while he on his part used the depreciatory term *sengaré* (my youngster) in speaking of the *daimiô*. They stopped for a couple of hours talking and drinking some Moselle with which I had provided myself at Nagasaki.

The *in-kio* began to talk eagerly to me about the very suspicious intimacy that existed between the Tycoon's government (*baku-fu*) and the French Legation, but as soon as old Matsuné, the principal councillor, perceived that his master was becoming indiscreet, he hurried him away on the pretext that it would be too late to fire the salute. So away they went, amid the thunder of seventeen guns, which was returned from one of the batteries. After he left the wives and families of the two princes flocked on board. They were not in the least afraid of us, and conversed with as much ease and readiness as European ladies. There was a Japanese officer on board, afterwards Admiral Hayashi Kenzô.

Noguchi, who had been ashore to have a hot bath and get shaved, had brought me an invitation to dine with Iriyé, the captain of the battery. So I took a boat and went off in spite of the wind and rain. My host had not yet returned from his duties, but his wife asked me to come in, and in about a quarter of an hour he made his appearance. Soon afterwards another artillery officer named Mori came in, and then two more juniors. Dinner was at once ordered. It consisted of innumerable courses of fish and soup, and lasted from six o'clock till eleven. We talked, drank hot *saké*, and sang by turns, and I had to answer a multitude of questions on all possible subjects. This gave me numerous opportunities of uttering appropriate wise saws and proverbial sayings, which gave my hearers unbounded delight, and inspired them with no small amount of respect for the philosophy of the western peoples. At half-past eleven the last guest retired, and after we had eaten a little rice, we went to bed in Japanese fashion. I was surprised to find that one could sleep comfortably without sheets.

On the following morning, after a good breakfast *à la Japonaise*, I rejoined the ship, and started in company with Round, and Wright and Dunn of the ixth regiment, who as I have hitherto neglected to mention, had come on board at Nagasaki, for the rifle range, in accordance with an engagement made on the previous day. A guard of honour of 25 men received us at the landing-place, and we were escorted by an officer of the Uwajima navy. Half-way we found another guard, which fell in and led us up a pretty stiff hill to the ranges. Some of our small-arms men were landed to exhibit their skill. We had to walk a short distance and climb the hills. There is not sufficient flat ground in Uwajima for a proper rifle range, so the butts were placed on the side of another hill separated from us by a valley about 700 yards wide. Here we found tents set us, and the *in-kio*, his own son, and the prince awaiting our arrival. Our men, who were not accustomed to shooting across a chasm of unknown depth and width, showed themselves less skilful than the Uwajima marksmen, who had the advantage of knowing their ground.

We got the shooting over by half-past one, and the whole party then proceeded to the *goten* or palace, which was outside the castle. It was an old building, dating from about 500 years back, but without pretensions to architectural style. We were not received at the great entrance, but at some temporary steps erected for the occasion which led up at once from the garden into the verandah. Here old Matsuné met us and conducted us into a long room, which was shut off on all sides by handsome folding screens covered with gold leaf. At one end of the room was a particularly large screen, which the prince said was a present to his ancestor from the great Taikô-sama. A table was placed down the middle of the room, with armchairs on the right side for the *in-kio*, the prince, and Matsuné, while on the left were seated Round and his officers. I sat at the head of the table to facilitate conversation.

The dinner was beautifully got up, every separate dish prettily arranged and decorated, but the most tasteful of all was a wild duck with all its plumage perfect, and the roasted meat cut up small and laid on the back between the wings, elevated in such a way as to convey the idea that the bird was swimming and flying at the same time. Other dishes consisted of huge crayfish, and there was a large baked *tai*, as required by etiquette, for each person. Each of us had a large porcelain cup to drink from, and the warm liquor was handed round in pewter vessels with long spouts, like flat teapots. The ex-prince exchanged cups with Round, myself, and the two redcoats in turn, and the same ceremony was afterwards gone through with the prince and his minister, old Matsuné.

There was a good deal of eating and *saké* drinking, and the *in-kio* presented me with a large shallow cup of red lacquer which I had first to empty. My companions left early, while at the *in-kio's* request I remained behind for some conversation on politics. He began by speaking of Hiôgo, as to which he had expressed his

opinion to Sir Harry Parkes in July last. But he was now in favour
of opening the place to foreign trade, and so was Shitotsubashi.
He had heard that negotiations were proceeding with the French
for its being opened next September, but he would prefer that the
arrangements should be made with us rather than with the French,
whom he did not like. I replied that I believed the French policy
was based upon the belief that the country needed a recognized
head, and that as they had a treaty with the Shôgun, who apparently was the most powerful political personage, they thought it
would be better to strengthen him as far as possible. The English
policy was different. We regarded our treaty as having been made
with Japan, and not with the Shôgun in particular. If with the latter, then as there was no actual Shôgun at the moment, our treaty
would have to be regarded as being in abeyance. We did not wish
to interfere, and were quite content that the Japanese should settle
their internal disputes among themselves.

"But," said *In-kio*, "if civil war becomes chronic, your trade will
suffer, and you will have to put an end to it for your own sakes."

"No," I replied, "for if we interfered and took a side, matters
would become ten times more difficult, and the foreign trade
would come altogether to an end."

The *in-kio* then remarked that his idea was for Japan to become
a confederated empire, with the Mikado for its head, and that this
idea was favoured by Satsuma and Chôshiû. I said I thought there
was no other way out of the difficulty, and I had written an article
in a Yokohama newspaper to that effect. "Oh," said the *in-kio*, "I
have read it," meaning the translation which has been already
mentioned. At last the ex-prince said, "Let us send for the women
and have some music. The captain will be jealous if he hears that
I produced them to you after he had left, so don't tell him, but if
he hears of it, you may say I was drunk."

Here the conversation was interrupted by the entrance of the
ladies of the harem, such a bevy of pretty women, some wives
and some not. All the children came in too. I had to drink *saké*
with all of the ladies, till I began to fear my head might give way.

Musical instruments were brought in, and a great deal of *saké* was drunk, greatly to the increase of friendliness and conviviality, but not to the advantage of the interchange of political views. In fact the *in-kio* gave himself up to enjoyment and would talk no more. He afterwards said in a casual sort of way: "You must not let it appear in the newspapers that I went on board the "Argus," for I have declined attending the meeting at Kiôto on the ground of sickness, and I should not wish the government to hear of it. I should not like to be at Kiôto just now." After the music had begun, I looked round and saw one of the officers of the "Argus," who had come in after the captain's departure, performing a Japanese dance. I proposed to him to dance a hornpipe, which he at once did, and the ex-prince, a man of the sober age of 49, got up, placed himself opposite, and tried to imitate the steps, holding up his loose trousers with both hands. The fun infected two of the ministers, who joined him in a three-handed reel.

After drinking a great deal of *saké* with the two princes and their ladies, I was carried off — no, led — to his own house by old Matsuné, where more *saké* was produced, and I was made acquainted with the rest of his family. After about an hour's conversation, I was glad to get to bed, for the fumes of the hot *saké* were beginning to have some effect on my head. Hayashi, young Matsuné, another Japanese and myself, slept in one room. Next morning I was roused before daylight by the report of a signal gun fired from the "Argus" to announce that she was ready to leave. I dressed hastily and went on board with young Matsuné, to whom I presented my opera glass as a souvenir. Noguchi and my boy Yasu, who had also been sleeping on shore, had not yet made their appearance, but Round refused to wait for them. So I begged Matsuné to send them somehow to Yokohama, and advance them any money which they might ask for, to be repaid to the Uwajima agent in Yedo. At half-past six we weighed anchor, and steamed out of the bay, full of regrets at being obliged to part from our kind, hospitable friends.

We reached Hiôgo about noon on the 11th of January, after visiting one or two unimportant places in the inland sea. I went on shore to inquire whether we could get coals, beef and vegetables. After arranging with the local officials to send some supplies on board, I walked about the town, and found the people quite accustomed to the sight of a foreigner. I met some two-sworded men, who protested that they were determined to prevent the opening of Hiôgo to foreign trade, but they were evidently joking. A Hizen man whom I came across declared that I was an old acquaintance, though I had never set eyes on him before. Afterwards Hayashi Kenzô and I went on board a Satsuma steamer that was lying in port, and made the acquaintance of her captain, Inouyé Shinzayemon. She had brought up from Kagoshima one of the leading Satsuma men named Komatsu Tatéwaki; he had gone up to Ozaka to meet Saigô, the greatest of all the Satsuma leaders. I immediately proposed to go up to Ozaka and see them, and letters were written by Inouyé and Hayashi to Godai Saisuké (our captive of 1863 at Kagoshima) to make the necessary arrangements. Next day, however, I heard that Saigô was himself probably coming to Hiôgo, and in the meantime Hayashi took me ashore to have a hot bath and some luncheon *à la Japonaise*.

Here for the first time I learnt how to put on a cotton gown (*yukata*) after the bath, and enjoy the sensation of gradually cooling down. We had just sat down to eat when it was announced that Saigô had arrived, and hastily swallowing our rice, we sallied forth to the other house-of-call of the Satsuma men. Saigô, as I had all along suspected, turned out to be identical with the man introduced to me as Shimadzu Sachiû in November 1865, and he laughed heartily when I reminded him of his alias. After exchanging the usual compliments, I began to feel rather at a loss, the man looked so stolid, and would not make conversation. But he had an eye that sparkled like a big black diamond, and his smile when he spoke was so friendly. I began about the employment of foreigners in Satsuma and the difficulties which might, under certain circumstances, arise from the residence of

British subjects outside the treaty limits and beyond the jurisdiction of the consular authorities. But this did not produce much in the way of response. So I bethought myself of another subject which was more likely to draw him, and inquired if Shitotsubashi had not lately received in person a letter addressed to him by the Emperor of the French. He replied "Yes." A short time ago he memorialized the Mikado to the effect that there was a letter from the French Emperor addressed to the Shôgun, the reception of which had been delayed owing to the late Tycoon's detention at Kiôto in connexion with the expedition against Chôshiû; that he now intended to summon all the foreign representatives to Ozaka, and would profit by the occasion to receive the letter in question. Shitotsubashi would accordingly come down to Ozaka on the 17th of the Japanese month (22nd January), and expected the representatives to arrive shortly afterwards. We (the Satsuma people) sent up a copy of the memorial to Sir Harry Parkes by the hands of Yoshii Kôsuké, but he had replied that he was uncertain whether he would accept the Tycoon's invitation, not having yet heard anything direct about the matter.

"But," I asked, "how can Shitotsubashi receive a letter addressed to the Shôgun. He is not Shôgun, is he?"

"Yes; he received his commission the day before yesterday."

"Well," I replied, "that is very unexpected. I thought he had to settle Chôshiû's affair first. But his influence must have increased immensely for him to have been able to manage this."

"Yes, indeed" — (emphatically) — "A man who was yesterday no better than a beggarly *rônin daimiô* is to-day *Sei-i-tai-shôgun.*"

"Who," I asked, "contrived it."

"Itakura Suwô no Kami" (a newly appointed member of the council). "Shitotsubashi is in great favour now with the Mikado, and he could become *Kwambaku* (grand vizier) if he chose. He has made his brother Mimbutayu, a younger scion of the Mito house, head of the Shimidzu family, which had become extinct, and he is going to send him as ambassador to France."

"Oh what business?"

"We have not the least idea."

"And for what is Shitotsubashi going to summon the foreign representatives to Ozaka?"

"We have not the slightest idea of that either," said Saigô.

"How odd that he should be able to do these things without consulting the *daimiôs*."

"The *daimiôs* ought to have been consulted, as we expected they would be henceforth on all political matters. The *Baku-fu* have got on so badly of late years that my prince is of opinion that they should not be left to ruin the country as they please. And when certain of the *daimiôs* were summoned by the Mikado to Kiôto, they expected to have a share in the government. Now they perceive that such is not the intention of the *Baku-fu*, and they don't intend to be made fools of. So they have one and all refused to attend. Echizen stopped there as long as he could, but went away at last."

"Then everything is over for the present?" I said.

"Well, we shall be able to find him out in the next three years, I suppose."

"Three years is a long time. But this council at Kiôto, was it not connected with the latter part of the decree giving power to the Shôgun to conclude treaties, where the Mikado says, 'There are points in the existing treaties which I wish you to rectify in concert with the *daimiôs*?'"

"Oh no!" said Saigô, "you are quite wrong there. It was intended, as I have said before, that the *daimiôs* should consult with the *Baku-fu* about government reforms."

"I suppose," I said, "that among other questions for discussion the Chôshiû affair and the opening of Hiôgo were included. What is the position with regard to Chôshiû? We foreigners cannot comprehend it?"

"It is indeed incomprehensible," Saigô replied. "The *Baku-fu* commenced the war without justification, and they have stopped it equally without reason."

"Is it peace, or what?"

"No. Simply that hostilities have ceased, and the troops have been withdrawn. There the matter rests."

"For us foreigners it is a great puzzle why the *Baku-fu* attacked Choshiû at all. It was certainly not because he had fired on foreign ships. If he really had offended the Mikado, surely your prince, with his profound affection for the 'Son of Heaven,' could have lent assistance."

"I believe the *Baku-fu* hated Chôshiû all along," replied Saigô.

"It is a great pity the council did not take place, because it is of the highest importance that the affairs of the country should come to a settlement within this year. We have a treaty with Japan, not with any particular person, and we don't intend to interfere with you in the settlement of your domestic disputes. Whether Japan is governed by the Mikado or the *Baku-fu*, or becomes a confederation of separate states is a matter of indifference to us, but we want to know who is the real head. I confess to you that we have serious doubts about the *Baku-fu*. We saw that they are not supreme, or rather not omnipotent when they asked us to let them off the opening of Hiôgo. Then the murder of Richardson and the impotence of the *Baku-fu* to punish his murderers showed us that their authority did not extend as far as Satsuma. Then when ships-of-war belonging to friendly nations were fired on by Chôshiû, we had to go and punish him because the *Baku-fu* could not do it. And we see now that Chôshiû has got the best of the late war. These things make us doubt the supremacy of the *Baku-fu* throughout the country, and we had hoped that the council would settle the difficulty. The *Baku-fu* will again be in a difficult position next year when, as we intend to do, we demand the opening of Hiôgo, if the daimios oppose it."

"My master does not oppose the opening of Hiôgo, but objects to its being opened after the fashion of other ports. We want it to be opened so as to be a benefit to Japan, and not solely for the private advantage of the *Baku-fu*."

"But how would you have it opened?" I asked.

"By placing all questions regarding Hiôgo in the hands of a committee of five or six *daimiôs*, who would be able to prevent the *Baku-fu* from acting exclusively for its own selfish interests. Hiôgo is very important to us. We all owe money to the Ozaka merchants, and we have to send the productions of our provinces to them every year in payment of our debts. Our affairs will be much thrown out of order if the place is opened on the same plan as Yokohama."

"I see now why you attach so much importance to Hiôgo. It is your last card. It is a great pity you cannot settle all your internal difficulties before the port is opened."

"When we sent Yoshii up to see Sir Harry Parkes, he told him if he came to Ozaka to ask for us. We could not go to call on him for fear of incurring suspicion. And Sir Harry replied that he would ask not only to see the Prince of Satsuma, but all the other *daimiôs* as well."

Saké and *sakana* (*i.e.* its accompaniments) were now introduced, and we were waited on by a good-looking girl who was said to be a sweetheart of Godai's. Saigô excused himself and retired for a few moments with my companion Hayashi, who was apparently a confidential agent of the Satsuma people. After the second course, as he seemed in a hurry to get away, I rose to go, but he would not hear of my leaving so early. I begged him not to stand on ceremony, but to leave whenever he chose, as I knew he had a long way to go. After a few minutes more, he rose, and saying, "In case Sir Harry wants to communicate anything to us, he has only to send a message to our house at Yedo, and we will despatch anyone he likes from Kiôto to see him," he took his departure. I thanked him very warmly for coming so far to see me, and we bade each other farewell. The feast was resumed, and after numerous courses, Hayashi and I went back on board the "Argus" by half-past seven. Next day we left for Yokohama. During our stay at Hiôgo we had walked freely about the town, and found the people perfectly civil. They were evidently becoming accustomed to the sight of foreigners, and scarcely took any notice of us as we passed through the streets.

CHAPTER XVI

First Visit to Ozaka

On reaching Yokohama on the 15th January 1867, I duly made my report to the chief of all I had seen, heard, and said, and took up my quarters on the following day at Yedo. The first news I learnt was that the Shôgun had invited all the foreign representatives to meet him at Ozaka, and that they would probably accept. His object, it was explained, was to break through all the traditions of the past eight years and to make the treaties of friendship which had been concluded by Japan with foreign countries more of a reality than they had hitherto been. But Sir Harry, who had now learnt enough of the internal political condition to convince him that the Shôgun's power was fast decaying, still hesitated, and it was only when he found a majority of his colleagues determined to go, that he made up his mind to join them. But he persuaded them that it would be well to have inquiries made beforehand as to the kind of accommodation that would be provided, and consequently deputed Mitford and myself to proceed thither in the "Argus." We were joined by Captain Cardew of the 2/ix, and reached Hiôgo on the 9th of February, after a two days' run. A couple of subordinate officials of the Shôgun's foreign department had accompanied us to make the necessary arrangements, and were landed at once to provide for our going to Ozaka without loss of time. We determined to go by land. The "Princess Royal," "Basilisk," "Serpent," and "Firm" were in port, having just arrived from visiting the Princes of Chikuzen at Fukuoka, and the Princes of Chôshiû at Mitajiri. Lord Walter

Kerr of the "Princess Royal" kindly gave me photographs of the four nobles and of two of the leading councillors of Chôshiû, which are here reproduced. Among them will be recognized Katsura Kogorô, already mentioned. On board the "Princess Royal" I met some native traders, who were greatly interested in the approaching opening of the port, and discussed various suitable sites for a foreign settlement. They also conveyed to me the news of the Mikado's death, which had only just been made public. Rumour attributed his decease to smallpox, but several years afterwards I was assured by a Japanese well acquainted with what went on behind the scenes that he had been poisoned. He was by conviction utterly opposed to any concessions to foreigners, and had therefore been removed out of the way by those who foresaw that the coming downfall of the *Baku-fu* would force the court into direct relations with Western Powers. But with a reactionary Mikado nothing but difficulties, resulting probably in war, was to be expected. It is common enough in eastern countries to attribute the deaths of important personages to poison, and in the case of the last preceding Shôgun rumours had been pretty rife that he had been made away with by Shitotsubashi. In connexion with the Mikado I certainly never heard any such suggestion at the time. But it is impossible to deny that his disappearance from the political scene, leaving as his successor a boy of fifteen or sixteen years of age, was most opportune.

Noguchi and my boy Yasu turned up here, having been forwarded from Uwajima. They were full of excuses, which were readily admitted.

We got away on the morning of the 11th, and Lieutenant Thalbitzer, a Danish officer from the "Argus," having joined us, we were a party of four. Ponies had been provided by the Japanese authorities, and we had an escort of nine men armed with swords from the corps which supplied the guards of the foreign legations at Yedo. Our steeds were small, ill-fed, and untrained, but each had a splendid running footman attached to it, who kept up the pace in magnificent style. Troops had been posted along the road for our protection, and the whole number thus detailed cannot have been less than 1,500. This gave us a novel and somewhat embarrassing sense of importance. The road is perfectly flat the whole way, and fairly straight until it approaches Ozaka, when it begins to make zig-zags which lengthened it unnecessarily. This plan was formerly adopted nearly all over Japan in the vicinity of *daimiôs'* towns for strategical purposes. As the roads nearly always run through the swampy rice fields, a hostile force is unable to march straight at its point of attack, but must follow the road, being thus constantly exposed to a flank fire from the defending force occupying the other arm of the angle ahead.

Soon after passing Ama-ga-saki we came in sight of the castle of Ozaka, a conspicuous object in the landscape by its shining white walls and many-storied towers, visible for many a league. At last we reached the city. Although our guides missed the route at first, and here and there a break occurred in the troops which lined the narrow streets, the crowd quietly made way for us, and stood in front of the houses without uttering a sound. At every corner there was an immense concourse, and the side-streets were filled with eager, gazing faces as far as the eye could reach. We crossed the great wooden bridge over the river which runs through the city, turned to the left along the embankment, and bending again to the right proceeded down a long, apparently interminable street until we finally reached our lodgings at the Hon-gaku-In monastery. Here we found some officials of the foreign department, and received calls from a few of the local functionaries. Everything had been done to make us comfortable, and the locality was the best that could have been selected. It was impossible to avoid contrasting this generous hospitality with the reluctant, almost hostile, reception accorded to us on the occasion of our visit in 1865. The times had evidently changed since the accession of the new Shôgun, and the recent death of the Mikado did not appear to have made any difference in his plans and intentions for the carrying-out of a conciliatory policy.

Preparations had been made by the officials for our accommodation to the best of their ability. After washing off the dust of our

long ride in a comfortable bathroom, we sat down to a dinner served
in imitation of western fashion, with French wines, including an
excellent bottle of Larose. Alas, it was the only one. The seats,
however, were mere four-legged wooden stools, and I suffered a
good deal from them during our stay. Afterwards we inspected the
bedrooms. The bedsteads were mere makeshifts, but there was a
plentiful supply of bedding, consisting of cotton quilts and stuffed
silk coverlets. The toilet service was made up of two ludicrously
small basins and, underneath the toilet table, a huge water pot; at
the side were a cake of almond soap and a bottle of eau-de-cologne.
But what seemed especially unusual was the deference of manner
and language exhibited by all the officials with whom we came in
contact. Hitherto I had experienced only familiarity approaching
to rudeness at the hands of government officers.

On the following morning we were visited by Suzuki, an official
of the Uwajima clan, who came with a message from the resident
Karô to beg that we would not visit them at their *yashiki*, but at
the same time he managed to convey the contrary impression. I
sent Noguchi to the Satsuma *yashiki* to invite Komatsu to call on
us, and to that of Uwajima to convey my thanks for the kindness
exhibited to my two servants. In the afternoon we went out for a
walk in the Shinsai-bashi-Suji, which is the principal street of the
city, preceded by a small band of one-sworded men, who emitted
a cry like a crow — *kau, kau* — to warn the people out of the way.
Dense crowds hovered on our footsteps, eager to catch a glimpse
of the strangers, for no Europeans had been in Ozaka since the
last Dutch mission from Nagasaki had passed through a few years
before. We were no less inquisitive, and made a great round, past
all the booksellers' and mercers' shops, till dark.

Our next visitor was Yoshii Kôsuké, whom I have already mentioned. He reminded me that we had met at Hiôgo in the autumn
of 1865 on board the steamer, when I had also seen Saigô for the
first time. Yoshii was a little man, very vivacious and talked with a
perfect Satsuma brogue. Every day we spent the greater part of our
time in sight-seeing, and the officials proved obliging in every way.

We had only to express a wish and it was immediately gratified. In a day or two we got Komatsu and Yoshii to tiffin. The former was one of the most charming Japanese I have known, a *Karô* by birth, but unlike most of that class, distinguished for his political ability, excellent manners, and a genial companion. He had a fairer complexion than most, but his large mouth prevented his being good-looking. They partook heartily of pâte de foie gras and pale ale, and at last became so merry that we feared they might make indiscreet revelations in the presenee of the Tokugawa servants who crowded the house.

On the next day Mitford and I returned their visit at the Satsuma *Kura-yashiki*, or produce agency, near the river bank. Yoshii received us at the door, and ushered us into a room where we found Komatsu, the agent and Matsuki Kôwan; the latter was one of the two prisoners taken by us in 1863, and I had some suspicion that he was not altogether to be trusted, as he was reported to have been in the Tycoon's service during the interval. So after the exchange of compliments I suggested that we might have some more private talk. It was a mistake on my part, however. Matsuki afterwards changed his name to Terashima Tôzô, or perhaps merely reassumed it, and held office pretty constantly since the revolution of 1868, chiefly in connexion with foreign affairs. So Komatsu, Yoshii, Mitford and I retired together into an inner room. They told us that the Mikado's death had taken place on the 30th January, though the date officially announced was the 3rd February. He had been succeeded by his son, a youth of fifteen, who, it was thought, had in him the makings of a clever man if properly educated in foreign and domestic politics. But unfortunately the *Baku-fu* would not allow him to be approached by any teachers who could improve his mind. During the new Mikado's youth, the conduct of public affairs would be carried on in his name by the *Kwambaku* (best rendered vizier). This officer is chosen from one of five noble court families, nominally of course by the Mikado, but in reality by the Tycoon and principal *daimiôs*. The present *Kwambaku* was a wise and good man, but too much disposed to listen to the counsels of the *Baku-fu*. They thought the new Shôgun's idea in inviting the foreign representatives to Ozaka was merely a counter move to the invitations which Sir Harry Parkes had accepted from the *daimiôs* of Satsuma and Uwajima. The Shôgun would probably talk a great deal about drawing closer the bonds of friendship, etc., but would avoid treating about the opening of Hiôgo. The *Baku-fu* in fact did not wish that event to take place, because it would let a flood of light into the minds of the Mikado and the court nobles. Komatsu said he had remonstrated with the *Baku-fu* for delaying to hand over the land at Hiôgo and postponing the notification of the tariff convention of last June, their answer being that they had not yet made up their minds on those subjects. Satsuma, he said, had purchased some land near Kôbé as a site for a *Kura-yashiki*, of which they would be willing to let us have the greater portion for a foreign settlement. Satsuma wished to see the place opened to foreign trade, but wanted it to be done in a proper manner. Many of the court nobles were also in favour of the measure; these were men of liberal tendencies, but not in favour with the *Baku-fu*, who had imprisoned some of them; they were not allowed to have access to the Mikado.

Affairs being in a critical condition, it was probable that the Shôgun would stop a long time at Kiôto. Were he to return to Yedo, he would lose his hold over the Mikado, and Chôshiû might make another dash at the palace. None of the *daimiôs* had proceeded specially to Kiôto for the investiture of the Shôgun, the absent ones being represented by their agents. Komatsu begged us to tell Sir Harry that it was not the desire of Satsuma and the other *daimiôs* who acted with him to upset the *Baku-fu*, but simply to restrain them from misusing their powers. They hoped, however, to see the Mikado restored to his ancient position as *de facto* ruler of the country. All the plans and hopes of Satsuma tended to the benefit of the country, and not to a revolution against the Shôgun. If Sir Harry on his arrival would propose to make a treaty with the Mikado, the *daimiôs* would at once give in their adhesion, and flock to Kiôto in order to take part in carrying out the great scheme. All that was necessary was for him to help them to this extent, and they would do the rest.

The conversation had now lasted so long that we thought it best to break off, for fear of exciting suspicion, and we returned to the other room, where a capital Japanese luncheon was spread out. To my great surprise we were joined by Inouyé Bunda, whom I had not seen since the bombardment of Shimonoséki. His face was now disfigured by a huge scar, the vestige of one of several wounds which he had received in the course of a party fight down in Chôshiû. He said his people had now got the steam up and would like to give the Shôgun another thrashing. He brought a message from the prince to Sir Harry inviting him to visit the province at the earliest opportunity. When Sir Harry last passed through Shimonoséki, he said, the French Minister was there, and that accident had prevented an intended interview. The Satsuma people expressed the hope that Mitford and I would visit Kagoshima as soon as possible.

We had a discussion with Shibata Hiûga no Kami, one of the Commissioners for Foreign Affairs, about Sir Harry's public entry into Ozaka, and settled all the details quietly and amicably. But when we came to the ceremony of presentation to the Shôgun some difficulties cropped up. He wanted the British Minister to make his bow outside the room in which the Shôgun would be, and we could not allow this. Our object was to insist on the forms being as like those of European courts as possible.

Noguchi, as I have said, belonged to the Aidzu clan, which furnished the best part of the Shôgun's fighting force at Kiôto. I had sent him there to see his people, and he returned with the news that some were coming down to call on me. Accordingly, late in the evening of the 17th, four of them appeared, named Kajiwara Heima (a *Karô*), Kurazawa Uhei, Yamada Teisuké and Kawara Zenzayemon, bearing as presents rolls of light blue silk damask, and lists of swords and other articles to be hereafter given to Sir Harry, Mitford, and myself. In making official presents the custom was that a list written on thick, light cream-coloured paper called *hôsho-gami* should accompany the articles, and often, if these were not ready, the list was handed over beforehand. We had nothing to give in return, but entertained them to the best of our ability. Kajiwara in particular distinguished himself by drinking champagne, whiskey, shelly, rum, gin and gin and water without blinking or shrinking. He was a particularly handsome young fellow, with a fair complexion, and had perfect manners. We gave them a letter of introduction to Captain Hewett of the "Basilisk," as they wanted to see a foreign man-of-war. This was the foundation of a close friendship between myself and the Aidzu clan, which survived the war of the revolution and the completest possible difference of opinion on Japanese internal politics. But they never resented the part we took, clearly seeing that all the English wanted was the good of the Japanese as a nation, and that they were not partisans of any faction. Our new friends came a couple of days later to tiffin, when they were regaled with champagne and preserved meats, greatly to the elevation of their spirits. It ought to be noted that in those days it was quite the proper thing to get drunk at a dinner party, and a host whose guests went away sober would have been mortified by a feeling that his hospitality had not been properly appreciated. One of them got very tight, and began to talk things unfit for the ears of boys or maidens, while another produced a packet of indecent pictures, which he generously distributed among the four of us. In return for this entertainment Kajiwara invited us to go and drink *saké* with him in the evening. We at once accepted, but had some trouble with the foreign department officials from Yedo, to whom it appeared an improper violation of all precedent for members of a foreign legation to attend a feast given by a *daimiô's* man, even though the *daimiô* belonged to the Shôgun's party. We could therefore trust them to make every effort behind our backs to prevent the entertainment coming off.

The afternoon was spent in visiting the boats in which it was proposed to bring the British Minister and his suite to the temporary Legation, and a long weary tramp of it we had, but at last we got to the place where they would leave the men-of-wars' boats. Embarking here, we made an experimental trip ourselves, and came to the conclusion that it would not do. To begin with, the distance was very great, and poling against the stream was a slow method of progression; next, instead of showing themselves to the populace, the minister and his staff would be almost hidden from view, and would be taken through a succession of narrow, obscure, and not very clean canals, to a very short distance from their lodgings, to which they would have to proceed on foot. We found a dense crowd had collected at the landing-place to see us, although it was quite dark. We had been more than a week in the city, and the curiosity of the inhabitants seemed not a whit abated, though we had traversed the city in all directions, and not a day passed without our taking a long walk. Noguchi, who had gone with the Aidzu men to find out where the symposium was to be held, was not yet back, so reconciling ourselves to the idea that the officials had succeeded in putting it off, we sat down to a dinner of terrapin soup and boiled terrapins. In the middle of it, however, Noguchi appeared to announce that all was ready. The guard that usually dogged our steps when we went out had all retired to rest for the night, so we got away unaccompanied except by one man carrying a lantern. The streets were by this time quite deserted, and we hugged ourselves with the consciousness of an adventure. No European had yet been abroad in the streets of a Japanese city at night as a free man. We had to walk a couple of miles, and then turn down by the river till we came to a house close to the great bridge. Here we found our friends awaiting our arrival. Blankets were spread for us on the floor at the upper end of the room, while the Aidzu men sat on cushions opposite to us, a row of tall candlesticks occupying the centre. Tea was served by some very ancient females, and we began again to fear a disappointment, for the invitation had been accompanied by a promise to show us some of the most celebrated singing and dancing girls of the city. However, when the *saké* was brought up, they descended from the upper storey, where they had been engaged in completing

their toilette. Some of them were certainly pretty, others decid-
edly ugly, but we thought their looks ruined in any case by the
blackened teeth and white-lead-powdered faces. In later times I
became more accustomed to the shining black teeth which were
then the distinctive mark of a married woman, as well as of every
"artiste" old enough to have an admirer, so much so that when
the empress set the fashion by discontinuing the practice, it was
long before I, in common with most Japanese, could reconcile
myself to the new style. I have always thought Japanese dancing, or rather posturing, extremely uninteresting. It is a sort of
interpreting by more or less graceful (or, as one may look at it,
affected) movements of body and limbs, of the words of a song
chanted to the accompaniment of a kind of three-stringed lute.
It is some help to know the words of the song beforehand; they
are no more comprehensible when sung than the sounds given
forth by the singers in Italian opera are to the majority of their
audience. But no foreigner, unless he be an enthusiast, would
ever take the trouble to educate himself to appreciate this form
of art. He can enjoy the beautiful in other ways at much less cost
of time and mental exertion. Then it takes a long apprenticeship
to accustom the European ear to music constructed with a set of
intervals that are different enough from ours to make nine-tenths
of the notes seem out of tune. This form of entertainment is universal all over the east, in India, Burma, Siam, China and Japan,
with local variations, and is, to my uncultivated taste, everywhere
equally tedious. Our Yedo officials had found us out, and did
not cease to urge our return, until at eleven o'clock we gave way
to their importunity and said good-bye to our hosts, after only
a short stay. I daresay they kept it up to a much later hour. This
was the evening before we left Ozaka.

CHAPTER XVII

Reception of Foreign Ministers by the Tycoon

On our return to Yedo we were horrified to learn of the death by his own hand of poor Vidal, the junior student interpreter. No motive was assignable for the terrible act, except ill-health. Insane he certainly was not. A more lucid intellect it would be difficult to find. He had abilities of a very high order, but was a prey to a torpid liver, which seemed always to embitter his existence. His first nomination was to Siam, but before he had taken up his appointment he was transferred to Peking. After a year or two there, finding the climate did not suit him, he obtained a change to Japan. But even there he was not content with his lot, and preferred annihilation.

The next few days were spent in visiting Atami and Hakoné in company with some friends from Yokohama. There is nothing worthy of record about this excursion, except that Atami, which then contained only a couple of hotels, now (1887) possesses at least a dozen, and has become a fashionable winter resort, much frequented by the higher classes living in Tôkiô (Yedo). The cost of transport then was much less than it would be now. We paid the coolies who carried our baggage over to Hakoné, a distance of about ten miles, 1 3/4 *ichibus*, about 2 shillings and 4d per man. At that time there existed a barrier at the eastern end of the village, at which all travellers had to exhibit their passports to the men on guard. The notice-board at the guardhouse, among other provisions, stated that dead bodies, wounded persons, and individuals of suspicious aspect were not allowed to proceed without the production of a passport. A lady of our party accomplished the difficult feat of riding on a Japanese pony down the steep and badly paved road which descends from the top of the pass to Odawara. We established ourselves in the official inn, where we were received with due respect and cordiality by the innkeeper. It was a one-storied building spread over a considerable area, and containing ten or fifteen rooms of the regulation size, namely 12 feet square, besides a huge kitchen and an entrance hall. Here we passed the night, and on the following day Noguchi procured for us packhorses and coolies at the government rates, which were 1 horse load 464 cash, 1 coolie load 233 cash, for a distance of ten miles. Now 6,600 cash were equal to one *riô*, that is four *ichibus*, or at par rates about 5s 4d, so that the official rate for the coolie was about two and a fifth pence for the whole distance or a little over the 1/5 of a penny per mile. The coolies were obliged to perform the labour as corvée, and if they were not in sufficient number, the population of the post towns had to hire men at ordinary rates to let them out at the government tariff. It was a heavy tax, and one of the first reforms of the new government established after the revolution was the abolition of this system. At Hodogaya I parted from the rest of the party, who returned to Yokohama, and went on to Kanagawa, where I slept at the *hon-jin* or official hotel, occupyihg the best rooms, which were reserved for *daimiôs* and high officials of the government. I rode in a *kago* or palanquin from Hodogaya, just five miles, and was two hours accomplishing that short distance. It was, however, the ordinary rate of travelling in those days. One of the native legation guard went ahead, also in a *kago*, preceded by a big bamboo and paper lantern on a pole, then came my *kago*, followed by a coolie carrying my baggage in a couple of wicker boxes slung on a pole (*riô-gaké*), and a second guardsman. Noguchi probably walked. Next morning when I came to discharge the bill for my whole party, including rooms, *saké* and *sakana*, supper and breakfast, I found it amounted to about 8s 6d, and I gave one *ichibu* (say 1s 4d) to the hotelkeeper as *cha–dai* or tea money, which was considered quite enough. In Japan the charge for a night's lodging, called *hatago*, used to include everything, rice, tea, sleeping accommodation, fuel, candles, and use of the hot bath. The only extras were *saké* and *sakana*, which a liberal-minded traveller ordered "for the good of the house," but if he was of an economical turn, he contented himself with the regular two meals, which were quite enough to satisfy his appetite. *Sakana* (fish) is more played with than eaten, and is merely the excuse for *saké*. The comparison with a European hotel bill, with its charges for candles, firing and bath, is striking. Moreover, in Japan, you give no tips, for none are expected, and the tea money takes the place of the charge for the room you occupy.

It was after my return from this journey that Mitford and I removed to a little house outside the legation, situated in a pretty garden on the rising ground which overhangs the side road leading from the Tôkaidô to Sen-gaku-ji. It was in reality a small monastery named Monriô-In, and we occupied the guest apartments, having each a bedroom and one sitting room. No palisade surrounded it, and our only protection was a hut at the gate which held three or four of the *betté–gumi*. We thought ourselves very plucky in thus braving the risks of midnight assassination, when the legation grounds below us were patrolled all night, and sentries passed the word to each other as the hours struck. Here we spent several months together, living entirely on Japanese food, which was brought three times a day from a restaurant known as *Mansei*, much frequented by our friends the Satsuma men.

Mitford devoted himself with unflagging diligence to the study of the Japanese language, as he had before at Peking to that of the Chinese, and made rapid progress. I began to compile for his use a series of sentences and dialogues which some years afterwards were published under the title of *Kwai–wa Hen*. It was convenient to be outside the legation compound, because I could receive visits from the retainers of *daimiôs* without obstruction. I used to go a good deal to the Satsuma *yashiki* in Mita to get political information from two men named Shibayama Riôsuké and Nambu Yahachirô; the former met his death towards the close of the year in a remarkable manner. The *yashiki*, having gained evil repute as the refuge of a number of *ronin* and other disorderly political characters, was surrounded and set on fire by the Shôgun's police. There was a fight, many were killed, but Shibayama was made prisoner. When brought up for examination, he boldly avowed that he had been the ringleader, and then drawing a pistol from the bosom of his dress, shot himself through the head. He was a capital companion, and I had more than one agreeable adventure with him.

Towards the middle of April the foreign diplomatic representatives moved in a body down to Ozaka. The French Minister, M. Roches, had already been there in March in furtherance of the special line of policy he was pursuing, and seen the Shôgun; doubtless promises of support had been given; at any rate, counsel had been offered. In fact, as it afterwards turned out, M. Roches so far committed himself with the *Baku-fu* that he found it impossible to remain one day longer in Japan after its final overthrow. On our side Sir Harry Parkes was resolved henceforth to treat the Shôgun as of no more importance than a vice-gerent; henceforward he was styled by us His Highness, while for the Queen we used a Japanese title placing her on full equality with the Mikado.

Sir Harry took with him to Ozaka the mounted escort under Captain Applin, and a detachment of 50 men from the 2/ix, commanded by Captain Daunt and Lieutenant Bradshaw. Lady Parkes was also of the party. The staff consisted of the secretary of legation, Sidney Locock, Mitford, myself (I was acting Japanese secretary), Willis, Aston and Wilkinson. We had persuaded Sir Harry to let Charles Wirgman come with us. We numbered about seventy Europeans, besides some thirty Chinese and Japanese, writers, servants and grooms. The Tycoon's government furnished all the fresh supplies required. Great offence was caused by this exclusive privilege, and Rickerby in the *Japan Times* poured out his wrath upon the head of our friend the artist. It was perhaps noy an unreasonable complaint from their point of view that no representatives of the mercantile community were invited to accompany the foreign ministers, but it is quite certain that they would have been very much in the way.

The British Legation occupied four spacious temples or monasteries at the further end of a street called Tera-machi, the other representatives being accommodated in perhaps somewhat inferior buildings nearer to its entrance. But the British Minister had taken the trouble to send down two of his staff beforehand to make all the arrangements, while the others were ready to be contented with what was provided for them by the Japanese Government. Mitford, Wirgman and I occupied one end of a temple (Chô-hô-ji) overlooking the city, while at the other end were Sir Harry's "office" and the temporary chancery. The whole mission messed together in the temple on the other side of the street, where Sir Harry and Lady Parkes had their abode. Next door was a temple given up to the officers of the guard and two student interpreters, and the fourth was set apart for guests. I had a charming set of rooms on three floors. The bottom was occupied by the Japanese writers and my retainers, the centre floor, consisting of two rooms, served as a bedroom and "office," and the top was a sort of parlour where I received guests, only twelve feet by nine, but large enough to accommodate a dozen persons, as it did not contain a single piece of furniture.

It was a busy time. I was employed from morning till night translating and interpreting, and remember that on one occasion I had to talk Japanese for eleven successive hours, as the chief had Japanese guests both at luncheon and dinner. For this reason I found no time to keep my journal, and what follows is a pure effort of memory, aided only as far as the dates are concerned by reference to printed sources.

A great part of our time was taken up with the regulations under which settlements were to be formed at Hiôgo and Ozaka, the conditions under which land was to be leased to foreigners, and the creation of a municipality at each place, and Sir Harry being the most practical man among the whole body of foreign representatives, the work fell in the main on his shoulders. The Japanese Government were evidently desirous of conciliating the representatives, and the negotiations proceeded with unaccustomed smoothness and celerity. No more angry discussions and heated arguments (in which the heat and anger of our chief were opposed to the stolid calm of the imperturbable Japanese Ministers) such as had characterized our official interviews at Yedo. At the word of the new Shôgun an entirely new line had been adopted, and serious endeavour was made to convert the treaty of friendship into a reality.

Then we had visits from Satsuma, Awa and Uwajima men, and tried to ascertain what was likely to be the out-turn of the political movement that had been in progress now for thirteen years. But on the whole everything seemed to point to the triumph of the Shôgun over his opponents. And one of the principal objects with which he had invited the foreign ministers to Ozaka was that he might make their personal acquaintance, and thus manifest his desire to cultivate friendly relations with foreign countries. Who put this into his head I do not know, but it does not seem *à priori* unlikely that a closer intimacy with the legations had been suggested to him by one of the representatives themselves. A good deal of time was consumed in discussing the etiquette to be observed at the audiences of the Shôgun, but in the end it was arranged that it should be entirely according to European fashion. The first interview was a private one. Sir Harry proceeded to the castle on horseback, accompanied by all the members of the mission, preceded by the mounted escort, and with a detachment of the infantry guard before and behind. A cloud of the Japanese guard called *betté-gumi* hovered on our flanks and kept back the crowd. A rather ludicrous incident was the presentation of arms by the soldiers who lined the open space in front of the castle to the officer in command of the escort, whose resplendent uniform had led them to mistake him for the minister. At the nearer end of the causeway crossing the moat there used to stand a wooden board inscribed with the Chinese characters for "alight from horseback," but as had been agreed upon beforehand, we took no notice of this and passed on through the gateway to the very door of the palace. If I recollect rightly, this was almost close to the gate. The palace unfortunately exists no longer, having been destroyed by fire during the retreat of the defeated *Baku-fu* forces early in February 1868. But it was reputed to be the most splendid example of domestic architecture then extant in Japan. It certainly was far superior to the Mikado's Palace at Kiôto. Wide and lofty matted corridors, partitioned off by painted screens, of choice cryptomeria wood, ran along the front of a succession of large rooms and away to the right by the side of the three large apartments constituting the *ôbiroma* or hall of audience. The other apartments had each a specific name, and the *daimiôs* were classified according to their right of waiting in one or the other for their turn of admission to the presence. Over these wooden screens were large panels of carved wood representing birds and animals surrounded by foliage, but somewhat too richly painted, very much in the style familiar to those who have visited the mausoleum of Iyéyasu at Nikkô.

We were conducted along the matted corridor by the Commissioners for Foreign Affairs, who had some difficulty in walking, as the court rules prescribed their wearing long wide trousers that extended far beyond their feet, so as to give them the appearance of moving on their knees, until we reached the further room, where the Shôgun was awaiting us. He shook hands with Sir Harry, and sat down at the head of a long table, with Sir Harry on his right and on his left Itakura Iga no Kami, who might be styled Prime Minister. The rest of the staff sat next to Sir Harry, and I had a stool between him and the Shôgun. He was one of the most aristocratic-looking Japanese I have ever seen, of fair complexion, with a high forehead and well-cut nose — such a gentleman. I felt somewhat nervous, not knowmg whether I had got hold of the forms of speech required by court etiquette, and remember making a ridiculous blunder over an observation of

Sir Harry's that all that was disagreeable in the past relations of Great Britain and Japan was now forgotten. There was no business talk on this occasion, and after the conversation was over, the whole company adjourned to a smaller apartment where dinner was served in European style. The Shôgun sat at the head of the table, and was very gracious. Round the walls hung paintings of the thirty-six poets, and Sir Harry having admired them, the Shôgun made him a present of one. Whiskey and water were produced after the repast, and I had the honour of brewing toddy for the great man. It was dark when we left.

A few days later there was a formal audience, at which the captains of the men-of-war were presented. We had arranged beforehand the address of Sir Harry and the reply of the Shôgun, who had been tutored also into saying a few words to each person presented to him. These somewhat resembled the Turkish Pasha's remarks as translated by the dragoman at the famous interview described in *Eothen*. To Captain Haswell, who had been on a polar expedition, for instance, he said what really amounted to "you had a long journey," but was interpreted in much more complimentary style.

I remember receiving a visit from Saigô and others of that party, who were not at all pleased at the *rapprochement* between us and the Shôgun. I hinted to Saigô that the chance of a revolution was not to be lost. If Hiôgo were once opened, then good-bye to the chances of the *daimiôs*.

The street in which the foreign representatives lodged was shut in at each end by solid wooden gates, at which a number of the *betté-gumi* were stationed on guard day and night, and it was impossible to get out into the city without an escort, as the guard had instructions to follow us wherever we went. This was very irksome to Mitford and myself, until we found out a gap in the wall which surrounded one of the temples, and from that time we used to make nocturnal excursions to all parts of the town, accompanied by my retainer Noguchi. The sense of a certain peril to be encountered, combined with a sort of truant schoolboy feeling, rendered these explorations into the night life of Japan very enjoyable. On one occasion young Matsuné joined us on an expedition to the quarter occupied by singing and dancing girls; it was a moonlight night, and the chance of detection by the guard was so much the greater. After getting through our gap, we doubled back, and passing behind the legations, got into a lower street running parallel to that in which we lived, where we ran along for some distance keeping close in the shadow of the houses, then darted into another street at right angles, turned to the right again until we felt sure of having baffled any possible pursuers, after which we walked on quietly, and crossing one of the long bridges over the river, found ourselves at our destination. A room had been taken in Matsuné's name, and some of the bepowdered and berouged girls were awaiting the arrival of the Japanese party they had expected to meet, when to their surprise and horror three Europeans were ushered into their midst. We were at that time objects of more alarm than interest to the women of Ozaka. The fair damsels starting up with a scream fairly ran away, and no assurances from our friend would induce them to return. The keeper of the house besought us to leave, as a crowd might collect, and if there was any disturbance he would get into trouble, and to we had to submit to our disappointment. But even the slight glimpse we had of the native beauties seemed to compensate for the risk run, for here in Ozaka no foreigner had ever been admitted to the quarter. On another occasion, when we were accompanied by some of the guard we had better success, and enjoyed the society of some *gei-shas* for several hours, the government officials having given their consent and even interfered, I believe, on our behalf. Matsuné, being a *daimiô's* man, was looked on with much suspicion. It seemed a plucky thing on his part to spend so much time with us, and even to accompany us in broad daylight to the tea-gardens opposite to where the Mint now stands. Everything was new and delightful in Ozaka, politics and diplomacy afforded unceasing interest and excitement, the streets, shops, theatres and temples were full of life and character of a kind thoroughly distinct from what we were accustomed to in Yedo and Yokohama, and the difference of dialect and costume imparted additional piquancy to the women.

During the whole five weeks we spent there we had not a single dull day. There was always something to do in the intervals of our official work, visits to temples and theatres, tea-drinking according to the elaborate ceremonial of the *cha-no-yu*, an excursion to the large commercial town of Sakai, the existence of which in such close proximity to Ozaka seems hard to explain. Near our residence was a florist's establishment, famous for its collection of orchids, which in Japan are cultivated more for their foliage than for their flowers; this taste is conditioned by the fact that in Loochoo, China and Japan there are very few species bearing conspicuous or fine blossoms, and the amateur makes the best of what is procurable. More attractive to the European was the exhibition of tree-peonies, which was going on during our stay. These flowers are now fashionable in England, but at that time were not much known; the magnificent pink or white blossoms of various shades, often as much as nine inches in diameter, are quite unsurpassable, and fully justify the Chinese title of "king of flowers." In Chinese and Japanese decorative art it is always associated with the lion, and has often been mistaken for the rose by European writers. Curio shops and silk stores also took up a good deal of our time, but the fabrics of the loom had not then attained the high artistic development of later years. We went about the city in every direction, and though frequently encountering men of the two-sworded class, never met with any instance of rudeness, while the common people were uniformly friendly to us.

The negotiations between the foreign representatives and the delegates of the Japanese Government proceeded satisfactorily though somewhat slowly, and about the middle of May had reached a stage at which it was felt that nothing more could be done for the present. All the ministers, therefore, made their preparations for returning to Yedo. Before leaving that part of the country Sir Harry made a trip across to Tsuruga, which had been talked of as a possible substitute for the port of Niigata, reported to be practically closed to commerce for one half of the year by the combined inconveniences of a bar at the mouth of the river on which it stands, and the persistent north-west gales that raise a most dangerous sea. It had been agreed between us and the Japanese that as a supplementary refuge for ships the harbour of Ebisuminato in the island of Sado should be opened if necessary, but only as an anchorage. If after an inspection of these two places the combined arrangement should appear unworkable, then some other port was to be substituted, either Tsuruga or Nanao. Sir Harry was accompanied by Lady Parkes and some of the staff. He proceeded by way of Fushimi, along the western side of the Biwa Lake, and returning by the eastern shore. The anti-Shôgun party made a great grievance of this journey, and fell foul of the government for having permitted the "barbarians" to approach so near to the sacred capital, Fushimi being practically a suburb of Kiôto, and the Satsuma people put in a written memorial on the subject, more to annoy the Tycoon's government than as a mark of real hostility to us. Of course we did not know of this until long after. I obtained leave to return to Yedo overland, and Wirgman became my travelling companion.

A proposal was made to Sir Harry by the Tycoon's government through Kawakatsu Omi no Kami to procure professors for English for a large public school to be established in Yedo on the basis of the existing *Kaiseijo*. Dr Temple was asked by Her Majesty's Government to furnish a sufficient staff at salaries which we in the legation thought quite adequate, but he took no trouble about the matter, and we thus lost the opportunity of giving an English turn to the higher class education of the country.

CHAPTER XVIII

Overland from Ozaka to Yedo

For centuries the interior of Japan had been closed to all Europeans, with the exception of the head of the Dutch trading factory at Nagasaki, who used to travel overland to Yedo at fixed intervals to pay his respects to the Shôgun and carry valuable presents to him and his ministers. Perhaps the best account of these tribute bearing missions is to be found in Kaempfer. But in the new treaties a provision had been inserted giving to the diplomatic representatives of foreign powers the right of travelling throughout the country, and Sir Rutherford Alcock had availed himself of this privilege a few years earlier, as he has recounted in his *Court and Capital of the Tycoon*. As a guide to succeeding travellers it cannot be said that his description of the journey was of much assistance. But the Japanese are great travellers themselves, and the booksellers' shops abound in printed itineraries which furnish the minutest possible information about inns, roads, distances, ferries, temples, productions, and other particulars which the tourist requires. Then a fairly good map was easily procurable, not drawn to scale, but affording every geographical detail that can be of any real service, and there was a splendid illustrated guidebook to the Tôkaidô containing all the legendary and historical lore that an Englishman accustomed to his Murray can desire. There are two great roads which unite the eastern and western capitals, namely the Nakasendô or road through the mountains, which, as its name implies, traverses the central provinces, and

the Tôkaidô or road along the sea to the east, which follows the
sea shore wherever practicable. Properly speaking this is not the
original name of the road, but rather of the administrative division
through which it runs, but practically it came to the same thing.
It was the latter which had been chosen for me as the principal
highway in the country, and the best provided with inn accommodation. Ever since the third Tokugawa Shôgun established the
rule that each *daimiô* must pass a portion of the year in Yedo, the
great highroads had become important means of internal communication. Posting stations were established at every few miles for
the supply of porters and baggage ponies, and at each of these were
erected one or two official inns called *hon-jin* for the use of *daimiôs*
and high functionaries of government. Around these sprang up
a crowd of private inns and houses of entertainment where the
daimiôs' retainers and travelling merchants used to put up. The
Tôkaidô was the recognized route for all the *daimiôs* west of Kiôto,
and of course for those whose territories lay along it. Then it was
the main route for the pilgrims who flocked annually to the sacred
shrines in Isé, and was the means of access to many other famous
temples; so that of all the roads in Japan it was the most frequented
and the most important from every point of view. Who that col-
lects Japanese colour prints is unacquainted with the numerous
delightful series of views devoted to its illustration, which present
such vivid pictures of Japanese life. One of the most famous of all
native novels is occupied with the adventures of a couple of merry
dogs on their way from Yedo up to Kiôto, and the list of its fifty-
three posting towns was one of the first lessons in reading and
writing which the youth of Japan had to commit to memory. On
account of its historical and legendary associations, to say nothing
of its famous scenery, it occupied something of the same place in
the imaginations of the Japanese that the Rhine formerly did in the
minds of English tourists before the Loreley rock had been tun-
nelled, and crowds of indifferent travellers were hastily whirled in
a few hours along an iron track on either side of the great stream
which at one time it was the fashion to "do" with dignity in a car-

riage and four. Carefully as one may study a map, there is no way of learning geography comparable to the pedestrian method, which, by a thousand associations of pleasure, fatigue and weather, fixes indelibly the minutest topographical facts, and enables the student of history to understand the vicissitudes of warfare.

Japan being a country where a peculiar political system had taken its birth from centuries of civil war, the more we saw of its interior districts, the more likely were we to arrive at a correct understanding of the problem which at that moment was being attacked by the rival parties. I do not pretend that any considerations such as these determined my application to the chief for permission to return to headquarters by land. Insatiable curiosity as to everythiug Japanese, a certain love of adventure, and dislike of life on board of a man-of-war were the real motives, the last perhaps as strong as any, and probably many persons would agree with me in preferring to spend a day in walking from Calais to Dover, if it were practicable, to taking their chance of rough weather in a steamer, even though it might not last for more than an hour and ten minutes.

Wirgman and I were by this time so accustomed to living on Japanese food that we resolved not to burden ourselves with stores of any kind, knives or forks, finger glasses or table napkins. Ponies were not procurable, so we bought a couple of secondhand palanquins, called *hikido kago*, such as were used by public officials, and had them repaired. They cost the small price of 32 *ichibus* each, or not £4. The pole was a long piece of deal, called by euphemism paulownia wood. A cushion of silk damask, thickly stuffed with raw cotton, was spread on the bottom, and there was then just room enough to sit in it cross-legged without discomfort. In front was a small shelf above the window, and underneath a small flap which served as a table. The sliding doors also had windows, furnished with a paper slide to exclude cold, and another covered with gauze to keep out the dust while letting in the air. If it rained, blinds made of slender strips of bamboo were let down over the windows. The body of the palanquin could also be enveloped in a covering of black oiled paper, in which a small aperture was left for the occupant to peep out of, a blind of the same material being propped up outside; this arrangement was, however, only resorted to on days of persistent rain. Each of us had a pair of oblong wicker-work baskets to hold our clothing, called *riô-gaké*, which were slung at opposite ends of a black pole and carried by one man over his shoulder. My bedding, which consisted of a couple of Japanese mattresses covered with white crape and edged with a broad border of common brocade known as *yamato nishiki*, and one of the huge stuffed bedgowns called *yogi* of figured crape with a velvet collar, with a couple of European pillows, was packed in a wicker box of the kind called *akéni*, and formed a burden for two men. To each package was fastened a small deal board on which my name and titles were inscribed with Indian ink in large Chinese characters. As escort we had ten picked men belonging to the native legation guard (*betté gumi*), and a couple of officials belonging to the Japanese Foreign Department (*gai-koku-gata*) were attached to us, who were instructed to make arrangements for our accommodation along the road. Last of all, a list was made out of the places at which we were to take our mid-day meals and sleep at night, the journey of 320 miles from Fushimi being calculated to occupy sixteen days.

On the 18th May, having exchanged farewell calls with the commissioners of foreign affairs, we got away from our temple lodging at nine o'clock in the morning. Willis, who was to join Sir Harry Parkes' party at Fushimi, accompanied us. We embarked at the Hachikenya wharf on the river side in a houseboat, the escort and *gai-koku-gata* in another, two open boats following with the luggage of the whole party. The stream was very strong, and our progress was correspondingly slow, but we felt that we were travelling in a dignified manner, and therefore repressed our natural impatience. Where the stream was deep enough close in shore, the boatmen landed, and towed us by a line attached to the top of a mast fixed in the front of the boat, while the steersman remained at his post to prevent us from running into the bank. When the towing path changed to the opposite side, the boatmen came on board and poled across to resume their labour as before. The river, which winds a good deal, is enclosed between lofty dykes, so that we had no prospect but the broad surface of the river itself and the tops of ranges of mountains peering over the bank. It was a fine day, and we were full of eager anticipations about the novel scenes we were about to pass through, every inch of the way being entirely new to us as far as Hakoné, and for myself the prospect of a fortnight's holiday was especially exhilarating after the hard work of the past five weeks.

By one o'clock we reached Suido-mura, a small village on the right bank about five miles above Ozaka, and landed to take our lunch. There was nothing to be had but rice and bean-curd, which did not constitute a very palatable meal. But *à la guerre comme à la guerre.* We passed a large number of crowded passenger boats descending the river, and ten barges laden with bales of rice. At half-past six we stopped at Hirakata, a somewhat more important place than Suido mura. Here we landed to dine off soup, fish and rice, the ordinary constituents of a traveller's meal. The charge for our three selves and three servants was less than an *ichibu,* and a second *ichibu* was given as *cha-dai* or "tea-money." Noguchi was paymaster, and gave whatever he thought right under this heading. The charge seemed extraordinarily cheap, which was explained by a regulation binding innkeepers to supply persons travelling in an official capacity at one quarter of the rates charged to ordinary people. We started again by moonlight, and as the night advanced, a thin mist rose and covered the surface of the broad river, imparting to the landscape that mysterious, sketchy indistinctness which is so characteristic of Japan, that none but native artists whose eyes have been educated to it from their childhood have ever been able to seize and represent.

The air now became as cold as it had been hot during the day time. We had blankets fetched from one of the baggage boats, and lay down to sleep in opposite corners of the boat. At two in the morning I woke and found that we were lying off the guardhouse on the right bank opposite to Hashimoto, which was held by troops of Matsudaira Hôki no Kami, a member of the Tycoon's Council, the other bank being in the charge of Tôdô, the *daimiô* of Isé. We had been as far as Yodo, where they turned us back because our pass had not been viséd here, and we did not reach Yodo again till four o'clock. It was still dark, the moon having set during the night. The river is here joined by the Kidzu-kawa, and is divided into several channels by islands lying in its course. We kept along the right bank, and arrived at Fushimi about six, where we found Sir Harry on the point of starting for Tsuruga. Here a generous member of his party gave us a last cigar. Our stock had been completely exhausted during the long stay in Ozaka, and for the rest of the journey we had to content ourselves with Japanese tobacco, smoked in tiny whiffs out of the diminutive native pipes, all inadequate to satisfy a craving nourished on something stronger. The worst of the Japanese pipe, with its metal bowl and mouthpiece united by a hard bamboo stem, is the rapidity with which it gets foul, necessitating cleaning at least once a day with a slender spill twisted out of tough mulberry-bark paper. Willis left us here, and joined the chief. Special precautions had been taken by the government to prevent Sir Harry turning aside to Kiôto, which it was thought his adventurous disposition might tempt him to visit.

After breakfast we started in our *kagos* for the journey overland. A crowd of *machi-kata*, who were a sort of municipal officers of all grades, dressed in their Sunday best, escorted us out of the town. Our road lay for a mile or so between the banks of the Uji-kawa and the low, fir-clad hills masked by clumps of graceful bamboo, and then leaving the tea plantations of Uji to the right, we journeyed along a level road winding through the hills to Oiwaké, where we joined the Tôkaidô. A kind of stone tramway ran from Kiôto all the way to Otsu, our next resting-place, for the heavy, broad-wheeled bullock carts, of which we passed a couple of score laden with rice for the use of the Tycoon's garrison at the capital. Oiwaké was famous for pipes, counting boards (*abacus*), and a species of comic prints called *toba-yé*, and lies at the foot of the hills separating the province of Yamashiro from the beautiful Biwa Lake. By the road-

side we had an opportunity of inspecting some tea-firing establishments on a small scale, like every other manufacturing enterprise
in those days. The fresh tea leaves were damped, then spread out
on a flat table heated from beneath by fuel enclosed in a plasterd
chamber, and twisted by hand. This new tea forms a delicious and
refreshing drink when infused after the Japanese method for the
finer qualities, with lukewarm water. At each establishment there
were not more than two persons at work.

At one o'clock we got to Otsu, and after lunch went to a monastery called Riô-zen-ji to enjoy the celebrated prospect of the
lake, but the mid-day heat had covered its surface with a dull grey
haze, and hid it entirely from view. We found everything nicely
arranged for us at Takajima-ya, where we rested for the mid-day
meal, while the escort and foreign office men in our train vied in
accommodating themselves to our wishes. From Otsu a level road
skirted the lake, and, soon after passing through Zézé, the "castle
town" of Honda Oki no Kami, we got out to walk. In crossing the
great double bridge of Séta we saw a couple of men in a boat spin-
ning for carp; the shallows here are crowded with traps, irregular
shaped enclosures of reeds planted in the mud, into which the
fish enter when stormy winds agitate the surface of the water and
deprive them of their equanimity. But before reaching Kusatsu,
where we were to put up for the night, we retreated into our *kagos*,
in order not to be overwhelmed by the crowd, and for the better
preservation of our dignity, which required that we should not be
seen on foot. At the confines of the town we were met by a deputation of the municipal officers and by the host of the official inn,
who escorted us in with great pomp, keeping back the inquisitive
multitude. Our bearers quickened their pace, not indeed to our satisfaction, for the *kago*, which is uncomfortable at all times, becomes
almost uninhabitable when the men get out of a walk.

At last we turned round a corner, and passing through a black
gate, before the posts of which were two neatly piled-up heaps of
sand, flanked by buckets of water, were set down in the wide porch
of the official inn. It was one of the most beautifully decorated

buildings of its kind that I have ever seen. That implies woodwork of the finest grain, plaster of the least obtrusive shades of colour, sliding doors papered with an artistic pattern touched up with gold leaf and framed with shining black lacquered wood, and hard thick mats of the palest straw edged with stencilled cotton cloth. In the principal room, only twelve feet square, raised six inches above the rest of the house, lay two thick mats forming a sort of bed-place, where the distinguished traveller was expected to squat without moving. The baggage was deposited in the corridor which ran round two sides of the apartment. There was no view from the windows, which looked out on a small courtyard enclosed by a sulky-looking, black wooden fence. Etiquette prescribed that a great man should neither see nor be seen. Our host came in with a small present, and bowed his forehead to the sill. After a few minutes he returned to give thanks in the same humble manner for the gift of two *ichibus* which he had received as *cha-dai*. We went in turn to the hot bath, where a modest, not to say prim, young damsel asked whether she might have the honour of washing our "august" back, but not being trained from our youth up to be waited on by lovely females during our ablutions, we declined her assistance.

At dinner time we ordered a dish oi fish and a bottle of *saké*, which had to be several times replenished before the artist had had enough. The people of the inn were astonished to find that we could eat rice, having been taught to believe that the food of Europeans consisted exclusively of beef and pork. When we went to bed, soft silk mattresses in plenty were spread on the floor, and the chambermaid placed within the mosquito net a fire-box with a bit of red-hot charcoal neatly embedded in white ashes for a last smoke, and a pot of freshly-infused tea. *O yasumi nasai*, be pleased to take your august rest, was the end of the first day.

In Japan travellers are in the habit of making an early start. A native usually rises before day, makes a hasty toilet by scrubbing his teeth with a handful of salt from a basket hanging over the kitchen sink, washes his hands and face without soap, swallows a hasty breakfast, and is on the road as soon as the sun is up, or even earlier. His principal object is to arrive at the town where he is going to pass the night at as early an hour as possible, in order to secure a good room and the first turn at the hot bath, there being only one tub and one water for the whole of the guests. In some out of the way places this is not even changed every day, and I remember on one occasion to have found the bath absolutely green with age and odorous in proportion. We were not expected to do as the vulgar herd, and did not get away much before half-past seven. Our average rate of going was about three miles an hour, and the day's journey not over twenty miles, but there were so many interruptions that we rarely reached our evening's destination before six o'clock.

First and foremost there was the mid-day meal (*o hiru yasumi*), which consumed at least an hour, and then our exalted rank required that we should stop to rest (*o ko-yasumi*) at least once in the morning and once again in the afternoon. Then we stopped again at every point of view to drink tea, and to taste every dish of cakes or other comestibles of which centuries of wayfarers had been in the habit of partaking before us. Thus on the third day we stopped at Mmé-no-ki to take tea at a house commanding a fine view of the legendary mountain Mukadé-yama (Centipede's Mount), and again for half-an-hour at Ishibé, where a big board was stuck up outside inscribed with "the little resting-place of the interpreter (the officer) of England." We lunched sumptuously at Minakuchi on fish, soup and rice, and so got through an hour and a quarter. At Ono, celebrated for pheasants' meat preserved in *miso* paste, we again drank tea, which was served out by pretty girls who made a great pretence of bashfulness. Wirgman's costume, consisting of wide blue cotton trousers, a loose yellow pongee jacket, no collar, and a conical hat of grey felt, gave rise to a grave discussion as to whether he was really an European, or only a Chinaman after all. At Mayéno, a centre of tea production, we stopped for another half-hour to taste several sorts of leaf at a tea-dealer's shop. This was a great act of condescension on the part of such distinguished personages, but we made up for this derogation from our dignity by having our purchases paid for by Noguchi, the real Japanese swell being supposed to know nothing about money, not even theoretically. The dealer declared that unless the leaf is picked and fired by virgins, it will not be drinkable, but I fear he was humbugging the innocent foreigner.

Many of the houses bore a notice-paper inscribed with Chinese characters meaning "Economy in all things," a laconic sentence which was interpreted to signify that the occupants had forsworn social entertainments and other unnecessary sources of expenditure. Wirgman made himself very popular by the sketches he threw off and gave away to the innkeepers, sometimes of ourselves as we appeared on the road, or of a bit of local scenery, or perhaps a pretty girl, whose bashful pride on discovering that her features had been perpetuated on paper was a pleasant sight to contemplate. It usually took same time before the waiting maids overcame what seemed to us to be their excessive modesty, but it was explained to us that women were not usually permitted to approach the dais-room, as noble swells had their own men-servants to attend on them. We regretted the exigencies of our lofty position, and pitied the *daimiôs* who have always to be correct and proper — in public. Another consequence of our supposed high rank was that in many towns the people knelt down by the side of the street as we passed along, being invited to assume that posture by the municipal officers who preceded us beadle-fashion, crying out *Shitaniro, shitaniro* ("down, down"). This honour used in those days to be rendered to every *daimiô*, no matter whether travelling in his own dominions or those of another nobleman, and also to the high officials of the Shôgun's government, as, for example, the governor of Kanagawa, to the great indignation of the European residents. The only reported instance of a foreigner ever submitting to this indignity was that of Mr Eugene van Reed, who is said to have fallen in with the train of Shimadzu Saburô on the day fatal to poor Richardson, and to have then and there conformed to the native custom. The practice had its origin, perhaps, in the necessity of protecting the nobles from sudden attack, combined with the rule of Japanese etiquette which considers that a standing posture implies disrespect. This latter fact was forcibly impressed on me at Fuchiû, where I went to visit the public school for the sons of *samurai*. Having taken off my shoes and laid my hat on the floor at the entrance, I was escorted into a room where about thirty youngsters were squatting on the floor, with Chinese books before them which they were learning to repeat by rote from the mouths of older and more advanced pupils, under the superintendence of half-a-dozen professors. I bowed and remained standing, but to my surprise no one acknowledged my salute; I had in my ignorance of propriety assumed what to the Japanese appeared an attitude of disrespect, and it was only on being admonished by one of the escort that I discovered my error, which being at once repaired, the professors returned my bow, made in proper form with head to the ground. I afterwards found it necessary to adopt Japanese manners, as far as was compatible with a certain stiff-jointedness that forbade my sitting on my heels for more than a very limited period, but could never resist the uneasy feeling that while I was pressing my forehead on the mats, the man opposite might perhaps be taking advantage of the opportunity to inflict a slight on the "barbarian" by sitting bolt upright. In fact, Japanese themselves were not exempt from a similar uncertainty, and they might sometimes be detected, whilst performing the obeisance, in the act of squinting sideways to ascertain whether the person they were saluting lowered his head simultaneously and to the same level.

Whenever we passed through a town of any importance, the population turned out *en masse*, eager to convert the occasion into a holiday. At Kaméyama, for instance, which is a *daimiô's* castle town, the streets were thronged with *samurai* and their children in gala dress, presenting a gay appearance; some of the young girls were extremely pretty, in spite of the quantity of white powder with which fashion condemned them to bedaub their faces.

Some odd methods of locomotion were practised in this part of the country, such as children riding in nets of coarse cord suspended from opposite ends of a pole carried by a man on his shoul-

der, women riding in pairs on packhorses, and in the flat plain
between Séki and Kuwana in small open omnibuses, not unlike
the costermonger's carts in which fruit is hawked about the streets
of London, but drawn by a man instead of a donkey; perhaps
half-a-dozen grown-up persons in one of these small vehicles,
the precursors of the *jinrikisha* which came into vogue in 1869.
Wirgman, who was too careless of his dignity (for he was travelling not as an artist, but in the quality of a *yakunin* or government
official), insisted in getting into one of these, and rode all the way
from Tomida to Kuwana, a distance of at least five miles, for three
tempôes, say 2 1/2 d. At a tea-house at Komuki we were presented by
our host with some teapots of very inferior Banko ware; this is the
famous unglazed pottery moulded by hand, and showing all over
its surface, both inside and outside, the marks of finger tips.

On the 22nd we reached Kuwana, a large town belonging to one
of the principal hereditary vassals of the Tokugawa family. Here
an enormous concourse of people had collected to see us make our
entry, and we had some difficulty in making our way through the
crush, until suddenly the procession turned aside through a gateway under a tower, and traversed the outer enceinte of the castle,
finally arriving at the official inn on the shore of the bay. Dealers
in Banko ware, curious stones from Mino and fans from Nagoya
came flocking in, and the evening was passed in bargaining.

The stage from Kuwana to Miya is by sea, across the head of
the bay of Owari. Nowadays (1887) people perform the journey
by steamer, but in 1867 we had to content ourselves with a rather
dirty boat, roofed in with planks. We left at half-past seven and
arrived at the termination of our voyage a little after eleven, but
as the distance is estimated at seven *ri* or 17 1/2 miles, we were
precluded from going further that day. I proposed, therefore, to
devote the afternoon to visiting Nagoya, of which Miya is little
more than a suburb.

It boasts a castle founded by Nobunaga towards the end of the
sixteenth century. It is famous throughout Japan for two huge
golden dolphins which surmount the donjon tower, and is one of

the finest extant specimens of that sort of architecture. But the foreign department officials had no instructions to let us deviate from the high road, and did not venture to take on themselves the responsibility for making other arrangements. They promised, of course, to see the governor of the town, and ask him to get permission which they represented was required before they could take us into the castle town of a great noble like the Prince of Owari, but it was all fudge. Shopkeepers flocked in laden with fans, metal work, lacquered porcelain and crape, with which we occupied the interval till an answer should be received from the authorities at Nagoya. A report of Wirgman's skill with the brush having spread, he was overwhelmed with quantities of Chinese paper and fans which, our host said, had been brought by the leading inhabitants who desired specimens of his art, and I wrote mottoes to his productions. The *saké* bottle furnished us with the necessary inspiration. But we found out at last that the fans thus decorated were being sold outside at an *ichibu* a piece, and refused to be imposed on any further.

In the evening we had in some singing and dancing girls, and having got ourselves up in native costume, invited the two foreign office clerks and some of our escort to join the party. One or two of the latter became so merry that they could not resist a temptation to perform buffoon dancing, and Sano, the biggest and most good-humoured, gave imitations of famous actors. We did not get rid of our guests until nine o'clock, by which time they had taken a good quantity of *saké* on board.

In passing through Arimatsu on the following day, famous for cotton *shibori*, dyed in the same way as the Indian *bandhana*, we called at the shop where the heads of the Dutch factory at Nagasaki had been in the habit of stopping from time immemorial on the occasion of their annual journeys to Yedo, and were shown a ledger containing records of the purchases made by them year after year. It was a matter of obligation to follow this time-honoured example, and we selected some pieces of the stuff, which oddly enough is called by the name not of the place where it is made, but by that of the last post-town, Narumi. Noguchi and the two foreign department officials did the bargaining, while Wirgman and I looked on and smoked in dignified silence as if we were utterly unconcerned about the prices. The owner of the shop was a distinguished person, evidently invested with a municipal function, in consequence of which he was allowed to have a few stands of matchlocks in his hall. Many of the houses were of more substantial construction than usual, thus testifying to the prosperity conferred by the local manufacture.

At Chiriû the landlord of the inn where we lunched came privately to Noguchi and asked him for four *ichibus* as "tea money," on the ground that Sir R. Alcock had given that sum in 1861, but his request was refused, and he was forced to content himself with what we had paid elsewhere, namely, half an *ichibu*. I always left such questions to his discretion, and have no doubt that he acted rightly. In the afternoon when the train stopped as usual to give the palanquin bearers a rest, the people of the *tatéba*, or half-way tea-house, presented us with buckwheat vermicelli, for which, as they assured us, the place was reputed famous. It was, however, inferior to what I have eaten in other places. Wirgman's fame having preceded him, paper, brushes and ink were brought, and he executed a masterpiece representing us eating vermicelli and drinking *saké* from a gourd which he had been careful to get replenished at Miya.

The bridge over the Yahagi-gawa being broken down, we crossed the river in a ferry boat, and were met at the entrance of the town by municipal officers and constables, the latter being furnished by the local *daimiô*, whose function was to walk at the head of the procession and to cry "Down, down." Down went the whole crowd of spectators, including men of the two-sworded class, all the more willingly perhaps because that was the only way they had of bringing their eyes to a level with the windows of our palanquins. For etiquette demanded that we should always ride in entering and quitting a town, the vulgar practice of proceeding on foot being allowable only in the more countryfied portions of the highroad.

The following day opened with what promised to be persistent rain, and we had to be fastened up in our palanquins with the oiled paper covering thrown over us; through a small opening we could just manage to see a few yards to right and left. All day long we ploughed our way onwards along the almost level road, which in places was flooded nearly six inches deep. At Arai there was then a guardhouse close to the shore of the Hamana Bay, where all travellers had to alight from their palanquins and walk through, taking off their hats and shoes in order to show respect while submitting to a searching examination. Over the *saké* on the preceding evening there had been a good deal of chaff about our being obliged to subject ourselves to this rule, which was said to admit of no exceptions. I was inwardly resolved not to submit, and was much relieved when the time came to find that the warden was satisfied with the *kago* door being opened about half-way as we were carried past; this slight concession had been arranged overnight by the foreign department officers, in order that the letter of the rule enforcing inspection might be observed, and we were quite contented, as the door was opened by a third party, so that our dignity as Europeans was duly saved by our not having to alight.

Some years ago a series of dykes and bridges exceeding a mile in length was thrown across the shallowest part of the bay. We had, however, to embark in boats so small that they would not hold more than a single *kago*. The spits which run out towards each other at the mouth gave the bay the appearance of a land-locked lake, until we got half-way across and the breakers became visible; nevertheless the sea at the point where we crossed was as smooth as a mirror. Two miles on the western side of Hamamatsu we were met by some retainers of Inouyé Kawachi no Kami, the local *daimiô*, wearing black hats as flat as a pancake, who, being himself a member of the Tycoon's Council, had no doubt given special orders regarding our reception, and at the entrance of the town they were joined by more. The procession was now formed in the following order. Two *machi-kata*, in green mantles with one in brown between them, marched a long way ahead to clear the street, followed by a couple of aldermen (*shuku-yakunin*) in single file on each side of the road, and a couple of *seishi* or heralds, whose fierce demeanour was delightful to behold, who roared out *shitaniro, shitaniro,* and warned some young *samurai* who displayed a disposition to approach too close that they must keep at a respectful distance. Then followed our *kagos*, with one of the native escort (*betté-gumi*) walking on each side. Then a constable (*dôshin*) carrying a spear, and behind him the rest of the escort, servants and baggage.

On arriving at the inn, we received visits from the head merchants, and were told that we were to be specially cared for, by orders of the *daimiô*, some of whose retainers kept watch and ward in the kitchen throughout the night, this being very spacious and situated in the front of the house. In leaving on the following day the procession was arranged in the same way, and as we passed the castle gates a high official stationed there handed his card to one of the *betté-gumi* to present to me. At the end of the town the escort was changed, and we were placed again in charge of the four black-hatted *seishi*, who did not leave us until we arrived at the boundary of Inouyé's, the *daimiô's*, territory.

After the rain of the day before yesterday the country looked especially beautiful; ripe fields of barley behind the rows of tall pine trees that lined the road stretched right away to the foot of the nearer hills, behind which rose range after range in the blue distance. We met yesterday and to-day soldiers of the 3rd regiment of the Tycoon's drilled troops marching to Kiôto to support the new policy of the head of the government, and perhaps to defend him against an armed confederation of the leading *daimiôs* of the west.

As soon as the local escort had turned back we descended from our palanquins to pursue our way on foot to the Tenriû-gawa, which we crossed by means of ferry boats. The river here is very wide and the current swift, and except during freshets is divided into two branches by a sandbank which occupies the middle of the stream. Wirgman had stopped behind to sketch, and I waited with one of the foreign office officials, who confided to me that

we should probably meet a "barbáre" on the road. By this I understood the *rei-hei-shi*, a high official of the Mikado's court who was
returning from a mission to the tomb of Iyéyasu at Nikkô. He was
of higher rank than any Japanese *daimiô*, and everyone on meeting
him had to get out of his palanquin and go down on his knees. My
informant hoped we should manage to avoid him, and I hoped so
too. The rest of the party having at last come up, we proceeded
by a short cut through the fields, which saved us a couple of miles
walking. We got to Mitsuké, where we were to lunch, some time
before noon. The streets were crowded with pretty girls, who had
turned out to see the foreigners. Our host, who had put on his
robes of ceremony, made his appearance, bowing low and bearing
a gift of dried white-bait fly, which when toasted and dipped in
soy is very palatable. Handsome Turkish carpets had been spread
in the bedroom. Two charming little boys about ten years of age,
with perfect manners, were told off to wait on us.

The *rei-hei-shi* was of course the principal topic of discussion.
He had not yet passed, and our followers were full of anxiety.
Noguchi said that all Japanese of rank, down to the lowest two-
sworded man, got out of his way, because his followers were in the
habit of extorting money on the pretext that the proper amount
of respect had not been paid to the great man. I was quite ready
to follow the example of the Japanese in avoiding if possible the
chance of an encounter. We were told that the *rei-hei-shi*, whose
rank by this time had been much diminished in the mouths of
our informants, was to stop the night at Fukuroi, the very next
town, only four miles further, so we hurried away hoping to get
to our own destination early in the afternoon. Two miles over the
tableland, then zig-zag down a beautiful hill covered with pine
trees, then two more over the rice field flat to Fukuroi, where
we changed the palanquin and baggage porters and hastened on
without stopping.

To-day, the 27th of May, the peasants were cutting barley and
planting out the young rice. I did the six miles more to Kakégawa
in two hours, including the last stoppage, which was considered

very quick going. A young Satsuma man who was on his way to Nagasaki called at our inn and gave me an account of the *rei-hei-shi* and the doings of his retainers, for whom he professed the greatest contempt. He said they were wretched citizens of Kiôto hired for the occasion, and dressed in a little brief authority. At Shinagawa, the last suburb of Yedo, they had seized eighteen people and fined them for exhibiting a want of respect towards the Mikado's messenger. It was rumoured that he would pass through about six o'clock, and spend the night at Fukuroi. Six o'clock came, but no *rei-hei-shi*; we passed the evening in expectation, and went to bed; still no *rei-hei-shi*.

Wirgman and I slept in separate rooms, Noguchi in a third, and all the escort but one were quartered at another house a little way off. At a quarter past one I was roused from sleep by a Japanese saying to me: "Mr Satow, Mr Satow, get your sword; they've come." My sword was an old cavalry sabre, not good for much but to make a show. I got up and groped my way through the black darkness to the sword-stand in the alcove and got the weapon. The Japanese led me by the hand, and we stood together in a corner of the next room, wondering what was going to happen. He said: "I wish the escort would come." Meanwhile violent noises were heard, as if of people breaking in. Bewildered by the darkness, I imagined them to be coming from the little garden at the back, on to which my bedroom looked. We remained still and breathless. In three minutes all was silent again, and I heard a voice cry "Mr Satow." It was Noguchi, who appeared with a light, and reported that the enemy had fled. Wirgman and my chancery servant Yokichi were nowhere to be found. The Japanese who had woke me proved to be Matsushita, the youngest of the escort. We proceeded then towards Noguchi's room; the wooden door opposite was lying on the floor, where the assailants had broken in. As we stood in the passage, others of the escort came in, all dressed in fighting mantles, with drawn swords in their hands and wearing iron forehead pieces. Seeing my scarlet sleeping trousers, they begged me either to hide myself or take them off, but the danger being past, I only laughed at them. Two of them went in search of Wirgman, and found him in an alley leading to the back of the house; they narrowly escaped being shot.

We began to feel cooler, and Noguchi narrated what had happened. He heard the noise of the front door being broken down, jumped up, tied his girdle, and stood in the doorway of his room, a sword in the right hand, a revolver in the left. Some men approached and asked for the "barbarians," to which he replied that if they would only come in, he would give the "barbarians" to them. They took fright at his attitude and determined tone, and fled. Altogether there were, he thought, about a dozen, two armed with long swords, the rest with short ones. On looking about, we discovered that the mosquito nets in the room diagonal to Wirgman's had been cut to pieces, the occupants having escaped. It was lucky for us that we had put out the lamps before going to bed, so that the assailants could not find their way.

Wirgman explained that on being awakened by the noise of people breaking down the doors and shouting for the "barbarians," he followed the people of the house, who took to their heels. A lantern that had been dropped by one of the "ruffians" led to the conclusion that they belonged to the *rei-hei-shi's* suite. No one was hurt, except one of the assailants, who in the hurry-scurry of running away was accidentally wounded by a companion. After everyone had related his own experiences, I retired to bed, while Wirgman called for *saké* and sliced raw fish, with which he and the escort regaled themselves until daylight.

On getting up in the morning my first step was to send for the two foreign office officials, and endeavour to obtain redress through them. The escort, who had not appeared on the scene till the danger was past, were now very anxious to distinguish themselves by some act of valour. I told the officials, with the full support of the escort, that they should either get the guilty men delivered up to me, or that I would go with my escort and take them by force. This was the attitude maintained until mid-day. I verily believe that if I had given the signal, the escort would have attacked the *rei–hei–shi's* lodgings. At last the official came back and said that the *rei–hei–shi's* people refused to give the men up to me; as an alternative they proposed to obtain a written apology, coupled with a promise to punish the assailants on their reaching Kiôto. To this I expressed my willingness to assent, in the hope that we should be able to pursue our journey before night set in. But the negotiations lingered, and this was not to be. So we sent for some musicians, and invited the two officials and the escort to a banquet. Wirgman and one of the escort entertained the company with dancing. Another of the escort got very drunk, and begged me to take him into my personal service on the same terms as Noguchi. We heard that the townspeople were delighted at the *rei–hei–shi* and his blackguards being so bothered by a couple of foreigners. No Mikado's messenger was ever before stopped on his road and talked to in our imperious manner. Four or five of the escort, when full of *saké*, started up the street in their fighting mantles and created great alarm in the minds of the *rei–hei–shi's* retainers, who, thinking they were to be attacked in earnest, begged for a guard from the *daimiô* of the town. The captain of the escort and two others in particular behaved in a delightfully swaggering manner. But in spite of all this, nothing was settled, and we had to stop a second night.

On the following morning on getting up, I was told that matters were nearly arranged, that the men who had attacked our lodgings were to be left behind in the custody of the *daimiô*, the people at the castle giving a receipt on his behalf. The morning wore on without the desired document making its appearance, and I feared they would slip through my fingers altogether. I got tired of waiting and went to sleep, from which I was awakened by one of the foreign office officials, who had been acting as go-between, bringing me a certified copy, signed by the governor of the town, of a written undertaking given by a leading retainer of the *rei–hei–shi* to remain there with three of the assailants. Another copy was given to him, and he started at once for Ozaka with it, accompanied by one of the escort. I was now asked whether I would permit the *rei-hei-shi* to depart, to which I gave my assent. We saw him and his retinue pass the inn; there were two large palanquins, half-a-dozen smaller ones, and about fifty ruffianly-looking fellows in green coats. We had thus remained on the field of victory. As soon as the *rei-hei-shi* was clear of the place, we started in the opposite direction about three o'clock in the afternoon. The *daimiô's* people offered to give us a body of men to escort us out of the town, but I replied that my escort was sufficient to ensure our safety. A guard of honour was drawn up in front of the inn as we left, and eight policemen accompanied us to the exit of the town.

Ultimately, some months later, these men and three others implicated in the affair were brought to Yedo and put on their trial. Two were condemned to death, and four more to transportation to an island. Sir Harry wanted me to be present at the execution of these two men, but I persuaded him to send some one else instead. To look on at the execution of men who have tried to take one's life would have borne an appearance of revengefulness, which one would not have liked. But I think that under the circumstances of those times the punishment was rightly inflicted.

Our next stage was to Nissaka, a pretty little town lying in a basin of hills. Beyond rose a steep ascent, which we climbed not without fatigue, to find ourselves on the top of a tableland running away to the sea on our right, while on the left hills rose ever higher and higher above the road, being cultivated up to their summits in tiny level plots cut out of their sides. At the highest point of the road we rested at a tea-house, where a kind of soft rice cake, bedaubed with a substance resembling extract of malt, was served to us by a diminutive girl. Though fifteen years of age, and consequently nearly full grown, she did not measure four feet in height.

On the further side of the tableland lay Kanaya, the next post-town, and beyond that the Oi-gawa, which had to be crossed before we could gain our stopping place for the night. A hundred naked porters hurried forward to carry our palanquins and baggage to the other bank. For ourselves there were a sort of square stretcher, carried on the shoulders of twelve men for greater safety, who made a point of plunging into the deepest part of the torrent to give us a greater idea of the difficulties they had to contend with. For the idea then entertained by every Japanese was that the force of the stream was too great for a boat to live in it, and that a bridge was impossible. As it has since been successfully bridged, the probability is that this belief was purposely inculcated on the people on the principle of *divide et impera*, and what more effectual means of division could be found than a river which was not to be passed but by taking off your clothes and running the risk of drowning in it while effecting the passage, to say nothing of the inconvenience of emerging half-naked on the other side; that is to say, unless you could pay to be carried.

Following the economical practice we had observed all along of limiting our tips to the smallest respectable sum, we threw a *bu* to the men, who clamoured loudly for its division, the share of each being somewhat over 2/3 of a penny. We did not get to the inn till eight o'clock. Our host was particularly polite, and thanked us profoundly for doing him the honour of stopping at his humble abode. We were still under the influence of the excitement produced by our recent adventures, so *saké* and fish were ordered in, and the liveliest of the escort were bidden to the feast. Some one distinguished himself by adding a new verse to the popular ballad then in vogue, expressive of our contempt for the "turnip-top" coated retainers of the *rei-hei-shi*, which was sung over and over again to the accompaniment of a lute played by an exceedingly ugly red faced damsel who waited on us.

The next day brought us to the large town of Fuchiû, formerly the residence of Iyéyasu after his retirement from the active government of the state early in the seventeenth century, and since re-christened Shidzuoka. It is an important centre of the tea and paper trades, and at the time we passed through was the seat of one of the principal universities of Japan, but greatly fallen from its ancient grandeur. On our way we had to taste various local delicacies, among which was a horribly tenacious kind of gruel, resembling bird-lime in appearance, made from the powdered root of the *Dioscorea japonica*, a species of wild potato. We found the streets so full of spectators that it became necessary to get into our palanquins to avoid the crush of curious sightseers. The town is also noted for a variety of articles of cabinet work and lacquered ware of the ordinary sort, and the room next to our apartment had been converted into a kind of bazaar in expectation of our arrival. The articles were of the class common enough at Yokohama, and not much cheaper; in fact the prices were such as befitted the supposed exalted rank of the travellers. In those days in Japan it was a well observed doctrine that "noblesse oblige" in the matter of payments.

Next morning when we rose at six, we got a beautiful view of Fuji, the "Peerless One," springing from the ground as it seemed almost behind the inn, and lifting its beautiful head into the pale blue sky, above horizontal wreaths and stretches of cloud. After breakfast we paid a visit to the "university," where we found about thirty youngsters seated on the floor in one room, with copies of some Chinese classic before them, learning to read by rote from the mouths of older and more advanced pupils. This instruction was given for about two hours each morning, and six times a month explanations of the text were imparted by professors. The headmaster, who was from the Confucian College at Yedo, used to be changed annually. And this, with the addition of learning to write with a brush, constituted the education of a young Japanese in the olden time. The system was one that cultivated the memory, but failed altogether to appeal to the reasoning faculties. Of course all this has long ago disappeared, and it is possible that this system of instruction is as obsolete in Japan as the dodo.

The great mountain having at last appeared on our horizon, we were to have its company for nearly every step of the rest of the journey. Near Ejiri we caught a delicious view of the summit appearing over the lower mountains on the left hand. At one o'clock we reached Okitsu, where we were to lunch. The inn stood close to the sea shore, and possessed an upper room commanding a magnificent view, in favour of which we abandoned the dignified glories of the *jô-dan* or dais. On the left the blue promontory of Idzu stretched away far into the ocean until it beeame almost invisible in the haze; on the right hand the low hills of Kunô-zan terminating in a low spit of sand covered with irregular growth of pine trees, the famous Miyo no Matsubara of the Japanese poets. From the back window we had a glimpse of the snowy peak of Fuji peeping over the tops of the intervening hills, and by craning our necks out sideways the double-topped head of the Futago-yama near Hakoné.

On leaving this spot, which we did with reluctance, we followed the base of the cliffs for two or three miles along the shore, when suddenly we turned a corner and Fuji came full in view; in front, the base of the great mountain was hidden by the low range which runs down into the sea near Kambara, and a white cloud encircled its middle. Wirgman sat down to make a sketch, from which he painted a picture which is still in my possession. Next we reached Kurazawa, famous for Venus-ear (*awabi*) and *sazai*, a big whorl with a curious spiral operculum. Of course we rested here awhile to eat of the local dish, washed down with repeated cups of *saké*, in which the guard joined us. Since the affair of Kakégawa we had become great friends, as men usually do who have shared the same perils. The road followed the sea-shore here to Kambara, and would be one of the most picturesque in Japan, but for the dirty uninteresting fishing villages which line nearly the whole of its length.

Next morning we were astir early, and crossing the low intervening hills, reached the banks of the Fuji-kawa at eight o'clock. Extensive preparations had been made at the official hotel for our reception, mats laid down to the entrance and red blankets spread on the floor of the dais. At the urgent entreaty of the innkeeper we turned in for a few minutes, and discovered that Wirgman was an ancient acquaintance of our host, having seen him when he travelled overland from Nagasaki to Yedo in 1861 in the suite of Sir Rutherford Alcock. We were shown into the best room with much ceremony, and when we had taken our seats on the floor, piled-up boxes (*jû-bako*) were brought in full of chestnut meal cakes, the speciality of the village, with a bit of pickled radish on the top.

Other "famous things" sold here are ink stones, bits of crystal with green streaks in them supposed by the common people to be grass, also agates. We crossed in a boat the narrow turbulent Fuji-kawa, running between wide beds of shingle. Nowadays you cross in the train. We then had a view of Fuji almost rising out of the sea and drawing its skirts up gradually behind it, curious but not so beautiful as when it is partly concealed by lesser summits which afford a standard of comparison. It looks in fact more like an exaggerated molehill than anything else.

We met on the road two little boys of twelve and fourteen years of age, who, having begged their way as pilgrims all the way from Yedo to the sacred temples of Isé and of Kompira in Sanuki, were now on their way home, carrying slung across their backs huge packages of temple charms done up in oiled paper. The road was terribly sandy and hot, and passing for the most part between the bamboo fences of cottagers' gardens, was the reverse of picturesque.

We had intended to sleep at Hakoné, but owing to delays for sketching, to say nothing of a huge feast of broiled eels and *saké* at Kashiwabara, did not manage to get beyond Mishima, at the western foot of the hills.

Next morning we started at half-past six to ascend the pass which climbs the range of mountains by an excellent road paved with huge stones after the manner of the Via Appia where it leaves Rome at the Forum, and lined with huge pine trees and cryptomerias. At a tiny hamlet more than half-way up some hunters came to present us with eggs, according to immemorial custom. Three hours brought us to Hakoné, the little mountain village standing on the southern border of the lake, surrounded by steep grassy hills. The warmth of the day tempted me to take a bath in the lake, which at first was strenuously opposed by the foreign official with us. It appeared that no boats were allowed on the lake, nor was any one permitted to swim in it, lest he should take the opportunity of swimming round at the back of the barrier gate, and so avoid the necessity of showing his passport. With considerable trouble I persuaded the objector to withdraw his opposition, by representing that my natatory powers were altogether insufficient for the purpose.

After a couple of hours spent in this charming spot, which nowadays has become a fashionable summer retreat of foreigners residing at Yokohama, we resumed our journey down the eastern side of the pass, already described in a previous chapter, and got to our inn at Odawara by five, little dreaming of what lay before me.

A letter from Sir Harry Parkes was at once delivered to me urging me to hasten my return, as there were important negotiations on foot. On conferring with the leader of the escort, I learnt that by starting at once and travelling posthaste through the night, I might get to Yedo next morning. Eight porters in relays of four would be able to carry the palanquin at the rate of about four miles an hour. So the men were ordered without delay. The Japanese on these occasions, to save themselves from being too severely shaken, wind a broad piece of cotton cloth tightly round the waist, and tie another piece round the temples. A third is suspended from the ceiling of the palanquin, to which the traveller clings with might and main. I had to adopt this arrangement, and in addition stuffed my palanquin full of bedding and pillows. Noguchi and two of the escort accompanied me to negotiate the changes of coolies at the various posting stations on the way, and by seven o'clock we were in motion. The porters maintained a constant crying "*eeya-oy*," "*eeya-oy*," in order to keep step with each other and render the swinging of the palanquin less unendurable. To sleep was impossible, as this noise continued all night. When the day broke we had done twenty-six miles, which was slower than I had expected. So we urged on the fresh men we got here, and accomplished the remaining twenty-two miles by ten o'clock. From sitting crosslegged so many hours I was almost unable to stand upright when I got to the Legation. And the vexatious part of it all was that the important conference, which I had hurried to be present at, turned out to be a mere complimentary visit of a crowd of officials for whom anyone could easily have interpreted.

CHAPTER XIX

Social Intercourse with Japanese Officials—Visit to Niigata, Sado Gold Mines, and Nanao

Our relations with government officials suddenly from this time onward assumed a character of cordiality which formerly would have been thought impossible. This was, of course, in consequence of very explicit instructions given by the Tycoon to his ministers to cultivate the friendship of the foreign missions, and especially of the British Legation, in order doubtless to counteract the intimate intercourse which was known to be carried on between ourselves and the retainers of Satsuma and Chôshiû. Each of the commissioners for foreign affairs in turn invited me to dine with him in Japanese fashion, and as I was extremely ignorant of Japanese etiquette, Noguchi used to accompany me on these occasions to be my tutor. An exchange of presents was always an important part of the entertainment, and this was a very troublesome business on account of the difficulty of buying anything at the foreign stores in Yokohama that was worth giving away as a specimen of English productions. Most of these officials lived in a very modest way. The rooms in which they gave their entertainments were usually upstairs, perhaps not more than twelve feet by fifteen, but as there was no furniture, there was plenty of space. On arriving at the house we were shown up a very narrow

staircase, and through an equally narrow door. Down we plumped
on our knees immediately, and bowed our heads to the mats to
the host, who did the same. Then ensued a contest of politeness,
our entertainer trying to get us nearer to the top of the room,
and we protesting that we were very comfortable where we were.
Of course it ended in my being put down in front of the recess
(*tokonoma*), which is the seat of honour, while Noguchi remained
where he was, just inside the door. Usually I was then allowed
to cross my legs in tailor fashion, owing to my joints not having
yet acquired the lissomness of the Japanese. Then Noguchi with
great solemnity unwrapping the present, would slide across the
floor and deposit it between the host and myself. In Japan you
don't use brown paper for parcels, but every household possesses
a set of cloths of different sizes, silk or crape for the smaller, of
cotton dyed green for the larger, which fulfil the same purpose as
paper. Then I pushed the present gently towards my entertainer,
saying "This is really a very shabby article, but as it is a production of my contemptible country, I..." To which he would reply,
"Really I am quite overpowered. What a magnificent article. I am
really ashamed to deprive you of it." And then all women folk,
the servants, and the children who were peeping in at the door or
round the corner of the balcony which ran along the front of the
room would crane out their necks to get a glimpse of the precious
rarity from the far west. Then the other guests, three or four in
number, would begin to arrive. If they were strangers, the following dialogue would take place. Each person putting his hands
together on the mat in front would bend over and almost touching
them with his forehead, say "I have the honour to present myself
to you for the first time. My name is so-and-so. I hope to enjoy
your friendship in perpetuity." To which either may add that he
has often heard of the great fame of the other, and longed for an
opportunity of meeting him.

When these bowings and prostrations are over, a small apparatus for smoking is brought in and placed before the guest, after
which tea and sweetmeats are served. Perhaps an hour passes in

this way, for the entertainment is provided from a restaurant, as the domestic who performs the office of cook in a household only knows how to boil rice and make commonplace stews; and in those days at least neither clocks nor punctuality were common. If you were invited for two o'clock, you went most often at one or three, or perhaps later. In fact, as the Japanese hour altered in length every fortnight, it was very difficult to be certain about the time of day, except at sunrise, noon, sunset and midnight. At last you began to hear a gentle clatter of dishes below stairs; the teacups, cakes and sweetmeats were removed, and a covered lacquered basin was set before you on a square tray, with a pair of chopsticks, the ends of which were neatly wrapped in paper. At the same time a girl put a basin half full of water down on the middle of the floor, with a small pile of diminutive flat cups by the side. Your host took one of these, held it out for a little of the hot *saké*, which is poured from a slender porcelain bottle, and having drunk it, slid forward to the basin to wash it. Having well shaken it, he crawled to where you were sitting, bowed profoundly, and presented the cup to you on his crossed palms. You bowed, and taking the cup between your own two hands deposited it on the floor, after which you were bound at once to present it to the damsel to be filled for yourself.

If your host, or one of the guests who has offered you the cup, wished to be very polite indeed, he waited before you with his hands resting on the floor in front of him while you emptied the cup, or at least took a good sip. When this ceremony had been gone through with all the guests, your host lifted the cover off his soup-basin, and invited you at the same time to follow his example. You drank a little of the soup, just dipped the end of the chopsticks into it by way of pretending to touch the meat, and laid down the bowl again; usually you replaced the cover. A number of dishes were brought in piled up with fish-cake, white beans boiled with sugar, raw, broiled and boiled fish, perhaps some boiled fowl or roast wild duck, cut up in small pieces, and these were served on small plates or saucers, and each person received a bowl containing a sort of pudding made of eggs, loach and the large seeds of the maidenhair tree. The raw fish, which was usually either *bonito* or sole, was sliced up very thin, and eaten with soy, raw laver (seaweed) and grated *wasabi*, which is the root of a plant belonging to the same order as the horse-radish, and resembling it in taste.

Towards the end of the feast a second water *souché* was brought in, and perhaps some broiled eels. The courses were not removed as each succeeding one was brought in, and the plates collected on your tray and the floor close by you till all the extent of the feast was exhibited. You ate very little, picking here a mouthful, there a mouthful, but you drank as much *saké* as you could stand, and sometimes more. After two or three hours of conversation, perhaps enlivened by some music and singing performed by professionals hired for the occasion, and you felt that you had had enough liquor you bowed to your host, and said that you would like some rice. This was the well-understood signal. A fresh tray was brought in with a large lacquered bowl for rice, and a couple more containing soups, accompanied almost invariably by the fish of ceremony called sea-bream, and the bigger it was the greater the honour. You had your bowl filled with rice, of which you were, however, not able to eat much, as your appetite had been nearly destroyed by the repeated libations of warm *saké*, so after a few mouthfuls you handed the bowl to the maid, who filled it half full of very weak tea, or on very formal occasions with hot water, and thus you managed to swallow the contents, aided by a piece of salted radish or vegetable marrow pickled in the lees of *saké*. That over, you carefully replaced the covers on their respective bowls, pushed the tray a foot or two away from you, and executed a bow of profound gratitude fo your entertainer. The feast was then removed downstairs, where all the portable parts of it were packed into a box of white wood-shavings and delivered to your servant, if you had one in your train, to carry home. Freshly infused tea was brought in, after which you thanked your host for the feast, and took your leave, being accompanied to the door of the house by the whole family, to whom you made as low a bow as possible before mounting your pony or entering your palanquin.

For the next six or seven weeks we were very busy arranging with the Japanese the details of a scheme for organizing their navy, with the assistance of a body of English officers who were to be sent out from England, as a counterpoise to the French Military Mission, which had been at work since the beginning of the year, and for the establishment of a college to be superintended by a body of graduates from English Universities. The former plan was successfully carried out, and some months later a mission under the command of Commander, now Admiral, Richard Tracey, arrived in Japan. The educational proposal, however, came to nothing. Ultimately the Japanese obtained the assistance of a leading American missionary residing at Nagasaki, and the present (in 1885) educational system was in fact established by teachers from the United States.

Sir Harry, as I have said before, had already visited Tsuruga, which was suggested as a possible alternative to Niigata as the port to be opened on the west coast, but before deciding this question, it was necessary to make a careful examination of Niigata itself. So in the latter part of July he started off on a voyage of inspection, taking Mitford and myself with him. I had Ono Seigorô, one of the legation writers, and my trusty Noguchi with me. We left Yokohama on the 23rd July in the "Basilisk," commanded by Captain, afterwards Sir William, Hewett, V.C. In less than four days we reached Hakodaté, where the usual visits were exchanged with the governor, a little dark-faced man named Koidé Yamato no Kami. A good deal was said about the coal mine at Iwanai on the west coast of Yezo, at which a commencement of working had recently been made under the superintendence of my friend Erasmus Gower. Admiral Keppel was already here in the yacht "Salamis," and on the 1st August we left again for Niigata, arriving there after a prosperous voyage of thirty-six hours.

From the sea the view of Niigata is very fine. In the background the mountains of Aidzu rise at some distance inland, stretching far away to right and left. In front lies a level plain, consisting mainly of rice fields, fringed with trees. The foreground is a sandy shore, rising into sandhills to the right of the river mouth, and at some distance to the west the prospect terminates in the lofty peaks of Yahiko yama. I landed immediately with Dr Wilson of the "Basilisk," and the sea being quite smooth we crossed the bar without difficulty. Inside the water is very deep, and some eighty junks were lying there at anchor. The town is situated a little way up the river, not quite close to the bank. We chose what seemed a convenient landing-place, and pushed ashore. Immediately a number of two-sworded officials made their appearance, and forming themselves into an escort, led the way to a Buddhist temple, the reception rooms of which had been prepared for the use of foreigners.

After we had waited for a few minutes the governor came in; he proved to be Shiraishi Shimôsa no Kami, an old acquaintance of mine when he held a similar post at Yokohama in 1864 and 1865. In those days we used often to have serious disputes about the claims of British subjects against defaulting Japanese merchants and questions of customs' duties, but I found him now in quite a different mood. He was very polite and cheery, and alluded with regret to the ridiculous arguments which in former days under a different régime he had been obliged to maintain against me. Now that the foreign ministers had visited the Tycoon at Ozaka all was to be changed, and our intercourse was to be really friendly. He had himself received from Kiôto a copy of instructions to that effect. After some further talk about the possibility of Niigata being made an open port, I arranged for him to call on Sir Harry on the following morning on board the "Basilisk," bringing all the maps in his possession, and took my leave.

On our way back to the ship we stopped at a new hotel, where we dined in Japanese fashion, and made some purchases of the curious lacquered articles called *mokusa-nuri*, which are manufactured in Aidzu, and China grass cloth woven in the villages further inland. This was not to be had in the shops, but was hawked about the town by people from the country. Here for the first time I saw the frozen snow, which in those days was the Japanese substitute for ice, and we found it a great luxury at that season of the year. Niigata was laid out in the form of the truncated segment of a circle, and intersected by canals, the banks of which were lined with willow trees, suggesting a Dutch model. The canals, however, were narrow and dirty, and better deserving perhaps the name of ditches. At this moment the feast of *Tanabata* was at hand, and the streets were crowded with little boys carrying paper lanterns of all sizes and colours, many of them adorned with clever sketches in colour representing Japanese historical traditions and popular customs.

On the following day the promised interview came off on board, and we returned the governor's visit in the afternoon at his official residence. He had hastily had some benchs constructed, which were covered with red cloth, the best substitute procurable for leather-bottom ehairs.

Old Shiraishi renewed acquaintance with me some twelve years later at Tôkiô, and used to give me lessons in the interpretation of the *utai* plays; his son became my librarian, and died in my house.

After a two hours' talk we started off to inspect an island in the river which it was proposed should be converted to the uses of a foreign settlement. Sir Harry, who was of an active inquisitive temperament, here signalized himself in the eyes of the natives by scrambling up to the top of a large shed, under which a junk was in course of construction, to get a view of the surrounding country, much to the horror of Mitford and myself, who were so orientalized by this time in our notions that we longed to see our chief conduct himself with the impassive dignity of a Japanese gentleman. This exploit being over, he dragged us all, including Hewett, about the town till half-past six, not to the improvement of the tempers of that gallant officer or of his boat's crew, who thus lost their dinner. I remained behind with Noguchi, dined again in

Japanese fashion, and spent the night on shore, in the enjoyment of a few hours' perfect freedom. In fact, I did not return to the ship till the following afternoon, and then had some difficulty in getting off, as there was a heavy swell on the bar, though outside there was neither wind nor rough sea.

From Niigata we crossed over to the island of Sado, the site of gold mines that have for a long period been famous. The Japanese proverb is that the "soil of Sado is the most effective of love-phil-tres." We had been told by the governor of Niigata that there was a good port here, where foreign vessels could lie, when the bar at the mouth of the Shinano River was too rough to cross owing to the northwest winds that prevail during the winter.

A letter had been sent off from Niigata on the previous day to announce the visit of the British Minister, and as soon as we let go our anchor some of the local officials came off to call. The mines however lay at Aikawa on the other side of the island, where the governor resided. He had sent over his own *kago* for Sir Harry to perform the journey in, but the chief did not relish either the idea of locomotion after this fashion, nor yet of walking across the island and of passing the night on the floor of a Japanese house in native quilts, and with nothing better than rice and fish to eat. So he decided to send me across in his stead, and proceeded round to Aikawa in the "Basilisk." This arrangement suited me down to the ground. It was much jollier to travel by one's self than to play second fiddle to one's chief always. The distance was about sixteen miles to Aikawa, and the officials made me extremely comfortable for the night.

Next day Sir Harry and a large party, including some of the officers of the "Serpent," Commander Bullock and W. G. Aston our interpreter, landed at Sawané, where I went to meet them, and we walked over the hills to the village near the mines, where I had put up. On his arrival at the house where I had lodged, which in fact had been prepared for his reception, one of those scenes occurred which were not infrequent in those days, when the Japanese tried to treat foreigners with indignity, and it became necessary to resent their impertinence. At the door he was met by one of two vice-governors, who ushered him into a side room. where the idea was that he should do "ante-chamber" till the governor deigned to receive him. But Sir Harry was equal to the occasion, and promptly turning round without saying a word, walked out of the house. I overtook him at the gate, and having found out what was the matter, was on my way back to tell the alarmed officials that the governor must receive the British Minister at the door of the house, when I met the two vice-governors hurrying after us with some ridiculous excuse. So we turned back, walking with immense dignity so as to give him time, and by the time we arrived back again the old fellow made his appearance beaming with smiles, as if nothing had happened. He was at once forgiven, and led the way into a large room where a long row of chairs extended down one side for ourselves, faced by three others for himself and the vice-governors.

We speedily became great friends and drank a quantity of *saké* together, Sir Harry and the governor vying with each other in the manufacture of the most high-flown compliments. After this the whole party adjourned to visit the gold mines, which were then, whatever they may be now, low-roofed burrows half full of water, and those who ventured in returned to the outer air again looking more like half-drowned rabbits than human Englishmen. I had never been able to see much pleasure in this sort of subterranean excursion, and carefully stayed outside. We got on board that night, and weighed anchor in order to proceed to Nanao in Noto. There a fine harbour was said to exist, which we thought could perhaps be substituted for Niigata.

Early on the morning of the 7th August we came in sight of the lofty mountains of Etchiû, which centre round the volcanic peak of Tatéyama, nearly 10,000 feet high, and at eleven o'clock reached the southern entrance of the harbour, which is formed by a considerable island lying opposite to a bay. The "Serpent" led the way, in discharge of the functions appertaining to her as a surveying ship, but we had to take great care on account of the numerous patches of shoal water, and did not come to an anchor in front of the town till half-past twelve. Nanao, or Tokoro no kuchi, at that time containing from 8,000 to 9,000 inhabitants, was rising into importance as a port for the few steamers belonging to the *daimiô* of Kaga, and was administered by a *machi bugiô* or prefect named Abé Junjirô. He was a young man who had been to Nagasaki and knew a little English, both of which facts in those days gave him a title to be considered travelled and learned, but he had no authority to speak on behalf of his prince. We therefore waited until the arrival of some more representative officials named Sano and Satomi, who were expected from Kanazawa, the capital of this daimiate. They turned up on board the "Basilisk" on the 9th August, and sat talking, or rather being talked to, by Sir Harry for five mortal hours. The chief topic was the question of the suit-ability of Nanao as a substitute for Niigata. What the Kaga people feared was that this would lead to its being taken away from them by the Tycoon's government, as in former times had happened in the case of Nagasaki and Niigata. But they did not venture to state this openly, and alleged therefore various other excuses, such as that the inhabitants were not accustomed to see foreigners, that the majority would object on account of the general rise in prices which would follow on the exportation of produce, and the *daimiô*, however willing to see the place opened to foreign trade, must of course act in harmony with the wishes of the people.

Sir Harry then gave up pressing the point directly, enlarged on the inconveniences of the anchorage at Niigata, the need of a port of refuge, and the "fact" that none existed nearer than Nanao. He said nothing of our having inspected Ebisu Minato in Sado with the view of using it as an alternative anchorage to Niigata. Would the *daimiô* object to foreign vessels anchoring at Nanao when the weather was bad at the bar of Niigata. The reply was that for the sake of humanity and of our friendly relations he would be unable to refuse this. Well then, as ships could not afford to lie a long time at Nanao doing nothing, would there be any objection to their cargoes being landed and stored till they could be transported to Niigata. No, probably not, in the interests of humanity. Who then, asked Sir Harry, should undertake the construction of the necessary warehouses? The reply was that either foreigners or the Kaga administration could do this as seemed most convenient. Well then, supposing that the people of Nanao should wish to buy any of the goods so stored by foreigners, would it not be a hard thing to prevent the sale? They said perhaps it might be, but to give such permission would lead to converting Nanao into a foreign trading port; nevertheless, if all the articles required were ordered beforehand, and not selected from those stored with a view to their transportation to Niigata, there could be no objection. But in actual fact, to speak frankly, they thought they could undertake the regulation of the port and the storage of goods without the assistance of the Tycoon's government. The territory of Nanao had belonged to the Maeda clan from very early times; it was the only good port in the three provinces of Kaga, Etchiû and Noto, and could ill be spared. They would dislike to share the local administration with the government, nor could they give it up to them altogether.

Sir Harry expressed his concurrence in these views, and then proceeded to talk about the means of transport for himself and his party overland to Ozaka. This subject had been discussed in the legation before our departure from Yedo, though when the governor of Niigata had asked Sir Harry whether it was not his intention to return by land from Nanao, our very diplomatic chief had replied that such an idea had never entered his head. They received his suggestion with no marks of cordiality, and drew on themselves a severe rebuke for their want of friendship towards foreigners, so different to the feelings displayed by certain other clans. This plain speaking completely spoiled their temper. They became very sulky and silent, and alleging hunger, probably with much truth, took their departure.

As soon as they had left the ship Sir Harry made up his mind to send Mitford and myself overland to Ozaka, while he went round by way of Nagasaki in the "Basilisk." It was, of course, evident that we could travel through the country in a much less formal style than would be necessary for him, and on our part of course we were only too delighted to get the opportunity of seeing a part of the interior where foreigners had never been before. I was therefore sent on shore to get hold of the prefect. Bullock was ordered to remain behind with the "Serpent" to make a complete survey of the bay. The Admiral, who had arrived from Niigata the day before us, got up steam in the "Salamis," and was off at half-past three, the "Basilisk" following a couple of house later.

The chief, who liked to keep us by him till the last moment, took us as far as the entrance of the harbour, where we put our traps into a boat belonging to the "Serpent." But just as we were pulling away, the "Basilisk" got ashore in a shallow place, and they signalled to us to return to her. Eventually we were released from dancing attendance on him, and reached the shore at eight o'clock in the evening.

We proeeeded to a house where I had more than once passed the night, and shortly received a visit from Sano and Abé, who were to make all the arrangements for our journey. Thither came also two officials of the Yedo Foreign Department, who had come from Yokohama with Sir Harry, and whom he had left behind with injunctions to facilitate the survey of the harbour by Bullock. But as soon as they heard that we were going overland, they conceived the plan of offering that one of them should accompany us, to spy upon our movements. They alleged that although everything might go well with us in the territories of the *daimiô* of Kaga, we should meet with difficulties further on. We should be unable to procure baggage and palanquin coolies; we might be attacked and killed. They had instructions in fact to accompany us wherever we went on shore, and that it was a law of Japan that foreigners must not travel without foreign department officials to look after them. To this I replied with equal weight that they were bound to respect the injunctions laid on them by Sir Harry, to whom they had been lent by the Tycoon's Council. He had told them to remain at Nanao for a specific purpose, while we had positive orders from our chief not to take them. We felt assured that the *daimiôs* of Kaga and Echizen, which was the territory that lay immediately beyond, would do everything to smooth our way; and as regarded the rest of the line of road, they might write to the Tycoon's people at Kiôto to send down the necessary instructions, and even take on themselves the responsibility of transmitting the orders direct to the authorities of the towns we should have to pass through.

As for the law they mentioned, I felt convinced that it had no existence. At best there was only a custom to that effect, which we could decline to abide by at our option. These considerations proved to them that argument would not help them, so they tried to work upon my feelings by representing that they would get into hot water with their superiors in Yedo if they suffered us to depart alone. But this also failed. Finally they washed their hands of the business, and begged to be excused from all responsibility for any difficulties we might encounter. This request was most readily granted, and they retired with a secret intention of getting Bullock to dispense with their services, while we betook ourselves to our beds with the consciousness of a victory achieved.

CHAPTER XX

Nanao to Ozaka Overland

Next morning Sano and Abé presented themselves with the welcome news that everything was ready for our journey, and made many apologies for the inconveniences we should have to put up with. They had provided a handsome palanquin for each of us, and ordinary ones for Noguchi and Mitford's Chinese servant, the philosophic Lin-fu. A guard was furnished of twenty two-sworded men carrying long staves, under the command of an officer named Tominaga. We got away at half-past eight. Looking out to sea, we perceived that the "Basilisk" had departed, and that the "Serpent" was lying peacefully at anchor. The foreign department officials did not show up, and it was to be concluded that they had made up their minds to submit. So we were perfectly free, away from our chief, from Tycoon's officials, from any other Europeans, embarked on an adventure in a totally unknown part of the country, which might end anyhow for aught we cared, but at any rate was of an altogether novel character.

As soon as we were clear of the town we got out and walked. It was a piping hot day. Each man of the twenty who formed the escort as he went along fanned himself with one hand, and wiped the perspiration from his brow with a towel carried in the other. It soon became evident that we were to be treated with great distinction, for we had not travelled more than an hour and a half before we were invited to rest and refresh ourselves with delicious water melons and tea; nectarines were also offered, but of such fearful unripeness that we dared not make their close acquaintance. An hour further we had again to rest. Every one was excessively polite; the peasants whom we met were made to crouch down and take off their hats. This was much more than could have been expected after the scolding Sir Harry had given to Sano and his colleagues on the previous day. The road lay up a gradually narrowing valley, cultivated principally with rape and hemp. At a quarter past one we stopped for lunch at a clean inn where they gave us a capital meal. After a nap we resumed our way at three o'clock down another valley, stopped to rest at half-past four, and reached our night quarters at half-past six, having accomplished eighteen miles. This was the village of Shiwo, prettily situated on the banks of a tiny stream, and close to the mouth of a valley, the view up which into the hills growing ever higher and higher was one of the charming prospects in which Japan abounds. After the hot bath, they served an excellent dinner with many polite apologies for its badness.

The next day brought us some sixteen miles further to Tsubata, where we joined the high road which traverses the dominions of the *daimiô* from one end to the other at no great distance from the coast. Here our escort left us, and a new set of men took their place. We were now passing through a more populous part of the country, and were objects of intense curiosity to the inhabitants. At Morimoto the front rooms of the houses on both sides of the street were filled with spectators sitting in rows three or four deep or on mats placed at the side of the roadway.

Shortly after leaving this place we caught a glimpse of the white castle walls of Kanazawa peeping through the pine trees. As soon as we came in sight of the town itself we got into our palanquins, and were carried to one of the first houses, where we met Satomi and another official named Tsunékawa. Crowds of spectators had assembled, and some of them were so eager to gratify their curiosity that they even stood in a muddy lotus pond which commanded a view of the back of the house where we were. Here delicious melons and apples were served with frozen snow from the mountains behind the town. Gold paper screens lined the walls, there were tables piled high with fruit and cakes, and in the recess behind the seat of honour a beautiful writing box of the finest gold lacquer, in case we wished to sit down and write letters. A most unnecessary piece of ceremonial preparation, one would say.

The officials asked us to proceed from here on foot in order that the people might see us better, but we preferred making use of our palanquins, as we had on our travelling garments, and were somewhat dusty and way-worn. The streets were thickly lined with spectators of all ranks and ages, among whom were some very pretty girls. Another charming resting place had been prepared for us, into which they obliged us to turn aside, although we had previously expressed our wish to go on straight to the inn. Continuing thence along the street, thickly filled with inquisitive but perfectly orderly townspeople, we crossed a bridge, and after turning a few times to right and left, at last reached our inn, rather tired with all the fuss and ceremony.

At the porch we were welcomed by Satomi, who had hurried on ahead to superintend our reception. He conducted us through several rooms into an inner room of great size, spread with a huge velvet-pile carpet and furnished with Chinese tables and scarlet-lacquered chairs such as the high priests of Buddhist temples occupy on grand ceremonial occasions. The host immediately presented himself, bowing his head to the floor as if he were saluting a pair of kings. Each servant who brought in the tobacco trays or tea bowed low to the ground, then advanced holding the article high in both hands, deposited it on the table, and then retiring backwards to the edge of carpet, knocked his head on the floor again before withdrawing. We were conducted in turn to the bath with great ceremony, and then put on our best clothes (which were neither new nor good) to receive visitors. The first to call was a special messenger from the *daimiô*, to express a hope that we had not suffered from the heat, and rejoicing at our fortunate arrival. Mitford replied with great dignity that we had not felt the heat. We were deeply grateful for the hospitality and kindness shown to us, and would like to call on the *daimiô* to thank him in person.

"My master," said the messenger, "is unfortunately indisposed, otherwise he would have been delighted to make your acquaintance." Mitford expressed a hope that he would soon recover. The real truth I imagine to have been that an interview between a *daimiô* and two foreigners would have involved far too important and complicated decisions on questions of etiquette for it to be lightly contemplated. The messenger added that he had been commanded by his master to offer us a small entertainment, and to accompany us in partaking of it. Mitford rose to even greater heights of flowery speech than before, and invented a message from Sir Harry Parkes (which if the chief did not actually charge us with, the omission could only be attributed to inadvertence), expressing his desire to swear eternal friendship with the *daimiô* and people of Kaga, which gave very great satisfaction to the messenger and everyone else present. Doctors were also introduced, whom the prince had deputed to attend on us in case we felt any ill-effects from the heat.

To this exchange of compliments succeeded a feast resembling in character what has already been described but far surpassing it in magnificence and the number of courses. Observing that our Japanese entertainers were not comfortable on their chairs, we proposed to banish the furniture and squat on the floor after the manner of the country, and thus facilitate the passing of the *saké* cup. After a considerable time had been passed in general conversation, and everyone's head was more or less heated, we introduced political topics, which were discussed very confidentially in the presence of a crowd of people.

The structure of a Japanese house is such that no secrets can be whispered; there is always some one listening behind a paper partition or on the other side of a screen, and if you wish to hatch a plot, your best way is to transfer your deliberations to the middle of the garden, where you can keep off eavesdroppers. However, as we could not do that on the present occasion, it seemed better to take all who chose it into our confidence. The gist of the conversation amounted to this — that the Kaga people wished to trade with foreigners, but did not wish avowedly to make an open port of Nanao, because the Tycoon's government would then try to deprive them of it; but they would agree to its being an anchorage for foreign vessels, ancillary to Niigata, and to goods being landed there, in which case everything else would naturally follow. If the Tycoon's government were to inquire what view they took of the question, they would reply ambiguously. Our answer was that of course we desired to act in harmony with the wishes of the *daimiô*, and would do nothing that could possibly be prejudicial to his interests. This proved very satisfactory to our entertainers, who declared the warm feelings of friendship for us which animated them, and a stratagem, the details of which I do not recollect, was agreed upon for keeping up secret and confidential communications with them after our return to Yedo. Both sides bound themselves to secrecy, and the party broke up.

The bedding, which was of the most magnificent description, was then brought in, piles of soft, quilted mattresses covered with silk or crape, and stuffed with silk wool, and a large net of silk gauze was hung up to keep off the mosquitoes. Then a freshly-infused pot of green tea, with teacups, on a small tray, and the necessary apparatus for smoking, were gently slid under the bottom of the mosquito curtain, and the people of the house wished us a good night's rest. In the morning the very first thing, before we were awake, the same elements of a comfortable existence were provided in the same unobtrusive manner.

The forenoon was spent in choosing lacquer and porcelain. On the previous evening an arrangement had been made for our visiting the neighbouring hills, but some hitch had occurred, and we were now asked to accept instead an excursion to Kanaiwa, the port of Kanazawa. It lay at a distance of about five miles, so we started on horseback about three o'clock. Our steeds were rather shabby-looking ponies, unshod, with saddles in the European fashion covered with thick black paper instead of leather, and painfully stiff bridles of badly tanned leather. Noguchi was mounted on a pony splendidly caparisoned in the native style, and the philosophic Lin-fu, who could not ride, was put into a palanquin. Though we had such a very short way to ride, it was supposed that delicately nurtured persons like ourselves would feel the fatigue, and three resting places had been prepared, two on the road and one at Kanaiwa itself. The so-called port proved to be an open roadstead at the mouth of an insignificant stream, quite useless except in perfectly calm weather.

At dinner that evening we had some further talk with a couple of officials. They had come to the conclusion, after thinking over the conversation of the previous evening, that it would be their wisest course to admit to the Tycoon's government the probability of a certain amount of trade taking place at Nanao. In that way no danger would arise of their getting into trouble for what would otherwise be smuggling. We approved of this proposal, and suggested their sending to Yedo some one authorized to treat with the government and the foreign representatives. In the course of conversation on the domestic politics of the country, they said that in their opinion the Tycoon's government ought to be supported, and not done away with altogether, as the Satsuma and Chôshiû people, with other clans, were believed to be advocating. But at the same time limits ought to be placed on its authority. They had read my pamphlet, and entirely approved of the suggestions it contained. After that, all one could say was that we entirely concurred in the views of the Kaga clan. As a matter of fact, these people were rather too remote from the main centre of political thought to be cognisant of or sympathise with the aspirations of the southern and western clans. They lay in an isolated position on the northern coast, in a part of the country that had always been looked upon somewhat as the home of ignorance and want of culture. They cared only for themselves. The lands held by the *daimiô* of Kaga were assessed at a much greater annual value than the fief of any other prince, which gave the clansmen an importance in the eyes of the rest of the world with which they were thoroughly satisfied; an alteration in the political organization of the country could hardly benefit them, and they were at bottom disposed to be contented with the *status quo*.

The British Legation, on the contrary, were determined that so far as their influence went, the Mikado should be restored to the headship of the nation, so that our treaties might receive a sanction that no one would venture to dispute, and for this purpose it was necessary that the constitution of the Tycoon's government should be modified in such a manner as to admit the principal *daimiôs* (or clans rather) to a share in the distribution of power.

Our hosts would have been contented to keep us longer, but we were due at Ozaka at a fixed date, and could not stay with them. We resumed our journey, therefore, on the morning of August 14. The landlord was very urgent with us that we should call in passing at a shop for patent medicines kept by a relation, to lay in a stock of a preparation called "purple snow" (*shi-setsu*), composed chiefly of nitre and perfumed with musk, and believed to be a remedy for most of the ills to which flesh is heir. The streets were again crowded with eager spectators. When just clear of the town we were forced to alight from our *kagos* for a parting feast at a restaurant on a height commanding a picturesque view of the castle, which planted plentifully with trees presented a park-like aspect very unlike the grim fortresses which in Europe usually go by the name. Here we spent an hour eating fish and drinking *saké*, and vowing eternal friendship with the Kaga clansmen, with whom previous to this visit we had had no intercourse whatever.

We lunched that day at Mattô, where I had a long talk with the mayor upon things in general, in the presence of a vast and attentive crowd, and reached Komatsu in the evening, having accomplished twenty miles. This was very fair going, considering the numerous delays and stoppages for refreshment. The next day we passed the boundary line between the territories of Kanazawa and Daishôji, where the escort was changed. At the latter town we found the streets entirely cleared, and crowds of people quietly sitting in the front rooms of the houses, among them many daughters of the best families in holiday garb, with wreaths of silver flowers on their heads, their faces nicely powdered with white lead, and their lips stained with the safflower dye which imparts such a curious metallic lustre to the skin. Here we took a formal farewell of Okada and Shimbô, two Kaga gentlemen who bad accompanied us during the previous days. Mitford's Chinese servant came in for a share in the general leave-taking, and philosophically remarked that he did not understand Japanese etiquette, which appears to consist chiefly in the performance of the *ko-t'ou*.

About three miles further we finally quitted the domains of the Maeda family, and passed into the territory of Echizen. There was no guard to meet us, only a couple of policemen, and it was proposed that we should retrace our steps to a tea-house half a mile back, to wait till an escort could be procured. To this we objected, saying that we were willing to go on without a guard. The *rusui* or head bailiff of the *daimiô* of Daishôji said that it would not be correct for his men to undertake our protection beyond the limits. Finally a compromise was effected. Okada and Shimbô, who in spite of the formal parting that had taken place at Daishôji, were still of the party, borrowed ten men from the bailiff on the distinct understanding that they were not any longer a guard, and walked on with us. Shortly afterwards we met an Echizen official of low rank (he was a *metsuké* or assistant clerk) , and our Kaga friends took their final leave of us, not without expressing the opinion that the Echizen people showed very little courtesy in not deputing some one of more exalted rank to offer us a welcome. But the fact was we were not welcome at all, as we speedily found, for although every possible pains had been taken to provide us with good food and quarters, the whole Echizen clan held aloof from us. For instance at Kanadzu, where we passed the night, the whole town was illuminated with coloured lanterns, and the spectators who crowded the main street went down on their knees in the usual respectful manner.

Very beautiful guest rooms had been prepared for us at a monastery, chairs and tables had been provided, and a couple of good little boys, of preternaturally solemn demeanour, sat on the floor behind us to fan away the mosquitoes. The superior civilization and resources of the country, as compared with Kaga, were exhibited by the production of beer and champagne. Next day we reached Fukui, the capital of the province, a town of about 40,000 inhabitants. Here again the streets had been cleared; spectators in their best were seated in rows in the shops, and looked just as if they had paid for their places, like the people who go to see the Queen open Parliament. I never saw so many pretty girls together anywhere. White brooms and buckets of water stood before each house, as a sign that the road had been swept clean and the dust laid. We were conducted to the monastery of the Hongwanji sect, a new and handsome building, where a large room had been prepared for us, and hung with silk crape curtains dyed with the Echizen crest. In the recess stood a beautiful vase containing a huge bouquet of lotus flowers, standing quite six feet high. The table was loaded with piles of fruit and cakes, and the usual Japanese luncheon was served, with champagne. No one approached us, with the exception of a young Japanese who had been in the service of a foreigner at Nagasaki and spoke a little English; but numbers of officials, some of high rank, collected in the passages to stare at us. We took no notice of them, adopting the perfectly cold and impassive manner of Orientals on their dignity. This was bad, but worse came behind.

Although on our quitting Fukui, they sent men before us to sweep the road ahead, our guards were rude, and chaffed about us among themselves. At Fuchiû, the town where we stopped for the night, a noisy crowd pursued us from the entrance of the town to our lodging, running along the other side of the stream which lay along the middle of the street. Arrived at the inn, we found the dais room shut up, and the matted floors spread with *shibu-kami*, a sort of thick, tough paper in sheets, which is laid down when any particularly dirty household business is to take place. It is the correlative of the dust sheets used in England to cover up furniture when a weekly cleaning takes place. We were, of course, indignant, but I think these, to us, offensive precautions had been taken in the belief that we were ignorant of Japanese manners and customs, and would walk in with our shoes on.

The day after this we crossed the boundary on the top of a hill called the Tochinoki Tôgé (Horse-Chestnut Pass), where we said good-bye to the rude Echizen escort, and were taken charge of by men belonging to Ii Kamon no Kami, the *daimiô* of Hikoné. A very moderate bill was presented to us for our board, lodging and coolie hire, which we paid, and we offered payment also for the extras in the shape of beer, champagne and fish, but could not induce the officials to accept it.

It is not very easy to explain why the Echizen people showed such an utter want of cordiality, but I think it may perhaps be attributable to the difficult position in which the clan then stood. Its head was closely allied to the Tycoon's family, being in fact descended from one of the sons of Iyéyasu, the founder of the Tycoonate. Although perfectly well aware of the difficulties in which the Tycoon was involved, he was not prepared to side with the Satsuma and Chôshiû party, which aimed at the restoration of the Mikado, and was probably acquainted with the policy of the British Legation, as supposed to be set forth in my pamphlet. Intimacy with foreigners had never until quite lately been a part of the government programme, and the Echizen people very likely thought it wiser to hold entirely aloof from us, in spite of the recent change of attitude on the part of the Tycoon, especially as the south-western *daimiôs* had never openly adhered to the policy of friendship with foreigners. The "expulsion of the barbarians" was still their ostensible party cry. So that on the whole I incline to the opinion that extreme caution was the keynote to the want of cordiality displayed by the Echizen folk.

We stopped that night at a little village among the hills called Naka-no-kawachi, where we could get nothing to eat but rice and tea. In ordinary years there are no mosquitoes here, owing to its elevation, and we had therefore considerable trouble in procuring mosquito curtains. The general aspect of the country reminded me closely of Scawfell Pass in Cumberland. At the further foot of the hills we passed one of those barriers, curious relics of a past full of suspicion, where no woman was allowed to pass, and where every man had to exhibit a pessport. At Nagahama we met an official of the Tycoon's government named Tsukahara Kwanjirô (brother of Tsukahara Tajima no Kami), with eighteen of the foreign guard, who henceforward charged themselves with our protection. Sir Harry Parkes had passed through here in May last in returning from his visit to Tsuruga, and we found the people disposed to be familiar and careless of our comfort. We felt that we were now little better than prisoners; farewell all jollity and all politeness on the part of the inhabitants. We hastened on as rapidly as possible, being now as anxious to get over the rest of our journey as we had in the beginning been disposed to loiter among a friendly population.

At Takamiya, where we lunched. we found the dais room closed against us, but I took the innkeeper and his servants roundly to task, and made them open it. After this, they recognized that we understood Japanese etiquette, and for their previous rudeness substituted perfect courtesy. As we were now about to quit the territory of Ii Kamon no Kami, we offered to settle our bill for lodging and coolie hire, but the official in charge refused to accept payment, alleging that he had received reiterated orders not to take anything from us. So we contented ourselves with addressing to him a letter of acknowledgement, and told him we would thank the *daimiô's* people on our return to Yedo. The local escort left us at Nakajiku, the boundary, and we were consigned to the care of the foreign guard, who concerned themselves very little on our behalf. The consequence of this was that the people crowded in upon us at every village, and were extremely rude in their behaviour. On our arrival at Musa I administered a quiet blowing-up to the commander of the guard, who promised that things should be better arranged for the morrow.

Next day we reached Kusatsu, where, to our surprise, we fell in with a couple more Tycoon's officials, whom I knew very well, Takabataké Gorô and a young fellow named Koméda Keijirô, the latter of whom spoke English remarkably well. They told us that they had come overland from Yedo with Hirayama Dzusho no Kami, one of the Tycoon's second council, and had been dropped here by him to look after us. He had charged them to say to us that the temple of Ishiyama, just below the Seta Bridge, which had been closed to Sir Harry in May, would be shown to us, and was well worthy of a visit. This temple in fact lay on the route which Tsukahara had already persuaded us to adopt. We were to take boat at Kusatsu, descend the river which flows out of the Biwa Lake as far as the rapids, then walk for about a couple of leagues (five miles), and take boat again to Fushimi. This, he said, was a much shorter and pleasanter route than that which Wirgman and I had taken in May. We therefore jumped at the offer made on the part of Hirayama, whom we voted a capital fellow, and some amicable conversation followed on Japanese politics, in which they tried to persuade us that the positions taken up by my pamphlet were all wrong, but without success.

After they left, Noguchi came to me and said that the road over the hills to Uji, instead of being only ten or twelve miles, as had been represented to us, was in reality much nearer five-and-twenty, so that we could not possibly get there by mid-day. A misgiving immediately arose in my mind that there was something concealed behind all this solicitude about our seeing temples. Probably the Tycoon's officials wanted to get us away from Otsu, which lay on the direct route, and the vicinity of Kiôto, in order to prevent trouble with the anti-Tycoon party, such as had occurred in May when Sir Harry passed through there. I therefore despatched Noguchi to probe Tsukahara, and sent for the posting officer to inquire about the distances. What he told me only confirmed my suspicions, which I then mentioned to Mitford. We therefore resolved to go by Otsu and to run all risks. We had invited Takabataké and the other man to dinner. Just before our guests arrived Noguchi returned, and I imparted my suspicions to him. He thought I was wrong. As soon as they came in, I announced to Takabataké our intention of taking the usual route. He was greatly disconcerted, declared it would be very inconvenient, nay impossible. I replied

that we were indifferent to temples and scenery, but extremely
fond of saving time in travelling; and as the road by Otsu was the
shorter, we would take it. Seeing that we were very firm in our
resolve, he retired from the room, and got hold of Noguchi, whom
he begged to use his influence. Noguchi thereupon called me
outside for a private conversation, and urged me to adhere to the
original arrangement. I replied that it was useless; we wanted to go
by the shorter route, and if altering the arrangements as to boats,
etc., cost money, we were willing to pay it. I returned to the dining-room, and my answer was communicated to Takabataké, who
thereupon called out Koméda. Koméda came back, and begged
me in turn to come out; as soon as we were alone, he said that he
wished to have a friendly talk, and confessed that the whole thing
was a plant. I said that we knew it before, and had felt convinced
that Tsukahara had been sent down from Kiôto by the Tycoon's
prime minister (Itakura Iga no Kami) to hoodwink us. If they had
told us the truth in the beginning, we would have complied with
their wishes; but that now it was too late to talk to us of going so
far out of our way merely to oblige them. We then returned to the
dining-room again, and tried to proceed with our meal.

The three Japanese were very crestfallen, and became still more
so when Mitford suddenly turned to Koméda and said to him in
English that if the private secretary (*ometsuké*) who had been sent
down from Kiôto on this particular business would address to hin
a letter stating explicitly the reasons why they wished us to change
our route, we would fall in with their wishes; otherwise we would
go by Otsu, even if the guard should refuse to accompany us. After
a little demur, they accepted his offer, as the easiest alternative,
and Takabataké went off to prepare the letter. We had great difficulty in obtaining a document to our minds. Takabataké produced
three drafts, one after the other, which had to be rejected, because
it was alleged in them that we were travelling without the permission of the government, and the phraseology was so confused that
it became impossible to make head or tail of it. At three o'clock
in the morning they at last brought the fair copy of what we had

insisted on being put down in black and white, namely that great complications had arisen at Kiôto in the previous May on account of Sir Harry's passing through Otsu, which was only six miles from the Mikado's capital, and begging Mitford as a favour to go by way of Uji. Great victory for us and corresponding defeat for the Japanese officials.

I had very little sleep that night, for we were on the move by a quarter to seven. We went in palanquins as far as the bridge of Séta, and embarking in a boat, proceeded down the river to Ishiyama-dera. As soon as we were sighted by the priests in charge, they ran to shut the gates in our face. So much for Hirayama's promise of admission. It was a very hot day. We left the river to ascend and descend a series of little hills for four miles, and then came out by the river again. Here we got a scanty meal of rice and tea, all that was procurable in such an out-of-the-way spot. Then along the path for a mile or so by the river, which roared over its rocky bed between steep schistose hills, and then climbed a very stiff ascent, trying in the extreme under the burning August sun. At every peasant's hut they told us that it was still four miles to Uji. Frequently we had to stop and wash out our mouths by some scanty stream trickling from the rock. But at last we reached the summit, and gained a magnificent view of the great plain below, in the centre of which lies the mysterious and jealously guarded Kiôto, like a Japanese Mecca, in which it was death for the heathen foreigner to set his foot. To the left lay Fushimi, with its network of canals and rivers, far away in front the sacred top of Atagoyama. At four o'clock we got to Uji, hot and tired, having trudged our weary way almost unceasingly since noon. We rested for a couple of hours at a charming tea-house on the bank of the river close to the broken bridge. At six we embarked in a comfortable houseboat, and drifted rapidly down stream to Fushimi, where we got a bath and dinner at the official hotel. Noguchi afterwards told me that he had overheard some men there talking about the advisability of murdering us. However, they lacked the courage to carry out their idea, and we got away safely at nine in a large boat. It was too hot to sleep inside, so I lay all night on the gangway which ran along the gunwale, overhanging the water.

Early in the morning we reached Ozaka, washed our faces in the stream, dressed, and betook ourselves to the temple we had occupied in the spring. Sir Harry turned up in the afternoon, with the news of the murder of two sailors of H.M.S. "Icarus" at Nagasaki, as they were lying in a drunken sleep on the roadway in a low quarter of the town. Before this new outrage the tale of our experiences paled altogether in interest.

CHAPTER XXI

Ozaka and Tokushima

The next few days were occupied almost exclusively with the question of what measures were to be adopted for the detection and punishment of the murderers of the "Icarus" sailors at Nagasaki. Sir Harry, as was very natural, took up the matter with great warmth, and used some extremely strong language to the principal minister of the Tycoon, a good-natured, yet not by any means weak, old gentleman named Itakura Iga no Kami. He seemed to be old, though probably not over five-and-forty. The rumour at Nagasaki had been that the perpetrators were Tosa men, and the suspicion was strengthened by the fact that a sailing vessel and a steamer belonging to Tosa, which were lying in the harbour, suddenly left before dawn, a few hours after the murder. It was suggested that the perpetrators had escaped in the sailing vessel, as she left an hour and a half before the steamer, and that they were transferred to the latter somewhere outside the harbour. As far as we could judge, the Tycoon's government seemed to entertain the same suspicions. The Tosa men had always had the reputation for being more savagely disposed than any other Japanese. The government promised to dismiss the two governors of Nagasaki, and to send a body of 500 men from Yedo to patrol the foreign settlement at Nagasaki to prevent anything of the kind recurring. Upon this Sir Harry accepted an invitation to see the Tycoon, who had come down from Kiôto to give an audience to the French Minister, M. Roches, about the recent arrest of some native Christians at Nagasaki. Sir Harry, Mitford and I went accordingly to the castle in palanquins, as the weather was very hot, and no good ponies could be procured. We were received in the private drawing-room (*shiro-in*). The Tycoon, who looked a little worn, had with him Itakura and Hirayama; the latter was a little old man of rather low origin with sharp cunning features, who had lately been promoted. We nicknamed him the fox, and he deserved it well.

After an hour's talk, on indifferent matters, we were joined by Admiral Keppel and his staff. This led to some conversation on naval affairs, but I came to the conclusion that His Highness took very little interest in the subject. After a while the Tycoon sent for Matsudaira Kansô, the ex-*daimiô* of Hizen, an oldish-looking man of forty-seven, and introduced him to Sir Harry and the Admiral. He had a sharp countenance, and spoke in a fitful, abrupt manner, constantly winking with both eyes. He had the reputation of being a time-server and a great intriguer, and certainly, up to the very moment of the revolution, which took place in 1868, he never allowed anyone to guess what side he would take. He sat next to the Tycoon on his left, and the only other mark of respect, other than that due to equals, which he employed in speaking was the word "kami," for "you." Sir Harry endeavoured to get an invitation out of him to visit his place at Saga, but he was too wary, and merely expressed the expectation that they might meet some day at Nagasaki; but that never came to pass. When the Tycoon was tired of talking we adjourned to the next room, where a Japanese luncheon was served, with cold *saké*; which was a sign that no one was expected to take more than enough.

Early that morning I had received a call from Saigô Kichinosuké, and here I insert a translation of a letter which he afterwards wrote to Okubo Ichizô giving an account of our conversation. The original was found many years afterwards among the papers of Iwakura Jijiû, and a copy was given to me in 1906, as I was passing through Tôkiô on my way home from Peking, by my old friend Matsugata Masayoshi.

Copy of letter addressed by Saigô Takamori to Okubo Toshimichi.

Yesterday morning at 6 I arrived at Ozaka, and on inquiring where was the lodging of the English, I learnt that it was at the temple where they were in the spring; so I at once sent to Satow to inquire at what time to-day it would be convenient for me to call. The answer was that I should come at 7 o'clock. I went at that hour, and found he had just woke, and I was shown upstairs. I said that hearing of the minister's arrival at Ozaka, I had been, as you know, sent as a special messenger to inquire after his health. The ordinary compliments having been offered, he said the mail to England was being despatched about ten o'clock, and that at half-past eleven the minister was going to the Castle. I said that I had no particular business, buthad only come to call in order to congratulate him on his arrival at Ozaka. As he must be very busy, I would not trouble him with a personal interview, and begged him to say so to the Minister. He replied that the Minister particularly wished to meet me, but as he was so much occupied he would ask to be excused that day. He said the Minister would remain two or three days at Ozaka, and particularly desired to meet me, and he thought he would be able to give me an interview in two or three days. He said he would sail from here on the 2nd of next month in order to return to Yokohama (or probably Yedo).

When I saw Satow, he said things were exactly as before and that there had been no change of any importance, and the position being just as before, it was entirely different from what Shibayama had suspected; therefore I told him that the Ozaka Commercial Co. has, as I said to you the other day, agreed with the French, and is planning to make great profits. [An obscure passage follows.]

I said I should like to try to discuss the settlement of Japanese affairs by the French, on which Satow replied that he would very much like to argue it. I told him the French said Japan must have a single concentrated government like all western countries, and the *daimiôs* must be deprived of their power. Above all it was desirable to destroy the two provinces of Chôshiû and Satsuma, and that it would be well to join in subduing them. I asked what he thought of this. Satow then answered that it might be seen from the two previous attempts at subjugation, that a government which had not been able to beat Chôshiû alone would certainly not be able to deprive all the *daimiôs* of their powers. I said: How could such weak people be helped. He replied that not a word could be said to that, and the argument was impossibie. If such an argument were publicly brought forward, there was no doubt that they would help the government to destroy the *daimiôs*. It was heard that the idea was that in two or three years' time money would be collected, machinery be provided, French assistance be invoked and war be begun. As the French would then send troops to give assistance, it would be dangerous unless an opposite great Power were got to assist. If a report were then spread that England would also send out troops to protect, it would be impossible for French auxiliary troops to be set in motion; he said that therefore it was necessary to come to a thorough agreement beforehand. In the first place the English idea was that the sovereign of Japan should wield the governing power, and under him the *daimiôs* should be placed, and so the establishment of the constitution (or national polity) would be similar to the system of all other countries. This was the first (word omitted here) thing of all. The sovereign of England had lately sent to the *Baku-fu* a letter addressed to the sovereign of Japan. This was a letter of condolence on hearing of the death of the late Emperor. This was to be delivered to the Emperor by the *Baku-fu*. It would be improper if no reply were made to it, but up to the present no reply had been received.

Although that was what they had declared with respect to the Emperor of Japan, at Kiôto H.M. did not take that view at all. It was maintained that the admission of aliens into the capital would be a defilement. As that sort of thing was undesirable, it would be necessary that a definite form of government vis-a-vis all countries carried on ordinary relations. If it was desired to consult with England, he would like to be informed, and as he was disposed to undertake the assistance asked for I replied that we would exert ourselves for the transformation of the Japanese government and we had no justification (?) vis-a-vis foreigners.

The French grabbed profit at Yokohama and entered into agreements for their own pleasure. England was a country based on commerce, and would strenuously oppose any attempt to hinder commerce, and was therefore extremely indignant.

The culprits who had killed two English sailors at Nagasaki were not yet known. We had heard it was rumoured to be the act of Nagasaki* men. He heard that Nagasaki was very badly spoken of. When Satow and others travelled overland from Echizen, Nagasaki men lay in wait for them at Fushimi. It was also said by many that they committed acts of violence at Kiôto, and gathered gamblers together. If it was Nagasaki men who had killed aliens at Nagasaki, it was to be much regretted as doing a great injury.

When they came to Echizen no one came to meet them. Though local governors came to meet them in the country, no one came to see them at the castle-town, but they were entertained hospitably with *saké* and *sakana*. Satow said he could not understand this. The above is a summary of the important points. Satow says he will come here to-morrow at ten o'clock, and I think there will be more conversation. I propose to stay two or three days longer, so please understand that. Satow's language about the *Baku-fu* is very insulting. I will tell you all in detail. Good-bye. 27th of 7th moon.

SAIGO KICHINOSUKE.
Okubo Ichizô sama.

---

* Substituted by Saigô for Tosa.

P.S. note by penman. — This copy of the letter contains obscurities, and some incorrect transcriptions.

Next day I went to see Saigô at the Satsuma agency, in order to learn from him how things were going on at Kiôto. He talked a good deal of a parliament of the whole nation, to be established as a substitute for the existing government of the Tycoon, which I found from my young friend Matsuné was a very general idea among the anti-Tycoon party. To me it seemed a mad idea. Saigô also revealed to me a plan conceived by the government for monopolizing all the trade of Ozaka and Hiôgo by placing it in the hands of a guild of twenty rich native merchants, which was no doubt copied from the old arrangement at Canton before the opium war of 1840.

This piece of news, when it was brought to him, inflamed the chief's wrath, who immediately got hold of the prime minister and insisted upon the scheme being abandoned. A new proclamation was issued, annulling the previous one establishing the guild, but as it was extorted by dint of great diplomatic pressure, I had very little belief in its being acted on. It was, and always has been, a Japanese idea to regulate commerce, both domestic and foreign, by means of the guilds, who pay for their monopoly, and make the most of it. Whatever may be the abstract merits of such a system, it is not altogether in accordance with western ideas, and we have never ceased to make war upon it whenever it crossed our path in eastern countries.

Another matter about which we had to speak very strongly was the wording of the Tycoon's reply to the Queen's letter, conveying the usual expressions of condolence on the death of the late Mikado. The ministers apologized very humbly for having made use of discourteous forms, and promised to take great care for the future. The style of official documents addressed to the British Minister was also a subject upon which we had never-ending disputes with the Japanese officials, and it was only after the revolution that I succeeded in getting these things done in proper form. Their object

was always by the use of particular forms and turns of phraseology
to convey to their own people the belief that the foreign representatives were the inferiors of the Tycoon's ministers; doubtless they
did not in their own country hold a rank at all approaching that of
the high functionaries they had to deal with, most of whom were
daimiôs, and it was a difficult matter, as it always has been in every
eastern country, to induce them to recognize the official position
of a diplomatist representing his sovereign.

I have said in an earlier chapter that one of my teachers at
Yokohama had been a retainer of the *daimiô* of Awa. During the
spring, when we were first at Ozaka, there had been some talk
about my going to pay the *daimiô* a visit at his capital, which lay
not far from that city, but owing to a misunderstanding it came
to nothing. On the present occasion the Awa people had sought
me out again, aud renewed the invitation, which I however persuaded them to transfer to Sir Harry and the Admiral. It had been
already agreed that the British Legation should proceed to the
province of Tosa in company with some special Commissioners
of the Tycoon, in order to discover, if possible, the murderers of
the two sailors belonging to H.M.S. "Icarus." Our wily old friend
Hirayama was selected, along with a couple of other officials, for
this business, and they wished to precede us by a few days in order
to make a preliminary inquiry. So when the projected visit to Awa
came to the ears of the ministers, they pressed Sir Harry to accept
it, as Tokushima lay in the direct route to Tosa, and also because
they believed that the *daimiô* was not a dangerous opponent, but
rather inclined to be a partisan of the Tycoon, if he took any side
at all. Sir Harry was pleased, because he liked these entertainments, and so the matter was settled to every one's satisfaction. I
took care to keep to myself the fact that the invitation had really
been intended for myself alone, the *daimiô* having heard about
me from my teacher, and being curious to see the writer of the
pamphlet on "English policy."

Sir Harry and Mitford went off in the "Basilisk" with Hewett,
the "Salamis" remaining behind to pick me up on the following

morning. She was to leave at eleven, so I had to pack up overnight, and start very early. I hurried off with the Legation writer Ono, leaving Noguchi in charge of the baggage, and as usual he was late. I waited some time, but still he delayed. I became impatient, and desperately started in a boat with only the writer. Just as we were passing the proposed site of the foreign settlelnent, Noguchi came alongside in a tiny skiff, without the baggage. Further down, near the mouth of the river, we changed into a larger boat, built to cross the bar, and got on board half-an-hour late. Two Awa officials had joined just before me, and to my great joy and relief the baggage boat came alongside a quarter of an hour afterwards. We weighed anchor precisely at noon, and steaming southward through the Yura strait got to the little harbour of Nei in Awa about six o'clock in the evening. The "Basilisk" was there already. Apparently no one awaited our arrival. Sir Harry therefore despatched me to Tokushima to find out what sort of reception he might expect. I got into a big native sailing boat with one of the Awa officials, while the other man hastened on ahead in another.

There was a fresh breeze, and we rushed along under the cliffs at a good pace until we found ourselves approaching the bar at the mouth of the river on which Tokushima is situated. It was already dark, and the breakers extended right across the entrance. The other boat, which had preceded me, now turned back, and as she passed the people on board shouted out that the passage was no longer safe. My pilot however disregarded the warning, and pushed boldly on. The passage was extremely narrow, between widely extended sandbanks on either side; the huge waves tossed about the boat, big as it was, like a child's toy. At last after some anxious minutes we got inside, and were now in comparatively smooth water, without having shipped a drop. A great deal of apparently unmeaning shouting and hallooing took place, and our boat was allowed to surge hither and thither, till we drifted back again to the sandbank, where we found the other Japanese; they had run their boat ashore in the most reckless way, narrowly escaping a drowning in the surf.

After mutual congratulations, we got into a houseboat and proceeded up the river to the landing-place, where I had to wait some time till a guard of soldiers could be brought down. This gave time for a crowd of spectators to collect, in spite of the advanced hour. At last the guard arrived; it consisted of cavalry, in long boots and conical hats, with white plumes of horsehair, commanded by a grizzled old warrior named Hachisuka Mimasaka, a descendant of the robber chieftain who founded the House of Awa, but a retainer for all that. They escorted me in solemn procession to a temple that had been prepared for our accommodation, by laying down red felt carpets and furnishing it with hastily constructed tables, chairs and bedsteads. It was evident that they had expected only a small party of three or four Europeans, but I explained to them that Sir Harry would not land without the Admiral, and neither of them could come on shore without the whole of his staff. So they had to make the best of it, and greatly extend their preparations before I would acknowledge myself satisfied. They had written up our official titles over the doors of the rooms intended for us, and mine had been rendered by "tongue-officer," a euphemism for interpreter; this I immediately had done away with, and my name substituted, for in Japan the office of interpreter at that time was looked upon as only fit for the lowest class of domestic servants, and no one of *samurai* rank would ever condescend to speak a foreign language. I had often to fight pretty hard with Japanese of rank in order to ensure being treated as something better than a valet or an orderly.

My good Awa friends, anxious to make me as happy as possible, had racked their brains in order to produce a dinner in European style, and a most dismal banquet it was; uneatable fishes in unsightly dishes, piles of unripe grapes and melons, heavy and tasteless sponge cakes, with coarse black-handled knives and forks to eat with. A wretched being, who had been to the United States as a sailor and had picked up a few words of low English, was put forward prominently to wait upon me, as if I were so ignorant of Japanese as to need an interpreter. It was explained that he was the only person in the clan who understood European manners and customs. I found him disgustingly familiar, and had to address a private remonstrance to one of the officials who had come down with me, who said that he was a privileged person "on account of his great learning." Nevertheless he administered a rebuke to the individual in question, who thereupon reverted to his native Japanese good manners.

I had entirely lost my appetite, owing to having been without food since the middle of the day. We proceeded to discuss various points of etiquette connected with our proposed visit to the *daimiô* at his castle. It was the first occasion on which foreigners of rank had been received within the walls of a native baron's fortress. It was finally decided that we should ride past the place where the notice to dismount stands, and get off our horses at the inner gate. The question of precedence at table was also decided. On one side were to sit the *daimiô*, his eldest son and a *karô* named Mori, Commander Suttie of the "Salamis," Major Crossman of the Royal Engineers, Lieutenant Stephenson (flag lieutenant); on the other Sir Harry Parkes, Admiral Sir Harry Keppel, Captain Hewett, Mitford and Mr Risk, the Admiral's secretary; I was to sit at the head of the table between Sir Harry and the *daimiô*. Separate and special individual presents were to be given to Sir Harry Parkes, to the Admiral and to myself, and a general present to all the others, to be divided among them as they liked. After all these knotty points had been disposed of, at a late hour I got to bed.

On the following morning I left early and went down to the mouth of the river to see whether it was possible to cross the bar in order to meet Sir Harry, but found that it was still impassable owing to the heavy swell that continued to roll in from the open sea. After wasting a good deal of time in this vain attempt, I returned to the town, and procured nine horses, with which I started off overland to Nei, where the ships were lying. The road was pretty good in places, but at times very narrow, and wound in and out among the hills. The ponies were sturdy little animals, and though unshod trotted over the stones without stumbling, but they had hard mouths, and would not obey the snaffle. At Nei I got a small boat and went on board. From Sir Harry downwards everyone was willing to risk the ride to Tokushima, in spite of the weather. We started at four, and in a couple of hours reached the town, in a heavy storm of rain and wind. The streams, which had been quite dry when I passed in the middle of the day, were now so swollen that the water came up to the ponies' girths. We were wet through. If we changed at the temple, there was the risk of getting wet again in riding to the castle. It was arranged therefore that we should go on as we were, and dress in an ante-room. Mitford and Aston were engaged in drying their clothes. I had got into a pair of pyjamas, and could not ride in that costume. So I tried to procure three palanquins for us, which took an unexpectedly long time to produce. Sir Harry lost his temper, and swore he would not be kept waiting for all the d — d *daimiôs* in Japan.

Numata (my old teacher) and the other Awa people manifested the most stoical indifference to all this wrath. Mitford volunteered to go on horseback, so they set out. Aston, as a punishment for not being ready, was forbidden by Sir Harry to join the party, a prohibition which caused him the intensest joy. At last my palanquin arrived, I got in, and the bearers went off at such a pace that I reached the castle at the same moment as the others. In the dark, for it was now nine or ten o'clock, the walls of cyclopean masonry, as we entered the gates and wound through the outer fortifications, seemed very imposing, though they were not so in reality. We had to alight outside the point at which I had agreed with the officials, but luckily no one seemed to be aware of the alteration. We got into the palace and were shown into rooms where we changed our dress; and the different garb worn by the various members of the party was very curious, no proper uniforms or evening dress at all. I could only muster a shirt, a white coat and trousers, no waistcoat, and no cummerbund. Sir Harry was the only one who kept his shoes on, as every one had got his feet wet in riding from Nei.

Everyone being at last ready, we were ushered through a series of wide passages into the banqueting room, and were met by the prince, who according to the agreement was clad in the ordinary costume of a gentleman, wide trousers, gown and mantle of silk. The introductions followed in the proper order of rank, and the prince led the way to the tables. The top one was oval, having been made months ago when it was expected that Mitford and I would be the only guests; the others were square. For the prince and his son there were elaborately carved chairs of old-fashioned style, for the rest of us there were three-legged chairs with semi-circular seats, very rickety and badly balanced. We were placed with our backs to the alcove (*tokonoma*), this being the seat of honour, on which the presents were laid out, a magnificent bronze about two feet high occupying the centre.

Sir Harry and the Admiral gave the prince a couple of revolvers, which seemed to afford him much pleasure, and the return presents, consisting of rolls of brocade, crape and so forth, were then announced by one of the attendants. Sir Harry, who had by this time quite recovered his equanimity, made himself very agreeable to the prince, talking on general topics, instead of dwelling on the "relations of friendship which happily unite our respective countries" and the usual diplomatic commonplaces. The prince, Awa no Kami, to give him his proper title, was a man of about forty-seven years of age, of middle height, and with a refined countenance, slightly pock-marked; his manner abrupt and imperious, but his good humour without limits. Awaji no Kami, the son, was about twenty-two, a little taller than his father, with a mild, fat countenance, a gentle and subdued manner; and he exhibited great deference towards his father.

The usual order of a Japanese dinner was reversed, the rice, soup and baked fish being first placed on the table. When this course had been removed, drinking commenced, a red lacquer cup being handed first to Sir Harry. I whispered to Sir Harry to call for the bowl to dip it in, and he returned it to the prince, who then offered it to the Admiral and to Captain Hewett, and then it travelled down the line to Stephenson, from whom it was returned to the prince. There was a good deal of picking at the various dishes of the banquet which was placed before us, and a great quantity of saké was drunk. After a while a play was announced, and in order to get a better view of the acting we moved our chairs down to the other end of the room, where tables with our plates and drinking cups were placed before us. The actors were retainers of the prince wearing the long trousers belonging to the court costume, but not otherwise dressed for their parts. In the first piece there was three characters — master, servant, and guest. The master tells the servant to imitate him in all things, which injunction he takes literally, and addresses the guest in exactly the same style as his master employs to him; this enrages the master, who cuffs the servant, and he in turn the guest. This sort of fun continues with variations until the master's patience is quite exhausted, and he kicks the servant out of the room.

The second piece is a well-known one, entitled "The Three Cripples." A rich and benevolent person advertises for cripples to enter his employ, and there enter successively a lame, a blind and a dumb man, gamblers who having become beggars have adopted these disguises in order to impose on the charitable. They are accepted, and having placed them in charge of three store-houses, their employer goes out. Then the three recognize each other as old comrades, and agree to open one of the store-rooms, which is full of *saké*, after which they will rob the other two. However, they get so drunk that when their master returns each forgets the part he had previously played; the blind man assumes dumbness, the lame one blindness, and the dumb pretends to be deaf. Their detection of course follows, with the natural consequences.

After the play was over we drew round the little tables, and the *saké* cup passed freely from hand to hand; Awa no Kami vowed that the Admiral was his father, and Sir Harry his elder brother, while Awaji no Kami expressed himself to me in a similarly affectionate manner. It was arranged that we should have a review of the troops on the following day, and about midnight the wind and rain having moderated we took our leave, getting back to our lodging at one in the morning. I found that even our servants had not been forgotten, presents having been sent to each one of them; not a single person was passed over. This was truly princely hospitality. I forgot to mention that before we started for the castle, a polite message of welcome was brought to Sir Harry from the prince, accompanied by a box three feet long, one deep and one wide, full of eggs, another of the same size full of vermicelli and a basket of fish. The trouble that had been taken to make us comfortable was very great, even after they had heard of the increased number they would have to entertain; they had gone to work to make bedsteads and tables, and even to build bathrooms.

The morning turned out finer than could have been reasonably hoped for after the storm of the preceding day, and after breakfast we started for the parade ground. Our way lay through the castle, and over a considerable stream which washed one side of the fortress. It was a very good ground, though rather small, but the prince explained that he could not enlarge it without pulling down some Buddhist temples, which would shock the religious feeling of the townspeople. Some five hundred men, divided into five bodies of varying strength, were put through their drill. Their uniform was in imitation of European style, black trousers with red stripes down the side, and black coats; happy the soldier who could muster a pair of boots, the rest had only straw sandals. On their heads they had hats of papier-maché, either conical or of dish-cover shape, with two horizontal red bands. They used the English infantry drill, with the quaint addition of a shout to indicate the discharge of their firearms. In the opinion of those who were competent to judge, they acquitted themselves very creditably. We viewed the evolutions from a sort of grand stand, with tables before us piled up with various delicacies. *Saké* of course formed part of the entertainment, and Hewett was singled out by the prince as assuredly the best toper of us all, on account of his jolly red face. Everyone this morning had remarked what a capital liquor is *saké*, it leaves no bad effects behind, from which it may be inferred that we had returned home on the previous night in a happy frame of mind and body.

About noon we took our leave. Sir Harry presented a ring to the young prince, and the Admiral put another on the finger of Awa no Kami, to their intense delight. On our way back from the drill ground we were taken to a temple on a hill commanding an extensive view, where we were entertained with a luncheon washed down with bad champagne procured in Yokohama for the occasion. The prince whispered privately into my ear that he intended to abdicate and pay a visit to England. To Sir Harry he said all sorts of friendly things about the opening of Hiôgo to foreign trade. The Admiral promised to bring the "Ocean" and "Rodney" to Nei in the coming winter to show him what English men-of-war were like. After returning to our lodgings we had a substantial lunch off the provisions brought from the ships, but our entertainers were not contented till they had made us sit down to a final feast prepared by themselves, just for five minutes, to drink a farewell cup and receive a parting message from the prince. At last we got away, some on horseback, others in palanquins, and in three hours after leaving Tokushima we were safely on board ship. Sir Harry was accompanied by four principal officials to the "Basilisk," where Hewett gave them some excellent champagne, and they went over the ship's side full of affectionate regrets at having to part from us. The "Salamis" left at once for Yokohama with the Admiral, Mitford, Aston and Crossman, while we remained to pursue our voyage to Tosa on the morrow in the "Basilisk."

CHAPTER XXII

Tosa and Nagasaki

Early on the morning of September 3 we anchored outside the little harbour of Susaki in Tosa. Inside were lying the Tycoon's war steamer "Eagle" (Kaiten-maru) and a smaller one belonging to the Prince of Tosa. We had fully expected a hostile reception, and preparations had been made for action. Shortly afterwards Takabataké Gorô and Koméda Keijirô came on board to say that Hirayama, the chief commissioner, was up at Kôchi. Gotô Shôjirô, the leading Tosa minister, also paid us a visit, but we told him to go away till we could get the ship inside the bay. Then arrived the other two commissioners (Togawa and an *ômetsuké*) to tell us that no evidence implicating any of the Tosa men had been discovered. The little schooner "Nankai," in which the assassins were supposed to have escaped from Nagasaki, was lying higher up the bay at Urado. Later on Gotô came on board with two other local officers. They promised to do all they could to discover the murderers, even if they should not be Tosa men. Sir Harry, who had quite made up his mind that the Tosa men were guilty, tried to browbeat them, adding oddly enough that with Tosa he could have none but friendly relations; the official discussions must take place with the Tycoon's government. After they left, Hirayama made his appearance; a long and stormy interview took place, in the course of which he heard a good deal of strong language, and was told that he was of no more use than a common messenger. He recounted to us in a plaintive manner the hardships he had undergone on the way down and since his arrival, for the Tosa people were extremely angry at the suspicions cast on them.

Later on Sir Harry sent me ashore to see Gotô, and detail to him all the circumstances which seemed to us to be evidence against his fellow clansmen. He renewed the assurances he had given in the morning, and said he felt certain my writer Ono and Noguchi were neither more nor less than government spies. The next morning I saw Gotô again, who renewed his protestations, and complained of Sir Harry's rough language and demeanour, which he felt sure would some day cause a terrible row. I was myself rather sick of being made the intermediary of the over-bearing language to which the chief habitually resorted, and told Gotô to remonstrate with him, if he really thought this; as for myself, I did not dare to hint anything of the kind to my chief. I also saw Hirayama, and arranged with him that I should be present at the examination of the officers of the "Nankai," who were to be sent down from Urado. At three o'clock two small steamers arrived, yet it was seven before the Tycoon's officials reached the "Basilisk" to say that everything was in readiness. As dinner was now announced, the inquiry was put off till the next day.

On the 5th September the examination was accordingly held in my presence. On the Japanese side the evidence went to show that the "Nankai" did not leave till ten p.m. on the 6th August, while Sir Harry's version was that she sailed at half-past four that morning, only an hour and a half after the schooner; and it was on this alleged fact that the whole of the suspicion against the Tosa men was founded. (It was proved at the end of 1868 that the murderers belonged to the Chikuzen clan, which was rather an unfortunate conclusion for him.) I reported this to Sir Harry, who was of course greatly dissatisfied. Gotô afterwards came on board to see Sir Harry and there was the usual talk about cultivating friendly relations between the English and Tosa. Sir Harry said he wished to send me as his envoy to call formally on the retired *daimiô* of Tosa, to which Gotô replied that Sir Harry could himself see the ex-*daimiô*, if we were on friendly terms. Otherwise, it was useless to hold any communications even by messenger. I knew perfectly well that I could easily manage to visit Kôchi, if left to myself, without the chief taking a roundabout way to get me there under the pretext of a mission to the old prince.

By this time my relations with the Japanese were such that I could have gone anywhere with perfect safety. A visit from Hirayama and his colleagues came next. The evidence taken was discussed, and Sir Harry said the inquiry must now be removed to Nagasaki, and that Hirayama ought to proceed thither to conduct it. Hirayama objected strongly, offering to send his two fellow commissioners, but it would not do, and he was finally forced to consent. The poor old fellow was almost at his wit's end. He became actually impertinent, and remarked that after all this murder case concerned Englishmen alone, while he had business to transact at Yedo which concerned all nations. I was much astonished to find that Sir Harry did not get into a passion on being talked to in this somewhat unceremonious way by a Japanese, but simply replied to it in a quiet argumentative tone. But a more curious thing followed.

After dinner Gotô came on board to have a talk on politics. He spoke of his idea of establishing a parliament, and a constitution on the English model, and said that Saigô entertained similar notions. That we had learnt at Ozaka. Then followed a good deal of abuse of the Tycoon's government, especially with reference to the proposed formation of a guild to control the foreign commerce of Ozaka and Hiôgo. We showed him the proclamation we had extorted from the government, intended to annul the previous one constituting these guilds. He replied that it was a mere blind, and I confess that I agreed with him. Sir Harry took a great fancy to him, as being one of the most intelligent Japanese we had as yet met with, and to my own mind Saigô alone was his superior by force of character. They swore eternal friendship, and Gotô promised to write once a month to report anything that might come to light in connection with the "Icarus" murder. Last of all he remonstrated with Sir Harry, at some length and in very explicit terms, about his rough demeanour on previous occasions, and hinted that perhaps others would not have submitted so quietly to such treatment. It was by no means a pleasant task for me to put his words into English, especially as Hewett's presence rendered the rebuke all the more galling, and Sir Harry at first seemed inclined to resent being thus lectured by a Japanese. However he managed to keep his temper, so no bones were broken.

Poor old Hirayama was made quite ill by the struggle he had had with the chief, but he did not venture to break his promise to proceed to Nagasaki and pursue the inquiry in person. I now received detailed written instructions from Sir Harry to follow the old fox, as we called him, to Nagasaki, to watch the proceedings and stimulate both the Tycoon's officials and the Tosa people to leave no stone unturned in their search for the murderers. Sir Harry himself was obliged to return to Yedo in the "Basilisk," and it was arranged that I should take a passage down to Nagasaki in a Tosa steamer, together with the incriminated officers of the "Nankai" and the officials named to conduct the inquiry. I was to be clothed with authority equal to that of the consul, but was not to interfere in any measures he might think fit to take. Sir Harry left on the 6th September, and I transferred myself to the Tosa steamer along with my writer and the faithful Noguchi.

There I spent the next day, after having seen the Tycoon's war steamer "Eagle" depart with Hirayama on board. In the middle of the night I was woken up by a messenger from Gotô, bringing an invitation for me to go up to Kôchi and make the acquaintance of the ex-*daimiô*. They had sent down a tugboat for me, so I went on board at once at four, after a hasty meal of rice and tea, and falling asleep on a locker, woke up at daylight to find myself already some way from Susaki. We did not anchor at Urado till half-past nine. The view outside of distant hills and a belt of pine trees fringing the shore reminded me strongly of the Bay of Point de Galle in Ceylon, where the eastern mail steamers used to call before the construction of the harbour at Colombo.

Kôchi Bay is in reality an estuary, with a very narrow outlet, much obstructed by rocks. We seemed to be running straight on to the sandy beach, when a sudden turn to the left put our head into the river, and we came to an anchor in fifteen feet of water inside a little cove. The river widens considerably above this point, but is so shallow that only boats drawing less than a foot of water can go up. I was transferred to a houseboat, which made very slow progress. At last, after traversing two or three broad lake-like reaches, we came in sight of the castle of Kôchi, rendered conspicuous from a distance by its lofty donjon four storeys high. Soon afterwards we turned up an embanked canal to the left, and touched the shore under a large new building on the outskirts of the town. Here I was met by Gotô, who told me that the ex-*daimiô* would shortly arrive. While waiting for his appearance I changed my dress, and was introduced to a host of Gotô's colleagues. At last the ex-*daimiô* Yôdô was announced, and I was conducted upstairs into his presence. He met me at the threshold, and saluted me by touching the tips of his toes with the tips of his fingers. I replied by a bow of exactly equal profundity. We then took our seats, he on a handsome Japanese armchair with his back to the alcove, and I on a common cane-bottomed wooden chair opposite, a little lower down to his right. Gotô and some of his fellow councillors squatted on the sill dividing the room from that next to it.

He began by saying that he had heard my name. I replied by thanking him for according me the honour of this interview. He then renewed the assurances already given through Gotô that if the murderers were Tosa men, they should be arrested and punished, and that even if it should appear that the guilty persons belonged to another clan, he would not relax his efforts to trace them out. He had received a letter from the Tycoon stating that he had heard there was strong evidence against Tosa, and advising him to punish the offenders. This of course he would be ready to do, supposing that the murderers were men of his clan, but he did not understand what the Tycoon meant by "evidence." I replied that we supposed the government to be in possession of proofs which they had not disclosed, as it was not likely that they were convinced simply by what Sir Harry had said to them. Perhaps, I added, they threw the suspicion on Tosa in order to get rid of an unpleasant discussion. This remark called forth from Gotô somewhat unmeasured expressions of indignation, and he announced his intention of giving the government a piece of his mind on the subject. Old Yôdô said that he had received a letter from a friend advising him to try and compromise the matter, as the English were greatly incensed at the murder of their men, but he would do nothing of the kind. If his people were guilty he would punish them; he could do no more; but if they were innocent he would declare their innocence through thick and thin.

Matsuné Dzusho (the chief man of Uwajima) had told Iyo no Kami that Sir Harry had said the Tycoon's government had assured him of Tosa's guilt. I replied again that from the language of the Tycoon's ministers we could not help inferring that they had independent grounds for their suspicions. Yôdô remarked that the only thing Hirayama had alleged was the supposed transfer of men from the schooner "Yokobuyé" to the steamer "Nankai," which had never been proved. I answered that this was all we had to go upon, but I should consider that we had good reason to blush if after all we had said the men should turn out to belong to another clan; at present I saw no ground for supposing that we were mistaken.

An argument then ensued between Gotô and myself as to the nature of suspiciousness in general, and what might be held to be sufficient justification for that attitude of mind; in the end he admitted that we were entitled, by our past experience, to mistrust all Japanese *à priori*, though he maintained that in the present case the rule did not apply. After this Yôdô and Gotô plied me with questions about the Luxemburg affair, the constitution and powers of parliament and the electoral system; it was evident that the idea of a constitution resembling that of Great Britain had already taken deep root in their minds. Later on a proposition was actually made to either Mitford or myself, I forget which, to enter the service of the Mikado and assist in organizing their parliament for them.

Huge dishes of fish were now placed on the table, and waiting women, *coiffées* in the exaggerated style of the *daimiôs'* courts, poured out the *saké*. While we drank and conversed, a pair of anatomical models of the male and female human being, life size, were exhibited and taken to pieces for my especial edification! Rice was afterwards served in the next room, Yôdô excusing himself on the ground of indisposition. The fact was, he preferred to remain alone with the *saké* bottle, of which he was notoriously fond. I had once in my possession a scroll of Chinese verses from his brush, signed "Drunken old man" (*sui-ô*).

Before taking my departure, I saw him once more for a few minutes, when he presented me with seven rolls of white crape. Under the circumstances I should have preferred to decline them, but Gotô argued that they were a part of the entertainment, and I could not refuse without being ungracious, almost discourteous. I therefore accepted, subject to the chief's approval, and we parted, with the same exchange of formal bows as before.

Yôdô was a tall man, slightly pock-marked, with bad teeth, and a hurried manner of getting out his words. He certainly looked very ill, and over-indulgence in *saké* would quite account for that. From some of the remarks he made, I gathered that he was free from prejudice, and not by any means conservative in his political notions. Still, it may be doubted whether he was prepared to go the same lengths as Satsuma and Chôshiû in the direction of change.

It was not considered advisable or safe for me to promenade through the town, and I made no attempt to insist on doing the sights. As I returned back to Urado in the gondola, multitudes of people followed in small boats, anxious to get a sight of the first European that had visited their part of the country since the wreck of the Spanish galleon in 1596, and even grappling with us in order better to satisfy their curiosity. No order was kept, and I was easily convinced that a walk in Kôchi itself might have given rise to a tumult.

Next day they took me to Susaki, and put me on board the "Shooeyleen," the steamer in which we were to proceed to Nagasaki. For the past two days I had been suffering from a whit-low on one of the fingers of the right hand, and felt utterly indiffer-ent to all that passed around me. Bad food, a dirty cabin, excessive heat, sullen fellow-voyagers were all accepted with the calmness of exhausted misery. The "Shooeyleen's" boilers were old, and we steamed along at the rate of two knots an hour. Luckily the weather was calm, otherwise there was every reason to think we must have gone to the bottom. Passing through Shimonoséki, I went on shore to ask after old friends, and found Inouyé Bunda, who was a perfect sink of taciturnity. There was no appearance here of guns or men-of-war, nothing to indicate that Chôshiû was still at war with the Tycoon; but all around were signs of peace and prosperity. The Tosa officers also landed, one and all, on some pretext or other, and the whole day was spent at anchor. Towards evening we set forth again in the same leisurely fashion, and reached Nagasaki on the 12th September late in the afternoon. Here I put up with Marcus Flowers, the consul. At dinner that evening I met for the first time the well-known Kido Junichirô, otherwise Katsura Kogorô, who came to the consulate together with Itô Shunsuké, whom I had known since 1864. Katsura was remarkable for his gentle suave manner, though under this there lay a character of the greatest courage and determination, both military and political. We had some talk after dinner about poli-tics, but I think they mistrusted me. At any rate they thought it necessary to assert that their prince was a much wronged, innocent and harmless individual, who had never entertained any schemes for overturning the Tycoon's government. But we had long been in possession of indisputable evidence that the abolition of the Shôgunate was the cardinal point in the policy pursued by the western *daimiôs* acting in concert.

On the following day Flowers and I went to meet Hirayama at the custom-house. The two governors were also present. Though they had been severely blamed by Sir Harry, they did not appear to be particularly disturbed by his censures. The Tosa steamer "Nankai" had left, in fact she steamed out of the harbour just after Sir Harry went off in the "Basilisk." On the 19th of August, as she was about to leave for Kagoshima, she was stopped, and an examination was held, which lasted through the night until the afternoon of the 20th, but without any evidence of complicity in the murders being elicited. The officers and crew were then entrusted to the charge of Iwasaki Yatarô, Tosa's agent (*kiki-yaku*), who undertook to produce them whenever they should be wanted. But she sailed the same evening, in defiance of Iwasaki's orders, at least so the Tosa people alleged. Nothing had been discovered with respect to the real criminals, and, as far as we could see, the governors had not exerted themselves to find out the guilty persons.

The 14th I spent with Itô and Katsura at a tea-house called Tamagawa, away at the back of the town close to the stream which flows down through it. We had a long discussion on Japanese politics, domestic and foreign, ending with the conclusion that Europeans and Japanese would never mix, at least not in our time. On my way back I called on Hikozô (the well-known Joseph Heco), who told me of a document, said to be signed by Satsuma, Tosa, Geishiû, Bizen and Awa, which had been presented to the Shôgun Keiki, requiring him to resign his office and allow the government to be reconstituted.

On Sunday the 15th I lunched with Hirayama. He said that Sasaki Sanshirô, the Tosa *metsuké* (equivalent to attorney-general, but not trained in law), was overruled by the Tosa society called the *Kai-yen-tai*, a sort of local navy league, who would not allow him to carry out the official orders received from his prince to have search made for the criminals. This was natural enough, as it was afterwards proved that the Tosa men were altogether innocent of the affair.

The 16th was spent at the custom house in the examination of the men of the "Yokobuyé," a Tosa sailing-vessel. It appeared certain that the "Nankai" did not leave Nagasaki till the evening of the 6th August. Two of the *Kai-yen-tai*, one of whom was the captain of the "Yokobuyé," were shown to have been at a house of entertainment opposite to the spot where the British sailors were murdered up to midnight. This looked suspicious, but I told the Japanese officials that if they did not disbelieve the statements that had been made, neither did I. The Tosa people did not want to make the "Yokobuyé" return, neither did the government officials seem to insist on her recall. As my plan was to throw on the government officials the responsibility of discovering the murderers, I did not urge it, but left it to Flowers, who was associated with me in the inquiry, to do so if he judged it necessary.

In the evening of the 18th I went to see Hirayama, and communicated to him my suspicions regarding a young fellow of forbidding countenance, who was with the captain of the "Yokobuyé" on the night of the murder at the house of entertainment referred to. I suggested that his companion should be sent for, and also the four men stated to have gone to Karatsu (in the north of Hizen, near the boundary of Chikuzen) in the "Nankai," and to have landed there. I advised that the keeper of the house of entertainment should be examined, and asked for copies of all depositions received, especially of the two Tosa men. What had fixed suspicion upon men of that province in particular was their general evil reputation as being predisposed towards assassination. The depositions were sent to us by the governors in the afternoon of the 19th, and on discrepancies being pointed out in those of the two Tosa men, they promised to send for one of them whose further examination appeared to be especially desirable. The translation of the depositions occupied me for the whole of the succeeding day. Then on the 21st I went to see Niiro Giôbu, a Satsuma *karô*, and asked him to make an inquiry about the murder among his own people. He said this had already been done, and offered to give me a copy of the record. As he said that nothing suspicious had been discovered, I declined his offer with thanks. But I hinted to him the possibility of the exclusion of all two-sworded men from the foreign settlement after dark, unless the murderers were discovered and delivered up by the combined clans, a measure which had been recommended to Flowers and myself by Sir Harry, for if the discovery were made by the government, it would be taken to be a proof of the complicity of his clan at least. He did not at all like this suggestion. Then I went to Sasaki Sanshirô, with whom I had travelled from Tosa. He said that the governors had lent a steamer to fetch the captain of the "Yokobuyé" and another man, and complained of Hirayama's supposition that he was lukewarm, seeing that he had given money to all the detectives in the place, and had offered a reward of 4,000 pieces of silver (worth £450) for the discovery of the murderer or murderers.

Next to Hirayama, to whom I proposed that he should order the Nagasaki representatives of all the clans to examine their men as strictly as the Tosa agents were doing, for as we had been ten days at work without being able to fix the responsibility on them, it was not unreasonable to admit the possibility of men of some other clan being guilty. I proposed that every two-sworded man should be called upon to give an account of his doings on the night of the murder, and that all the houses of entertainment should show their lists of guests on that date. There was, I said, no real difficulty in discovering the perpetrators. In consequence of all this one of the governors called the next afternoon. We proposed to him that the two-sworded men should be excluded from the settlement after dark, to which he added an amendment that if they had urgent business there in the evening, they should be escorted to and fro. The examination of all the clansmen and of persons who were in a house of entertainment close to the site of the murder was again urged by us. The governor also promised to have guard-houses erected at three points in the foreign settlement.

Two days later the same governor called again, and promised that the precautionary measures we had proposed to him should be taken. Nothing further was done until the 28th, when I attended at the custom house to hear the examination of two Tosa men who had been brought from Kôchi in the government steamer. It led to this result, that the governors declared that they found nothing to incriminate any of the men who had left Nagasaki in the "Yokobuyé" and "Nankai," and considered the Tosa people to be cleared of all suspicion as far as these two vessels were concerned. We rejoined that on the contrary we entertained very strong suspicions, not founded on any ocular testimony, but on circumstantial evidence, namely, that the murder was almost certainly committed by men in white foreign dress a little after midnight. That one of the two men with a companion were close to the spot where the murder was committed at the very moment, and that they were dressed in that fashion, and that no one else had been shown to have been in the brothel quarter in similar costume. We afterwards addressed a letter to the governors demanding the arrest of these two men on the above grounds, but we were not sanguine of obtaining their consent, as it was evident that the government officials were unable to exercise any control over the Tosa people.

Very little progress was made after this, as was natural enough, seeing that the Tosa people were entirely innocent of any share in the murders, as was afterwards proved. On October 6 I had an opportunity of conversing amicably with the vice-governor. I said that the Tosa people tried to throw obstacles in the way of discovering the criminals, instead of courting inquiry in accordance with Prince Yôdô's expressed wishes. That the government had lost much ground with foreigners in this affair. Firstly, the possibility of the murder being committed in such a manner showed the incapacity of the government to maintain order, and, secondly, it was not fitting that a body calling itself a government should allow *daimiôs* to enjoy such rights of extraterritoriality to the extent that was shown by the recent examinations at the custom-house. The vice-governor replied that he had nothing to do with these matters, to which I rejoined that this was precisely the reason why I had spoken to him about them. We received a refusal to our demand for the arrest of the two Tosa men. A few days later a drunken Englishman was cut about the head and an American wounded slightly in the arm by a Tosa man, who straightway gave himself up to his own authorities, and they reported the affair. Having failed entirely in our attempts to bring the crime home to the Tosa people, Flowers and I agreed that it was useless for me to remain any longer, and accordingly I returned to Yedo, leaving about midnight of the 12th October on board H.M.S. "Coquette," which had been lent by the Admiral to bring me back to Yokohama.

During my stay at Nagasaki we heard a good deal about the discovery and arrest of native Roman Catholic Christians of Urakami, a village near the town. Niiro Giôbu of Satsuma, who came to see me on the 12th October, said that besides the Urakami people, some of the inhabitants of a village close by, belonging to the *daimiô* of Omura, had been converted, and were now in prison at Nagasaki. According to Japanese law this was a capital offence. The Omura officials had hitherto conformed to the practice of the Nagasaki government with respect to the punishment of criminals, and desired to act accordingly in the present case. It was, however, reported that the governors intended to pardon all those who were willing to abjure, because the number of offenders was so large. This offended the Omura officials, who held that believing in Christianity was a very grave crime; further, that the proposal to let such criminals off on the pretext that they were too numerous to punish was revolutionary and subversive of good government, and they were endeavouring to induce all the *daimiôs* of Kiûshiû to join in a representation in that sense to the government at Yedo. This proposal was of course intended as a general manifesto against the Shôgun's government. I replied that he must quite well know that Christianity was not harmful to any country by whose people it was professed, and that even a Protestant government such as that of England would not be pleased to hear of Roman Catholics being persecuted on the ground of their religious belief, but if the only object of the remonstrance was to annoy the Shôgun's government, we should not disapprove of that by itself. On the general subject of Japanese internal politics, he said he did not believe that civil war would break out, or at least he pretended not to, though at the same time he acknowledged its possibility. Hirayama, to whom I said good-bye on the same day, told me that all the Christians of Urakami had been forgiven on their promising "not to do so again," and that they would be permitted to believe what they liked, doubtless on condition of their not professing their religion openly. He thought the Omura officials would also forgive their Christians. This opinion of his was, however, in contradiction to what I had heard from Niiro.

My stay at Nagasaki afforded me useful opportunities of making the acquaintance of *samurai* of various southern clans. I have already mentioned my introduction to Kido Junichirô.

The 14th I spent almost entirely in the company of Kido and Itô. A few days later Kido called to offer me the use of a steamer to Ozaka, if it suited me to return to Yedo by that route, but I deferred accepting, as my plans were not yet settled. Eventually arrangements were made for my being conveyed to Yokohama in one of H.M. ships, so that I was able to decline his obliging proposal. When Itô came to say good-bye on September 23, he was accompanied by a young fellow-clansman whom he wished me to take to Yedo, nominally as a pupil. This was Endo Kinsuké, one of the party of five Chôshiû men to which Itô had belonged, who went secretly to England in 1863, as already narrated. He bore the alias of Yamamoto Jinsuké. Itô's pseudonym was Hayashi Uichi, and Inouyé Bunda went by the name of Takada Harutarô. Amongst other interesting information given to me by Itô was that my friend Yamagata Keizô, who was one of the Chôshiû men that had accompanied me to Yokohama in October 1864, had been adopted by Shishido Bizen. It was his father, Yamagata Taiga, who wrote the pamphlet of which the title translated is the equivalent of "The present *daimiôs* are not vassals of the prince," *i.e.* of the Shôgun, and not Nagai Uta, to whom it was usually attributed. Itô was a pupil of the well-known patriot Yoshida Torajirô, the author of several books controverting the views of Yamagata and Nagai.

He said there were two schools of Chinese philosophy in Japan, namely, of Teishi (Ch'êng-tzu) and Oyômei (Wang Yang-ming), of which the first inculcates the duty of resisting tyrants, the second that of self-reformation. Yamagata belonged to the latter, hence his arguments against any attempt to disturb the existing political arrangements. (But the most widely diffused system in Japan was that of the philosopher Chu Hsi.)

Niiro Giôbu I saw four times. I dined with him once at a Japanese restaurant, when he said that he knew nothing of the engagement of Frenchmen by Iwashita Sajiémon, a Satsuma man who had gone to Paris for the exposition of 1867, and there came under the influence of the Comte de Montblanc. Directly he heard of it he wrote to Iwashita that the engagements must be cancelled, but his letter did not reach Paris in time. I said that of course we could not object to Satsuma employing Frenchmen, but as French views of Japanese domestic politics differed so widely from ours, and it was well understood that ours coincided to a certain extent with those of Satsuma, it was natural to ask whether this engagement implied a change of policy on the part of the Satsuma clan. Niiro replied that such a supposition would be quite natural, but that in fact no such change had occurred. Since the time when Osumi no Kami (father of the Prince of Satsuma, and virtual ruler of the clan notwithstanding his formal retirement from public life) had decreed the adoption of English methods, the whole province had become enthusiastic in their favour, and objected very strongly to the proposed introduction of Frenchmen. He was afraid he should have to send them home again. A few days later Niiro dined with Russell Robertson (assistant at the consulate) and myself at Robertson's house, when we engaged a French cook to serve the dinner. On this occasion no political conversation took place, but he told us that Saigô was Osumi no Kami's confidential man, and Komatsu Tatewaki one of the seven *shussei* (administrators) of the Satsuma clan. The prince, whose title was Shiuri no Taiyu, was 29 years of age, and his brother, Shimadzu Dzusho, 28. Altogether there were ten brothers and sisters, besides the three girls of the late prince,

Satsuma no Kami. My last talk with Niiro was on October 12, when he gave me information about the native Christians, already recorded.

Last year I had met at Robertson's house a doctor belonging to the Kurumé clan, and he now came with his son to ask permission to bring some of his fellow clansmen to call on me. This they did on the 8th October. Their names were Imaé Sakai, said to be connected with the government of the clan; Nagata Chiûhei, who was visiting Nagasaki for the first time in his life; and Tanaka Konoyé. Originally a Kiôto clockmaker, he had developed into a skilled mechanical engineer, and had constructed engines and boilers for a couple of Japanese steamers. After drinking a bottle of champagne together, we sallied forth to a Japanese restaurant, where we had a little feast in the style of the country, and a great deal of political talk. They said their principal reason for objecting to Hiôgo being opened as a port for foreign trade was that the tea consumed at Kurumé came from the provinces to the west of Hiôgo, and they feared it would be diverted to that place for exportation. With regard to internal affairs, I said I did not see how they could be settled without a war of some kind or other, as the *daimiôs* could not agree among themselves. A civil war might last twenty or thirty years, and greatly impoverish the country, while it would afford an opportunity to foreign powers to appropriate bits of Japanese territory by aiding one party against the other. But a foreign war, in which Kiôto became the object of attack, would lead to the reconciliation of their internal differences, and when peace came to be made we could conclude treaties with the Mikado, in which the constitutional position of the Tycoon might be defined.

Nagata, who was already drunk, shouted out: "You must not attack Kiôto, but destroy the *Baku-fu.*" This was the term, meaning "military power," by which the adversaries of the Tycoon were in the habit of speaking of his government. It appeared from this utterance that the men of Kurumé shared what was evidently the general feeling in the west of the country. Afterwards we adjourned to another restaurant, where a grand feast was served. More of the Kurumé clan came in, and the room was gradually filled with courtesans and musicians. Most of my friends got very drunk, so after about two hours of this festivity I left, and the party broke up. I also had a dinner with a Tosa man named Yui, who was captain of the "Yugawo."

Another acquaintance I made was that of Hosokawa Riônosuké, younger brother of the Prince of Higo, who came to call on Flowers. He had a fat round face, was about 25 years of age, and intelligent. He tried to pump me about the Tosa affair but failed, and when he proceeded to talk politics I held my tongue, for Higo was supposed not to belong to the Satsuma party. He then invited me to visit him on board his steamer and have a long conversation, but when I went at the appointed hour on the following day he was absent. However, next day two of his men called to apologize for his breaking the engagement, and he also appeared in person to tell me of the desire cherished by the Higo people to invite Sir Harry Keppel, the Admiral in command of the China squadron, to some point off their coast to display naval evolutions; for the clan having ordered an iron-clad man-of-war and two smaller war steamers to be built in England, wanted to learn how they should be manœuvered. He was at great pains to prove that he was on the best of terms with Kido (*alias* Katsura), and that the Hosokawa brothers loved the English more than they did any other nation, for all their steamers, besides 16,000 rifles of different patterns, had been bought from us. I replied that their inviting the Admiral to a place off their coast and not to the castle at Kumamoto, was like sending for a troupe of tumblers to perform before one's house, into which one would not care to admit them. If a man were prevented from inviting a guest to his own house, it would be more courteous to go and call on him than to ask him to come half-way, and that Riônosuké at least ought to come to Nagasaki and visit the Admiral first of all. He said he intended going to Shimonoséki with one of the Higo *karô* (councillor) to arrange an alliance between Higo and Chôshiû.

Endo presented himself on the 12th, but instead of coming straight to me, he sent in his card by my Aidzu retainer Noguchi, who read it and at once discovered who he was. We embarked in the course of the evening, and steamed out of the harbour at eleven p.m. through the inland sea, and without calling anywhere, arrived at Yokohama at midnight on the 16th.

CHAPTER XXIII

Downfall of the Shogunate

B efore leaving Yedo I had taken a lease of a house known as *Taka-yashiki* (high mansion) on a bluff overlooking the bay, at a monthly rental of 100 *ichibus*, equal to £6 13s. 4d. It was the retired home of a Japanese gentleman of rank, who had abdicated his position in favour of his eldest son, and had bought a piece of ground to build himself a residence after his own taste. Consequently it was one of the oddest houses imaginable, consisting of a number of small rooms of varying sizes, and the garden was laid out in little hills and grass-plots, planted with trees and shrubs. The only flowers were those of the camellia and St John's wort bushes (Hypericum Chinese), for herbaceous borders are almost impossible to manage in Japan, owing to the heavy summer rains, which beat down all plants that have not woody stems. The whole covered about two-thirds of an acre. There was an upper storey, where I had my bedroom and apartments for the entertainment of Japanese guests, and three staircases provided means of escape in case of attack from the midnight murderer. Downstairs was a room for the reception of European visitors, and two waiting rooms for callers, one more for the accommodation of my head man and my own study. This was nine feet square, with a circular window commanding a view of the sea, and a square one at the side overlooking the garden. It was fitted up with numerous small cupboards and shelves for the accommodation of books and papers. It held a writing desk, a small table, a chair for myself and one for my Japanese teacher, and a stool for the Chinese teacher attached to the legation. There were also a large bathroom, a kitchen, and a two-storeyed building beyond where my head man lived, and where the young Japanese to whom I intended to teach English were to be lodged. My food was entirely in the Japanese style, sent in from the well-known house called Mansei, but I continued to drink English beer. The household consisted of my head man (the Aidzu *samurai*, Noguchi, who has been already mentioned), whose function was to superintend everything, pay my bills, arrange for necessary repairs, and receive persons who came on business which did not require a personal interview with myself. Next to him came a small boy of fourteen who waited at table and acted as valet. He was of the *sumurai* class, and so entitled to wear sword and dagger when he went abroad. Then there was a woman of about thirty years of age, whose duty it was to sweep the floors, open the sliding shutters in the morning and close them at night, and sew on my buttons. As there was hardly any furniture, she had very little dusting to do. I was to engage a man to go, not run, on errands, perhaps cook the rice for the whole family, and make himself generally useful. Lastly came a gatekeeper, who had also the duty of sweeping the garden, and a groom or running footman. When I went out walking or on horseback, I was accompanied by a couple of the mounted escort that had been attached to me by the Tycoon's government since my journey overland from Ozaka in the earlier part of the year.

Thus established as a householder after my own liking, able to devote myself to Japanese studies and to live intimately with Japanese and thus become acquainted with their thoughts and views, I was perfectly happy. In my jourual I find noted down a dinner on November 6 with Nakamura Matazô at the Sanku-tei near Shimbashi, with *geisha* of course to pour out the *saké* and entertain us with music and bright conversation, and on the 7th a dinner of broiled eels and rice at the Daikokuya, Reiganbashi, with Yanagawa Shunsan, a teacher at the foreign language school (*kaiseijo*). The political ferment threw a great deal of work on me in interpreting for Sir Harry in his talks with government people, and in translating official papers from and into Japanese, and these duties often occupied me from nine o'clock in the morning till nine in the evening, with only short intervals for meals.

In the dead of night on November 16 Ishikawa Kawachi no Kami, one of the commissioners for foreign affairs, came to impart to Sir Harry the momentous news that the Tycoon had resigned the direction of government into the hands of the Mikado, and in future would simply be the instrument for carrying out His Majesty's orders. We had heard from other sources that he had abdicated, and that the office of Shôgun would cease to exist. Already on the 14th Ogasawara Iki no Kami had told us confidentially that the programme of the future consisted of a council of the great *daimiôs*, decision by the Tycoon subject to the approval of the Mikado.* The actual date of Keiki's resignation was November 8.

At an interview with Sir Harry two days afterwards, Iki no Kami read out a long paper explaining the causes which had led to the Tycoon's decision to surrender the government into the hands of the Mikado. He went into a long retrospect of affairs from the commencement of the renewed intercourse with foreign nations. The blame was, of course, thrown on the agitators for political change. Keiki, it said, had not resigned the chieftainship of the Tokugawa clan, but had simply abolished the office of Shôgun. The new arrangement would not involve any change in the previous agreements about the opening of the new ports which had been entered into earlier in the year. Two of the Council of State, Nui no Kami and Hiôbu Taiyu, were off to Kiôto.

Katsu Awa no Kami told us that he was afraid that the Tycoon's party would precipitate events, and cause the outbreak of civil war. Kanéko Taisuké, a retainer of Sakai Hida no Kami, told us that the *daimiôs* were collecting troops at Ozaka. Satsuma had

---

* For the detailed circumstances of this event I must refer the reader to Chapter V. of my friend Mr J. H. Gubbins' valuable volume *The Progress of Japan, 1853-1871.*

5,000 men, and Chôshiû and Tosa men, under the command of Môri Nagato, were also encamped there, so that we should find ourselves in a hornets' nest when we went down to superintend the opening of the ports. The Tycoon had ordered 4,000 or 5,000 men to be despatched thither. The Council of State had informed his chief and Matsudaira Hôki no Kami that in future they might be Tycoon's or Mikado's men as they liked. A secret circular had been sent round among the *hatamoto* (retainers of the Tokugawa chief holding fiefs assessed at less than 10,000 *koku* of rice) inciting them against Keiki, by accusing him of having poisoned the previous Shôgun Iyémochi, and calling upon the faithful to assemble at Mukôjima, a suburb of Yedo. The *sampei* or drilled troops were clamouring for their pay. Civil war at Kiôto was inevitable.

Truly it seemed as if the end of the old régime had come.

A week later Iki no Kami circulated another paper to be substituted for the first, in which he had vented a little too much abuse of the anti-Tycoon party. Matters had quieted down very much in the interval. Kanéko also came to us and confessed that there was no foundation for the rumours he had previously reported. Last night there arrived a letter from Gotô Shôjirô, brought by Gotô Kiûjirô, one of the aliases of him whom we afterwards knew so well as Nakai Kôzô, and a companion. They produced a copy of the Tosa memorial of last month, advising the Tycoon to take the step he had since adopted, and proposing various reforms. Of these the most important were the establishment of an assembly composed of two houses, the erection of schools of science and literature in the principal cities, and the negotiation of new treaties with foreign powers. They asked me for detailed information about parliamentary practice, which I did not possess, so I put them off by promising that they should get it from Mitford when we went to Ozaka for the opening of the ports. They were succeeded the following day by a messenger from Yoshii Kôsuké of Satsuma, to report that all was going on well, and that they hoped to be "favoured with a call" as soon as we reached Ozaka. Saigô and Komatsu had gone down to Kagoshima to fetch either Osumi no Kami or Shiuri no Taiyu.

We had now become acquainted with the Satsuma agents in Yedo; the *rusui* (as the principal representative of a *daimiô* was called) Shinosaki Hikojirô scoffed at the notion that the Tycoon had given up the reins of government because he thought it would be better for the country at large to be ruled by an assembly; the fact was that he could not help himself. Messages arrived by post from Tosa and Satsuma, the "two or three clans acquainted with the dispositions of foreigners" mentioned in the Mikado's most recent edict respecting foreign affairs. This seemed to indicate a pretty strong desire to gain our support. We now prepared to start for Ozaka. On the 27th November I went down to Yokohama with my little pupil, Tetsu, dressed like a drummer-boy. Mitford and I sailed on the 30th at daylight in H.M.S. "Rattler," Captain Swann. On December 2, as we were steaming up the Kii channel, we encountered a strong north-west breeze, against which the ship could only do two knots, so deficient in boiler-power were the British men-of-war of that period. We anchored off Ozaka in the afternoon, and as no boats put off from the shore, we had to conclude that the bar was impassable. However, we managed to get ashore about noon, and proceeded to call on the governors at their official residence opposite the castle. It is a remarkable proof of Mitford's linguistic powers that he was able to carry on the conversation in Japanese entirely unaided, although he had been in the country no longer than twelve months.

Our mission was to find quarters for the legation, and after consultation with them we went to inspect a *yashiki* behind the castle, which had been occupied in the spring by Iga no Kami, Keiki's principal minister. We arranged for its repair, and for the construction of a temporary barrack for the mounted escort and a detachment of fifty men of the 9th regiment, who were to arrive as a guard. Everything was to be ready by the 18th if possible. This peaceable and entirely commercial city was full of two-sworded retainers of *daimiôs*. Finding that Saigô had not yet returned from Kagoshima, and that Yoshii was in Kiôto, we wrote to the latter asking him to come down to see us, but he replied that he was too busy, and recommended us to wait until Saigô came back. We visited the site of the intended foreign settlement, where we found bonded warehouses, a custom-house, a guardhouse and a palisade being erected, the object of the latter being to cut off the foreign residents from the city. This proceeding was altogether contrary to treaty stipulations, and we lost no time in lodging a protest with the governors.

On December 7 we called on two of the Council of State and their colleagues of the second council (Inaba Hiôbu Taiyu, Matsudaira Nui no Kami, Nagai Hizen no Kami and Kawakatsu Bingo no Kami), who were on their way to Yedo, and had orders from the Tycoon to stop at Ozaka to see us. They gave us no information worth mentioning, but asserted that he had long ago been intending to take the step of surrendering the government to the Mikado. This of course we did not believe, our view being that he was tired of being badgered by Satsuma, Chôshiû, Tosa and Hizen, and that in order to give unity to his own party, he had resolved to call a general council, which possibly might reinstate him by a majority of votes, and thus establish his authority more strongly than ever.

On December 12, having transacted all our business at Ozaka, we started in palanquins for Hiôgo. Mitford walked as far as Ama-ga-saki, which he reached in 3 3/4 hours, and I in a palanquin took half-an-hour more. By three o'clock in the afternoon, after travelling six hours, we had got only half-way. So we betook ourselves to Shanks' mare. Mitford's Japanese teacher Nagazawa and our escort had to trot in order to keep pace with us, and we got on board the "Rattler" soon after six. Having dined with Captain Swann, we went ashore again, and took up our quarters for the night at the municipal office (*sô-kwai-sho*). Next day we called on the newly appointed governor, Shibata Hiûga no Kami, to discuss various business details. He told us that there had been a week of feasting at Kôbé in honour of the anticipated opening of the port, with processions of people dressed in red silk crape, with carts which were supposed to be transporting earth to raise the site of the proposed foreign settlement. Its situation appeared to us entirely satisfactory. Fêtes at Hiôgo itself were also projected. These we took to be marked signs of goodwill on the part of both government and people, and to promise a great extension of friendly intercourse between Japanese and foreigners.

The same day we returned to Ozaka by boat, accompanied by Noel (afterwards Admiral Sir Gerard Noel), first lieutenant of the "Rattler." There we found the whole population occupied with festivities in honour of the approaching opening of the city to foreign trade. Crowds of people in holiday garb, dancing and singing "*Ii ja nai ka, ii ja nai ka*" (isn't it good), houses decorated with rice-cakes in all colours, oranges, little bags, straw and flowers. The dresses worn were chiefly red crape, a few blue and purple. Many of the dancers carried red lanterns on their heads. The pretext for these rejoicings was a shower of pieces of paper, bearing the names of the two gods of Isé, alleged to have taken place recently.

On the 14th we received a visit from our Satsuma friend Yoshii. He told us that the coalition, which was determined to push matters to the last extremity in order to gain their points, consisted of Satsuma, Tosa, Uwajima, Chôshiû and Geishiû. Higo and Arima were inclined to join, Hizen and Chikuzen indifferent. On the whole, it might safely be said that all the western clans were pretty much of one mind. Osumi no Kami (who suffered a good deal from *kakké*, a sort of dropsy of the legs) was too ill to come to Kiôto, and Shiuri no Taiyu was to take his place, arriving in a few days. Saedani Umétarô, a Tosa man whose acquaintance I had made at Nagasaki, had been murdered a few days ago at his lodgings in Kiôto by three men unknown. The Tycoon had about 10,000 troops at Kiôto, Satsuma and Tosa about half that number between them, part in Kiôto, part in Ozaka. Other *daimiôs*, such as Geishiû, would also bring up troops. The Chôshiû question would be difficult to settle peacefully, as the Tycoon's party included a large number of men who wished to force on a renewal of the war in order to effect the complete destruction of that clan.

I took occasion to say that the murder of our sailors at Nagasaki was by no means disposed of, and that one of the first demands to be laid by us before the new government would be for the punishment of the murderers; that no money compensation would be accepted, and that the Japanese, if they wished to remain on good terms with foreigners and to avoid a disaster, had better prevent the occurrence of such incidents. Yoshii replied that if internal affairs were not placed on a sound footing on the present occasion, the *daimiôs* would wreak their wrath upon foreigners, in order to provoke bad relations between the Tycoon and the treaty powers. I responded that they would not gain their object, as we could no longer hold the Tycoon responsible for the acts of persons over whom he had no real control.

On the 16th I received a visit from two Uwajima men, Sutô Tajima and Saionji Yukiyé, the former a man of high rank in his clan, the other an official whom I had met when I was at Uwajima in the spring of the year. They had come up to Ozaka as precursors of Daté Iyo no Kami, who was expected to arrive early in January. They represented him as greatly pleased with the existing prospect of the establishment of a parliament, regarding which the old prince had talked to me on more than one occasion. I mentioned the Nagasaki affair in similar terms to those I had used to Yoshii, and assured them that the question of reparation was by no means abandoned, but was simply in abeyance for the present, and I explained that we were on as good terms with Tosa as before.

No sooner had they gone than Nakai came in to say that Gotô had arrived the previous evening, but was too busy to call on us. We offered to call on him instead of his coming to us, a proposal which was joyfully accepted, and meeting Gotô in front of the Tosa *yashiki* (agency), we turned in there with him. Our first topic was the murder of our two sailors. We said that though the particular suspicion against Tosa was removed by the discovery that there was no foundation for the report of the "Yokobuyé" and "Nankai" leaving the port together on the nigrht of the murder, the fact that our men had been killed by Japanese still remained, and that we should not rest until redress was afforded, not in the shape of a pecuniary indemnity, which some people appeared to suppose would satisfy the British Government, but by the punishment of the criminals, and that we were content to wait until the establishment of the new constitution gave us an opportunity for presenting our demand with effect. He replied that the recent murder of two of his own subordinates inspired him with sympathy for our feelings, and that both the ex-Prince Yôdô and he himself held that no stone should be left unturned to discover the criminals. I then asked him to take charge of a gun which I wished to present to Yôdô as a small return, though not of any great value or beauty, for his kindness to me. We then discussed the constitution which he proposed for the new government, and particularly the senate he desired to see established. The upshot of the conversation was that he promised to come down from Kiôto to see the chief on his arrival, and to stay a few days at Ozaka in order to learn more from Mitford and myself about the English form of government. All we could do on that occasion was to give him some information about the composition of the Cabinet, and the method of carrying legislation through Parliament.

Gotô said he wanted to employ a foreigner, such as myself for instance, to collect information for him, and with whom he could consult. I replied that I was content to serve my own government, and could not take service under that of any other state, but that if the clan wanted the services of an officer they should apply to the minister for the loan of one.

The idea of taking *pay* from a Japanese, however highly placed, did not suit me, and I was resolved, in case I quitted Her Majesty's service, not to seek another career in Japan.

That evening we, that is, Mitford, Noel and I, devoted to a *diner en ville* in the Japanese fashion at a sort of "Trois frères" called Tokaku, and about half-past six we started forth. It was expected that the streets would be full of merry-makers, and the two men of my escort who were detailed to accompany us wished that the rest of them should be summoned to attend us. But I threw the burden of decision on their shoulders by saying that I thought the two of them would be enough for anything, and no more was heard of that proposition. So we issued into the streets, and dived through all sorts of back lanes to find a shorter cut, for my instinct seemed to show the road, but our escort triumphed after all, and they brought us to the place of entertainment by what proved to be a circuitous route.

Some difficulty was experienced in making our way through the crowds of people in flaming red garments dancing and shouting the refrain *ii ja nai ka*. They were so much taken up with their dancing and lantern-carrying that we passed along almost unnoticed, but I was half afraid the escort (*betté*) would provoke a quarrel by the violent manner in which they thrust people aside in order to make way for us; on the contrary, the crowd did not offer any rudeness to us, and let us pass without hindrance. On reaching Tokaku we found the principal rooms occupied by festival makers and the rest of the house shut up. Our messenger had been just that instant turned away with a refusal to receive us. While we stood there trying to persuade the people of the house to give us a room, a herd of young men and boys trooped in, shouting and dancing, and tossing about in their midst a palanquin occupied by a fat doll clad in the most gorgeous robes. All the feasters in the house came out to meet them, one cannot say at the doors, for in Japan there are no doors, but on the thresholds in which the sliding screens run that divide the different parts of a house. After a violent united dance executed by all present, the troop disappeared again. The number of pretty girls who appeared as dancers was much larger than previous experience had led us to suppose Ozaka could possibly contain. We could not prevail on the Tokaku people to take us in, but they gave us a guide to a house about "five minutes" walk distant. There we found the doors locked, the explanation being that all the inmates had gone to the dance. We began to despair of success, and contemplate the possibility of having to return to our quarters and sup on whatever cold food "the philosopher" (Mitford's Chinese servant Lin-fu) could give us. Luckily however the guide, a little man on sturdy legs, said he knew of a house called Shô-ô-tei (Hall of the Old Man of the Pine Tree), where we might as well call, since it lay on our road home. So we went there, and after waiting a few minutes were shown into a very good room, where we had our meal, waited on by the women of the house, who carried on the conversation and passed the wine cup, offices usually discharged on such occasions by *geishas*. The entire absence of fear or dislike on the part of the Ozaka women was very remarkable when compared with the cold and often hostile reception we were accustomed to meet with in Yedo. Curiosity apparently triumphed over every other feeling; and besides, the attendants mostly had their teeth dyed black, a sign of mature age, instead of wearing them as they are naturally, and probably felt immune from attempts at flirtation. We got home early, very pleased with our adventure.

Noel returned next day to his ship, and we moved over from our lodgings in Tera-machi to the quarters prepared for the whole legation behind the castle. The main building was large enough to accommodate the minister and three or four members of what he delighted to call "the staff," a military term picked up during his campaigns in China. The outbuildings were given up to Mitford, the officers of the detachment from the 2/ix regiment shared a second, guests were to be put up in a third, the mounted escort in a fourth, and the fifth I reserved for myself; a temporary shed was provided for the infantry guard.

After settling in, we went to call on Saigô, with whom we found Iwashita Sajiémon, just back from Europe, accompanied by his friend the Comte de Montblanc. The conversation turned on the murder of the two bluejackets of H.M.S. "Icarus." Saigô paid me the compliment of saying that I gave little hits, but hard ones. Opinion seemed to be divided as to the probability of more such murders being committed. I used to find that men who desired the progress of Japan, and were actuated by friendly feeling towards its people, maintained that the attacks on foreigners would cease, but that unprejudiced observers did not give one much encouragement to leave off the practice of carrying revolvers. We gave them clearly to understand that the "Icarus" affair could not be disposed of by the payment of a sum of money by way of "indemnity." They were anxious to disprove the possibility of there having been a plot on the part of Tosa and Satsuma men to murder Mitford and myself when we passed through Fushimi in the previous August. (Fortunately we changed our route for other reasons.) But I had no doubt myself of the fact. Noguchi had told me when we reached Ozaka that he had overheard some men, whom he believed to be Tosa *samurai*, expressing their regret at having failed to carry out their project, and when I told Gotô at Susaki that I had heard this story, he replied that being in Kiôto at the time he too had heard such a report, and took measures to prevent the scheme, if there were one, from being carried out. Saigô tried to show that it could not have been true, and asserted that Gotô was not then in Kiôto. We assured him that we did not think it probable that men of either Satsuma or Tosa would desire to take the lives of foreigners, but that the clans contained ruffians who sometimes took such ideas into their heads quite independently of their chiefs.

Ishikawa Kawachi no Kami, a commissioner of foreign affairs, came to see us on the 18th. He told us that no date had been fixed for the assembling of the *daimiôs*, and no one of them could be blamed if he arrived at Kiôto later than the others. Even supposing that the few who were already there, or were about to arrive, should discuss matters and come to a decision, how could they enforce it? Objections would surely be raised. We came to the conclusion from this conversation that civil war was after all not unlikely to break out, and that the omission to fix a date for the assembly was part of the Tycoon's plan for embarrassing his opponents.

Letters which arrived overland from Yedo on the 20th reported the general impression to be that there was no more a Tycoon, and that Keiki was nobody. So much did distance and report by word of mouth change the look of the situation. Itô Shunsuké's opinion was that war would begin almost immediately, with the object of depriving the Tycoon of a part of his domains, which were far too large for the peace of the country. He had only seven battalions of infantry in Kiôto, all reinforcements having been countermanded in the belief that no cause for war existed. Of course Hiôgo and Ozaka would not be the most peaceful places of residence for foreigners if war did break out, and our Legation, situated just at the back of the Ozaka castle, would be endangered, as that fortress was certain to be the centre of a severe conflict in arms. He wanted to know whether Sir Harry's arrival and the opening of Hiôgo and Ozaka to foreign trade could not be deferred, and whether Saigô had written to the chief to make this proposal. I said "No, of course" (though I did not know). Then, said he, their object must be to open these two places, and so content foreigners, while the Japanese went on with their plans for the reformation of the government. Some one however must be appointed to represent Japan at Ozaka and Hiôgo. I suggested the present governors, but he replied that they would immediately be expelled when the crisis arrived. I rejoined that as long as the insurgent forces did not attack the residences of foreigners, they might do as they liked with the Tycoon, but that if they interfered with us they would have a couple of English regiments and all the foreign men-of-war to fight against, as well as the Tokugawa troops. Itô did not think they would wish to do this, and promised to let me know beforehand when the actual day for taking action became imminent. A body of Chôshiû men was coming up under the command of Môri Heirokurô and Fukumoto Shima, Katsura (*i.e.* Kido) and Kikkawa Kemmotsu being obliged to remain at home to carry on the administration of the province.

Sir Harry arrived on December 24, took a look at the legation quarters, and then went back to the ship that had brought him down. There was a fine confusion all day. I received a letter from Shinosaki Yatarô comparing the present condition of the country to an eggshell held in the hand, and begging me to persuade Komatsu and Saigô to keep the peace. On Christmas Day Kasuya Chikugo no Kami, a commissioner of foreign affairs, called. He said that the *daimiôs* of Hikoné, Bizen and Geishiû, all three men of importance, were in Kiôto, and he appeared to be doubtful what was going to happen. My old friend Hayashi Kenzô, who had made the cruise in H.M.S. "Argus" with me in January, called on the 28th, and reported that 1,500 Chôshiû men had disembarked at Nishinomiya on the 23rd, under the command of Môri Takumi. He also seemed uncertain whether there would be any fighting, but he thought that Saigô and Gotô were trying to keep the peace. My protégé Endo naturally went off to Nishinomiya to see his clansmen, and doubtless to report what he had learned in Yedo to Môri Takumi. The latter had the reputation of being a man of capacity, which was perhaps the reason why he had retired into a private position (*in-kio*) early in life. On the 29th Iga no Kami came to see the chief, accompanied by Nagai Gemba no Kami, who had the credit of being almost the only adviser of the Tycoon at the moment, though of course Iga no Kami was admitted into their secrets. All the governors of Ozaka and Hiôgo were present, and the only subjects of discussion related to the arrangement for opening these places to trade on January 1. "All the governors" is the phrase, because the practice in those days was to duplicate nearly every administrative office.

Next day the two great men came again, and the Nagasaki murders were the topic of conversation. It appeared unlikely that we should obtain any satisfaction. It was however agreed that old Hirayama should again go to Nagasaki, in spite of Gemba's efforts to get him let off this disagreeable errand. The Foreign Office had written approving Sir Harry's action, and he seemed inclined to keep this question hanging over the Tycoon's government as a perpetual nightmare. He told them in the strongest language that we would never desist from pressing the matter until the murderers were seized and punished. Our callers asked a great number of questions about the English constitution, just as Gotô had done, so that it appeared as if both parties were desirous of getting our advice. Then Sir Harry told them that unless they got all troops away from Ozaka, where they might come into collision with foreigners, he would send for a couple of regiments. I could not help feeling that it was unfair of him to meddle in this way in Japanese domestic affairs and thus add to the Tycoon's embarrassments, for as the *daimiôs'* forces had taken Ozaka merely as a stage towards advancing on Kiôto, where else could they go except to the capital? Following on this move, he sent me the following day to Koba Dennai, the Satsuma agent, to explain why he wished their troops to be removed. Koba replied that there were only two hundred and fifty, but doubtless they could be sent elsewhere, and he would write to Saigô on this point. From there I went on to see a Chôshiû man named Nagamatsu Bunsuké, who had come over from Nishinomiya, and was stopping with the Geishiû people. A proclamation was out announcing that the Chôshiû forces, having been ordered to come up to the neighbourhood of the capital, were allowed to borrow the use of the Geishiû *yashiki*, and to be quartered also at the Nishi Hongwanji temple. Nevertheless, they had no wish to come to Ozaka, and thought it a great piece of luck that the English Minister had proposed to the Tycoon's people what they themselves happened to desire most particularly. I found it impossible to get any explanation from Nagamatsu of the real reason for their coming.

Iga no Kami had told us that by a messenger who left Geishiû on the 15th, instructions were sent ordering them not to come, but he went by sea, thus missing a Chôshiû messenger who arrived there by land to report that they were starting in compliance with the orders previously given. (This was evidently a mere fiction.) He also said that on the 20th three Chôshiû steamers full of troops put in at Mitarai in Geishiû, and asked for Geishiû officers to accompany them. This request was refused, and they were advised to return home, which they declined to do, alleging their prince's orders; without a recall from him they were unable to go back to Chôshiû. This was the Geishiû story, which it was impossible to believe. I felt certain that it had been concocted between the two clans, and was simply in accordance with the general plan of campaign. That the Tycoon should have sent orders to countermand the movements of Chôshiû troops was pretty clear proof that when the original instructions were given (if they really were given), the present change of policy on the part of the government was not contemplated — as Iki no Kami had pretended to us — but in reality had recently been forced on them by the confederate *daimiôs*. It had been intended by the chief that I should go down to Nishinomiya to ascertain how the land lay, but having learnt all that the Chôshiû man was willing to tell me, I was relieved from the necessity of undertaking a toilsome journey.

That day, the last of the year 1867, despatches arrived from the Foreign Office sanctioning my appointment as Japanese Secretary, with a salary of £700 a year, in succession to Eusden, transferred to Hakodaté as consul.

CHAPTER XXIV

Outbreak of Civil War (1868)

On New Year's Day salutes were fired at Tempôzan, the fort at the mouth of the Ozaka river, and at Hiôgo, in honour of the opening of the city and the port to foreign trade. Many Japanese had been under the impression that it had been deferred, owing to the notification about the west coast port, *i.e.* Niigata, which they took to mean Hiôgo because of its situation west of Kiôto. I conceived a plan for taking the chief up to Kiôto to mediate between the contending parties, and to prevent the Japanese from cutting each other's throats, and I proposed to go ahead of him to Fushimi in order to make the necessary arrangements with Saigô and Gotô. But this ambitious scheme was frustrated by the rapidity with which events developed at Kiôto.

Rumour was very busy during the next few days. First, we heard that the two princes of Chôshiû had been reinstated in their titles. The Tosa *in-kio* (Yôdô) landed on the afternoon of January 1, and went up to Kiôto at once without stopping at Ozaka. It was said that the Tycoon's position was weak, for he had no support except from Aidzu and one or two of the smaller clans. Chôshiû's people had taken military possession of Nishinomiya, and were patrolling the surrounding country, as if afraid of being attacked. My man Noguchi told us that the Chôshiû troops had left Nishinomiya, and marched ten miles to Koya on the road to Kiôto. All the Aidzu men at Ozaka had gone up to Kiôto. The prince was dissatisfied with the Tycoon's leniency in the Chôshiû business, and intended to resign his office of guardian of the Mikado's person (*Shugo-shoku*). On the 4th January there were symptoms of a great disturbance at Kiôto. The ministers of the other Treaty Powers came to visit the chief and impart their views of what had passed. For the most part these were of very slight value, for they were very much in the dark as to the internal condition of Japan. Von Brandt, the Chargé d'Affaires of the North German Confederation, was so little acquainted with the geography of the country as to confound Geishiû and Kishiû. Endo, who had come back from Nishinomiya, told me that Môri Takumi was already at Kiôto with part of the Chôshiû force, and that another part had occupied Fushimi in conjunction with Satsuma troops. But more significant than anything else was the fact that Satsuma, Geishiû and Tosa were guarding the imperial palace in the place of Aidzu. There was some talk of the Tycoon intending to come down to Ozaka, and boats were said to have been embargoed at Yodo to convey his drilled soldiers down the river. That the object of the *daimiô's* was not to fight the Tycoon, but only to extort concessions from him. They proposed to deprive him of a million *koku* of lands as a punishment for the transgressions of the Tokugawa family. It was certain, Endo said, that the Chôshiû question was settled, and that the guards of the palace had been changed. Noguchi's story was that Aidzu, disgusted with the Tycoon, sent in his written resignation, but that it was intercepted by Kuwana. The Tycoon however had heard of Aidzu's intention, of which he informed Iga no Kami directly after the return of the latter from Ozaka, and sent him his dismissal. Then the three clans above-mentioned seized the environs of the palace. The *daimiôs* thereupon proceeded to the palace to discuss the situation, but the Tycoon refused to attend. He would neither fight nor take any decided action; his sole aim was to arrange matters peaceably. Noguchi evidently was reflecting the war-like disposition of his clan. Ishikawa Kawachi no Kami gave a somewhat different account, but it was clear that up to that moment there had been no disturbance of the peace. The *Kwambaku* Nijô, a nephew of the Tycoon Iyénari, who died in

1841 aged 52, was said to have been dismissed, and either Konoyé or Kujô appointed in his place. Chôshiû's troops had entered Kiôto on January 2.

Ozaka was not perturbed by the events that had passed at the capital, and on the 5th I was able to give an entertainment to my Japanese escort at a restaurant in the city. We had two charming *geishas* to attend on the party, one looking as if she had just stepped out of a picture, the classical contour of the face, arched nose, small full underlip, narrow eyes, and a good-hearted expression of countenance. The other personally more attractive according to western notions of beauty, but with a little of the devil in her eyes. Lastly, there was an old *geiko* or musician of six or eight and twenty, a clever woman. The streets were still illuminated at night for the festival, and crowded with dancers.

On the 6th the mystery was cleared up by Ishikawa, who came to tell me that on the 3rd Satsuma had proposed to abolish not only the Tycoon, but also the *Kwambaku, Tensô* and *Gisô*, the three offices intermediary between the Mikado and the Tycoon. The new administration would consist of *Sôsai*, which sounded like secretaries of state; *Gijô*, which he thought meant a cabinet; and thirdly *Sanyo*, resembling our under-secretaries of state. This looked rather like what we had suggested to Gotô as the framework of the future executive.* He said that this proposal had met with great opposition from others besides the *fudai daimiôs*, who were afraid that the extremists might go further and abolish the Mikado. I endeavoured to reassure him on this point. "It is not," he continued, "a proposal which can be discussed over the table, and fighting must decide." It seemed from his account that the Tycoon personally did not object, but his followers objected for him, while he seemed willing to make every possible sacrifice in order to secure peace.

---

* But it was not quite correct. The *Sôsai* were to be a sort of partners in the office of Minister-President, as we should call it, and *Gijô* were to be the heads of administrative departments.

From a letter of January 4 to my mother, I find that on the 1st Locock, Mitford and Willis, the legation doctor, and I were to have gone over to Hiôgo to dine with the Admiral, whose steam-launch was to come to Ozaka to fetch us. So we went down to the foreign settlement, and, having no other resource, got into a large Japanese boat managed by a single little boy with a paddle. At first we proceeded very slowly, but a sailing boat gave us a tow, after which we shoved off and had to depend again on the small boy. It was bitterly cold, with a north-east wind. I sat in the bows, holding up a railway rug with my teeth. Two of the others protected themselves with umbrellas, and Mitford's Chinese servant, the faithful Lin-fu, hoisted a mat on a pole. So we sailed down the river to the port at its mouth. No signs were to be seen of the launch, so we tried to hire a Japanese boat to carry us across the bay, the distance being only eleven miles and the wind fair, but one and all refused, on account of the gale they would have to encounter in coming back. So we were compelled to put our luggage into a boat and return. The distance from the fort to the Legation was about seven miles and a half, but it took us several hours, as we had to call in at the newly established vice-consulate in the foreign settlement. We dined all together at the Legation, the chief being confined to his room with a sharp attack of lumbago, which had not, however, prevented his making a formal entry into Ozaka on horseback, accompanied by the mounted escort and the guard of fifty infantry detached from one of the regiments stationed at Yokohama.

By January 7 all was over with the Tycoon. That morning Moriyama, the ancient Dutch linguist who used to interpret between the foreign ministers and the *Rôjiû*, came to communicate the news of Keiki's withdrawal from Kiôto. At first I feigned to suppose that he was coming down to see the French Minister. "Not at all, he is coming here, deprived of the office of Shôgun." He had already made up his mind to do this four or five days before, but was persuaded to countermand the orders given for his departure, whereat the commissioners for foreign affairs stationed at Ozaka had rejoiced greatly. But now the orders had been repeated, and would be carried out. We sauntered out to look at the preparations made for his arrival. Small bodies of drilled troops were marching about headed by drummers, and field-pieces were placed so as to sweep the narrow streets. We saw men in all sorts of military costumes with their heads muffled up to protect them from the cold, not presenting a very martial appearance. We went on to the restaurant on the river bank, where in the spring we had been often entertained *à la Japonaise*, and found it full of Aidzu men, whose arms were piled outside. There was a *karô* inside, on whom I paid a call. He ascribed the Tycoon's withdrawal to his unwillingness to fight under the walls of the palace, and described the leading *daimiôs* as being at loggerheads, Satsuma desiring to carry out their plans by main force, and Tosa preferring to rely on reason; but their objects were identical. It was not Kaga, but Tosa, that was endeavouring to negotiate an arrangement between Satsuma and the Tycoon. He talked a good deal about forms of government, and thought that Gotô's plans would be delightful, if feasible, but the nation was not yet ripe for fundamental changes. I agreed with him that representative government would be a curious substitute for the despotic form of authority that had existed hitherto. Mitford and I went out again about two o'clock to have another look at the preparations, and wandered over the Kiô-bashi bridge on to the Kiôto road. Here it was evident that the Tycoon was expected to arrive at any moment. There were wonderful groups of men in armour, wearing surcoats of various gay colours, armed with spears and helmets. Here we found Kubota Sentarô, the commander of the Tycoon's drilled troops, with a couple of colleagues, one of whom told Mitford in bad Japanese that they were very brave and intended to die. I whispered to Kubota that a brave man did not retreat in this fashion. He repeated the explanation of the Tycoon's objection to fighting at the steps of the throne, and perhaps endangering the person of the Mikado. I replied that he should not have given up the guard of the palace. Kubota alleged the Mikado's orders. I suggested that if the Mikado ordered that there should be no fighting, that order must be obeyed. The significant rejoinder was: "Yes, by the Tycoon, but not by his retainers."

We had just got to the end of the street that ran by the castle moat when the bugles sounded to arms, and we saw a long train of drilled troops advancing. We stood on one side opposite to a man wearing a gorgeous red surcoat, till the troops should pass. On they went, followed by a herd of men in fantastic costumes (*Yû-geki-tai*, "brave fighting men"), some wearing helmets with long wigs of black or white hair reaching half-way down their backs, others in ordinary helmets, basin-shaped war-hats (*jin-gasa*), flat hats, armed, some with long spears, short spears, Spencer rifles, Swiss rifles, muskets, or the plain two swords. Then a silence came over the scene. Every Japanese knelt down as a group of horsemen approached. It was Keiki and his train. We took off our hats to fallen greatness. He was muffled in a black hood, and wore an ordinary war-hat. What could be seen of his countenance looked worn and sad. He did not seem to notice us. Iga no Kami and Buzen no Kami, members of his council, who came next, on the contrary nodded gaily to our salute. Aidzu and Kuwana were also there. Then followed other *yû-geki-tai*, and the procession closed with more drilled troops. We turned round with the last of these, and hurried on to see the entrance into the castle. On the way we met the chief, who had come out to have a look at the Tycoon, to whose downfall he had contributed as far as lay in his power. The defiling across the bridge over the moat was an effective scheme of colour, and the procession entered by the great gate (*ôté*). Every one dismounted except the Tycoon. Rain fell, in much accordance with the occasion.

The chief insisted, much against my own feeling, in sending to ask for an interview on the morrow. In the letter I sent, I spoke of Keiki as Tycoon Denka (His Highness the Tycoon). The reply which came back styled him simply Uyésama, the title borne by the head of the Tokugawa family before his formal recognition as Shôgun by the Mikado's Court.

Endo came back with the following information. Arisugawa and Yamashina, both princes of the blood, Ogimachi and Iwakura, court nobles, were appointed *Sôsai*; the princes of Owari, Echizen, Geishiû, Satsuma and Tosa were appointed *gijô*. Ohara (a court noble) and various others were to be *Sanyo*, besides three from each of the great clans. Satsuma in this way was represented by Iwashita, Okubo and Saigô. Those of the other clans were not known to him. The titles of the Prince of Chôshiû and his son had been restored to them. The palace was guarded by Satsuma and Geishiû, Chôshiû's troops held the city of Kiyôto. A Satsuma steamer had left for Chikuzen to bring back the five court nobles who had fled in 1864, Sanjô (afterwards prime minister for a series of years), Sanjô-Nishi, Mibu, Shijô and Higashi-kuzé (subsequently minister for Foreign Affairs).

It was difficult to accuse Keiki of cowardice. No one had ever yet expressed such an opinion of him, and the probability was that he could not put confidence in the courage of his troops. How a new government which did not include the Tokugawa chief could hope to succeed one did not see. He must either join the *daimiôs* or be destroyed. Perhaps the latter alternative was what his adversaries designed. Keiki had declined to see the chief on the following day, and it looked as if the audience would have to be deferred. The policy advocated in the *Sakuron*, translated from my articles in the *Japan Times*, seemed to govern the situation. The opening of Yedo to foreign trade must evidently be postponed, as Locock had declined the responsibility of superintending the execution of the arrangements.

On the morning of January 8 the chief became very impatient, and about noon ordered me to prepare a note to the effect that Locock and I should go to the castle and arrange for an audience. Its despatch was delayed by a private note from Koba Dennai asking me to name an hour for an interview with him. At three o'clock our note was to have gone in, when in came Tsukahara and Ishikawa to inform us that the French Minister was to see the Tycoon, as we still called him, at once, and that Keiki could receive Sir Harry to-morrow at any hour he chose to name. On hearing that he had been outstripped by his colleague, his wrath was unbounded; he claimed priority on the ground of superior diplomatic rank, and ordered out the escort. We proceeded to the castle in pouring rain. I was a little behind the others, and entered the audience chamber just as Roches and Sir Harry were exchanging words about what the former stigmatized as a breach of *les convénances* in interrupting his interview. But he got as good as he gave, and the audience then proceeded, after Aidzu and Kuwana had been presented and ordered to retire. Aidzu was a dark-complexioned man with a hooked nose, about thirty-two years old, of middle stature and thin; Kuwana an ugly young person, apparently twenty-four years of age, pock-marked and of dwarfish proportions. The old fox Hirayama sat behind the Uyésama and took notes. Shiwoda Samurô, who spoke French well, interpreted for Roches and I for Sir Harry simultaneously the words which fell from Keiki's lips. He gave but a lame account of the events of the last few days, professing at one moment to have withdrawn his troops from the palace in accordance with an imperial order, while refusing to recognize another such order, which he felt was equally dictated by Satsuma. Perhaps this was natural on his part, for it abolished his office and forbade him access to the palace. He had had it hinted to him that he should also resign his rank of *Naidaijin*, and offer to surrender two million *koku* of lands; but he had resolved not to heed the suggestion, on the ground that this property belonged to him apart from his office, just as much as the lands of Chôshiû, Satsuma and the other *daimiôs* belonged to them. He appeared to feel that the *daimiôs* had stolen a march on him by preparing their plans beforehand, instead of proceeding with the general congress of princes at which each should be free to speak his own mind; in other words, he was vexed at having been taken in by a stratagem. That the proposal of a congress was merely intended to throw dust in his eyes was pretty evident. He explained the order for the withdrawal of the Aidzu palace guard by saying that other *daimiôs*, amongst them Satsuma and Geishiû, held some of the gates under Aidzu, and that they introduced cer-

tain proscribed court nobles into the precincts after the *Kwambaku*
and other dignitaries had retired for the day on the morning of
January 3rd., and that at noon the same day these persons issued
the proclamation setting up the new government. This he said was
a preconcocted matter; they had it all ready on paper, and took
these measures without consulting anyone. At one time he seemed
to say that the five great *daimiôs* were divided among themselves, at
another he spoke of the decrees as having been agreed to by them
all beforehand. After finishing his account, he asked the opinion
of the two ministers. Both expressed admiration of his patriotism
in surrendering power, and the justice of his desire to settle all
questions by a general congress, Roches in very flattering terms,
Sir Harry more moderately, asking also some pertinent questions,
which were answered without much frankness. Keiki gave as his
reason for coming down to Ozaka his fear lest a tumult should arise
in the vicinity of the palace, and his desire to appease the indignation of his followers. It was his intention to remain at Ozaka, but
could not say whether the opposite party would attack him there.
To another question as to the form of government that had been set
up at Kiôto, he replied that the Mikado ruled nominally, but that
Kiôto was occupied by a set of men who did nothing but quarrel
among themselves, anything but govern. Yet he did not appear to
claim that he himself possessed any authority, and he did not know
whether the other *daimiôs* would rally to his support. Some of those
who were at Kiôto had been disgusted at the congress not having
come into existence, and had returned to their homes; others who
were confounded by the audacity of the five still remained there.
Our inference, of course, was that they were not of his party.

The Uyésama finally said he was tired, and so put an end to the
conversation. One could not but pity him, so changed as he was
from the proud, handsome man of last May. Now he looked thin
and worn, and his voice had a sad tone. He said he would see the
ministers again in order to consult with them. The commissioners
for Foreign Affairs gave us a paper announcing Keiki's resignation of
the office of Shôgun, and the change of his title back to Uyésama.

It turned out that what Koba wanted was to ask whether I could tell him what the Uyésama's plans were; was he returning to Yedo in order to gather his forces together, or remaining at Ozaka with the intention of undertaking a "ruffianly" expedition to the capital. I sent back a reply by Itô that I knew nothing of Keiki's intended movements. To suppose that I would supply information on such points showed great simplicity.

The diplomatic body being intent on the observation of neutrality between the contending parties, held a meeting on the morning of January 9 at the Prussian Legation to frame a declaration, and a request to be informed where the government was being carried on. The French Minister did his best to make the former a declaration of non-partizanship with the *daimiôs*. Shiwoda his interpreter and I had to translate it into Japanese, which we did separately. His version was very literal, and he rendered "divers partis" by a term which could only be applied to conspirators. I also wished the translation to be in free Japapese, not adhering slavishly to the wording of the original, and we had a quarrel over this point. After Shiwoda left me, Ishikawa came in, to whom I showed me version, in order that whatever were the result, no doubt should be possible as to the attitude of the British Legation. Up to a late hour at night nothing was settled, except that the interview with the Uyésama, which was to have been immediate, was put off. On the following morning, after the two translations had been compared, the chief suggested an alteration in the French original which removed the cause of dispute. Then Locook and I went round to the other ministers and got them to accept my translation. While we were at the French Legation Hirayama and Kawakatsu came in, and they took the paper away with them to prepare the Uyésama's reply. A difference had arisen between Roches and Sir Harry as to relative precedence. The former was only minister plenipotentiary, while our chief was envoy extraordinary and minister plenipotentiary. According to all rules he was senior, but the other ministers held that Roches, having arrived first in Japan, had precedence. This decision did away with Sir

Harry's claim to be *doyen*, and his reason for asserting a right to have audience before any of his colleagues. The latter pretension was, of course, one that could in no circumstances be upheld.

At three o'clock the whole diplomatic body assembled at the castle in the *o-shiro-jô-in*, all the other apartments being occupied by Aidzu, Kuwana and Kishiû. The same ceremony was observed as at an European court. Behind the Uyésama stood his pages; at his left Aidzu, Kuwana, Makino Bitchiû no Kami, Matsudaira Buzen no Kami (two councillors of state), and a noble person whom I took to be Ogaki, then Hirayama and Tsukahara. On his right were a number of *ô-metsukés*. In Japan, as in China, the left was the position of honour. Close to His Highness stood Iga no Kami, on whom devolved the task of reading the translation of the Diplomatic Body's address. The reply was a very long one, spoken by the Uyésama himself. He began by explaining his policy, vindicating his retirement from Kiôto, and expressing his determination to abide by the decisions of a general council. His reply to the particular question asked by the ministers was that foreigners should not trouble themselves about the internal affairs of Japan, and that until the form of government was settled he regarded the conduct of Foreign Affairs as his own function. The commissioners for foreign affairs, who were probably apprehensive that they might to-day become nonentities, were obviously relieved. They became joyful, and somewhat triumphant. The audience was over in an hour and a half. After the delivery of his speech the Uyésama went round the row of foreign ministers and spoke a few words to each. To Sir Harry he said that he hoped for a continuation of his friendship, and for his assistance in organizing the Japanese navy. The chief replied in florid style that his heart was the same as it had ever been towards him, and that he trusted the sun shining through the windows was an omen of his future, a metaphor which I found some difficulty in putting into Japanese. However, the Uyésama pretended to take it all in. One of the private secretaries, Tsumagi Nakadzukasa, came in the evening to assist me in translating the answer into English.

From Kuroda Shinyémon I received the correct text of the Kiôto decrees. He told me that the *daimiôs* were unanimously awaiting Keiki's reply to the demand for two million *koku* of lands and the surrender of a step in court rank. They expected to be joined by the other western *daimiôs*, and also by the northern ones. I advised that they should not fight if they could help it, but if they judged it necessary, to do it at once. He nodded assent. It was intended that in three or four days the *daimiôs* would declare their intentions to the foreign ministers. It showed, I thought, a good deal of courage on the part of a Satsuma man to come all the way past the castle sentries to our legation, and to spare him this risky proceeding I promised to go and see him at his own quarters.

Ishikawa brought me a document purporting to be a protest of the retainers of Awa, Hizen, Higo, Chikuzen and other great *daimiôs* against the violent proceedings of the Satsuma party, and insisting on the convocation of a general council. As far as could be inferred from their language, it did not appear that war was contemplated by either party. We heard that in a day or two Owari, Echizen and the court noble Iwakura would come down to receive the Tokugawa answer to the demands already mentioned. The troops of Sakai Uta no Kami of Obama in Wakasa, a powerful adherent of the Uyésama, had been sent to Nishinomiya, where there were probably Satsuma and Chôshiû troops. Endo however was of opinion that war would certainly break out. He said that a hundred of Satsuma's people arrived from Kiôto last night to escort thither the five court nobles who had been recalled from exile.

On the 12th I went to see Kuroda Shinyémon and Koba Dennai, and gave them copies of the address of the foreign diplomatic representatives to the *ci-devant* Tycoon as well as of his reply. They acknowledged the authenticity of the protest of Awa and the other eleven clans, and said that there were others who had disapproved of his restoring the sovereign power to the Mikado. From this it was evident to me that the reason why the five clans were in such a hurry to act was that they wanted to carry out their plans before the others arrived. Kaga was said to have left Kiôto in order to muster his forces for the assistance of Keiki. It now became evident that the Tokugawa party were preparing for war. Kishiû's men were at Tennôji, Sumiyoshi, and Kidzu, close to Ozaka. Aidzu had occupied the castle of Yodo, a few miles south of Kiôto on the direct road, with 500 of his own troops, and 300 of the *Shinsen-gumi,* a recently raised body of Tokugawa infantry, had also proceeded thither, while all along the road small detachments were stationed. Owari, Echizen and Iwakura were expected on the 18th January, but it was possible that the five clans might march on Ozaka before that date.

Koba Dennai invited us to the Satsuma *yashiki* on the 14th, so Mitford and I went there, and there we met Terashima Tôzô (formerly known as Matsugi Kôan), who had arrived from Kiôto that morning. He explained that it was thought better to delay issuing the Mikado's announcement to foreign countries of his having assumed the government until the question of a surrender of territory by the late Tycoon, which Owari and Echizen had undertaken to arrange, should be settled. (It must be understood that in conversation with Japanese this title was never employed, as it was only invented for foreign use. Either Tokugawa, or the *Baku-fu,* was the term we employed.) It had been originally proposed that only Aidzu and Kuwana should come down to Ozaka, in order to return by sea to their respective countries, but as they were unwilling to come alone, Keiki was allowed to accompany them. The territory to be surrendered by him was to form the nucleus of a national treasury, and it had been proposed by Tosa and some other clans that each *daimiô* should sacrifice a smaller proportion for the same purpose, but Satsuma objected to this latter part of the scheme. The Mikado's notification would be in archaic Japanese,* stating that he was the head of the confederated *daimiôs,* That he alone was the sovereign of Japan, that the office

---

* This was stated in reply to a question about the court language. When the document eventually was delivered, it was found, as far as my memory serves me, to be framed in classical Chinese.

of Shogun was abolished, that the government was entrusted to a general council of *daimiôs* subject to his supervision, and lastly that the treaties were to be remodelled in his name. We quite agreed with him that to issue the announcement in the present undecided state of affairs would be premature. A civil governor had been appointed for Kiôto, and a night patrol to arrest marauders and disturbers of the public peace. Of course Keiki's plan of calling a general council of *daimiôs* to deliberate on the state of the country was put forward because he was certain of securing a majority by the aid of those of them who were his own vassals, and that he would get a vote carried in favour of reinstating him in his previous position of authority. This stratagem had been defeated by the bold stroke of Satsuma getting possession of the Mikado's person.

Next day Sir Harry paid a visit to the castle with the object of pumping the Uyésama about his plans for the general council and the new form of government, but he was anticipated by inquiries about the British Constitution, which took up all the time available, and he was only able to get in a question or two at the end. These the Uyésama adroitly parried by saying that the events he narrated on the last occasion of their meeting had upset all his arrangements.

The escort was ordered, and we were obliged to leave. As we were going, Aidzu came up and saluted the chief with great cordiality, who replied that he was very fond of making the acquaintance of *daimiôs*, and already knew several. He hoped to know more of them. Could the Prince of Aidzu tell him whether the Prince of Awa was at Kiôto or Ozaka. Aidzu replied that he did not know. The chief rejoined that last year he had been to Awa's place, and had been very civilly treated. This rather broad hint, however, produced no effect.

The same day there came to see me a young Tosa man, of Kishiû origin, named Mutsu Yônosuké, with whom I discussed the question of the recognition of the Mikado's government by the foreign ministers. I explained that it was not for the foreign representative to take the first step. We had received assurances from the Tokugawa chief that he would continue to carry on the administration, and as no communication had yet come from the Kiôto side, we had to go on holding official relations with him. If the Kiôto government wished to assume the direction of affairs they should inform the *Baku-fu* that they were going to notify their assumption of foreign affairs to the ministers, and then invite the latter to Kiôto. This would be to all the world a clear proof of the position held by the Mikado.

Mutsu replied that he had not come as a messenger from Gotô, but was merely giving his individual views. He hought a prince of the blood should come down to Ozaka and hold an interview at the castle with the foreign representatives, at which the Tokugawa chief should attend and resign the conduct of foreign affairs, on which the prince of the blood would deliver the Mikado's declaration of policy. Of course he would be escorted by *daimiôs* and their troops. I warmly approved his suggestion, and at his request promised not to divulge it to anyone.

The next day Mitford and I went again to the Satsuma *yashiki*, and found that a list of questions to be put to us had been sent down from Kiôto. We gave one answer to everything, namely, that it was only necessary for the Mikado to invite the ministers to Kiôto, and compel the ex-Tycoon to abandon his claim to conduct the foreign affairs of the country. They proposed to make Keiki withdraw his answer of the 10th. I gave them copies of Sir Harry's Note conveying the Queen's condolences on the death of the late Mikado, and of Itakura's reply; but they were not able to say whether the Note had been communicated to the court. The *daimiô* of Higo had arrived and proceeded to Kiôto. Bizen was to garrison Nishinomiya. The five exiled court nobles were expected to arrive that evening, and would go up to Kiôto by the river.

Echizen and Owari came down from Kiôto and went to the castle, as had been announced several days previously. The former sent a message through the Japanese Foreign Department to ask when his retainers might come to see our guard go through their drill. We replied that they did not drill. Perhaps they had heard of the mounted escort being exhibited to the Tycoon on some previous occasion. We should have preferred to have this request made to us direct.

On the 23rd Ishikawa came to tell us that our Japanese guard was to be increased by one hundred men in consequence of disturbances that had occurred at Yedo. On the night of the 16th, he said, some Satsuma men had attacked the Shiba barracks of Sakai Saémon no jô, *daimiô* of Shônai in the north, but were beaten off. On the next day but one Sakai's people went together with some troops which they had borrowed from the government, intending to demand the surrender of the men concerned in the violence of the 16th, but before they reached the Satsuma *yashiki* fire was opened on them with field pieces and small arms, to which they replied. In the end the *yashiki* was burnt to the ground. Some of the defenders were killed, others captured, and some escaped to a Satsuma war vessel that was lying in the bay. This at once attacked a government ship, but the result of the fight was unknown. At any rate, the other *yashikis* of Satsuma and of Shimadzu Awaji no Kami had also been burnt. It was possible that the Satsuma people who had escaped might try to revenge themselves by creating disturbances at Ozaka. Though it was not likely that they would attack the castle, it was thought desirable as a measure of precaution to station some troops where we were. The chief's answer was that they must first write all this officially to him and await his reply before sending a single man to the Legation. To alarm us still further Ishikawa told us a story of boatmen having reported that the student interpreters we had left at Yedo had been fired at from the Satsuma *yashiki* in the street called Tamachi, the date of the letter which brought this news being January 14th. As this was two days before the Satsuma attack on the Sakai *yashiki*, we did not give credit to his tale. What we thought was that Keiki had returned a refusal to the ultimatum of the *daimiôs*, and feared they would attack him at Ozaka. Echizen and Owari returned to Kiôto that day, but we did not hear what had been the result of their mission. On the 24th the Admiral arrived with news from

Yedo confirming all that Ishikawa had reported. His account of it was that on the night of the 17th the Satsuma people had contrived to set a part of the castle on fire, and carried off Tenshô-In Sama, a princess of theirs who had married the last Tycoon but one. Thereupon the government people attacked all the Satsuma *yashikis* in Yedo and burnt them, and the occupants getting on board their steamer put to sea. In the meanwhile, the "Eagle" and other government vessels received orders to get up steam and attack her. A sea fight ensued, which ended by the "Eagle" and the Satsuma steamer disappearing in the offing. The former was met by H.M.S. "Rodney," the Admiral's flagship, returning next day with her fore-yard gone, and the latter was seen off Cape Oshima, south of the province of Kishiû, on the 23rd. The story that our student interpreters Quin and Hodges had been fired at about the 12th as they were passing in front of the Satsuma battery in a Japanese boat was true, but no harm was done.

CHAPTER XXV

Hostilities Begun at Fushimi

O n the evening of the 27th a great blaze was seen in the direction of Kiôto. Endo said it was at Fushimi, three miles from
the capital, and that the ex-Tycoon's troops and those of Satsuma
and his allies were fighting there. The government ship "Kaiyô-
maru" with others were blockading Satsuma vessels at Hiôgo. On
the preceding day a couple of battalions had been seen parading
for the march to Kiôto, and were probably among the troops
engaged at Fushimi. Report said that Keiki himself would take
the field in a few days. Willis' servant, the faithful Sahei, who
passed through Fushimi the same day, saw bodies of Satsuma
men waiting about in the streets and warming themselves at fires,
but he could not say for certain whether there were any other
imperialists with them. A little on the nearer side of Fushimi
were the *shinsen-gumi*, and behind them large bodies of infantry,
all apparently eager for the fray. During the succeeding night the
Satsuma *yashiki* on the Tosa-bori canal, where we used to meet
our friends, was burnt down. Some accounts said it was set on fire
by the occupants before they stole away, others that the Tokugawa
troops sent three or four shells into it and so caused the blaze. At
any rate the Satsuma people got into boats and went down the
river, pursued by the Tokugawa men, who fired at them from
the banks, and killed two of the fugitives. Sir Harry went to call
on Itakura, who told us that the town of Fushimi had been set
on fire by Satsuma troops, who were opposing the entry of the

Uyésama's forces into Kiôto. Fighting began at four o'clock, and
the result was not yet known. Another detachment marching up
the Toba road, which follows the right bank of the river, fell into
an ambuscade and was forced to retire. He could not tell us when
the Uyésama would start. The troops that had been opposed at
Fushimi were his advanced guard, destined to occupy the castle
of Nijô in Kiôto, as he was returning there shortly, having been
invited to do so by Echizen and Owari. All the other *daimiôs*
were tired of the arrogant conduct of Satsuma. Probably it was
his troops alone which had fought at Fushimi. Ishikawa gave me
a copy of a letter from the commandant at Fushimi, who writing
to Tsukahara and Buzen no Kami mentioned that guns had been
lent for the destruction of the Satsuma *yashiki*. It was reported that
Tsukahara had disappeared, and it was conjectured that he had
been shot during the imperialist attack on the official residence of
the governor of Fushimi, but we could not ascertain that he had
been seen farther on than Yodo.

Next day the chief went to Itakura's house just inside the Tama-
tsukuri Gate near our legation, where he saw Nagai Gemba no
Kami. Nagai told us that up to last night the Tokugawa troops had
been repulsed on both points of their advance, and were going to
try another road, the Takéda kaidô, further to the west. To us it
appeared that they ought to have done better, as they were 10,000
to 6,000. They reported the enemy force to consist of Satsuma
and Chôshiû men, assisted by *rônin*, which probably meant the
men of other clans, but the remaining *daimiôs* appeared to be
preserving a neutral attitude. The Uyésama's commander-in-chief
was Takénaga Tango no Kami. The denunciation of Satsuma's
crimes was carried by the advanced guard, whom Gemba no Kami
described as the Uyésama's "retinue." He still maintained that
the Uyésama had not wished to have recourse to arms, but was
forced into it against his will. Still Gemba no Kami could not give
a satisfactory explanation of the firing on the Satsuma steamer
"Lotus" as early as the evening of January 26. The same evening
reports came in that the Tokugawa troops had retired 7 1/2 miles

from Fushimi, and had destroyed the bridge over the Kidzu-kawa river below Yodo, to obstruct the further advance of the Satsuma forces. Seven boat-loads of wounded had come down the river.

From what we heard on the morning of the 30th, it appeared that the prospects of the Tokugawa party were not very encouraging. In the afternoon great fires were distinctly visible from the hill by the castle, in the direction of Hirakata and Nashimoto, about half-way between Ozaka and Fushimi, which showed that the battle was approaching nearer. A consultation was held by the chief with the Legation staff, the result of which was that we were to hire as many boats as possible to convey the archives to the British squadron, and when they were placed in safety we should be able to await the development of events with calmness. After dinner Sir Harry went to see the French Minister, and returned about half-past nine with information that a circular was to be addressed to the foreign ministers announcing that the Uyésama could no longer defend them, and they must take their own measures for the protection of their flags. At eleven came an official messenger with the circular, who promised to get us as many boats as possible on the following morning to move our baggage; and after packing up the archives we went to bed. At four o'clock in the morning, Locock woke me with the news that a note had come from the French Minister to say that the enemy would enter the city early in the day, and that we must run off at daylight with what we could carry. So we all got up, frightfully cold though it was, and packed up our belongings. No boats had arrived. At daylight my Japanese escort came to say that with the greatest difficulty they had managed to procure one large boat; on this the archives were placed, and started off about nine. Then came Ishikawa, who said he was powerless to help us. The imperialists had not yet appeared, but he considered it advisable for us to get off at once. So Sir Harry and I went off with him to look for the porters, whom we met outside the great gate of the castle. Just at that moment we saw a curious procession going in. It consisted of a palanquin like a *mikoshi*, one of those gods' litters carried in religious pageants, a large umbrella held over it and two men with lanterns on long poles in front. Ishikawa let out that he thought it was conveying a messenger from the Mikado. He and I came back with the porters, and brought the greater part of the baggage down to the bank of the stream behind the legation, but still there were no boats. So we went off to the governor's residence and tried to interest the officials on our behalf. They appeared to be in a state of extreme perturbation, and declared that it was impossible to procure any boats. Ishikawa almost shed tears, and vowed that he would never again try to get boats and porters for the legation; it was none of his business. We agreed therefore to deposit the greater part of the baggage inside the castle. Luckily however this proved unnecessary, for when I returned to our quarters I found the chief radiant with joy, five boats having arrived in the interval. About ten o'clock therefore we were able to make a start for the foreign settlement, but I stayed behind with the six men of my Japanese escort, capital fellows who had stuck to me ever since we made the journey overland from Ozaka to Yedo in 1867. I had to procure boats for my own baggage, which by an oversight had been left behind, and to get the stores removed to the castle. However, more boats arrived than had been expected, so I put all the baggage on board, including even a huge pot of mince-meat. Unluckily, a fine gold lacquer cabinet of Mitford's, for which he had recently paid 800 *ichibus*, was overlooked. About noon I started for the foreign settlement in great triumph. There was even a house-boat (*yakata-bune*). I asked a man whom I had never seen before for whom this was intended, and was greatly flattered when he replied innocently that it was for Satow-*sama*. This enabled me to go down comfortably instead of walking the whole distance. On the way we all nodded and dozed, for we had had no proper night's rest. From time to time we were challenged by the posts on the banks, but no attempt was made to stop us. On arriving at the settlement I found the wind was blowing too strongly from the west to allow of our passing the bar at the mouth of the river. The chief, Locock, Willis and Wilkinson were all fast asleep. Captain

Bruce, commandant of the infantry guard, and the constable had gone off again to the Legation to endeavour to recover the remainder of our property that had been left behind, and I got Lieutenant Bradshaw a boat with the same object. Towards evening they returned. A steam launch from the squadron was lying off the settlement, and the Legation was located at the vice-consulate there. It was bitterly cold, and we were glad to get to bed, after what was a very good dinner considering the circumstances. The other foreign representatives were at Tempôzan, at the mouth of the river, in miserable huts, and with very little to eat. We felt pity for them, mingled with pride, when we compared our situation with theirs. Rumours were flying about among the townspeople that Keiki had been declared a rebel (*chô-téki*).

About nine o'clock on the following morning (February 1), Locock and I took an escort from the 2/ix detachment and went off to the castle to see what was the state of things there. In front of it there was a great crowd, and all the gates seemed deserted. We knocked at the governor's door, but got no answer, a clear sign that he and his people had taken to flight. The crowd laughed. We sent in to the castle by one of my Japanese escort to inquire who was there, and were told in reply that Keiki had departed, leaving it empty. We went on to the Legation, where we found everything just as we had left it. We got back by noon, and as we were at lunch there came in a detachment of thirteen Frenchmen, who in return for being stoned by the crowd had fired and killed some eight or nine people. This was looked upon as a wholesome lesson to the rabble not to cry out abuse of foreigners, but nevertheless was much to be regretted, as it would tend to make the foreign colleagues believe Ozaka unsafe for themselves. During our walk to the castle and back we had observed no signs of hostility, a fact which seemed to show that the population were able to distinguish between nationalities. The French Legation had been pillaged and the furniture smashed.

After lunch, Sir Harry, Willis and I went down to Tempôzan, the chief to call on his colleagues, Willis to attend to the wounds of some Aidzu men who had been brought down from Kiôto, where they had fought against the imperialists. The colleagues were furious with Sir Harry for havihg been so fortunate as to save all his baggage and archives, and for having had the pluck to remain four miles nearer the supposed danger than they had. A rather angry discussion ensued. Sir Harry declared that he would not leave Ozaka unless he was able to carry off every atom of Legation property, and he did not know when that might be possible. They, on the contrary, said that having struck their flags, it was their intention to move across to Kôbé (Hiôgo), and await the course of events. I went to make friends with some of the Aidzu wounded, who were waiting for boats to put them on board of Tokugawa ships. They asserted that they would have beaten the enemy if they had been properly supported, but Tôdô had turned traitor at Yamazaki (on the right bank of the river, nearly opposite Yodo), which was the most important point of the defence, and Keiki's general Takénaga had gone over to the enemy at Yodo itself. Moreover, the drilled infantry were useless; if one man ran the rest followed like a flock of sheep (as we should say). They estimated the Satsuma force at the low figure of 1,000, but said the skirmishing of the enemy was very good, and they were armed with breech-loaders. Keiki had run away, they knew not whither, but probably to Yedo. We found that the fort at Tempôzan, and one a little further up the river, which had hitherto been under the charge of Kôriyama (a Kiûshiû *daimiô*) had been dismantled, the guns in the former being spiked, and the ammunition embarked in the Tokugawa warship "Kaiyô-maru," which left at noon. Keiki was believed to be on board of her. Old Hirayama was in the fort at Tempôzan, but studiously concealed himself. Chanoine (many years afterwards for a brief period French Minister of War) and another officer of the French military mission had arrived the previous night from Yedo, but had had to leave again, greatly disappointed that they had come too late for the fair. Obviously it had been intended that they should act as advisers to Keiki's commander-in-chief. The town of Sakai was reported to have been burnt, and also the houses round the Namba-bashi bridge over the Yamato-gawa, but it was not known whether by accident or intentionally. No Satsuma men had yet entered Ozaka. The French Minister was our authority for a story that Keiki, on finding that the majority of the *daimiôs* were arrayed against him, had surrendered the castle and city of Ozaka to Echizen and Owari, because they had been kind and polite to him when they came on their mission from the court! The Aidzu men were very grateful to Willis for the assistance he gave in attending their wounded, and apparently regarded the English as the best and kindest people in the world. It was resolved by Sir Harry that he should go to Hiôgo in order to avoid a quarrel with his colleagues, and I volunteered to remain at Ozaka with Russell Robertson as acting vice-consul, and half the guard from the 2/ix under the command of Bruce, so that the honour of the flag might be maintained. It was certain that Noguchi and my Japanese escort would stand by me, and we were determined to fight to the last if we should be attacked, but that I did not anticipate. I despatched the Chôshiû student Endo Kiôto-wards to urge that the *daimiôs* should forthwith make their declaration of policy to the foreign representatives, as Mitford and I had given the draft of a notification to our Satsuma friends, and there was also my private understanding with Tosa on that subject. The Aidzu soldiers at the fort said that Satsuma men had been found in the castle in disguise, and that there even were some amongst Keiki's drilled troops; cunning devils they must have been if all we heard was true.

Accordingly on February 2, the chief went away to Hiôgo to arrange for H.M.S. "Rattler" to convey Locock to Yokohama, where he was to be in the charge of the Legation, and also for his own temporary withdrawal to Kôbé. About half-past eight in the morning we saw from the vice-consulte a puff of white smoke ascend in the direction of the castle, followed by dense clouds of black smoke. The report soon spread that the castle was on fire, and so it was in fact. After breakfast Locock and I took forty of the 2/ix guard, with Bruce and Bradshaw, and went off to see the fire and find out whether our Legation had been burnt. We marched along the bank of the river to the Kiôbashi gate of the castle, and turning in there, found that the granaries and the *hommaru* (inner circle) had been set on fire, but no one could tell us by whom this had been done. The wind was blowing from the north, and sparks had spread the conflagration to some of the huts previously occupied by the drilled troops on the south side. We walked round to Tama-tsukuri, where we found that the Legation buildings were being plundered by people of the lowest class. We pursued some of them, but were not in time to put an end to the devastation. All the furniture had been destroyed, and the godown sacked. Unfortunately this contained Mitford's beautiful *étagère*, which had no doubt been carried off. There was an immense crowd in front of the castle, and men were pouring in and out of the gates, but they offered no opposition to us, and did not stone us as we might have expected them to do. The mob had, of course, destroyed the official residence of the governors as far as was possible.

We got back to the vice-consulate about mid-day, and found there Endo, who had already returned from his mission. He said that two or three hundred of the Chôshiû folk were already in the castle, and that an official had been left behind to hand the place over to Owari, but the flames broke out before the ceremony could be completed. Whether the fire was started by the rabble or by Keiki's followers he did not know. The only imperialists who had yet arrived were Chôshiû men.

About two o'clock we left the foreign settlement in a lifeboat with Locock and Wilkinson, who were to be embarked on board H.M.S. "Rattler" and proceed to Yedo. Halfway down the river we met the steam-launch, with two other large boats, bringing the chief and Captain Stanhope of H.M.S. "Ocean," who, seeing what they took to be a general conflagration of all Ozaka, had come to take us away and haul down the flag. How angry I was! We were not in the slightest danger, either of being attacked by the victors or from the burning of the castle, and I would have answered with my life for the safety of every person left with me. Had I not received repeated assurances from Satsuma, Tosa and Chôshiû that our Legation would be respected. However, there was no help for it; orders had to be obeyed. We found great difficulty in procuring barges, and had to send the steam-launch out to seize as many as we wanted. We secured three, into which we packed everything, including the vice-consul's furniture; the archives and the baggage of the 2/ix having been already started off. Everything was got away by half-past six, and we eventually crossed the bar in safety. The steam-launch, in which I was, grounded three times, and finally stuck fast, but Captain Bullock of H.M.S. "Serpent" fetched me off in his gig. Willis, who, with the safe containing the Legation funds, was in a boat towed by the "Serpent's" pinnace, did not get on board till midnight. Then she took all the barges in tow, and steamed over to Hiôgo.

Next morning we landed there, and got the baggage on shore. Most of the party found accommodation at the consulate. I took possession of the district administrator's house, which had been occupied by some custom-house officers. The caretaker objected. I insisted however that as we had been turned out of Ozaka by the *Baku-fu*, we had the best right in the world to the abandoned accommodation of the *Baku-fu's* officials. So I had my baggage carried in and set up house there. Our chief had quartered himself at the consulate, and the other five foreign representatives, French, Dutch, American, North-German and Italian, occupied the custom-house, a large two-storeyed building in foreign style, which the officials would otherwise have set on fire to prevent it falling into the hands of the victors. The governor, an old acquaintance of ours named Shibata, had chartered the steamer "Osaka" at $500 a day (say £100) to convey himself and his staff back to Yedo, whither he started the same afternoon.

Satsuma's man Godai, I learnt, had gone to Ozaka the previous night, or early that morning, in order to assure the chief that he might safely remain there, but of course he came too late. The next thing one heard was that it had been intended to declare Keiki a rebel if he did not withdraw his troops from Ozaka, Kiôto and other points between the two cities, and that Satsuma, Geishiû, Chôshiû and Tosa were charged with the duty of using force to compel obedience if he refused to listen to the advice offered to him by Echizen and Owari in the first place. This seemed to explain his hasty flight, but from any point of view, European as well as Japanese, it was disgraceful. After informing the diplomatic representatives that he regarded himself as charged with the direction of foreign affairs, the only further intimation they received from his officials was that he could no longer protect the Legations, but he never so much as hinted that he was about to abscond. I was also informed that it was intended to invite the ministers to Kiôto, and Keiki had been ordered to transmit the invitation to them, which of course he omitted to do. In fact the policy of the Tokugawa government from the very beginning of their relations with the outer world of Europe had been to keep foreigners from coming in contact with the Kiôto party; and in this they were heartily assisted by Roches, the French Minister. I well recollect how, when we went to the castle to see Keiki after his retirement from Kiôto, some of the commissioners for foreign affairs jeered at me, saying, "Of course you now expect to get to Kiôto, but don't be too sure," or words to that effect.

A report having been circulated that somebody, either Satsuma or Tokugawa people, were going to blow up the martello tower which stood at the end of the dry river bed between Hiôgo and Kôbé, boats were sent from H.M.S. "Ocean," the French flagship "Laplace" and the "Oneida"; the door was locked and the key taken away.

CHAPTER XXVI

The Bizen Affair

On February 4, Bizen troops were passing through Kôbé from the early morning, and about two o'clock in the afternoon the retinue of one of their *karô* shot an American sailor who had crossed the street just in front, which according to Japanese ideas was an insult that deserved mortal chastisement. After that they attempted the life of every foreigner whom they met, but fortunately without any serious results. What at a later time became the foreign settlement was then an open plain; at the upper edge of it ran the high road, and as the Bizen people passed along they suddenly opened fire, apparently from breech-loaders. Then every foreigners was seen scurrying across the plain for safety. The American marines immediately started in pursuit, our guard of 2/ix was called out, and some French sailors were landed. Half of our guard under Bruce were despatched to occupy the entrance from Kôbé into the foreign quarter, and the other half followed in pursuit. On reaching the Ikuta-gawa stream-bed, at the eastern extremity of the plain, we perceived the Bizen men marching in close column about 600 or 700 yards ahead, so we passed through the gap in the river bank and opened fire. There were at least half-a-dozen civilians with us, all armed with rifles, who likewise fired. Willis, Mitford and I had only our revolvers. At the first volley from our side, the enemy turned into a field by the side of the road, and fired at us from below a bank. On our returning their fire, they all took to flight. We pursued them, every now and then firing at one or other who had failed to get under cover, but finally they took to the hills and disappeared completely. Sir Harry, followed by his mounted escort of ex-policemen, galloped some distance down the road in the direction of Nishinomiya, but was unable to catch sight of the foe. If any of them had suffered from our fire, he must have been carried off by his comrades. Willis found an old peasant woman lying by a bank with a bullet wound through both ankles, whom he brought back and cured of her hurt. Then we took prisoner a wretched porter, who escaped with his life by a mere miracle, for at least fifteen revolver shots were fired at him at close quarters as he rose from his place of concealment, without his receiving a single wound. We opened the baggage which had been dropped by the fugitives, but found nothing of value, only three small weapons, representing a cross between a matchlock and a howitzer, and a few carpenters' tools. From the porter, whom we led home as our prisoner, we ascertained that the detachment consisted of two Bizen *karô*, Ikéda Isé and Hiki Tatéwaki, who were on their way with about 400 men to reinforce the garrison of Nishinomiya, and that some of them had remained behind at Hiôgo. On returning to the settlement we found a quantity more baggage which had been dropped in Kôbé by the men whom Bruce had intercepted. Sentries were then posted along the main street of Kôbé as far as the first barrier gate, where a strong guard was stationed with a howitzer. A line of sentries was also drawn round the north and east sides of the plain. From some of these, who were Americans, sailors or marines, an alarm was raised about ten o'clock. Great alacrity was displayed by the naval people; field pieces were landed and numbers of small-arms men. After all, no enemy made his appearance to justify so great a stir being made. I proposed to Sir Harry that we should issue a manifesto declaring that if Bizen's people did not satisfactorily explain their behaviour, the foreign powers would make it a quarrel with Japan as a whole. He induced his colleagues to agree to this, and I started our prisoner back to his people with a copy, though I did not feel much confidence in its reaching its destination. About half-past one, a hundred Chôshiû men sent down for the protection of Kôbé and Hiôgo against Tokugawa troops arrived just outside our post in the middle of the village, and were within an ace of being fired on by our guard. Luckily I came up at the moment, and went to an inn at which they had billeted their rank and file, to arrange that they should withdraw, which they did very readily.

During the afternoon, four steamers belonging to Chikuzen, Kurumé, Uwajima, and one it was thought to the Tokugawa, were seized at Hiôgo and Kôbé, to hold as a "material guarantee."

The morning of February 5 brought me again an invitation from Yoshii to visit him at Ozaka and talk over affairs, but it was impossible, for I had too much on my hands. The "Whampoa," a steamer belonging to Glover & Co., of Nagasaki, had arrived, and a rumour was invented and spread that she was conveying 800 Satsuma troops, so I was sent off in a boat to stop their landing. There was not a single Satsuma man on board. Some men of Awa in Shikoku had decamped in boats from Hiôgo, and our people pursued them, but as they were only a few in number and very miserable in appearance, they were not molested. We then issued proclamations, with the wording of which I was entrusted, explaining why we had seized the steamers, a second exhorting the people to go quietly about their business, and a third announcing that all unarmed persons would be allowed to pass our posts. About one o'clock a Dutchman (appropriately enough in accordance with popular notions) raised an alarm that the Japanese were advancing to the attack. The report spread as far as the quarters of the Foreign Representatives at the custom-house, where von Brandt was making a great fuss about a body of at least three hundred armed men that he asserted were menacing Kôbé from the hills close by on the north side. I had a look at them through his glass, and certainly saw men, but if they were armed, I was sure they were friendly Chôshiû men. So I got leave to take Lieutenant Gurdon of H.M.S. "Ocean" with ten men, and we started out to explore, and to paste up our proclamations wherever we found one of Chôshiû's. The only people on the hills turned out to be peasants. The Chôshiû troops were billeted at Shôfukuji, a large temple, or Buddhist monastery, about two miles away among the hills, so it was manifest that they were keeping their engagement to us. We marched through Hiôgo, and pasted a copy of our first notification on the door of the Bizen official hotel (*honjin*), and the whole series of four on the house where their troops had passed the night of the 4th. Having accomplished all this, we returned to relieve the anxiety of our fellow foreigners.

Just as I got back I met Yoshii and Terashima, who had come down to have a talk. The chief gave them a short interview, at which he advised them to send off at once and get the Mikado's messengers to come down with their notification to the Foreign Representatives. They wanted him to let 300 Satsuma troops pass through our lines, but he refused, on the ground that as we did not know anything officially from the Mikado, we could not recognize Satsuma as acting under His Majesty's orders. So they agreed to bring their men into Hiôgo by another route. Then I went off with them to their *honjin* at Hiôgo, and they told me a good deal about the course of recent events. Theirs had been a continuous course of victory from the very first, for being like "rats in a bag," they had to fight hard for their lives, and were compelled to be victorious. At Fushimi they had had a desperate fight, but after that they pressed on and drove the Tokugawa forces into Yodo. This place, as well as the long bridge over the river, was fired by the retreating troops. Aidzu's men fought very bravely. The plan of the *Baku-fu* was to get the Satsuma and Chôshiû soldiers engaged with Aidzu and the *Shin-sen-gumi* (a body of armed *samurai* recently raised), and then to creep round to the imperialist right with the drilled infantry and seize Kiôto. Higo too was only waiting for signs that Satsuma was getting the worst of it, in order to seize the palace, but now he was very humble. The number of Satsuma and Chôshiû men actually engaged was about 1,500, the remainder being employed in the defence of the city. Anyhow, as the roads to be held were very narrow, large bodies could not have been employed to any advantage. They loaded their field-pieces with bags of bullets, which did great execution on the enemy. About twenty Satsuma men were killed, and the entire list of casualties did not exceed 150. They took a good many prisoners, and captured numbers of guns and small arms, etc. Tôdô's defection was a great help to the imperialists. His men had been fighting against them, but when the Mikado's standards, the sun in gold on a red ground and the moon in silver, were displayed, they lost heart and changed sides. Another of their advantages was their good skirmishing. Ninnaji no Miya, a prince of the blood, also known as Omura no gosho, was the commander-in-chief. They anticipated that all the clans as far as Hakoné would submit, and that Sendai would join them. Kishiû already showed signs of a desire to come to terms, and Ogaki had submitted, as indeed had nearly all the other clans who had fought, with the exception of Aidzu. They said that Iwashita, Gotô and Higashi-Kuzé, the latter one of the five runaway court nobles, were to come down to Kôbé to communicate the Mikado's proclamation to the foreign representatives. It would be the desire of the new government to show perfect impartiality in its relations with foreign states, but as the English had been the good friends of the Kiôto party, they would always be regarded with particularly grateful and amicable feelings. I remained with Yoshii and Terashima till half-past ten in the evening. They seemed to admit that we had acted within our rights in seizing the steamers, and while I was with them they wrote and despatched long letters to their own people at Ozaka, explaining the affair and enclosing our notification. They also wrote up to Kiôto urging that no time should be lost in despatching the Mikado's messengers with the announcement to the foreign ministers.

Early on the morning of the 6th Satsuma troops came over from Nishinomiya in large boats, and were landed at Hiôgo, in accordance with our agreement of the previous day.

Some retainers of Omura in Hizen, Watanabé Noboru and Fukuzaka Kôzô, came to inquire about our intentions with regard to their steamer which had been seized, and was now held by the

French. The steamer belonged to Uwajima, and was only borrowed by Omura for this trip. So I gave them copies of our manifesto against Bizen, and another one explaining why the steamers were seized, and they declared themselves quite convinced that we had acted rightly. Our bluejackets however and the Americans and French also, were getting us a bad name by committing all sorts of petty pilfering.

I went to call on Katano, commander of the Chôshiû troops, who said that the two Bizen *karô* had gone to Ozaka or Kiôto, he did not know which, after the affray on the 4th, the rank and file remaining behind.

It was on February 7th that the Mikado's messenger, Higashi-Kuzé, accompanied by Iwashita, Terashima and Itô, with a small retinue, arrived at Hiôgo in a little steamer belonging to Geishiû. As soon as I received the note informing me of this, I went over to the chief, on whom devolved the task of seeing his colleagues, and arranging with them the place and hour of meeting. Apparently they were greatly annoyed, especially the French Minister, at finding themselves as it were ignored, and that their English colleague had thus become the channel of communication between the Mikado and themselves. They tried to pump him about the contents of the imperial message, but he did not tell them even the little he knew. It having been decided that the interview should take place at the custom-house at noon on the following day, I went over to Hiôgo and informed Iwashita. There had been a report that 300 Bizen men had entered the town, but I could not find a trace of them. All our marines had been withdrawn on account of the difficulty experienced in forming mixed posts, and the Americans now had charge of the gate in the middle of the town, so that they would henceforth be responsible for all the petty pilfering that went on. I found them most unpleasantly strict, and because I had no pass they obliged me to go a long way round in order to reach my destination and get back again.

So on the 8th of February the fateful communication was made by Higashi-Kuzé at the place and hour previously fixed. Higashi-

Kuzé was a small man even for a Japanese, with sparkling eyes, irregular teeth, which were not yet completely freed from the black dye (*o-haguro*) worn by court nobles, and with a stutter in his speech. The document was drawn up in classical Chinese, and might be thus translated: —

> The Emperor of Japan announces to the sovereigns of all foreign countries and to their subjects that permission has been granted to the Shôgun Tokugawa Yoshinobu* to return the governing power in accordance with his own request. We shall henceforward exercise supreme authority in all the internal and external affairs of the country. Consequently the title of Emperor must be substituted for that of Tycoon, in which the treaties have been made. Officers are being appointed by us to the conduct of foreign affairs. It is desirable that the representatives of the treaty powers recognize this announcement.
>
>   February 3, 1868.   MUTSUSHITO
> (L.S.).

This document was very ingeniously framed. It assumed as a matter of course that the treaties were binding on the Mikado, and therefore only mentioned them incidentally, in saying that the Mikado's title must be substituted for that of Tycoon. After the translation had been made and shown to all the ministers, a fire of questions was directed against the envoy, who answered them well.

Roches asked whether the Mikado's authority extended throughout the whole of Japan, to which he replied coolly that the rebellion of Tokugawa prevented that from being the case at present; but it would gradually extend all over the empire. Roches' interpreter (who was a Tokugawa man) then made a wilful mistake

---

* Keiki, by which he was usually spoken of, is the pronunciation of the two Chinese characters with which his name Yoshinobu was written.

by representing the envoy to say that "if all the people submitted to the Mikado, he would be able to govern the country," whereas he really said, "the people will all submit to the Mikado as a natural consequence of his taking the reins," as we ascertained on repeating the question. With regard to the Bizen affray, the Mikado's government undertook to protect the lives and property of foreigners at Kôbé for the future, and to satisfy the demands of the Foreign Representatives for the punishment of Bizen. On these conditions, it was agreed that the marines and bluejackets should be withdrawn to the ships, and the steamers released. Ozaka was not as yet perfectly quiet, but normal conditions would soon be restored, and foreigners would be formally invited to return there. On the part of the Mikado's government the envoy desired to know whether the Foreign Representatives would report the announcement to their governments and proclaim it to their people. This was tantamount to asking for "recognition." Roches became very angry, and said: "We must not throw ourselves upon the necks of these people," whereupon the Italian Comte de la Tour and the German von Brandt raised their voices against him, and replied that so far from doing anything of the sort we had waited till they came to seek us (not knowing, of course, of our secret negotiations at the Satsuma *yashiki* in Ozaka). On this, everyone said he would report to his government, and that satisfied the envoy. A great deal of desultory conversation went on while he was waiting for the gunboat to convey him back to Hiôgo, but on no particularly important topic. Itô said to me that it was all right about our going to Kiôto, that there would be no difficulty. I pretended to be indifferent, though in truth I was very eager to get a view of the city and its famous buildings, from which foreigners had been so jealously excluded for over two centuries.

Next day Higashi-Kuzé, at his own request, went to visit H.M.S. "Ocean."

A joint note was sent in to him demanding reparation for the Bizen offence, namely a full and ample apology and the capital punishment of the officer who gave the order to fire. The ministers, and especially M. Roches, insisted that the fact that they were under fire increased the gravity of the offence — as if their presence there could have been known to the Bizen troops passing through on the march. Itô seemed to think that the government would agree to make the Bizen *karô* perform *harakiri*. He said that Chôshiû had relinquished to the Mikado the territories he had conquered in Kokura (on the south side of the strait of Shimonoséki) and in the province of Iwami. Katsura (*i.e.* Kido) and Itô wanted him to go much farther, and resign to the Mikado all his lands, retainers and other possessions, except so much as might be required for the support of his household. If all the *daimiôs* would do this, a powerful central government might be formed, which was impossible with the existing system. Japan could not be strong as long as it was open to every *daimiô* to withdraw his assistance at his own pleasure, and each prince to drill his troops after a different fashion. It was the story of the North German Confederation over again; the petty sovereigns must be swallowed up by some bigger one. The *daimiôs* of Matsuyama and Takamatsu in Shikoku, who were partizans of the Tokugawa, would be destroyed, and their territories imperialized. Tosa was charged with the execution of this measure, having offered to undertake the duty. It was probable that Himéji, a few miles west of Hiôgo, would also be attacked by the imperialists.

A notification, signed by Iwashita, Itô and Terashima, as officers of the Foreign Department, was placarded about the town, informing the people that the Mikado would observe the treaties, and enjoining on them proper behaviour towards foreigners. It was given out that Roches, with his interpreter Shiwoda, would leave that evening for Europe, Baron Brin, the secretary, remaining in charge. The official declaration made the day before by the Kiôto envoy had quite thrown him on his beam-ends, and he could not bear to stand by and see his policy turn out a complete failure. His intention was to proceed first to Yokohama, where I suspected that he would try to rehabilitate his reputation as a diplomatist by some of his artful tricks. However, he thought better of this

idea, and remained in Japan until matters shaped themselves so
that he could accept the Mikado's invitation to Kiôto, and so
decently recognize the new political arrangements. The other
ministers behaved very correctly, having very little to do but to
follow Parkes' lead.

The foreign ministers had another interview on February 10 with
Higashi-Kuzé, who was accompanied by Iwashita and Gotô. They
told us that Itô was to act temporarily as superintendent of customs
and governor of the town of Kôbé. It seemed curious, we thought,
that a man of certainly not very high rank should be thought fit
for this double post, and that the common people should be ready
to obey him, but the Japanese lower classes, as I noted in my diary,
had a great appetite for being governed, and were ready to submit
to any one who claimed authority over them, especially if there
appeared to be a military force in the background. Itô had the
great recommendation in his favour that he spoke English, a very
uncommon Japanese accomplishment in those days, especially in
the case of men concerned in the political movement. It would
not be difficult, owing to the submissive habits of the people, for
foreigners to govern Japan, if they could get rid of the two-sworded
class, but the foreigners who were to do the governing should all of
them speak, read and write the Japanese language, otherwise they
would make a complete failure of their undertaking. But as the
samurai were existent in large numbers, the idea was incapable of
realization. Looking back now in 1919, it seems perfectly ludicrous
that such a notion should have been entertained, even as a joke, for
a single moment, by any one who understood the Japanese spirit.

Gotô was to proceed to Kiôto with the joint note about the Bizen
business, and there was every reason to expect that the court would
agree to the infliction of the capital sentence, but they would probably desire to let the *karô* Hiki Tatéwaki perform *harakiri* instead
of having him decapitated. At least that was what I heard privately
from my Japanese friends, who also asked that, until the question was finally disposed of, foreigners should abstain from visiting Nishinomiya, where Bizen men were stationed. Everything

was now reported to be quiet at Ozaka, and we looked forward to returning there in a few days.

Gotô Kiûjirô, as he had called himself previously, now resumed his real name of Nakai, and was attached to the Foreign Department. He was a very cheery and gay personality, always ready for any kind of fun and jollity, and when an entertainment had to be got up, it was to him that its organization and conduct were entrusted. In this way he earned the nickname of *Gaimushô no taikomochi*, "jester of the Foreign Department."

On the 11th, Higashi-Kuzé with his staff came to the consulate to talk business with Sir Harry and von Brandt, a talk which lasted three hours. We exhibited to them all the Treaties, Conventions and Agreements respecting the opening of the ports, all of which had to be confirmed by the chief minister for Foreign Affairs, Ninnaji no Miya, a prince of the blood, in the name of the Mikado. There was much said by way of question and answer about the recent transactions at Kiôto, which ended in their promising to furnish a detailed narrative, rebutting the statements made by Ogasawara Iki no Kami and other supporters of the former régime. The general council, which Keiki complained had been violently anticipated by Satsuma, ought to have met on December 15. The western *daimiôs* waited a considerable time after this date, but none of the others arrived, so they were compelled to take action. The demands made on the *Baku-fu* were that, together with the governing power, they should surrender as much territory as would suffice to maintain that power. They estimated that 2,500,000 *koku* of lands would then be left to the Tokugawa family, besides the territories of the *fudai daimiôs* and most of the *hatamoto*. Tokugawa had declined, but offered to surrender 800,000 *koku* of lands, and to continue his subsidy for the support of the imperial establishment. When leaving Kiôto however he had agreed to make the surrender demanded of him, though this was strenuously opposed by Aidzu and Kuwana. Then when Echizen and Owari came down to Ozaka, they invited him back to Kiôto to conclude these arrangements, but it was never intended that Aidzu and Kuwana should form the van of his retinue, and that was how it happened that fighting ensued. At the date of this conversation nearly all the *daimiôs* west of Hakoné had been reduced, or had given in their adhesion, or would soon be compelled by force to submit to the Mikado, and thus about seven out of the eight million *koku* of lands possessed by Tokugawa would be actually in the hands of the Mikado. If Tokugawa then submitted, he would be left peaceably with the remainder of his possessions. It was to be feared however that he would endeavour to regain what he had lost, and in that case the Mikado's party would destroy him. It was intended to despatch forces against him by the north-eastern road (which passes through the provinces of Echizen and Kaga), by the central road through Shinshiû, and by the Tôkaidô. Ii Kamon no Kami of Hikoné and later adherents to the Kiôto party would be placed in the van of the imperial forces, in order that their fidelity might be tested. The *daimiôs* of the north had nothing to thank Tokugawa for, and there was no reason why they should support him. Awa had submitted, and was assisting in garrisoning Hiôgo. Prisoners taken in Kiôto during the recent fighting would be returned to their homes on the restoration of peace, instead of being put to death according to the ancient Japanese custom in civil war.

We understood that the Mikado's party intended to call upon the Foreign Powers to observe strict neutrality.

A report went about that Nambu Yahachirô and Shibayama Riôsuké, old friends of mine in the Satsuma *yashiki* at Yedo, had been put to death, the one by crucifixion the other by simple decapitation, and I felt that I should like to do something to avenge them, for to western minds the idea of taking the lives of prisoners was revolting.

We heard that old Matsudaira Kansô, the retired *daimiô* of Hizen, Mr Facing-both-way as he was universally regarded, was expected to make his appearance shortly at Kiôto. Also that the

---

* Hayato no Shô, who went to Europe for the French Exhibition of 1867.

governors of Nagasaki had departed, and that the town was occupied by Satsuma, Geishiû and Tosa, Hizen holding the batteries.

The mail which reached us on February 13 brought a letter from Iki no Kami to Sir Harry very diplomatically framed, in which Keiki's failure to reach Kiôto was attributed entirely to the machinations of Satsuma, and a hope was expressed that a momentary success on the part of the latter would not cause the violation of engagements of long standing. He entirely burked the question put to him by Locock, as to the course the chief should take in case the Mikado sent an envoy to the Foreign Representatives. The news came from home that Mukôyama,* had complained at the Foreign Office of Sir Harry having applied the title of "Highness" to the Tycoon instead of "Majesty"; to this Lord Stanley replied that he understood there was a higher title than that of *Denka* in use in Japan, and that consequently *Denka* could not mean "Majesty," which was the highest designation applicable to any potentate. It was also a noteworthy fact that in this letter of Iki no Kami *Heika* (which is synonymous with "Majesty") was reserved for the Queen, *Denka* being used of the Tycoon. As modern slang would have it, this was giving away the whole show.

Godai and Terashima came to see me, after which they had a long talk with the chief on political matters. They told him that in three weeks or a month's time affairs would have made sufficient progress at Kiôto to enable the government to invite the Foreign Representatives thither in order to enter on friendly relations. They also asked for the loan of a surgeon to attend to their wounded at Kiôto. The chief replied that the alleviation of suffering in the case of any human being was always a pleasure, and that as the Legation doctor had looked after the wounds of Aidzu men, no objection could exist to his treating the hurts of others; but his consent would depend upon the nature of the reply the ministers received about the Bizen affair. The question of the Legation returning to Ozaka was mooted, and Buddhist temples were offered for our accommodation as the buildings which we had occupied behind the castle had been too much knocked about to be fit for a residence; but this would not matter much, as they would be occupied only temporarily. Godai and Terashima were very anxious that I, and I alone, should visit Ozaka at once. (In fact I believed I could have gone anywhere that I liked, for instance to Kiôto the next day, by only expressing a wish.) Godai wanted to buy an English man-of-war with which to attack Yedo; it was a curious notion that we had H.M. ships for sale. I advised them to get their Note demanding neutrality on the part of all Foreign Powers sent in at once, because then they could request the American Minister to prevent the "Stonewall Jackson" being delivered to the Tokugawa people, as well as the two iron-clads from France which were expected. Godai said further that Uyésugi and Saské, two *daimiôs* of Déwa province, had asked to have the duty of chastising Aidzu entrusted to them, and their request had been granted.

Next day they brought Notes from Higashi-Kuzé enclosing copy of the instructions he had received from Daté Iyo no Kami (Uwajima) and Sanjô Sanéyoshi (one of the fugitive court nobles) accepting on behalf of the Mikado's government the terms of settlement of the Bizen affair laid down by the Foreign Representatives, namely the capital punishment of the officer who had given the order to fire on foreigners and the apology. The ministers expressed themselves gratified with the promptness of the reply, which was received twenty-four hours before the expiration of the delay accorded. They said they would wait three or four days for the letters of apology and for the announcement of detailed arrangements for carrying out the execution. Godai and Terashima stated that if Bizen were to refuse to surrender the ofiicer, the Mikado's troops would compel obedience. They also brought a Note from Ninnaji no Miya, ratifying the Treaties and all subsequent engagements in the name of the Mikado, and notifying his own appointment as Chief Administrator of Foreign Afrairs, with Daté, Sanjô and Higashi-Kuzé as his assistants. There was also a Note demanding strict neutrality on the part of the British Government and its subjects, and a like Note to each of the other Representatives. Facsimiles of the Mikado's notificatioin to the Treaty Powers were also handed to those of the ministers who had not yet received it. The request for Willis to go to Kiôto to treat the wounded was repeated and granted, and a proposal made by myself to accompany him was accepted with alacrity.

News was received that day from Nagasaki that the withdrawal of the governor Kawadzu Idzu no Kami had been quietly effected on the night of the 7th, and a provisional government formed on the following day of all the *daimiôs'* agents in the port, thirteen clans in all. The direction of local affairs had been offered by the governor to Hizen and Chikuzen, but they declined undertaking such a responsibility without the co-operation of the other clans. All the subordinate custom-house officials and interpreters, as well as 500 troops raised at Nagasaki for defensive purposes, were taken over by the provisional government, so that the business of the port had not been interrupted for a single day. A few fires broke out, but were soon extinguished.

CHAPTER XXVII

First Visit to Kioto

The next day was taken up with our preparations for Kiôto, including the purchase of sufficient stores for a fortnight. Saionji Yukiyé of Uwajima called, and I offered him a passage to Ozaka in the gunboat which was to convey Willis and myself to the starting-point of our journey. A Satsuma man named Oyama Yasuké,* whom I had known in Yedo, came to announce himself as commander of our escort. That European surgical skill was very necessary for the treatment of the wounded can be seen from the fact I find recorded in one of my letters home, that the Japanese surgeons had sewn up all the gunshot wounds, and some of their patients died from this cause. The prospect of visiting the city from which foreigners had been rigidly excluded ever since the ports were opened in 1859 was enticing, especially as we were now being invited thither by the very people who, we were told by the Tycoon's officials, had all along tried to keep us out.

Sir Harry was now in high spirits and in very good temper. We had no more of the interviews with Japanese officials at which he used strong language, and interpreting for him, which used to be a painful duty, was changed into a labour of love. Success makes a man kind, and certainly Sir Harry had been successful. By the departure of the French Minister he became the *doyen* of the

---

* Afterwards Field-Marshal Oyama. Commander-in-chief in Manchuria in 1904-5 in the Russo-Japanese War.

diplomatic body, and the rest of his colleagues followed his lead with perfect unanimity, for they had begun to see that his policy was the right one to adopt. It was his influence that induced his colleagues to join him in issuing declarations of neutrality in the conflict between the Mikado and the Tycoon, which among other things prevented the delivery to the latter of the American iron-clad ram "Stonewall Jackson," bought with Japanese money. These declarations were subsequent to the departure of M. Roches to Yokohama, and while his secretary Baron Brin was in charge of the French Legation.

We started about nine o'clock in the morning of February 16 on board the gunboat "Cockchafer," having in our train Noguchi, a boy-pupil named Tetsu, one of my Japanese escort named Matsushita, and Willis' servant the faithful Sahei. Off the Ozaka bar we found the Satsuma steamer "Keangsoo" and another engaged in disembarking a large body of troops. On landing at the city we found lodgings had been taken for us at a Buddhist temple close to a burnt Satsuma *yashiki* called Takamatsu, and no sooner had we seated ourselves than a messenger arrived, in the person of Koba Dennai's secretary, to ask us to stop two or three days in Ozaka so that Willis might see some men who were ill of fever, and that boats to convey us up the river were not obtainable. We replied that Willis had not made any preparations for treating fever patients, and had brought appliances for wounds only; that we supposed boats were as numerous at Ozaka as they had been before the recent fighting up-river, and that we could not understand this delay being interposed, after we had been so urged and hurried by Iwashita and Terashima, who had wished us to start even a day earlier than we had found possible. So the secretary went out, and Yasuké after him. They stayed away a whole hour, and we came to the conclusion that the permission to bring us into Kiôto had been revoked, resolving to return to Kôbé rather than waste our time at Ozaka. At four o'clock Oyama returned, bringing with him an old, ugly, mis-shapen fellow named Ijichi Shôji, who appeared to be one of the Satsuma generals. After bestowing on us a vast quantity of complimentary phrases, this individual brought out in a jerky St Vitus' dance sort of way the same sort of excuses as had been made by Koba's secretary. To this we returned the same answer as before, with the addition that if they found it inconvenient to receive us in Kiôto, we would go back at once to Kôbé. This decided attitude induced Ijichi to give orders at once for boats to be got ready, and we then went off to see the castle ruins. There was a notice at the front gate refusing entrance to any but Satsuma and Chôshiû men, but as we had one of the former clan with us we found no difficulty in gaining access. Passing through the gate we came upon a wide scene of desolation. The white-plastered towers and wall of the inner moat were gone; all the barracks and towers of the outer wall to the south likewise; only the stones of the gateway to the right remained. We passed into the *hommaru* or keep, through the gateway constructed with huge blocks of stone, the largest measuring 42 by 16 feet and 35 by 18 feet. Nothing was left but the masonry, giving somewhat of the look of the ancient Greek Cyclopean walls of Tiryns. The magnificent palace itself had disappeared; all that there was to show where it had once stood was a level surface covered with half-calcined tiles. The way to the foundation tower of the *ten-shi* remained clear, and we mounted to the summit. Here in the exfoliation of the stones were traces of a former conflagration; a plaster wall built right round had escaped not only the flames, but also the explosion of the great magazine close underneath. Four doors in this wall gave on to the outer parapet, from which the view of the river, with its three great bridges, winding through the city to the sea, and the hills on the further side of the bay surpassed anything I had ever seen. In the opposite direction the stream could be distinguished here and there as it meandered through the fields down from Fushimi. The interior of the castle had been completely destroyed, with the exception of a few rows of store-houses, which had escaped through being situated to windward of the flames. The three concentric walls of masonry, including the one from which we looked, reminded one of the appearance that West's Tower of Babel would have presented if viewed from above. We sounded the well, whence is drawn the famous *ô-gon-sui*, or golden water, and found the depth to be 140 feet. Issuing again from the gate at the base of the *tenshi*, we came upon a quantity of burnt armour and helmets piled up round a store-house which the flames had spared; some had been melted by the violent heat into an irregular mass of metal. There were also piles of thousands of matchlock barrels, with a few rifles among them. Curious to see what had become of our temporary legation buildings, we took our way out of the ruined Tamatsukuri gate. The whole place, exceptiug the houses that had been occupied by Mitford and myself, was level with the ground, and even they had been gutted so completely by the rabble as to be quite beyond the possibility of repair. It was a melancholy sight.

On returning to our lodging we found Godai, who with many profuse apologies conducted us to a house close by which was better fitted for inhabitation by human beings.He explained that we could not start for Kiôto before the following morning. From what he said it appeared that delay in issuing the permission from the Imperial Court for our entrance into Kiôto was caused by Ninnaji no Miya's having unexpectedly gone there himself, but as he, Godai, had at once despatched a messenger, the pass would be received at Fushimi the next evening before our arrival there. This arrangement being accepted by us, *saké* and its accompaniments were ordered in, and half-a-dozen singing girls attended to help us pass away the time.

February 17, at ten o'clock in the morning, saw us start in a houseboat from the stairs below the burnt Satsuma *yashiki*. The party, seven in number, included our merry friend Ōyama, and another officer in command of a guard for our protection. Although we had only just breakfasted, *saké* and various dishes were soon introduced, and the entertainment was repeated all through the day at short intervals. It was a fine morning, and the scenery was as beautiful as on the previous occasion in May, when Willis, Wirgman and I had made the same journey. Conversation naturally turned for the most part on the incidents of the recent fighting. The Tokugawa forces had been pressing all day along Toba road until four o'clock, when they made an attempt to force the Satsuma position. The attack was met by a steady fire from a field-piece planted in the middle of the path (for the so-called road was very little wider), and from three others in position on the left, while troops concealed in the brush-wood opened on them with musketry. This unexpected reception threw the Tokugawa men into confusion, and they retired precipitately leaving numbers of dead and wounded on the ground. The imperialists at Fushimi, on hearing the sound of firing in the direction of Toba, from which place they were about a mile distant, attacked the Tycoon's troops as they formed outside the governor's residence, and the fighting lasted till the middle of the night. The officers on the Tycoon's side set the example of flight, and their men could not resist the temptation, so that the rout became general. After Yodo was passed no more fighting occurred on the road to Ozaka. At Hirakata the drilled infantry broke into the storehouses of the townspeople who had run away, and disguised themselves in the finest garments they could find; other townspeople pursued the marauders and killed six of them.

We passed Hirakata at four, but did not reach our hotel at Fushimi till midnight. Tôdô was holding his old post at Yamazaki, and Kaga occupied Hashimoto. Dear old Yoshii was at our hotel to welcome us, and more respectably dressed and shaven than I had seen him for a long time past. A fresh supply of *saké* was produced, and we kept up the conversation till past two in the morning. These late hours did not prevent our being ready to start at ten o'clock, escorted by a company of eighty-eight men. Large palanquins of the sort called *kiri-bô kago*, that is "with a Paulownia-wood pole," used by personages of the highest rank, had been provided for us, but Willis, who was 6 feet 3 high and big in proportion, was not able to double himself up inside, and preferred to walk. The route lay through Fushimi for some way, issuing on to the Takéda road, fifteen feet wide, then ascended to the top of a dyke constructed to keep the river within bounds, crossed a bridge and so into the city of Kiôto. At a temple by the roadside we fell in with Komatsu, who had followed us from Fushimi, and by one o'clock we arrived at Sô-koku-ji, a Buddhist temple close to the Satsuma *yashiki* at the back of the imperial palace. Shiuri no Taiyu, the Prince of Satsuma, paid us a visit of welcome, accompanied by his confidential adviser Saigô. After shaking hands with us both, he sat down in a chair placed at the end of the table by the door, while we occupied chairs behind the table in a position of greater dignity. All his attendants squatted on the floor. After the exchange of a few complimentary speeches he took his leave, and we accompanied him as far as the door. The grounds of Sô-koku-ji were extensive, and well planted with trees, the temple itself a fine example of wood architecture, the state apartments divided off by splendid gold paper screens decorated with landscapes in Indian ink, the coffered ceilings fifteen feet above the floor. To suit the convenience of us westerners a table and chairs had been provided, and a luxurious feast was served immediately after the prince had taken his leave. In the afternoon Willis went to look after the wounded, while I took a walk down to the bookshops in Sanjô-dôri, accompanied by an escort. It was not until I reached this point that the populace seemed to be certain that I was a foreigner; one little boy asked whether I were not a native of Loochoo. The Tokugawa Castle of Nijô struck me as insignificant compared with many a fortress belonging to a small Fudai *daimiô*. It was then occupied by the troops of Owari; the *yashiki* which had been the head-quarters of Aidzu as military governor of Kiôto was tenanted by a few of Tosa's troops. The men who had accompanied me about the city took the liberty of sitting down with us to dinner, and showed great want of good manners. It was evident that they took a departure from the polite social observances characteristic of the Japanese to be an evidence of what was held to be civilization, *i.e.* in their own words *hiraketa*.

Next day I went to ask Saigô about the settlement of the Bizen affair. He replied that Hiki Tatéwaki, the *karô* who was riding in the palanquin, could not be regarded as free from blame, and that he would be imprisoned in the charge of three clans. The officer who had been riding on horseback would be executed. The Mikado's inspectors (*kenshi*) would attend, the sentence would be pronounced, and a copy would be furnished to the foreign Representatives. Afterwards the sentence and an account of the proceedings would be circulated throughout the country for the information and warning of others. Saigô said the Mikado's government hoped to be able to keep the whole of Japan in order, so as to prevent the necessity ever arising for foreigners to take the law into their own hands. I said that this view was shared by Sir Harry; that in regard of the Bizen outrage he had felt confident that an envoy would be sent from the Mikado, and he had therefore resisted the solicitations of those around him, who had urged that a force should be despatched against the Bizen people at Nishinomiya; he preferred to leave the opportunity open to the Mikado. Saigô also explained the reference in the Mikado's proclamation regarding the observation of the treaties, to the "reform of abuses," to mean that the new government would propose a revision of those agreements. I mentioned three points on which changes were desirable, firstly, the residence of the foreign ministers being fixed at Yedo (for it was naturally supposed that the government of the country would in future be conducted from Kiôto); secondly, the confinement of foreigners to a radius of ten *ri* (245 miles) round treaty ports; and thirdly, the circulation of all foreign coin throughout the country. While abolishing the ten *ri* limit, it should be made obligatory on a person travelling about the country to carry a passport signed either by the Minister or the Consul, and countersigned by the governor of the port from which he set out. This last proposal was in fact one made by the Japanese themselves.

In the afternoon we went to return the call of the Prince of Satsuma. As during his visit yesterday, he scarcely opened his lips, but Willis said that he had treated Sir Harry in the same way when he went to Kagoshima in 1866, and that it was supposed he was advised by his councillors not to talk, lest he should make a fool of himself; a probable though not very charitable explanation. We spent the afternoon in exploring the city, which had been little more than half rebuilt after it was burnt in 1864 in the Chôshiû attack on the Palace.

Next day I went with Yoshii to call on Gotô, to whom I spoke about the Bizen affair. He told me pretty much the same thing as Saigô, but less decisively. He talked of executing the man who used his spear before the firing began. Then he discussed the new constitution, and said he despaired of getting a deliberative assembly, because the majority would always be stupid and wrong-headed. I advised him to make the experiment nevertheless; if the members ran their heads against a block of stone, they would learn reason from the blow. He seemed to favour the idea of governing by a *junta* composed of the prime minister and the cleverest men in the country, in default of one man of heroic mould, who should rule autocratically. Of course he included himself among "the cleverest men" (*jinketsu*). During this put of our conversation Gotô had excluded Yoshii, as well as Saionji of Uwajima, who happened to be calling on him, and Yoshii expressed his annoyance to me afterwards at having been treated with so little confidence. I pacified him by saying that we had been discussing the settlement of the Bizen affair. After these two were admitted some general conversation ensued among them, from which I gathered that it was by no means decided as yet who was to be what, and that the chief men of the different clans found it difficult to manage each other, that mutual jealousy, and especially jealousy of Satsuma, prevented their pulling together. I gave them a hint to use in revising the treaties, namely, the establishment of mixed courts for trying cases between foreigners and Japanese, instead of deciding them according to the laws of the defendant's nationality. I also called on Katsura (Kido), but we did not meet till the next day, when he came to our lodging in company with a Chôshiû naval captain named Shinagawa, who for some time past had been living in Kiôto as a Satsuma man. Yoshii also turned up, but the conversation flagged until Willis came back from the hospital, and during lunch a heated argument arose as to the best way of preventing affrays from happening between Japanese and foreigners. Katsura and I had previously agreed that the Japanese Government should discuss the procedure with the foreign representatives; foreigners should be informed that to break through a procession is an offence in Japanese eyes, and Japanese on the other hand should be taught that they must not use weapons, but simply arrest offenders and hand them over to their own authorities; further, that when a *daimiô's* train was to pass along a thoroughfare, constables from a mixed force of westerners and Japanese should be stationed to keep the road clear. Willis dissented from this view, and maintained that the only way to preserve the peace between foreign rowdies and Japanese bullies was to keep them apart, and to carry the high road round at the back outside Kôbé. My argument against this, in which Katsura concurred, was that a change of road would give rise to a great deal more ill-will between the opposite nationalities than the murder of a few foreigners, and that from what we had hitherto seen in this country a little fighting would open the eyes of the Japanese and make us all better friends than before; in fact, we held it was better to apply caustic at once than to let the disease linger on and attempt to cure each symptom as it presented itself. We did not settle the question, but I noted down what precedes as being a Japanese view.

In the evening I went to call on Okubo Ichizô, a Satsuma *karô*, who was one of the councillors of the Home Department. Last year he and I had sent presents to each other, but had never met, so I wished to make his acquaintance. Instead of merely exchanging formalities, we had some interesting conversation. He said that 7,000 infantry were being sent forward to Hakoné, and 5,000 to a pass on the Nakasendô. Satsuma and Chôshiû were determined to prosecute the war, and perfect unanimity prevailed among the *sanyo* (councillors). Even Echizen and Higo, who at first had been opposed to the employment of force, were now working hand-in-hand with the other clans. The *daimiô* of Ogaki, who was a councillor of the Finance Department, until recently an adherent of the Tokugawa, had expressed his hope that the expedition against Yedo would soon be sent on its way. Probably the Mikado would accompany the army in person, a step which would greatly weaken the rebels. He thought that the return of M. Roches to France would have the effect of determining the Tycoon to submit, as he would have no one to rely on for material assistance. If he submitted, his life might be spared, but Aidzu and Kuwana must lose their heads. At Ozaka the discovery had been made of the diary kept by a confidential adviser of Keiki's, in which the false hopes that had given rise to the expedition against Kiôto at the end of last month were plainly expressed; the other clans were represented as getting tired of Satsuma, and even Chôshiû to be divided into two parties, one for war the other for peace; that Gotô Shôjirô was inclined towards making terms with the Shôgun, and that the Court desired to see him back in Kiôto. But, said Okubo, Keiki was in too much of a hurry, and now the whole situation had completely changed; those who previously had wavered were now convinced of the *Baku-fu's* weakness, and were eager to be first in striking a blow at the Tokugawa. At his request I explained to him as well as I could the working of our executive government in combination with the parliamentary system, the existence of political parties and the election of members of the lower house. The Bizen affair he said was pretty well settled, and his account agreed in the main with what Saigô and Gotô had told me. Next day however there arrived a very peevish letter from the chief, complaining that the Bizen business did not appear to be nearing a settlement, that sufficient preparations had not been made at Ozaka for the reception of the Foreign Representatives, that he doubted whether he would ever go there at all, and winding up by ordering Willis and myself to rejoin him by the 24th at latest. This gave me one day more at Kiôto, but it considerably upset Willis' arrangements, as he had calculated on a fortnight's stay. Okubo having called to return my visit, and Yoshii also, I took the opportunity of urging on them the necessity of settling Bizen at once. They replied that they did not belong to the department concerned, but undertook to see Gotô and Higashi-Kuzé, and repeat to them what I had said. I had to go, but left Willis to await further orders. On the 23rd Saigô came to say good-bye to me, and present me with two large rolls of red and white crape and two of gold brocade. He said there was no possibility of my carrying back the final decision of the Bizen affair. When he was gone, Yoshii came in; he told me Sir Harry perfectly well understand the cause of the delay, and had consented to wait a week. A letter had gone from Higashi-Kuzé to him, which had probably crossed his to me. The final decision would probably be arrived at on the morrow or the day after. Daté (Uwajima) and Gotô would go down next day to Ozaka, and Higashi-Kuzé would follow with the sentences of the Bizen men as soon as they were made out. Both Saigô and Yoshii begged that Willis would stay five or six days longer.

The war news was that the town and territory of Kuwana had submitted to the imperial messenger, but the retainers replied that they could not undertake for their prince, who was in Yedo, having accompanied Keiki thither. Everyone in Kiôto hoped that the Yedo people would resist instead of peaceably submitting, for the western men were all "spoiling for a fight."

At three o'clock in the afternoon I therefore set out alone. It took me a long time to get through the city to the Gojô bridge, as I completed my sight-seeing as I went, and I did not reach Fushimi till dark. There I found Oyama's elder brother, who was Satsuma agent (*rusui*), and from words dropped by Notsu, the captain of my escort, I learnt that the orders to march on Yedo were expected to be issued in a day or two. At nine o'clock we embarked for Ozaka in a fifty *koku* flat-bottomed boat, long and narrow, with a roofing of coarse straw mats supported by rafters resting on a pole laid from one end of the boat to the other, horribly uncomfortable, and especially so when crowded. We got to our destination at 6.30 next morning, and I crossed to Hiôgo in the gunboat. Notsu said that in the recent fighting the heads of all the wounded who could not escape had been taken off, a proceeding hardly reconcilable with what we had been told about the resolution to spare the lives of prisoners; unless, indeed, it was done to put them out of their pain.

The next entry in my journal is of February 29th, when Daté came over from Ozaka. On arriving he went to the consulate by invitation from the chief to have lunch, and began to talk about the Foreign Representatives being presented to the Mikado, who was to be brought down to Ozaka, perhaps by March 13. We had to stop this interesting communication in order that he might go to call on the other ministers. In the evening I went to see him, when he told me M. Roches had asked to see Saigô, Okubo, Komatsu and Gotô, as he understood they were the leaders of the Kiôto movement; this had greatly annoyed the dear old man, who resented being ignored in that fashion, and said he hated Roches and his interpreter. Roches had sent to say he would call next morning, and it was with difficulty that I persuaded him to receive the visit, instead of going on board H.M.S. "Ocean" on Sir Harry's invitation. Inouyé Bunda, whom I saw that day, told me the French consul at Nagasaki had refused to pay duties to the provisional government, and had threatened war, especially against Satsuma and Chôshiû. We had a good laugh over this exhibition of impotent wrath.

CHAPTER XXVIII

Harakiri—Negotiations for Audience of the Mikado at Kioto

Next day Daté introduced to the Foreign Representatives Sawa Mondo no Kami, one of the five fugitive court nobles of 1864, who was proceeding to Nagasaki as governor, together with the *daimiô* of Omura, who was to furnish his guard. Sawa wore rather a forbidding expression of countenance, not to say slightly villainous, but for all that had the look of a good companion, and a year or two later, when he was minister for Foreign Affairs, we liked him greatly. Omura Tango no Kami, to give him his full title, was a weak, sickly looking man, who did not utter a word during the interview, and seemed even afraid of speaking to a foreigner. Sawa's son, a dissipated-looking young man, with the white complexion of a woman, was also present. After the compliments were over, these three were turned out of the room, and we learnt that the Bizen affair would be wound up by the decapitation of the responsible officer. Early that morning the chief had been asking my opinion about the advisability of granting a reprieve, or rather a mitigation of the penalty. Mitford learnt from von Brandt that the colleagues knew him to have leanings that way, and that he was believed to have put forward Polsbroek, the Dutch Political Agent, to advocate clemency. Mitford and I had however agreed previously that lenience would be a mistake, and that was the view I maintained in reply to Sir Harry. Daté and Sawa came to dinner that evening with the chief, an arrangement which he fancied he had kept secret from his colleagues, but they knew of it as soon as the invitation was accepted. Afterwards there was a long conversation which lasted until midnight, a principal topic being the proposed visit of the Mikado to Ozaka. Daté said the object of the excursion was to open the mind of the young sovereign by showing him something of the outer world, and also a big English man-of-war. Of course, he added, if the foreign diplomats were there at the time, they might be presented. Parkes said the Mikado might receive the Diplomatic Body as a whole, but not each minister separately, his object being to secure priority of presentation for himself, as he had already written home for new credentials. Daté suggested that the capital might possibly be moved from its present position to Ozaka, as it was situated at a spot hemmed in by mountains, to which all supplies had to be transported by water. My own belief was that Satsuma and Chôshiû wanted to get the person of the Mikado into their own hands in order to make him march with the army, and secondly to have him on the seacoast in order to be able to cut and run whenever it might become necessary. This was confirmed by the fact that the Mikado had issued an order announcing that he was taking the field in person. In reply to a question as to the fate of the ex-Tycoon, Daté said it would depend on circumstances, which no one could foretell. The people of Ozaka, aware of the anti-foreign policy of the late Mikado and the former political opinions of Chôshiû, supposed that since the Court and Chôshiû had come into power, foreigners would be generally obnoxious, not any longer having the Tokugawa power to defend them; that was the reason of the populace having wrecked the various legations. Perhaps the Bizen people had been actuated by the same notions. This last suggestion furnished an additional ground for our refusing to reduce the capital sentence.

By this time M. Roches had come back to Kôbé, to the great annoyance of his colleagues, who considered that he had played a trick on them in leaving his secretary here as Chargé d'Affaires, in order that he might not be unrepresented, and at the same time playing the part of French Minister in Yedo.

It did not cause us, that is Mitford and myself, much surprise when in the afternoon of the next day Godai and Itô came to ask for the life of Taki Zenzaburô, the retainer of Hiki Tatéwaki, who had been condemned to perform *harakiri* as the penalty for ordering his soldiers to fire on foreigners. A long discussion took place between the foreign ministers which lasted for nearly three hours, in which Sir Harry voted for clemency, but the majority were for the sentence being carried out. It was half-past eight o'clock in the evening when Godai and Itô were called back into the room and told in a few words that there was no way but to let the law take its course. So we started at nine o'clock, Mitford and myself, with a single representative of each of the other legations. We were guided to the Buddhist temple of Sei-fuku-ji at Hiôgo, arriving there at a quarter to ten. Strong guards were posted in the courtyard and in the ante-chambers. We were shown into a room, where we had to squat on the matted floor for about three-quarters of an hour; during this interval we were asked whether we had any questions to put to the condemned man, and also for a list of our names. At half-past ten we were conducted into the principal hall of the temple, and asked to sit down on the right hand side of the dais in front of the altar. Then the seven Japanese witnesses, Itô, Nakashima Sakutarô, two Satsuma captains of infantry, two Chôshiû captains, and a Bizen *o-metsuké* took their places. After we had sat quietly thus for about ten minutes footsteps were heard approaching along the verandah. The condemned man, a tall Japanese of gentleman-like bearing and aspect, entered on the left side, accompanied by his *kai-shaku* or best men, and followed by two others, apparently holding the same office. Taki was dressed in blue *kami-shimo* of hempen cloth; the *kai-shaku* wore war surcoats (*jimbaori*). Coming before the Japanese witnesses they prostrated themselves, the bow being returned, and then the same ceremony was exchanged with us. Then the condemned man was led to a red sheet of felt-cloth laid on the dais before the altar; on this he squatted, after performing two bows, one at a distance, the other close to the altar. With the calmest deliberation he took his seat on the red felt, choosing the position which would afford him the greatest convenience for falling forward. A man dressed in black with a light grey hempen mantle then brought in the dirk wrapped in paper on a small unpainted wooden stand, and with a bow placed it in front of him. He took it up in both hands, raised it to his forehead and laid it down again with a bow. This is the ordinary Japanese gesture of thankful reception of a gift. Then in a distinct voice, very much broken, not by fear or emotion, but as it seemed reluctance to acknowledge an act of which he was ashamed — declared that he alone was the person who on the fourth of February had outrageously at Kôbé ordered fire to be opened on foreigners as they were trying to escape, that for having committed this offence he was going to rip up his bowels, and requested all present to be witnesses. He next divested himself of his upper garments by withdrawing his arms from the sleeves, the long ends of which he tucked under his legs to prevent his body from falling backward. The body was thus quite naked to below the navel. He then took the dirk in his right hand, grasping it just close to the point, and after stroking down the front of his chest and belly inserted the point as far down as possible and drew it across to the right side, the position of his clothes still fastened by the girth preventing our seeing the wound. Having done this he with great deliberation bent his body forward, throwing the head back so as to render the neck a fair object for the sword. The one *kai-shaku* who had accompanied him round the two rows of witnesses to make his bows to them, had been crouching on his left hand a little behind him with drawn sword poised in the air from the moment the operation commenced. He now sprang up suddenly and delivered a blow the sound of which was like thunder. The head dropped down on to the matted floor, and the body lurching forward fell prostrate over it, the blood from the arteries pouring out and forming a pool. When the blood vessels had spent themselves all was over. The little wooden stand and the dirk were removed. Ito came forward with a bow, asking had we been witnesses; we replied that we had. He was followed by

Nakashima, who also made a bow. A few minutes elapsed, and we were asked were we ready to leave. We rose and went out, passing in front of the corpse and through the Japanese witnesses. It was twelve o'clock when we got back to the consulate, where we found Sir Harry waiting up to receive our report.

The newspaper reports which reached England of this execution, and of the subsequent execution by *harakiri* of eleven Tosa men at Sakai gave a very distorted view of the facts. Charles Rickerby who was the owner and editor of the *Japan Times* of Yokohama was responsible for the attempts to mislead public opinion in both instances. He invented an account of the proceedings witnessed by Mitford and myself which was entirely false, and wound up by saying that it was disgraceful for Christians to have attended the execution, and that he hoped the Japanese, if they took revenge for this "judicial murder" would assassinate gentlemen of the foreign Legations rather than anyone else. As for being ashamed of having been present at a *harakiri* on the ground that it was a disgusting exhibition, I was proud to feel that I had not shrunk from witnessing a punishment which I did my best to bring about. It was no disgusting exhibition, but a most decent and decorous ceremony, and far more respectable than what our own countrymen were in the habit of producing for the entertainment of the public in the front of Newgate prison. The countrymen of this Bizen man told us that they considered the sentence a just and beneficial one. As regards the case of the Tosa men at Sakai, no punishment was ever more righteously inflicted. These Japanese massacred a boat's crew of inoffensive and unarmed men, who were never alleged to have given the slightest provocation. Twenty were condemned to death, and one could only regret that Captain du Petit Thouars judged it necessary to stop the execution when eleven had suffered, for the twenty were all equally guilty, and requiring a life for life of the eleven Frenchmen looked more like revenge than justice.

A few days afterwards all the ministers returned to Ozaka. We went over on board H.M.S. "Ocean," Captain Stanhope. She was an iron-clad, of 4,000 tons, carrying 26 muzzle-loading rifled guns of the Woolwich pattern, enough to blow any vessel on the station into tiny fragments. With us went Daté and Polsbroek, and the transport "Adventure" conveyed our baggage. Our former temporary residence having been destroyed by fire, we were accommodated at temples in Naka-dera-machi, and were fortunate enough to light upon some of the furniture stolen by the mob after we decamped in January. The townspeople recognized us as "the foreigners who ran away the other day," but they were very civil, and did not shout after us as they rudely did in the last days of the ex-Tycoon's occupation of the city. From Yedo we heard reports that the feeling among Tokugawa people was that he should be compelled to perform *harakiri* and that his principal advisers should be beheaded, in order to appease the imperialists. It was difficult not to feel a certain degree of sympathy for him, mingled with resentment, for he had let us believe he would fight at Ozaka, while he had made up his mind to beat a retreat. If he had told us the truth we could have remained there tranquilly, for we were well assured of the friendliness of Satsuma and Chôshiû.

The "Ocean's" steam launch landed us at the foreign settlement, and we marched through the city with our guard of the 2/ix to our new quarters. There had been a great deal of talk about the Mikado being brought down to Ozaka to see some steamers and to meet the foreign ministers, but I hoped this would not happen. If we were to have an audience of His Majesty, we ought to have it at Kiôto, otherwise the ceremony would lose half its significance. In the afternoon Iyo no Kami and Komatsu paid friendly visits to Sir Harry. It was evident that we were in a fair way to regain the diplomatic ascendancy of which we had been deprived by the recall of Sir Rutherford Alcock in 1864. When Daté and Higashi-Kuzé called next day on the foreign representatives they came to us last of all, which was convenient. Sir Harry spoke to them about the proposed audience of the Mikado. They acknowledged the advantages that would result from its taking place at Kiôto instead of at Ozaka, but were evidently not prepared to promise that immediately. The American, Prussian and Italian Representatives had told Daté that they wished to leave in three days' time, thus causing some amount of consternation in the minds of the Japanese, who desired to keep them for the audience, while they fully appreciated what the chief told them, namely that the three Representatives who wanted to get away would not stop for an audience which was to be merely incidental to the Mikado's visit to some Japanese steamers. It would be unsuitable to the dignity of the Representatives to be presented to His Majesty while at Ozaka on a visit made ostensibly for a different purpose. I myself greatly hoped that the way in which the chief had put the matter would induce the Japanese to invite the ministers at once to Kiôto. That would be the consummation of the imperialist theory and scheme. Von Brandt had said privately that he would not accept even if asked, but publicly had said he would, while the American Minister was apparently of the same way of thinking. Sir Harry had proposed that the Mikado should receive the whole Diplomatic Body together, on one day, and not accord separate audiences until they could present credentials, and this suggestion had been readily adopted.

On the 7th March an important conference was held between the Foreign Representatives and high Japanese functionaries, Daté, Higashi-Kuzé, Daigo Dainagon a court noble appointed governor of Ozaka, and *karôs* of Owari, Echizen, Satsuma, Chôshiû, Tosa, Geishiû, Hizen, Higo and Inshiû, practically all the great territorial nobles of the west. It is a remarkable fact that the princes of Echizen, Bizen and Inshiû, now ranged among the enemies of the Tokugawa, were descended from the founder of that house. The conference took place in the vast hall of the Buddhist temple of Nishi Hongwanji. After the Japanese Ministers had expressed their good wishes for the extension of friendly intercourse between Japan and foreign countries, and declared that the *daimiôs* there represented heartily supported the foreign policy of the Mikado, discussions arose about the ministers going up to Kiôto for an audience of the Mikado, about exchange of foreign coin for

Japanese and the sale of land in the foreign settlements at Ozaka and Hiôgo (Kôbé). We were told that letters were expected from Kiôto in a day or two fixing a date for the audience, so that the ministers could go up one day, see the Mikado on the next, and come down again, thus being absent only three days from Ozaka. M. Roches was of course deadly opposed to accepting any such arrangement. Van Valkenburg the American, von Brandt and de la Tour the Italian seemed unwilling to commit themselves too deeply with the imperialists. The chief tried hard to conceal his determination to accept the invitation in any case, while Polsbroek put on an appearance of indifference. Roches attempted to get an unconditional refusal conveyed to the Japanese Ministers, but was unsuccessful thanks to the watch I kept over his interpreter Shiwoda, and finally the decision was left to depend on the contents of the letters expected from Kiôto. Yamanouchi Yôdô, the older Prince of Tosa, was reported to be very ill at Kiôto, and the services of Willis were asked for on his behalf. This request was readily acceded to by the chief, and Willis started the same evening accompanied by Mitford.

My personal relations with the Awa clan had long been of an intimate character, and it was therefore no surprise when Hayamidzu Sukéyomon, formerly Awa agent at Yedo and now at Ozaka, came to call on me on March 8, bringing a present of silk for Major Crossman in return for the treatises on artillery which the latter had sent to Awa no Kami. It was with great regret that I learnt from him of the death of that friendly and hospitable old gentleman on January 30th. His son and successor, who had been kept at home till the period of mourning expired, was now expected at Ozaka on his way to Kiôto. Hayamidzu brought a budget of Yedo news which mostly proved afterwards to be little better than mere gossip, such as that Itakura was reported to have committed suicide by *harakiri* because the other ministers of state differed from him in opinion; that the *fudai daimiôs* and *hatamoto* talked of compelling Keiki to disembowel himself; of cutting off the heads of Aidzu and Kuwana in order that those two families might escape destruction. He had not heard of Keiki being allowed to retire into private life (*in-kio*), and thought it absurd to suggest such a step under existing circumstances. His conduct had been too shabby for him to become entitled to such consideration. On the 7th February Hori Kura no Kami, one of the second council, had performed *harakiri*, after having vainly endeavoured to persuade Keiki to take that step, and offering to accompany him in the act. All Yedo applauded Kura no Kami and said Keiki ought to follow his example. The *Baku-fu*, said my friend, had no desire to fight. The Awa clan was now supporting the Mikado and was taking part in the expedition to subjugate Tokugawa, and would like to make a declaration to the foreign representatives such as was made by the other clans on the previous day.

In the afternoon I went to Daté to inquire whether he had any news from Kiôto about the invitation of the ministers. He said they would be asked to start on the 11th, but the date of the audience not having been fixed, the invitations could not be sent out. I advised him to go at once to invite each of the ministers and to say that the day after their arrival in Kiôto would be appointed for the audience, because he and Higashi-Kuzé had written asking for that arrangement to be made, and therefore no doubt existed that it would eventually be done. So off he started, beginning with the French Minister, who kept him to dinner, but declined going to Kiôto until he could perceive actual evidence of the Mikado's supremacy. He was answered that even were the *Baku-fu* to be restored with all its original powers, the Mikado being undoubtedly the sovereign of Japan, and the Shôgun only his vicegerent, no offence could possibly be given by being received in audience by the former. From him Daté went to the Italian, Prussian, American and Dutch Representatives. The first three refused on the ground of pressing business at Yokohama, but the last said he would act in the same way as the British Minister. And when Iyo no Kami came to our chief, he accepted the invitation.

CHAPTER XXIX

Massacre of French Sailors at Sakai

Unfortunately just at this moment news was received that a boat-load of Frenchmen had been massacred by the Tosa troops at Sakai. This put an end to the conversation and to all hope of going to Kiôto for an audience. Two men were reported killed on the spot, seven missing, seven wounded, while five escaped unhurt. The account received by Daté just as he left the French Legation was that only one had been killed. It was evident to everybody that the execution of the Bizen officer had not had the effect of a warning. Confusion, despair; hopes dashed to the ground just on the point of fulfilment. No better accounts being given by Daté and Higashi-Kuzé on the following morning, and the missing sailors not having been given up, the Foreign Ministers resolved to withdraw their flags. When the two Japanese Ministers called on the French Minister to express their deep regret, he refused to see them, and addressed a letter to the Japanese authorities demanding the surrender of the missing men by eight o'clock the following morning. The French, Italian, Prussian and American representatives embarked. We and the Dutch political agent remained on shore. But on the morning of the 10th the British flag was formally lowered, and Sir Harry went on board the "Ocean," leaving Russell Robertson and myself at the vice-consulate, with Lieutenant Bradshaw and six men of the 2/ix. The dead bodies of the seven missing French sailors having been found, Daté and Higashi-Kuzé went on board the French flagship "Vénus" to inforn M. Roches. But by some curious blunder the boxes containing the corpses were sent first to the British transport "Adventure," where they were mistaken for cases of "curios" belonging to our Legation, and how the discovery was made of the real nature of the contents I never heard, but they did not arrive at the French flagship till late in the afternoon. I saw Daté on his way back, who said he was greatly pleased with the moderation with which the French Minister was treating the affair. Next day Sir Harry landed, and carried off Bradshaw and his men. He instructed me to call on Daté and say to him that the Representatives would consult together after the funeral as to the reparation to be demanded from the Mikado's government, and that if they were unanimous the Japanese might feel assured that the demands were just. In that case the best thing they could do would be to accept them without delay. On the other hand, if the requirements of M. Roches exceeded the bounds of justice, the other ministers would refuse to join him, and the Japanese Government could then appeal to the French Government and those of the other Foreign Powers. In Sir Harry's own opinion a large number of the Tosa men ought to suffer death, but he did not approve of pecuniary indemnities. Having given me these instructions he went off to Hiôgo to attend the funeral of the murdered Frenchmen, eleven in all. Robertson and I called on Daté to deliver the chief's message, and after having executed our commission, we went with Komatsu and Nakai to a Japanese restaurant and had a feast in the usual style. We got home about seven o'clock, and as the day was still young we took it into our heads to give ourselves an entertainment, and with a guide carrying a lantern went to the quarter of the town where such amusements are provided, to a house to which I knew that a foreigner had been introduced, and that by Tosa people. The master said he was afraid of his trade being injured if he received foreigners, but suggested our applying to the local authority for permission. While we were still in the shop a Tosa man came down from a room upstairs, and on seeing us asked for his sword, but the people of the house refused to give it, and led him away. It never entered my head that the master of the house wished to get rid of us on account of his Tosa guests. So we went to the municipal office, and came back again with the desired permission, but the landlord was still not satisfied. We were conversing with him when the same Tosa man came down sword in hand, and squatting down before us with a threatening air, demanded to know who we were and what we were doing there. I replied that we were English officers and was proceeding to explain what we wanted, but he interrupted by fiercely questioning our right to be present. One of his companions roused by the disturbance came downstairs and carried him up again, the women taking his sword and hiding it. The peaceful man then came to us, and was offering an apology, when the madcap descended again with a naked weapon in his hand, at least that was Robertson's impression. His friend rushed to stop him; a struggle took place on the stairs and we bolted through the door into the street. The master of the house came out after us with our lantern, saying that our guide had disappeared, and as he was not to be found, the old man had to escort us home.

Mitford and Willis arrived back from Kiôto on the 12th, Sir Harry's letter giving permission for the latter to remain having crossed him on the way. Having made arrangements for his going back again, we went on board the "Adventure" to see the chief, and while we were there Daté and Komatsu arrived to tell him what the French Minister's demands were: namely, 1st, the execution of all the men concerned in the massacre (about twenty Tosa men and twenty townspeople armed with fire-hooks, they told us); 2nd, $150,000 for the families of the murdered men; 3rd, apology of the principal minister for Foreign Affairs at Ozaka (this was Yamashina no Miya, a Prince of the Blood); 4th, apology of the Tosa *daimiô* Yamanouchi Tosa no Kami on board a French man-of-war at Susaki (the port of Tosa); 5th, the exclusion of all Tosa armed men from treaty ports and cities. These had all been agreed to. We then returned ashore and started Willis on his way back to Kiôto.

Next day we moved over to Hiôgo on board H.M.S. "Adventure." All the Foreign Representatives had addressed Notes to the Japanese Government counselling them to comply with the French demands. Hasé Sammi, a Court Noble, arrived as an envoy from the Mikado to the French Minister bearing a message of condolence. He afterwards saw Sir Harry and arranged with him that he should go to Kiôto for an audience of the Mikado, as soon as this affair was disposed of. M. Roches had not fixed any date, but it was expected by the Japanese authorities that everything would be finished by the 16th. M. Roches seemed to be harping on one string, that it would be regrettable if any single representative went to Kiôto by himself, and Komatsu, who told us that he had expressed himself to Hasé in that sense, thought that this was intended as a hit at Sir Harry. However, Polsbroek had also promised the Japanese that he too would go up to Kiôto as soon as satisfaction for the Tosa outrage were afforded. Next day Daté arrived at six o'clock with Komatsu and went on board the French flagship to deliver to Roches the Note accepting his demands. The 5th demand was understood to mean not merely that no Tosa troops should garrison treaty ports and cities, but that no Tosa *samurai* of any class should be allowed at the treaty ports. This appeared to be too severe, and we held that it would have to be modified. After he had finished with Roches, Daté came over to see Sir Harry and to tell him what had been arranged. Two officers and eighteen rank and file were to perform *harakiri* at Sakai at 2 p.m. the next day, and Yamashina no Miya was simultaneously to call on Roches to deliver the apology, and also invite him to Kiôto. On the day after that the prince was to call on Sir Harry, at the same hour, on board H.M.S. "Ocean" at Kôbé. We were to leave Kôbé for Ozaka on the 19th, pass the night of the 20th at Fushimi, and enter Kiôto the next day. On the 22nd we were to receive visits, and have audience of the Emperor on the 23rd. This was only a private and confidential arrangement with Daté, and would only become official after Yamashina no Miya delivered the formal invitation. In accordance with this programme the Prince, who was a first cousin once removed of the Mikado, and principal minister for Foreign Affairs, came to Kôbé on the 18th to call on

Sir Harry and Polsbroek. We learnt from him that Roches had begged off nine out of the twenty condemned men, taking only one life for each of the murdered Frenchmen,* and that he had decided to go to Kiôto having heard from Daté that Sir Harry would accept the invitation. The Miya was dressed in the same costume as the other court nobles we had seen, a purple silk robe (*kari-ginu*) and a small black-lacquered wrinkled hat perched on the top of the head. His age might be about fifty, and he wore a short beard and moustache. His teeth bore marked signs of having been once dyed black. He was accompanied by Higashi-Kuzé, a son of the latter, and by Môri Heirokurô, son of Môri Awaji no Kami; this young man was to go to England with the son of Sanjô Sanéyoshi and young Nakamikado. It was expected, they said, that the Mikado would move down to Ozaka about the end of the month, and remain there until Yedo was finished with. Keiki had sent an apology through his relative Echizen, but it was not considered satisfactory, and military operations would be continued.

---

* This statement was not exact. The fact was, as we learnt afterwards, that Captain du Petit Thouars, commanding officer of the "Dupleix" to which ship the murdered sailors belonged, who had been deputed by the French senior naval officer to witness the execution with a party of his men, finding that the completion of the proceedings would involve the detention of his men on shore after dark. raised his hand after the eleventh man had suffered. The nine whose lives were spared were grievously hurt, we were afterwards told, and no wonder, considering what the spirit of the Japanese *samurai* was. Patriotic death poems by the men who suffered the extreme penalty were afterwards circulated among the people. The following are prose translations of some of these:

Though I regret not my body which becomes as dew scattered by the wind, my country's fate weighs down my heart with anxiety.

As I also am of the seed of the country of the gods, I create for myself to-day a glorious subject for reflection in the next world. The sacrifice of my life for the sake of my country gives me a pure heart in my hour of death.

Unworthy as I am I have not wandered from the straight path of the duty which a Japanese owes to his prince.

Though reproaches may be cast upon me, those who can fathom the depths of a warrior's heart will appreciate my motives.

In this age, when the minds of men are darkened, I would show the way to purity of heart.

In throwing away this life, so insignificant a possession, I would desire to leave behind me an unsullied name.

The cherry flowers too have their seasons of blossoming and fading. What is there for the Japanese soul to regret in death?

Here I leave my soul and exhibit to the world the intrepidity of a Japanese heart.

CHAPTER XXX

Kioto—Audience of the Mikado

On March 19 the whole legation crossed to Ozaka in H.M.S. "Adventure." I left my Japanese escort behind, as they would have been in the way at Kiôto, and probably, being Tokugawa retainers, in fear of their lives the whole time. Our party slept at the vice-consulate, and next day we rode up to Fushimi, escorted by Komatsu and a couple of Hizen officers, one of whom named Nakamuta was the commander of the "Eugénie," a steamer recently acquired by Nabéshima. The party on horseback consisted of Sir Harry, Lieutenant Bradshaw and myself, with the legation mounted escort. We went nearly the whole way at a foot's pace, the road being in fairly good condition, but the bridges at Yodo having been burnt during the recent fighting we had some difficulty in getting across the Kidzukawa, which falls into the river there. We got to Fushimi about six o'clock, and found comfortable quarters prepared for us in the guest rooms of a Buddhist monastery, where we were well looked after by some Hizen officers. The rest of our party, together with the infantry guard of the 2/ix, were to come up in boats, starting at three o'clock in the afternoon, and travelling through the night. They gradually reached Fushimi next morning, and we managed to make a start about ten o'clock. The first half of the way we were escorted by Hizen men, who were then joined by Owari troops, and here we were met by Gotô and our cheery little friend Nakai. The streets were crowded with spectators, who observed perfect order. Chi-on-in, a very fine Buddhist monastery at the foot of Higashi-yama, had been prepared for our accommodation, and guards were posted consisting of Higo, Awa and Owari troops. We found the Owari officials who were in charge to attend to our comforts very dilatory people, and as yet quite unacquainted with foreigners and their requirements. The apartments assigned to us were magnificently decorated, altogether in the style of a feudal noble's palace, such as we had seen at Tokushima the previous year. Shimadzu Osumi no Kami (father of the Prince of Satsuma) had occupied them for some time when he first visited Kiôto. As soon as we settled in, a grand feast of many dishes in Japanese style was served up to us, but of course we had brought our own cooks and utensils with us, for most of us were unaccustomed to Japanese food. Old Yôdô of Tosa, whom Willis had been attending, was reported to be out of danger and in a fair way of recovery.

The 22nd March was spent by the chief in making a round of visits. It took the Owari folk three hours to get us the necessary palanquins and bearers. We called first on Yamashina no Miya, who was very affable and jolly, his dirty beard shaved off, and his teeth dyed black in correct style; he was dressed in the costume called *nôshi*, and wore the tiny black lacquered hat as before. The conversation turned upon the delightfulness of the occasion which had brought the British Minister to Kiôto. Just after leaving the prince's residence we were stopped in the road to let Ninnaji no Miya pass. He was on horseback, a stoutish, swarthy, thick-lipped young man, with his hair just beginning to sprout; for until recently he had been in the Buddhist priesthood. Our next visit was to Sanjô, who had had his title of Dainagon just restored to him, a pale effeminate-looking undersized man of thirty-three years of age. He discoursed very formally on the happiness it gave to all the Court people to see foreign ministers in Kiôto. From there we went through the enclosure known as the Nine Gates, past the Imperial Palace. It was surrounded by a finely stuccoed wall four feet thick at the base, with gates like those of a Buddhist temple, very neatly thatched with small shingles. Iwakura, whom we called on next, had his temporary residence just inside and opposite the Kugé Mon gate on the west of the palace. He was a severe-looking oldish man, but frank in speech. He told the chief it was true that the Mikado and Court Nobles had hated foreigners hitherto, and talked of "barbarian-expelling" (*jô-i*), while the *Baku-fu* was all for "opening the country." But now that was completely changed. They had specially to thank the English for having been the first to recognize the truth that the Mikado was the sovereign. Itô told me that after we had left the house Iwakura expressed to him a fear that he might have given offence by speaking too frankly about the former attitude of the Court towards foreigners. We then went to the Hizen *yashiki*, and saw the prince, a young good-looking man of about twenty-four years of age; he had been appointed to the department of Foreign Affairs, but we would not discover that he had any great aptitude for official work. Daté and Higashi-Kuzé luckily were not in when we called. We also visited the younger Chôshiû prince, Nagato no Kami, whom we easily recognized by his likeness to the photograph taken when Admiral King was in Chôshiû. At the other houses we had been accommodated with chairs, but here we had to squat on the floor in Japanese fashion, and when we rose to leave it was with difficulty that we could straighten our knee joints. We exchanged with him hearty expressions of goodwill and congratulations on our ancient friendship. On returning to Chi-on-in we found Daté aud Gotô who had come to discuss the details of the audience that was to take place on the morrow. They expressed much anxiety lest the Mikado should find some difficulty in making his speech to the minister, as he had not up to the present ever spoken to any one but inmates of the Palace, and it was only ten days since he had first shown his face to a *daimiô*. So we finally arranged that His Majesty's speech should be written down, that he should try to repeat it, and then hand the copy to Yamashina no Miya, who would read it out, and hand it to Itô for translation. The document was finally to remain in Sir Harry's possession. Then the latter would reply direct to the Mikado through Itô acting as interpreter. The only member

of the legation staff to be admitted to the audience was Mitford,
as he alone had been presented at court in England. He was to be
introduced by Yamashina no Miya, and the Mikado would salute
him with the word *kurô*, which might be freely rendered by "Glad
to see you." The *Shishinden* where the audience was to take place
was, they told us, a large hall 28 yards deep by 36 in length, with
a floor of planking, with a dais and a canopy for the Mikado, and
another dais, rather lower, specially arranged for the ministers.
Daimiôs who were received in audience had, we were assured,
to kneel on the bare planks. The three foreign representatives,
Roches, Sir Harry and Polsbroek were to assemble in one room,
and be thence conducted into the presence of the Mikado.

It was now our turn to suffer an assault at the hands of the
fanatics of patriotism, from which our constant advocacy of the
rights of the sovereign afforded us no protection.

It was arranged that we should start from Chi-on-in for the
palace at one o'clock on March 23. The procession was to be headed
by the mounted escort, led by Inspector Peacock and Nakai, then
Sir Harry and Gotô, myself and Lieutenant Bradshaw, the detachment of the 2/ix, followed by Willis, J. J. Enslie, Mitford in a
palanquin (being unable to ride) and five naval officers who had
come up with us. We descended the whole length of the street
called Nawaté opposite to the main gate of Chi-on-in, but just as
the last file of the mounted escort turned the corner to the right,
a couple of men sprang out from opposite sides of the street, drew
their swords, and attacked the men and horses, running down
the line and hacking wildly. Nakai observing what was passing
jumped down from his pony and engaged the fellow on the right,
with whom he had a pretty tough fight. In the struggle his feet got
entangled in his long loose trousers, and he fell on his back. His
enemy tried to cut off his head, but Nakai parried the blow, receiving only a scalp wound, and pierced the man's breast with the point
of his sword at the same time. This sickened him, and as he was
turning his back on Nakai he received a blow on the shoulder from
Gotô's sword, which prostrated him on the ground, and Nakai

jumping up hacked off his head. In the meanwhile the troopers on the left had turned, and some of them pursued the other villain, who rushed down the street from which Sir Harry and I had not yet emerged. I had only just arrived at a comprehension of what was taking place; my presence of mind had deserted me, and as he passed my sole idea of defence was to turn my pony's head round to ward off the blow aimed at me. It was a narrow escape, as I afterwards found, for the animal received a slight cut on the nose, and was also wounded on the shoulder an inch of two in front of my knee. As soon as I recovered my equanimity I moved up to the head of the procession. There I saw Sir Harry Parkes, in his brilliant uniform of an Envoy and Minister calmly sitting on his horse in the middle of the cross-roads, with Inspector Peacock close by, also on horseback, and a crowd of Japanese spectators. The Japanese infantry, 300 men of Higo, who had led our procession had disappeared, as had also those who had originally brought up the rear. But our Japanese grooms stuck to us with the greatest cool pluck. Behind me was the infantry guard of the 2/ix, facing to the left. Upon them he hurled himself, cutting one man over the head and inflicting a severe wound, but here his career came to an end, for one of the soldiers put out his foot and tripped him up, and others drove their bayonets into him. Nevertheless he managed to get to the end of the line, where being stopped by Mitford's palanquin, he fled into the courtyard of a house, dropping his sword outside. Here he was found by Bradshaw, who discharged a pistol at his head, but the bullet struck the joint of the lower jaw, and did not penetrate the bone. On this he fell down in the yard, and became nearly insensible. Our wounded were too numerous to admit of our proceeding to court. Nine of our escort were wounded, and one of the 2/ix guard, besides Nakai and Sir Harry's Japanese groom. We therefore procured bearers for the palanquins which had been abandoned by their frightened porters, and returned to our quarters without any further mishap. When the wounds were examined it was found that none were in a vital part, though there had been much loss of blood. A cut into the knee of one man, and the almost complete severance of the wrist of another were the worst cases. It was a great piece of good fortune that we had such an experienced surgeon as Willis with us. The captured assailant appeared to be a Buddhist priest, at least his head was shaven. Assisted by a retainer of Sanjô's we examined him. He expressed great penitence, and asked that his head might be cut off and exposed publicly to inform the Japanese nation of his crime. His wounds were attended to by Willis, and he was carefully deposited in the guard-room. Nakai brought the head of the other man back with him, and kept it by his side in a bucket as a trophy; it was a ghastly sight; on the left side of the skull a terrible triangular wound exposed the brain, and there was a cut on the right jaw which apparently had been dealt by the sword of one of the escort.

My diary contains no further entry until the middle of May, and letters I wrote to my parents narrating the incidents which befel us at Kiôto have not been preserved. A very full account of this affair, written by Mitford to his father, was communicated to the *Times*, and the despatch of March 25 in which the chief reported the whole affair was included in a volume of "confidential print" and has not been published. See also *Memories* by Lord Redesdale, ii. 449. A briefer narrative based on official documents is to be found in vol. II of *The History of Japan* by F. O. Adams. As long as we remained at Kiôto I was so busy with interpreting between the chief and Japanese high functionaries and in translating documents that my journal had to be neglected, and my memory of what occurred over fifty years ago, left unrecorded at the time, is scarcely full enough to afford material for completing this chapter unaided.

It will readily be comprehended that this fanatical attack on the British Minister, who had proved himself a cordial friend of the imperialist party, caused a feeling of utmost consternation at the Court as soon as the news was received there about four o'clock in the afternoon. The French Minister and the Dutch Political Agent had punctually reached the Palace, where they were kept waiting for the arrival of their colleague. As he failed to make his appearance their reception was hurried through, and on leaving the audience chamber they received the notes Sir Harry had sent off informing them of what had happened. About six o'clock in the evening there came to him straight from the court Tokudaiji, Echizen Saishô, Higashi-Kuzé, Daté and the Prince of Hizen to express the deep regret of the Mikado. The minister replied that he would leave the matter in the hands of the Mikado's government. He considered that a graver outrage had been committed upon the Mikado than upon himself, and he felt assured that the government would know how to vindicate the honour of their sovereign. They manifested a degree of feeling and concern which showed that remonstrance from him was not needed to make them sensible of the gravity of the offence. They reproached themselves for not having taken better precautions for his safety, and deplored the disgrace attaching to themselves for an outrage committed on a foreign representative specially invited by the Mikado to Kiôto. He added that of course their apologies would take a written form, but he recurred to arguments he had previously addressed to various members of the government as to the necessity of an enactment which should attach the penalty of an ignominious death to all *samurai* who committed murderous attacks on foreigners instead of allowing them to die with credit by their own hand; as in the case of the eleven men who were executed for the murder of the French seamen at Sakai. He urged also that the Mikado's government should make known by public proclamation that His Majesty really desired to cultivate friendly relations with foreign powers. It was their duty to eradicate the spirit of hostility towards foreigners to which so many had fallen victims, and which was fostered by the erroneous idea entertained by a certain class that in attacking foreigners they were doing the Mikado good service. Accordingly the written apology was delivered next day, together with a copy of the sentence depriving the prisoner of his rank as *samurai*, and passing a sentence of decapitation on him. Sanjô, Iwakura, Tokudaiji, Higashi-Kuzé and other ministers called to offer their regrets, and promised that the proclamation should be posted on the public notice-boards which were a feature in every town and village. They offered also in case any of our wounded should die, or be deprived of their livelihood by inability to perform their duties, to provide suitable compensation.

This affair having been satisfactorily disposed of, the chief agreed to have an audience of the Mikado, which took place on March 26th. Of course we were not able to make such a show as on the 23rd, since most of the mounted escort were incapacitated by the severity of their wounds. On the other hand extraordinary precautions were taken for the security of the party in passing along the streets. As had previously been arranged, of the legation staff only Mitford was presented. The minister and he ascended the *Shishinden* by steps at the north end, entered by the door on the south, and issuing from it after the audience descended by steps at the south end. Those of us like Willis and myself, and the other members of our party walked through the courtyard past the hall of audience, and rejoined them as they came down again. The Mikado was the first to speak, and his speech ran as follows: —

I hope your sovereign enjoys good health. I trust that the intercourse between our respective countries will become more and more friendly, and be permanently established. I regret deeply that an unfortunate affair which took place as you were proceeding to the palace on the 23rd instant has delayed this ceremony. It gives me great pleasure therefore to see you here to-day.

To this the minister made the following reply: —

Sire,
Her Majesty the Queen is in the enjoyment of good health. I shall have great pleasure in reporting to my government Your Majesty's inquiries and assurances of friendship. The condition of the foreign relations of a state must ever be dependent upon

its internal stability and progress, and Your Majesty is taking the best measures to place the foreign relations of Japan upon a permanent footing by establishing a strong general government throughout Your Majesty's dominions, and by adopting the system of international law universally recognized by other states. I am deeply sensible of the manner in which Your Majesty has been pleased to notice the attack made upon me on the 23rd instant, and I appreciate the exertions of Your Majesty's ministers on that unfortunate occasion. The memory of it will be effaced by the gracious reception which Your Majesty has given me this day.

The foreign representatives left Kiôto the following day. Saégusa Shigéru, the captive of our bow and spear on the 23rd, was executed that morning. Three supposed accomplices before the fact were sentenced to perpetual exile, but we were never convinced of their guilt. If it had been proved against them they ought to have suffered the same penalty, but the chief did not care to press the point.

It was Sir Harry's wish that I should remain at Ozaka to keep up communication with the court, but I persuaded him to leave Mitford there for the purpose. Two motives actuated me. I wished to get back to my newly acquired house at Yedo, and Mitford knew much more than I did about English parliamentary institutions, which was a subject in which the leaders of the *samurai* class at Kiôto, and especially Gotô Shôjirô, were greatly interested. For their hope was to base the new government of Japan on a representative system.

CHAPTER XXXI

Return to Yedo and Presentation of the Minister's New Credentials at Ozaka

On March 31 I arrived back at Yokohama with the chief, and went up to Yedo on April 1 to find out what was the state of things there. I took Noguchi and my six Japanese escort men with me. The latter were lodged in a building by the gate of my house. My chief source of information was Katsu Awa no Kami who had been the head of the Tokugawa navy. To avoid exciting attention I used to visit him after dark. The van of the imperialist army had already arrived in the neighbourhood of Yedo, the advanced posts being at Shinagawa, Shinjuku and Itabashi. Slight skirmishes with detached bodies of disabanded Yedo troops had taken place on the Kôshiû and Kisô roads, which had delayed the arrival of the imperial forces for a day or two. Small parties of Satsuma and Chôshiû men wandered about the streets of the city unmolested, and a smaller Satsuma *yashiki*, near our legation, was re-occupied on March 7 by a few soldiers of that clan. Arisugawa no Miya, the commander-in-chief, was reported to be still at Numadzu, half a day's journey west of the top of the Hakoné pass. Keiki was residing in retirement at the Tokugawa mausoleum of Uyéno, straining every effort to keep his retainers in a submissive temper towards the Mikado, by means of notifications to the people and a body of armed police. Already as early as March 4 a proclamation had been issued declaring that the

ex-Shôgun was determined to submit to any orders which might
be given to him by the Mikado, and that no opposition was to
be offered to the imperial troops. Aidzu and his clansmen had
retired to their home at Wakamatsu in Oshiû, after dismantling
all the clan establishments in Yedo. Nearly all the other *daimiôs*
who had been residing in Yedo until recently had either returned
to their territories or gone to Kiôto to give in their allegiance to
the Mikado. The *hatamoto*, or retainers of Tokugawa below the
rank of *daimiô*, were daily following their example. The people of
the city, ignorant of the demands about to be made on Keiki, and
mindful of the misfortunes some of them had experienced when
the Satsuma *yashiki* were attacked in the previous December, were
apprehensive of a general conflagration. Some had removed their
household property, but the shops were still open, and the panic
was by no means general. The forts in the bay of Yedo were handed
over to the imperialists on April 4, after the guns bearing on the
city had been dismounted. This was the news on the 8th. On the
12th I went up again for a three days' stay, and found the city much
quieter, owing to a feeling that the terms offered to Keiki would be
such as he could accept. Katsu, who was now commander-in-chief
of the Tokugawa forces, told me that he and Okubo Ichiô had
charge of the negotiations. On the other side Saigô represented
Arisugawa no Miya, the imperialist commander-in-chief who was
still at Sumpu. The demands made on Keiki were that he should
surrender all arms and munitions of war, all vessels of war and
other steamers, evacuate the castle of Yedo, and execute those of
his officers who had been foremost in prompting and conducting
the attack on Fushimi; when these demands were compiled with
the Mikado would show clemency towards the ex-Shôgun. The
nature of the further conditions covered by the word "clemency"
was the subject of negotiations between Katsu and Saigô, which
took place at a house in Shinagawa. Katsu was willing to agree to
any arrangement that would save the life of his chief and secure
sufficient revenue to support his large body of retainers. He had
hinted to Saigô that less favourable terms would be met by armed

resistance. Keiki also desired to retain possession of his steamers and munitions of war, and had addressed a petition to the Mikado on this subject. Saigô, carrying this petition and Katsu's verbal proposals, had returned to Sumpu to lay them before Arisugawa. From there he had journeyed to Kiôto, but was expected back on the 18th. Katsu said he was ready to fight in defence of Keiki's life, and expressed his confidence in Saigô's ability to prevent a demand being made which might not only be a disgrace to the Mikado, but prolong the civil war. He begged that Sir Harry Parkes would use his influence with the Mikado's government to obviate such a disaster. This the chief did repeatedly, and in particular when Saigô called on him at Yokohama on April 28, he urged on him that severity towards Keiki or his supporters, especially in the way of personal punishment, would injure the reputation of the new government in the opinion of European Powers. Saigô said the life of the ex-Shôgun would not be demanded, and he hoped that similar leniency would be extended to those who had instigated him to march against Kiôto. Keiki was still at the monastery at Uyéno, but some of his late advisers, whom he had ordered into strict seclusion (*kin-shin*) had secretly fled. Amongst these Katsu mentioned Ogasawara, late chief minister for Foreign Affairs, Hirayama, whom we used to call "the old fox," Tsukahara, an official whom we greatly liked, and Oguri Kôdzuké no Suké, a finance minister. The most remarkable statement Katsu made to me was that at a conference between the ex-Shôgun's ministers and M. Roches in February the latter strongly urged resistance, and that the officers of the French Military Mission were persistent in advising the fortification of the Hakoné pass and other measures of a warlike nature. On the whole Katsu was of opinion that he and Okubo Ichiô would be able to arrange satisfactory terms, if they could manage to escape the hot-heads of their own party who were threatening their lives.

By this time the first division of the imperialist naval force had arrived to co-operate with the army which had advanced by land. There seemed to be little likelihood of fighting, but even a peaceable settlement would be disadvantageous to the prosperity of the city. Now that the *daimiôs* whose wants had been supplied by the merchants and shopkeepers had left for their country homes, the population would naturally decrease. It was a sad thing that Yedo should decline, for it was one of the handsomest cities in the Far East. Though it contained no fine public buildings, its position on the seashore, fringed with the pleasure gardens of the *daimiôs*, and the remarkable huge moats surrounding the castle, crowned with cyclopean walls and shaded by picturesque lines of pine-tree, the numerous rural spots in the city itself, all contributed to produce an impression of greatness. It covered a huge extent of ground, owing to the size of the castle, and the large number of official residences, intersected by fine broad well-gravelled streets. The commercial quarter was actually smaller than the city of Ozaka.

Newspapers, to a large extent in the nature of gazettes, had lately been started in Kiôto and Yedo, and contained a great number of interesting political documents, which I had to translate for the information of my chief. Previously we had been obliged to rely on such manuscript copies as we could obtain from our friends in *daimiô's yashikis*, and the supply was limited. Nor were the papers that came into our hands altogether trustworthy. There was as much forgery of memorials, manifestoes and correspondence as in any other part of the world in a time of political excitement. There were rumours about this time that the capital would be transferred from Kiôto to Ozaka, an arrangement we felt inclined to welcome, for it would have been very inconvenient to establish the foreign legations at Kiôto, so far inland and away from our sources of supply, subject to great cold in winter and excessive heat in summer. Even at Ozaka, close to the sea, the climate was almost unbearable in July and August. But as everyone knows, Yedo was after all constituted the centre of government, and its name changed to Tôkiô.

During this period my time was passed half at Yedo gathering information and half at Yokohama making translations and drawing up reports. Bread and beef were unprocurable at Yedo, and I could not afford to set up a cuisine in European fashion, so while there I used to have my food brought in from a well-reputed Japanese restaurant close by, and came to like it quite as well as what I had been accustomed to all my life.

As early as the end of November 1867 Sir Harry had applied to Lord Stanley for letters of credence to the Mikado. No time was wasted in their preparation and despatch, and they reached him at the end of March 1868, but it was not till the middle of May that things had quieted down at Yokohama sufficiently to allow of his leaving that part of the country. By that time Sidney Locock and his family had left for home, and his successor Francis Ottiwell Adams had arrived. We started from Yokohama in the Admiral's yacht "Salamis" on May 15, Sir Harry, Adams, J. J. Quin the senior student interpreter, and myself. Next afternoon we anchored in the harbour of Oshima, between the island of that name and the southernmost point of the province of Kii. On a neck of land there was a small village, very dirty, stinking and labyrinthine, surrounded by prettily wooded hills, where we started several pheasants in the course of a walk. At dusk we weighed anchor, and reached Hiôgo at nine o'clock the next morning, where we found H.M.S. "Ocean" and "Zebra" already in harbour. We had passed H.M.S. "Rodney," the flagship of Admiral Sir Harry Keppel, on the way up the Kii channel. These ships were assembled off Ozaka to give *éclat* to the presentation of the first letter of an European sovereign to the rightful sovereign of Japan. We got to the Ozaka bar about noon, and afterwards Adams, Quin and I went ashore with the baggage. The chief did not land until the 18th, when a salute was fired from the fort in his honour. We then became busily occupied with the arrangements for the presentation of the minister's credentials, of his staff and a large number of naval officers. We took up our quarters at the vice-consulate for the sake of convenience in communicating with the squadron outside the bar. The 22nd was fixed on as the day for the ceremony. Then the credentials had to be translated into Japanese, and the number of officers to be presented had to be agreed upon. I had to be present, much to my annoyance, for I possessed no diplomatic uniform. The chief offered me the loan of a sort of staff jacket of blue serge fastened in front with frogs, and an old pair of trousers with gold lace down the sides, but I put them away in a cupboard and went to Court in plain evening dress. As soon as Sir Harry landed he was visited by Gotô, one of the two *samurais* who had fought in our defence at Kiôto on the 23rd March, and by Daté. With the latter we had a discussion about the recently published edict against Christianity; it revived the ancient prohibition, but in less stringent terms. Daté admitted that the wording was objectionable, and said that he had caused it not to be exhibited on the public notice-boards at Ozaka and Hiôgo. He had tried to get the expression (translated "evil" or "pernicious" sect) altered, but said it would be impossible to suppress the proscription of Christianity altogether. Sir Harry responded that religious toleration was a mark of civilization, and to us he said privately that the presentation of the Queen's letter was a good opportunity which we ought to turn to account. Afterwards I had a long talk with Nakai on this subject, and suggested that instead of specifically mentioning Christianity the decree should merely forbid "pernicious sects" in general. It was clear that the Japanese Government would not be induced to revoke the law completely, for that would be to give a free hand to the Roman Catholic missionaries at Nagasaki, who had already made themselves obnoxious by the active manner in which they had carried on their proselytism. It was however agreed that Sir Harry should meet Sanjô, Daté, Gotô and Kido on the following day to dispose, if possible, of this question, but Nakai warned me that not even the heads of the government (*sôsai*) could make a definite promise; they were not absolute, as he said. So on the 19th we had a palaver at the Nishi Hongwanji, at which Yamashina no Miya, the president of the Foreign Board, was present, besides those already mentioned, and several more. They defended what had been done on the ground that the hostility to Christianity was still intense, and that in popular opinion it was allied to magic or sorcery. This I knew myself to be a fact. I had once been asked by a Japanese to teach him "Kiristan," which he believed would enable him to discover what his wife was doing in his absence from the house. They admitted however that an error had been committed in describing Christianity as a pernicious sect, and said that this wording would be altered. To have published nothing would have been tantamount to toleration, "silent approval" as the Japanese expression goes, and upon this they could not venture. On the 24th Sir Harry recurred to the subject with the same set of ministers, with whom Iwakura was joined. Perhaps it was on this occasion that a young *samurai* of Hizen, Okuma Hachitarô, whom we had not met before, assured us that he knew all about the subject, for he had read the *Bible* and the *Prairie-book*. It appeared that he had been a pupil of Dr Verbeck, an American missionary at Nagasaki. Sir Harry gave them a copy and a Japanese version of a despatch on this subject, which had been received from Lord Stanley. The other foreign diplomats took the same line, but their united remonstrances produced little effect, and the measure of exiling to other parts of the country some four thousand Japanese of all ages and both sexes mostly from the village of Urakami near Nagasaki, was unflinchingly carried out.

The presentation of the minister's letters of credence took place on the 22nd. Admiral Keppel landed in the morning accompanied by his flag-Captain Heneage, and Captain Stanhope of the "Ocean"; Commander Pollard and Lieutenant Kerr in command of a gunboat; Pusey, commander of the "Salamis"; his secretary William Risk, and Garnier, flag-lieutenant, and joined us at the vice-consulate. The legation party included the chief, Adams, Mitford, who had just been gazetted second secretary, and myself. Our procession consisted of a hundred marines from H.M.S. "Rodney" and the same number from H.M.S. "Ocean," twelve palanquins in which such of us rode as had legs flexible enough, four of the legation escort on foot, and two bodies of Japanese troops who preceded and followed us. We arrived punctually at

one o'clock at the Nishi Hongwanji, assigned for the performance
of the ceremony. The theory of the Mikado's presence at Ozaka
was that he was at the head of the army operating from Kiôto
against the rebellious Tokugawa chief at Yedo, and he was therefore obliged to put up with such accommodation as he could find
in the Buddhist monasteries, which were not very imperial in their
appointments. We were ushered into an ante-chamber which was
merely a part of the hall of audience divided off by screens. Down
the middle ran a long table covered with cloth of gold, about
the only piece of splendour in the place; on one side of this we
took our seats, the Japanese ministers for Foreign Affairs on the
other. Tea, and sweetmeats piled on wooden trays were brought
in for our refection, and we had to wait about half-an-hour before
the chief of the ministry entered the room and made the polite
speeches necessary on such an occasion. In a few minutes more
we were informed that everything was ready, whereupon the
second and third ministers proceeded to usher us into the throne
room. This was an apartment of considerable size down each side
of which there ran a row of wooden pillars supporting the roof.
On a dais at the extreme end sat the Mikado, under a canopy
supported by black-lacquered poles, and with the blinds rolled up
as high as was possible. We advanced up the middle of the room
in double column, the one on the right headed by the Admiral
and composed of naval officers, the other headed by the minister,
and consisting of the legation staff. Everyone made three bows,
first on advancing into the middle of the room, the second at the
foot of the dais, the third on mounting the dais, which was large
enough to afford place for us all. The Mikado rose and stood under
the canopy from the moment that we began to bow. The principal
minister for Foreign Affairs and one other great personage knelt,
one on each side of the throne.

In front of the throne, on each side, stood a small wooden
image of a lion; these are of great antiquity and are much revered
by the Japanese people. Behind the throne a crowd of courtiers
were ranged in a double row, wearing little black paper caps and

gorgeous brocade robes of various hues. As the Mikado stood up, the upper part of his face, including the eyes, became hidden from view, but I saw the whole of it whenever he moved. His complexion was white, perhaps artifically so rendered, his mouth badly formed, what a doctor would call prognathous, but the general contour was good. His eyebrows were shaven off, and painted in an inch higher up. His costume consisted of a long black loose cape hanging backwards, a white upper garment or mantle and voluminous purple trousers. The proceedings were as follows: the minister stood in front of the Mikado's right, with the Legation behind him in order of seniority, the Admiral with his personal staff and the other naval officers on the imperial left. Sir Harry then recited his address, which he had got by heart; it seemed truly absurd when one at last stood face to face with the recipient. Then Itô, who discharged the functions of interpreter on the occasion, read the translation, and we all bowed. Sir Harry stepping forward put the Queen's letter into the hand of the Mikado, who evidently felt bashful or timid, and had to be assisted by Yamashina no Miya; his part was to receive it from the Mikado. Then His Majesty forgot his speech, but catching a word from the personage on his left managed to get out the first sentence, whereupon Itô read out the translation of the whole that had been prepared beforehand. Sir Harry then introduced each of us in turn, and next the Admiral, who presented his officers. The Mikado expressed the hope that all was well with the squadron under his command, and we retired backwards out of the presence into the ante-chamber, bowing as we went, and congratulating ourselves that everything had passed off without a hitch. In the evening we went to dine with Daté, who gave us a banquet cooked as nearly in European fashion as he could manage. Next day we celebrated the Queen's birthday in advance by firing salutes, and a large party of Japanese nobles went on board the "Rodney" to lunch with the Admiral. Yamashina no Miya proposed the Queen's health, which was responded to enthusiastically by everyone present. Many of the guests were intelligent and well behaved, but the Prince of

Chôshiû, who insisted on my sitting next to him, behaved like a great baby, and drank more champagne than was good for him. One felt however that Japanese princes could not be blamed if they were weak-minded, their education being planned so as to produce that result. The son of the Mikado's maternal uncle was possessed with a huge desire to see an European cat, while another great man wanted to get sight of a negro, and we had great difficulty in satisfying their wishes. The principal minister for Foreign Affairs, who had of course to be saluted, desired that as little powder as possible should be used, because the sound of a violent explosion hurt his ears. One of the great attractions was the "Rodney's" band, which played a great deal of noisy music for the benefit of the Admiral's guests, and the bandmaster of the "Ocean" gained great applause by composing a march and a Japanese national anthem, which be dedicated to the Mikado. The conference held at Ozaka on the following day (a Sunday), at which among other things the Christian question was discussed, lasted for six hours, and that meant six hours for me of interpreting from English into Japanese and from Japanese into English. So it was a certain amount of relief to me when on the 25th we reembarked on board the "Salamis" to return to Yokohama. The Mikado left Ozaka on the 28th and returned to Kiôto, the submission of the ex-Tycoon being held to justify this step.

CHAPTER XXXII

Miscellaneous Incidents—Mito Politics

Adams and I set up housekeeping together in the First Secretary's house at Yokohama, but I still kept on the Japanese *yashiki* I had rented at Yedo, and spent a great deal of time there watching the course of events. From time to time I returned to Yokohama to report to my chief, or else reported to him by letter. I was very busily occupied in making translations from the official gazette that was now being published at Kiôto and the popular newspapers that had started into existence at Yedo. One of these contained documents of the highest interest, the terms communicated to Keiki on April 27, the acceptance of which by him involved his retirement to Mito on May 3, and the provisional recognition of Kaménosuké (Tayasu) as the head of the Tokugawa clan. The castle of Yedo was occupied by the imperialist forces, and the troops of Satsuma, Chôshiû and other clans moved freely about the city. On June 23 I went up to Yedo for a three days' stay with Adams; I found there in the local papers interesting communications which were probably fictitious. Thus one, said to be written by a retainer of the Miya of Chi-on-in, where the British Legation had been lodged in March, who though regarding the expulsion of foreigners as perhaps difficult of achievement, recommended that the organization of the army be diligently taken in hand, in order that foreigners might be humbled and kept in subjection. He also deprecated audiences being granted by the Mikado to foreign diplomatic representatives. Another such paper professed to represent the views of Chôshiû "irregular troops" and protested against audiences being granted, because such friendly treatment of foreigners would prevent the nation from affording hearty support to the Mikado when the time should arrive for "expelling the barbarian." When I mentioned these publications to my friend Katsu, he replied that a council of court and territorial nobles (*kugé* and *daimiôs*) was held at Kiôto about the end of May, at which the former expressed the opinion that a favourable occasion for expelling foreigners from the country had now presented itself; their attempt to introduce Christianity at Nagasaki might be alleged as the justifying ground of the measure. That the *daimiôs* were silent and that the Mikado, on being referred to, took no notice of the proposal. Katsu was not very accurately informed, but it is a fact that on May 14 the principal members of the government and *daimiôs* in attendance on the Mikado at Ozaka were summoned before His Majesty at the Hongwanji, and were informed that Christianity was on the increase at Urakami, a village near Nagasaki; he asked for their opinion as to the best way of dealing with the matter, and it was understood that their replies would be published in the government gazette. Daté denied to Mitford that part of the story which said that the meeting was for the purpose of considering whether an anti-foreign policy might not be resorted to. It was difficult for us to obtain accurate information, and probably every Japanese in the position of Katsu or Daté experienced similar difficulty. I do not think however that these documents ever saw the light, and the suggestion is very natural that some of them were of such a character that it was considered advisable to suppress them. The formal appointment of Kaménosuké, a mere boy of six years of age, took place on June 19, and the leading men of the Tokugawa clan waited on him the following morning to present their felicitations. The situation and extent of the territory to be left to the clan had not then been determined. Katsu told me that Sanjô, who had arrived in Yedo on the 13th, was waiting for the reinforcements expected from the south and west before announcing a decision on these points.

He gave me such statistics about the revenue hitherto accruing to the Tycoon's government as showed, to his satisfaction at least, that it would not be possible for the Mikado to derive any income from forfeiture of that revenue, and there was danger of his government falling to pieces for want of funds. Higashi-Kuzé, who was then in Yedo, said to me that the revenue to be granted to the Tokugawa would not be fixed until that part of the clan still in arms against the Mikado was entirely reduced to submission. The war was being vigorously prosecuted near Niigata in Echigo and in the neighbourhood of Aidzu. I myself saw a considerable body of southern troops march into Yedo on June 25, which effectually contradicted the hopes of the Tokugawa people that the imperialists were weakening, and that some of the western clans, in particular Higo, were likely to afford them sympathy, if not actual support.

M. Roches finally left Yokohama on June 23, having been succeeded by M. Outrey, with the intention of visiting Ozaka and Nagasaki on his way home. His policy had proved a complete failure, as far as supporting the Shôgun against the Mikado was concerned. He had succeeded however in procuring for French engineers the construction of the arsenal at Yokosuka and the engagement of a French military mission, which were continued for several years after the establishment of the new government.

Noguchi had an elder and a younger brother, the latter of whom had joined the followers of the Tokugawa who after the withdrawal of Keiki to Mito had gathered themselves together in the mausoleum enclosure at Uyéno. Thence they issued forth at night and assassinated imperialist soldiers from time to time. At last it was decided to attack them in their stronghold, aud early in the morning of July 4 an advance was made which led to the destruction by fire of a considerable part of the city lying between the outer moat and the main gate of Uyéno, and also of the great temple building which occupied the centre of the enclosure. The burial places of the Shôguns were not damaged. Rinôji no Miya, the imperial prince who had always resided there in the character

of abbot, and whom the recalcitrant Tokugawa men talked of raising to the throne as Mikado, was carried off by the survivors at the
end of the day. The fighting began at eight o'clock in the morning
and was over by five o'clock in the evening. During this affair I was
at Yokohama, having been kept there since my last visit to Yedo at
the end of June. At the beginning of that month Willis and I were
in Yedo together for a few days, while he attended to wounded
men of the Satsuma and other clans, such as Toda, Chôshiû and
Bizen. The latter occupied Tôzenji, which had formerly been the
British Legation, and he recorded in his report the fact of his
being received and treated by the Bizen men with great courtesy,
which showed that they entertained no feelings of hostility against
foreigners, and regarded the death of Taki Zenzaburô as a just
retribution for the attack on foreigners at Kôbé in the previous
February. The condition of these wounded men was deplorable,
for at that time Japan had no experienced surgeons, and the treatment of gunshot wounds was of a very amateurish character. There
were but few cases of sword-cuts. Subsequently some of the more
urgent cases were at Willis' suggestion sent down to Yokohama,
and towards the end of July there were 176 patients in the building
appropriated as a military hospital. Under the previous government it had been a school for instruction in the Chinese classics.
Two-thirds of the number were Satsuma men, Chôshiû and Tosa
soldiers together made up a fourth. About 40 had been wounded
in the recent fighting at Uyéno, the others had received their inju-
ries in the expeditions to the north of Yedo against Aidzu. Willis'
services were so greatly appreciated that the minister was asked in
October to lend them again to the troops which had been fighting
in Echigo. This arrangement was facilitated by the fact that he
was now vice-consul at Yedo, a post which he was unable to take
up because the opening of the city to foreign residence and trade
had to be deferred; and he was relieved at Yokohama by Dr J. B.
Siddall who had been appointed medical officer to the legation
early in January.

On the 29th July I went to Yedo with Adams, and spent four days in visiting Okuma, Katsu and Komatsu, but though I must have reported to my chief the result of the conversation with these persons of importance, I have no record, except of voluminous translations from the Japanese of anti-Christian pamphlets and political documents of all kinds. I went alone to Yedo again on August 17, and next day called on Okuma, whom I found in bed looking very ill. From him I learnt that fighting had commenced on the 13th at Imaichi, near Nikkô. The imperialists were victorious and were still advancing on Aidzu, 75 miles further. A messenger who left Echigo on the 8th reported that Niigata was still held by Aidzu men. Subsequently to the capture of Nagaoka by the imperial troops more fighting had taken place, in which both sides lost heavily. The imperialists were holding their ground, and expected further reinforcements which would enable them to advance on Wakamatsu, the capital of Aidzu, at the same time as the divisions from Shirakawa and Akita. The Prince of Hizen, Okuma's own chief, had been urged by his troops in Shimotsuké, where Imaichi is situated, to lead them against the enemy, but his councillors (*karô*) had dissuaded him from taking the field. Since the beginning of the year several constitutions had been framed and issued one after the other, and about this time I was engaged in translating the newest edition, which bore the date of June. It showed marked traces of American political theories, and I have little doubt that Okuma and his fellow-clansman Soyéjima, pupils of Dr Verbeck, had had a considerable part in framing it. "The power and authority of the *Daijôkan* (*i.e.* government), threefold, legislative, executive and judicial," was the wording of one article. By another it was provided that "All officers shall be changed after four years' service. They shall be appointed by a majority of votes given by ballot. When the first period for changing the officers of government arrives, half of the present staff shall be retained for an additional space of two years, in order that there be no interruption of the public business." In this we seemed to hear an echo of the "spoils system." Okuma explained that the "executive" represented the executive department in the United States Constitution, "consisting of the president and his advisers," but that in fact it was the head of the Shintô religion, finance, war and foreign departments. It is needless to say that this state paper has long ago been superseded by the existing Itô constitution of 1889. Then I went on to Katsu. He said that Sumpu (now called Shidzuoka) was to have been formally handed over to the Tokugawa family two days previously, but as a matter of fact it had always formed part of their possessions. He took down from a shelf a memorandum in which he had noted down some years before the names of the ablest men in different clans. Many of them were already dead. Satsuma and Chôshiû accounted for the largest number; of the Tokugawa clan there were very few. All our friends of Satsuma, Chôshiû and Tosa were among the number of those still living. While I was there Tsumagi Nakadzukasa, who had given me a dinner a couple of months earlier, came in. He had returned a few days before from Mito, where he had left Keiki, employing his leisure in the composition of Japanese poetry, and not expecting to be invited at present to take a share in the government. This was an absolutely baseless notion on his part, if he in reality entertained it. He had sent an affectionate message to Katsu, which Tsumagi appeared to be afraid of delivering in my presence, but it proved to be nothing more than a warning to care for his personal safety, which was said to have been threatened by the hot-headed younger Tokugawa men. He said that about 500 Mito men had gone to join Aidzu. The outcome of their conversation was that there was nothing in the existing political situation to cause them anxiety. The Tokugawa people were desirous of getting Katsu to take office under Kaménosuké, but he was unwilling. I asked him whether he had heard of a general feeling of dislike towards the English. That he replied was an old thing, dating from the time when Sir Harry used to advise the Shôgun's ministers to refrain from attacking Chôshiû. The idea was no doubt fostered by Roches, who told them that unless they asked the

British Government to lend naval instructors, the English would back up the *daimiôs'* party, and the want of confidence in British friendship was the reason why Dutchmen had been engaged to bring out the "Kaiyô-maru," a ship of war constructed in England for the Prince of Higo by Glover & Co. of Nagasaki, which had come into the possession of the Mikado's adherents. I had heard from Komatsu and Nakai that imperialist troops landed from the "Kaiyô-maru" at Hirakata about the 5th or 6th August had gained a victory there over a mixed force of Sendai men and Tokugawa *rônin*, and this was confirmed by Tsumagi. On the 19th I walked as far as the Nihon-bashi, the bridge in the centre of the city from which all distances were measured by road, and from there to the huge hotel at the foreign settlement constructed under the supervision of the Tokugawa government for the accommodation of foreigners. The commercial quarter was very lively, the streets were crowded, especially by *samurai* belonging to the imperialist forces, but the neighbourhood of the *daimiôs' yashikis* below the castle was like a city of the dead. On the 20th I had a visit from Kawakatsu Omi, an ex-commissioner for Foreign Affairs. He said that the Castle of Sumpu was little better than a ruin, and that there were no houses which could receive the Tokugawa retainers. He would like to become a retainer of the Mikado (*chô-shin*); his family was not originally in the service of the Tokugawa family, but was of more ancient descent. He would be satisfied if he was made a minister of public instruction. Midzuno Wakasa, a former governor of Yokohama, and Sugiura Takésaburô, another Tokugawa man, would probably be employed by the imperialist government to make all the arrangements with regard to the foreign settlement at Yedo. Mimbu Taiyu, the younger brother of Keiki, then still in France, was to be fetched home to succeed the late Prince of Mito, who had died just about the time of Keiki's retreat thither. About a hundred and thirty *hatamotos* went up to Kiôto in February and by surrendering to the Mikado, secured the possession of their lands. He regretted that he had lost everything through not following their example. The Tokugawa family were to retain 700,000 *koku* of lands, which would enable them to keep a good many retainers, but not all the 30,000 who had hitherto belonged to the clan as *go-ké-nin*. My own Japanese escort, who belonged to the body of *betté-gumi* created several years before to act as guards and escorts for the foreign legations, 300 of whom were to be kept together for that purpose, all wanted to become Mikado's men.

On the 21st Komatsu and Nakai came to call on me. They said the troops sent by way of Hirakata to Tanagura in Oshiû had been completely victorious, and that more would speedily follow. In fact, while we were talking, 500 Satsuma men marched past the house along the main-road by the seashore in order to embark for the north. Kido, who had gone to Kiôto to report the state of affairs at Yedo, was expected back soon. They thought that a good deal of pressure would be necessary to induce the very conservative Kiôto Court to bring the Mikado there. That afternoon I called on Okuma, who was still very unwell, and, like most of the Hizen people, not disposed to be communicative. From him I went to Nakai, who showed me the draft of the state paper by which Gotô overturned the late government in the previous October. It differed slightly from the published copies, in that it contained proposals for the engagement of French and English teachers of language, to get military instructors from England, and to abolish the Tycoon and reduce the Tokugawa clan to the same level as the others. These were all struck out on reconsideration in order to avoid exciting a suspicion that Gotô and his political allies were too partial to foreigners, and provoking the hostility of the *fudai* and *hatamotos*. He had also the drafts of a letter from Higashi-Kuzé to Sanjô, in which, among other things which strengthened the Aidzu resistance to the imperial troops, he reported that foreign vessels anchored at Niigata and supplied the rebels with arms and ammunition; and Higashi-Kuzé said that on his informing the foreign representatives of this, they replied that they would put a stop to the practice. I pointed out to Nakai that this must be a mistake. The Ministers having issued proclamations of neutrality had nothing to do with their enforcement, and that if the Japanese authorities wished to put an end to this traffic, they had merely to notify to the foreign representatives the blockade of the port of Niigata, and that a vessel-of-war was stationed there to prevent communication with the shore. This must have appeared a very strange doctrine to him, but international law was a complete novelty in Japan in those days. He also showed me the draft of Komatsu's letter to Kiôto about the treatment of the Nagasaki Japanese Christians, embodying the arguments recently used to him by Sir Harry, and advocating the adoption of milder measures.

Next day I went again to see Nakai, and found with him a very attractive Satsuma man named Inouyé Iwami, who was greatly interested in the development of the resources of the island of Yezo. He was full of schemes for its colonization from Japan, and for the introduction of the European system of farming under the supervision of a German named Gaertner. He said that Shimidzudani, a young Court noble of about 25, was to be governor of Hakodaté, and that he intended to make him learn English. We discussed various leading personalities with considerable freedom — I hinted that Higashi-Kuzé, in spite of his rank, was not the best representative man to send to Europe as Ambassador. I thought Daté or Iwakura or even Kansô of Hizen would do better. He replied that Iwakura could not be spared. The most important and interesting suggestion he made was that the Mikado must move to Yedo, and make it his Capital, as otherwise it would not be possible to keep in order the rebellious clans of the north. Both he and Komatsu, who joined us later on at a restaurant on the river, approved of what I had suggested about the blockade of Niigata.

On the 23rd I dined with Komatsu and Nakai to meet Okubo, the Satsuma statesman who had suggested the removal of the Capital from Kiôto to Ozaka earlier in the year. I have no doubt that the final decision to make Yedo the centre of government, and to change its name to Tôkiô or Eastern Capital was largely his work. He was very taciturn by disposition, and the only information he vouchsafed was that Daté was to go to Sendai to endeavour to persuade the *daimiô*, who was the head of the Daté family and all its branches, to abandon the cause of Aidzu. Komatsu talked a good deal about the English naval instructors who had been engaged by the previous government, whom he evidently wished to get rid of, and I encouraged him to dismiss them, for I felt it would not be fair to insist on their keeping these officers in their service during a period of civil war, when the British neutrality proclamation prevented their making use of them. Komatsu told me that their plan was to retain the services of the commissioned officers, but to send the petty officers and seamen back to England.

About two months before this time some Higo men had called on me, and said they were going north to Tsugaru. They argued that any other system than feudalism was impossible in Japan. Now I heard that the Higo clan had privately sent messengers to Wakamatsu to endeavour to effect a reconciliation between Aidzu and the *daimiôs* of the west and south, but Aidzu replied that matters had gone too far, and the questions at issue must be decided by the sword. I thought it likely that these envoys from Higo were the men who had been to see me, as the ideas which they entertained seemed to be similar.

The translation of the June Constitution, which superseded one that had been promulgated in March, had given me a great deal of trouble. I was unable to decide upon the best name in English for the second department. It might be Imperial Council, Privy Council, or Cabinet. It appeared that the officials of this department were merely secretaries to the two prime ministers, and had no real executive authority; and that the administration was divided into this nameless department and the other four which followed it. This was Okubo's explanation. It was, however, pretty evident that this constitution was not to be the final one, and it seemed to me to contain in itself the elements of change. There were so many appointments that were held by dummies of high birth, while the real work was done by their underlings. The ancient ranks and precedence had been practically done away with, and I could not help thinking that the court and territorial nobles (*kugé* and *daimiôs*) would have to be struck out of the list of officials. There was hardly one of them fit to occupy the place of head of a department, and yet these appointments were confined to them, no commoner being eligible.

The 25th August was chiefly occupied with arrangements made with Nakai for the opening of Yedo on October 1, by instructions from the chief, the abolition of the absurd existing rules about passports for foreigners proceeding to Yedo, and for ordering one of the naval instructors there to buoy the channel. The ex-Tycoon's government had arranged to have a huge hotel built for the accommodation of foreign visitors, and the owners would have liked to let it, but it seemed unlikely that any foreigner would undertake to run such an establishment on his own account, and I advised that they should engage a man from Yokohama to act as steward for the proprietors, make out the visitors' bills and purchase the necessary wines and provisions.

It was evident that the imperialists were gathering their forces for a combined attack on Aidzu, and as Nakai said, if they could not crush him with their troops they now had in the field, they never would succeed. An American sailing barque named the "Despatch" was hired for $3,000 to carry men to Hirakata. On August 25 I saw 200 men march through Shinagawa to embark for the north; on the 22nd a large body of Chôshiû men arrived, and were billetted in Sen-gaku-ji, the temple in which the 47 Faithful *Rônins* were buried. And Nakahara Naosuké, a Satsuma man, usually believed to be their admiral, but in reality an artillery officer, had been sent to Echigo with four companies of artillery, and great things were expected of him.

August 26 I went to see Katsu, and found him greatly relieved in his mind as the result of a visit paid to him on the previous day by Komatsu. He said that the Castle of Sumpu had been handed over to the head of the Tokugawa clan on the 18th, but that the territories assigned to him had not yet been vacated by their previous possessors, who were very difficult to move, so that the lands at present available did not exceed 80,000 *koku* in extent. He hoped Kaménosuké, by which he, of course, meant the guardians of the six-year-old child, would not go to any great expense in building or in engaging crowds of retainers. He said that the "Kaiyô-maru," flagship of Enomoto Idzumi, who commanded the Tokugawa fleet, was supplied with provisions by that clan. Enomoto, otherwise known as E. Kamajirô, was a naval officer who had been trained in Holland.

I asked him whether the son of the late Prince of Mito was dead, or whether he was to be set aside in favour of Mimbu Taiyu. On this he gave me the following account of Mito politics, which had been a puzzle for many years to foreign observers.

Noriakira, commonly called "the old prince of Mito," was the younger son of Harutoshi, and his childhood's name (*zokumiô*) was Keisaburô. His elder brother Narinobu was the heir, and his portion as a younger brother was only 200 *koku*. Being averse to society on account of his deafness, he spent his time in wandering about the country and acquainting himself with its actual condition, and no doubt then formed the habits of simplicity and frugality which distinguished him in after life. On the death of Harutoshi, Keisaburô's elder brother succeeded him, but dying shortly afterwards, left the prince-dom vacant. By that time two parties had gradually formed themselves in the Mito clan, one which supported the ancient Kiôto policy of the author of the *Dainihonshi*, the other which, fearing Keisaburô, had formed an alliance with the Court of Yedo, at that time ably directed by Midzuno Echizen no Kami, father of Idzumi no Kami until lately a member of the *Go-rôjiû* (Council of State). The latter party schemed to set aside the claims of Keisaburô in favour of an adopted heir from the then Shôgun's family. A will of the late prince was however discovered, in which he declared his desire that the claims of blood should be respected, and his brother Keisaburô be appointed as his successor. The will was backed up by a strong party known as the *Tengu-ren*, and Keisaburô became prince of Mito. This was in 1834 when he was about 30 years of age.

The new prince was bent on carrying out certain reforms which the luxurious habits of the age appeared to him to render necessary. With this object he obtained a relaxation of the ancient rule which required the head of the house of Mito to be a resident in Yedo, the more easily because he had rendered himself obnoxious to the *Go-rôjiû* by the ostentatious manner in which he seemed to reprove their pomp and luxury by the simplicity of his own dress and manner of life, and retiring to his province on the pretext that it was necessary for him to superintend personally the government of the clan, he devoted his time to drilling troops in the only fashion then known in Japan. Openly advocating the supremacy of the Mikado, and non-intercourse with the western world (*Kin-ô, jô-i*), he secretly introduced into the province every Dutch scholar he could find, and made himself acquainted as far as was then possible with the resources of European science. With incredible labour he constructed from drawings contained in old Dutch books a frigate, which long lay at Yokohama for the protection of foreigners, but had he believed been since broken up. The report of his doings having been brought to Yedo, it was represented to the *Go-rôjiû* that the drilling of men and building of warships were merely preparations for carrying out the traditional Mito policy, and that the prince was plotting rebellion. In 1844 he was compelled to retire into seclusion, and he was succeeded by his son, the late prince, then a mere boy.

In 1851 a Dutch man-of-war made its appearance at Nagasaki, and caused no slight consternation at Yedo. It was said that the Nagasaki Dutchmen were becoming restive, and that the ship was merely a precursor of the English, who at that time bore the detestable reputation of being a nation of pirates ready for any violence. Succeeding events proved to the Shôgun's government that Japan was in danger of being forced into relations with European Powers; the advent of Admiral Perry and his squadron heightened their alarm to such a degree that they yielded to the voice of public opinion, and inviting the old prince of Mito to Yedo admitted him again into their councils.

In 1858 the Shôgun Iyésada died, and the old prince of Mito wished to secure the succession to his seventh son, who having been adopted as heir to the house of Shitotsubashi was in a legitimate position to become the Shogun's heir. It was at this moment that Ii Kamon no Kami came into power, and though it is uncertain whether he had a previous understanding with the Ki-shiû family that they should furnish an heir, it is certain that he found them ready to comply; and his influence was strong enough to force old Mito to retire a second time into private life, and to order Echizen, Tosa and Uwajima, who had supported the Mito claims, to resign their *daimiates* to their sons. The assassination of Ii Kamon no Kami a couple of years later by Mito men was the consequence.

Other influences were then at work in the west. The Kiôto policy and the expulsion of foreigners had been warmly espoused by Satsuma and Chôshiû. Hence the bond of union between them and the *Tengu-ren* section of the Mito men, who on hearing that civil war had broken out at Kiôto, made their appearance before the castle of the prince, and demanded that he should carry out the clan policy. This action proving unsuccessful they raised the standard of rebellion on Mount Tsukuba in Hitachi, whence they were expelled by the forces of the Shôgun after some hard fighting. Their fate among the mountains of Kaga was a well-known tale. Takéda Kô-un-sai, who had been driven by the force of circumstances to join them, and several hundred of his comrades were beheaded at Tsuruga. The remainder of the *Tengu-ren* fled to Kiôto, where the ex-Tycoon, at that time still bearing the name of Shitotsubashi, took them into his pay. Now that the revolution of the previous January had so completely changed the face of affairs, these men had returned to their native province, headed by Takéda Kinjirô, a grandson of Kô-un-sai, and their political opponents, whom they styled *Kan-tô* (traitors), finding themselves on the losing side, and likely to be in a perilous minority, since the *Tengu-ren* were backed up by the imperialists, had gone off to Echigo, to the number of some five hundred. The *Tengu-ren*, out of gratitude to their former protector, had determined to set aside the heir in favour of Mimbu Taiyu, Shitotsubashi's younger brother, and had despatched agents to bring the latter back from Paris.

That day Nagaoka, younger brother of Higo, arrived by sea with a large number of retainers, and on the 29th the Prince of Awa marched in great pomp with about 600 men. On the 28th I had a great feast with Komatsu, Inouyé Iwami and young Matsuné of Uwajima. One of the party drank so much *saké* that he lay down on the floor and went to sleep. In half an hour's time he woke up quite sober, and was able to repeat the process.

From September 8 to October 17 Adams and I were absent on a wild-goose chase after the Russians who were reported to be occupying the northern coast of Yezo, in the course of which H.M.S. "Rattler," in which we had embarked, was wrecked in Sôya Bay. But as this was not concerned with the progress of political events in Japan, it seems unnecessary to occupy space in narrating our experiences. We were rescued by the French corvette "Dupleix," Captain du Petit Thouars.

CHAPTER XXXIII

Capture of Wakamatsu and Entry of the Mikado into Yedo

November 6th was celebrated with much pomp and ceremony as being the Mikado's birthday. A review of the 2/x regiment was held at Yokohama to which Sir Harry invited Sanjô, now promoted to the rank of *Udaijin*. The foreign men-of-war joined with the Kanagawa fort in firing a royal salute, which the party viewed from my upstairs verandah overlooking the bay. Besides Sanjô we had Nagaoka Riônosuké, Higashi-Kuzé and Madé-no-kôji. A luncheon at the minister's residence followed, and the swords of honour sent out from England for presentation to Gotô and Nakai in recognition of their gallant conduct on the 23rd of March were handed over. Nakai at once girt his on, and strutted about with a gold-laced cap on his head, to his own great delight and the intense amusement of the rest of the company. As it happened to be the second day of the Yokohama races it was proposed that the whole party should adjourn to the race-course. Sanjô and Higashi-Kuzé, who had on white *maedaré* and black-lacquered paper caps, declined. I rode down with Madé-no-kôji and Nagaoka, who enjoyed themselves immensely. On returning home I took Nakai in with me and gave him tea; in exchange for this he informed me that news had been received of the capture of the outer castle of Wakamatsu, and that only the inner ring and citadel remained in possession of the defenders; also that the Mikado would arrive at Yedo about November 27.

Next day I went up to Yedo on board a Japanese steamer belonging to the Yokosuka arsenal with Sanjô, Higashi-Kuzé, Nagaoka and Nakai. By a mistake of Nakai's about the hour of leaving I kept the party waiting for me at the custom house and a mounted messenger had to be sent to fetch me. I hurried down and found them sitting quietly smoking. They protested against my apologising. How different from some Europeans!

On the 8th Mitford and I went to call on Katsu. His wife had gone off to Sumpu, but he remained to do the "head muck-and-bottle-washing" (*miso-zuri*) of the clan. He hoped to obtain the Shimidzu lands, amounting to 110,000 *koku*, for feeding the retainers who had lost their lands and pay. Instead of the lands promised in Oshiû, part of Mikawa and the whole of Enshiû had been conceded, but the *daimiôs* hitherto entitled had not yet given up possession. Keiki had preceded Kaménosuké to Sumpu. Katsu also had a story that Brunet, one of the French military instructors, went off in the Kayô-maru, when the Tokugawa naval squadron left the Yedo anchorage on the night of October 4. We doubted this, as we knew that he had just received promotion in the French army. Nevertheless it turned out to be a fact. He was accompanied by another officer named Caseneuve, and several other Frenchmen.

We also visited Nakai, who gave us a first-rate dinner from the hotel. He said that the citadel of Wakamatsu was captured on October 29. He had also received a letter from Kido placing the question of the Mikado's coming to Yedo beyond a doubt. And as we returned to my house we found that great preparations were already being made in anticipation of His Majesty's arrival, roads being re-made, bridges rebuilt, and ward-gates being constructed in side streets where they had never existed before.

One of my *betté* Sano Ikunosuké called to present his thanks for having been selected by the court to remain one of the Yedo guard for foreigners; all my sixteen men had been engaged for this service. He said that the Shimidzu domain had been granted provisionally to the Tokugawa family for the purpose mentioned by Katsu. To-day (November 9) was the last day on which men of the Tokugawa clan could send in their names for service under the Mikado. In some cases they would receive about half their former revenue, but others would be better off than before, because their allowances, though nominally diminished, would be issued in rice instead of in money at a low fixed rate. That evening Mitford and I dined with Nagaoka at the Higo *yashiki* in Shirokané, close by our legation, Higashi-Kuzé and Nakai being the other guests. It was a dinner in European style served from the hotel in a picturesque two-storeyed house, built in the garden so as to command a view over the *nagaya* in the direction of the bay. In the garden there were some splendid trees and pretty shaded nooks. Hosokawa himself was there, very fat and amiable, very small eyes and a tendency to "fly catching." On the 10th I went back to Yokohama.

At an interview on November 16 between all the Foreign Representatives, Higashi-Kuzé and Térashima, the Japanese ministers stated that the castle of Wakamatsu had surrendered on the 6th November to the imperial forces. The two princes, father and son, in robes of ceremony and preceded by a retainer carrying a large banner inscribed with the word "surrender" (*kô-fuku*), and followed by the garrison, likewise in robes of ceremony and with their heads shaven, came to the camp of the besiegers and gave themselves up. The castle and all the arms it contained were handed over, and the two princes retired into strict seclusion (*kin-shin*) at a Buddhist monastery in the town. Nakamura Hanjirô, the chief of the staff (*gun-kan*) wept when he went to take delivery of the castle and its contents. It was a pleasure to us to see how the countenances of some of those who had to listen to the story fell, for they had counted on a desperate resistance on the part of Aidzu to defeat the imperialist party and frustrate the policy of the British Legation. Now that this exciting episode was at an end, the speedy submission of the other northern clans could be counted on with confidence. The detailed report made by the

Hizen clan, dated November 16, published in the *Kiôto Gazette*, shows that the garrison included *samurai* soldiers 764, troops of a lower class 1,609, wounded 570, outlaws from other territories (*rônin*) 462; women and children 639, officials 199, civilians 646, personal attendants of the princes 42, and porters 42. There was no record of the number of men killed in the defence. On November 19 I went to Yedo with Captain Stanhope, Charles Wirgman the artist, and Dr Siddall, after breakfasting with Du Petit Thouars on board the "Dupleix." Adams and William Marshall went up by road. On our arrival possession was at once taken of Siddall, by a Japanese doctor named Takéda Shingen, and he was carried off to the military hospital established at the Tôdô *yashiki* in the Shitaya quarter. On the 21st Adams, Mitford, Marshall and Wirgman went to the Yoshiwara and had a feast in fine style at the Kimpeirô, part of which was furnished in western style for such Japanese guests as liked it. The admission of Europeans into that quarter of the town, from which they had until then been jealously shut out, was hailed as the dawn of a day of friendly intercourse of the frankest character. Next evening I gave a great entertainment at my own house. There were three *geishas* from Shimmei-mae and two *taiko-mochi* (jesters). We kept it up boisterously till midnight. The jesters performed a foreigner and his escort arriving at the Kawasaki ferry on the way to Yedo, and meeting with the usual obstruction at the hands of the men placed there to guard the crossing. My escort men also exhibited some comic scenes, much to their own satisfaction and to the delight of the household, who were admitted to a room at the top of the stairs. Letters arrived from the chief to say that he wanted a stand erected for himself opposite to the gate of our former legation buildings, in front of Sen-gaku-ji, for him to see the Mikado pass in (he was expected to reach Yedo on the 27th), and that Higashi-Kuzé and I must go down to Yokohama on the 24th to see himself. We wrote in reply to say that a stand was altogether an impossibility, seeing what Japanese etiquette was in such matters, and that I could not leave Siddall alone in Yedo without some one to interpret for him. So next day Wirgman and I went over to see Siddall, and found that the Tôdô *yashiki* had now been turned into a general hospital. Here we fell in with old Ishigami, the Satsuma doctor who married a daughter of old Freiherr von Siebold by a Japanese mother, a very cheery person. After lunch we went with him and a crowd of other Japanese doctors to Uyéno, intending to get in and examine the scene of the fighting that took place on July 4, but the gate was shut in our face, and though we waited and argued patiently for a whole hour with the sentries, we could not convince them that we might safely be admitted. I think our Japanese companions felt even more annoyance than we did. The gateway was riddled with bullets, and it was evident that a pretty stiff fight had taken place there in July.

We stayed the night at the hospital, and spent a jolly evening with Ishigami and another doctor named Yamashita. Next morning, in spite of the bitter cold, we went round the wards with the doctors. All the state apartments of the *daimiô's* mansion (*go-ten*) had been converted into wards, and provided with iron bedsteads and hair mattresses. There was a very plucky little Tosa boy, probably a drummer, who had had his foot amputated. Then our attention was attracted to an aristocratic-looking little surgeon from Chôshiû, with his sleeves turned up like ruffles over a pair of delicate little wrists. At noon there came the two brothers Notsu, Shichizayémon and Shichiji, who persuaded Wirgman and myself to go to the Yoshiwara with them, instead of keeping an engagement with Nakai. Siddall compounded *mistura vini gallici*, and after partaking of this we started on a journey of exploration. It was a terribly cold day, with a gale from the north-west coming straight down the plain from the snowy peak of Asama-yama and other mountains of Shinshiû. The Yoshiwara lay right out in the middle of the rice-fields, occupying a considerable extent of ground. It was entered through a narrow gate at the end of a long causeway. After passing this gate, we were introduced into the upstairs rooms of a rather shabby house, evidently much frequented by the Satsuma clan. *Geishas* were of course sent for, and

the *saké*-cup circulated merrily. Towards nightfall it was proposed
that we should visit the Kimpeiro, a hideous house furnished in
what was regarded as European style; but we stayed there only a
few minutes, and then returned to the house where we had first
been entertained. Here we had more drinking, dancing and playing at *nanko*. In this game a wooden chopstick is broken up into
six pieces, of which each player receives three. He puts in one
palm as many as he thinks fit, and guesses at the total of what his
hand and the hand of the other player contain. If he guesses right,
the loser has to drink, and his turn comes to give the challenge.
Evidently this is the way to get speedily drunk. We stopped there
till a message came from Ishigami to say that he was awaiting us
at another house to drink sober again. We went in search of him
to a restaurant on the river bank, the Yu-mei-rô, where much
singing, dancing, drinking and *nanko* followed, till we had had
enough of it, and came home by boat to the hospital, accompanied
by three of the *geishas*. Next afternoon the artist and I said good-
bye to Siddall, and walked over to Nakai's, but not finding him at
home, we went to the hotel for refreshment, where we sat down
in the garden and found ourselves overwhelmed with melancholy
at the ugliness of the building. For five cups of tea and a bundle
of Manila cheroots the manager charged us a dollar, to the surprise and horror of the Japanese boy who waited on us. To him it
appeared an exorbitant demand. The cheroots were perhaps worth
20 cents, which left 16 cents for a cup of tea. On getting home to
Takanawa we found that Rickerby, the proprietor and editor of the
Japan Times, had just arrived in a boat from Yokohama to witness
the ceremony of the following day.

November 26, 1868. About ten o'clock in the morning the
Mikado passed into Yedo, having slept at Shinagawa. Mitford,
the artist, Rickerby and I saw the procession from the open space
recently created in front of the new gate of what had previously
been Sir Harry Parkes' diplomatic residence, now transformed
into a sort of foreign office. The display could not be described as
splendid, for the effect of what was oriental in the courtiers' cos-

tumes was marred by the horribly untidy soldiers with unkempt hair and clothing vilely imitated from the west. The Mikado's black-lacquered palanquin (*hôren*) was to us a curious novelty. As it passed along the silence which fell upon the crowd was very striking. Old Daté, who rode between it and the closed chair in which the Mikado was really seated, nodded to us in a friendly manner. Rickerby wrote and published an excellent newspaper account of the whole show a few days afterwards in the *Japan Times*. In the afternoon he and I walked to Kai-an-ji, a Buddhist religious house at Shinagawa, celebrated for its very pretty plantations of maple. From there we proceeded to a house of entertainment, the Kawasaki-ya, close by, to drink *saké* and crack jokes with the girls about the Prince of Bizen, who had passed the night there. The house was full of troops from the west, but they scarcely took any notice of us, and in fact all those we met on the road ignored us completely. It must be said that whenever I went out into the streets of Yedo I was always accompanied by my Aidzu *samurai* Noguchi and from four to six of my personal escort of the *betté-gumi*.

On the 28th Sir Harry and Dr Alford the Bishop of Victoria, Hongkong, came up to Yedo, and were entertained in European style at the new foreign office by Daté and Higashi-Kuzé. Machida and Môri, young Satsuma men, were also of the party. Both had been in England and spoke English, the latter, who was only about one-and-twenty, particularly well.

Next day Mitford and I went to call on Nakai. We met there Machida, and Yamaguchi Hanzô, a Hizen *samurai*, who brought with him a man who had just returned from Shônai. He reported that Shônai had submitted on the 4th instant, and that two foreigners, one an American, the other an Englishman, both from Hakodaté, were present as spectators. Nakai, who was a member of the local government of the city, now called the Tô-kei-fu instead of Yedo, had given in his resignation because he found that the governor-general instead of placing confidence in himself and the other officials, was in the habit of upsetting their arrangements on the complaint of a few wretched tradespeople.

Wirgman and I went down to Yokohama on the 30th, walking as far as Namamugi-mura (where Richardson was murdered in 1862), whence we took boat across to the foreign settlement. At Kawasaki-ya in Shinagawa we fell in with Notsu Shichizayémon and Ijiû-in, with two Kurohané men and one from Utsunomiya, companions on the occasion of our visit to the Yoshiwara, of whom the Satsuma men were on their way home. There was a large consumption of *saké* and Japanese dishes, and much Doric Japanese spoken. Further on, at Mmé-yashiki or Bai-rin, as it had now become the fashion to call this very pleasant half-way house between Yedo and the ferry at Kawasaki, we found Oyama, who was like the others returning to Kagoshima as the civil war was practically at an end. We drank many parting cups together, and then walked with him to his hotel at Kawasaki. The road was full of homeward bound Satsuma men and Tokugawa people going to Sumpu. A report had got about that difficulties had arisen between Satsuma and Higo, and that the latter in conjunction with Arima and Chikuzen were going to fall upon the great clan; that in consequence of this the troops were rushing off as fast as possible to forestal the attack. Another rumour, much credited by the French Legation, was that Aidzu surrendered only on condition that the Satsuma troops should be withdrawn from the east and north of the country; and the Mikado come to Yedo. But as others besides the Satsuma fighting men were also going home, these stories were easily discredited. On December 3 I went back to Yedo, half-way in a *kago* (common palanquin) from Kanagawa, and on foot from Kawasaki. At Bai-rin I met Midzuno Chinami, hurrying back from Shimoda where he had been put ashore from H.M.S. "Manila." Here was the late governor of Yokohama, who last year used to ride in a state palanquin (*nagabô*), with a large cortége and preceded by running footmen crying *shitaniro*, "down on your knees," now travelling in a wretched cheap hackney *kago*, without a single retainer. For all that he seemed cheerful enough. A good deal of my time in those days was passed in the compilation of an English-Japanese dictionary of the spoken language and in reading Japanese novels. On the 4th I went over to the hospital, where I found Siddall with his hands full, wounded men from Echigo having begun to arrive. Willis had gone on from Echigo to Wakamatsu to look after the Aidzu wounded, of whom there were nearly 600 in the castle when it was surrendered. My new pony "Fushimi," a present from Katsu before he left Yedo, carried me splendidly; the imperialists who crowded the streets appeared to admire with envy a black chimney-pot hat which I was wearing. On the 5th I went there again to pass the night with Ishigami and Yamashita. They complained bitterly of one Mayéda Kiôsai, who had been appointed chief of the hospital, and said that the patients had threatened to cut his head off because he spent his time in driving about the city in a carriage and pair instead of attending to his duties. The reflection came naturally that you cannot make a silk purse out of a sow's ear, or give the standing of an European physician to a Japanese half-educated apothecary.

On December 9 I went to the hotel to dine with Machida. The indispensable Nakai was there, also Okubo and Yoshii. The latter had left Wakamatsu on December 1st. Willis was there looking after the wounded, of whom he said there were at least two thousand on the Aidzu side alone. Snow was lying deep both in Echigo and Aidzu. Shônai was pacified, and the whole country might now be said to be at peace, a state of things which of course was displeasing to anti-imperialists, whether among diplomatists or merchants. Information had arrived that the murderers of the two sailors of H.M.S. "Icarus" in August 1867 had been discovered; they were from Chikuzen and the party to which they belonged was said to number nine in all. This of course would be welcome news to the Tosa people. It was strange that retainers of Chikuzen, who entertained Admiral King so hospitably in January should have been guilty of such a wanton crime. The newly issued paper money, known as *kinsatsu*, was much discussed, and it was evidently creating a great ferment among the people. Uchida, the mayor (*nanushi*) of Kanasugi, who had been to see me a few days earlier, said that a refusal to receive these notes in the payment of taxes was the only obstacle to their free circulation. Nakai denied the correctness of the statement that taxes might not be paid with them, but he thought that in the end it would be found necessary to establish a proper banking system by giving authority to the great firm of Mitsui to issue notes against a reserve of coin or bullion. It was a matter of vital importance to the imperial government, which had not found any money in the Tokugawa treasury, and the Mikado had always been kept very poorly supplied by the Shôgun's ministers.

CHAPTER XXXIV

Enomoto with the Runaway Tokugawa Ships Seizes Yezo

On December 11 Machida came to me with a report from Hakodaté that the Tokugawa pirates, as they were styled after their refusal to surrender and their exodus from Yedo Bay on October 4, had landed at that port from the "Kaiyô-maru" and her consorts. The rebels were led by a member of the French military mission sent out in 1866 who had gone off with them when they left the bay, and it was very annoying for the French Legation that this officer should have violated the neutrality proclaimed by the Minister, and have joined rebels against the authority of a sovereign with whom France maintained friendly relations. A fight had ensued near Hakodaté, in which a large number of imperialists were killed or wounded. The Yokohama foreign press however represented that the Mikado's men had won the victory at a place about 15 miles from the port. According to despatches received from the consul the rebels had had by far the best of it. The foreign residents were in a great state of alarm. The consul wrote thus: "As the enemy approach we shall retire towards the hill; if he comes nearer, we shall go up the hill, and should it come to the last extremity we shall have no resource but to put our trust in an over-ruling Power." Nakai came on the 13th to talk about the new paper money, and the difficulties with foreigners to which it would give rise. Tom Glover's opinion was quoted in favour of a paper circulation, but he did not himself agree that a merchant, who was naturally an interested party, should be regarded as an authority on currency. This paper money had been issued to the troops, who forced the shop-keepers and the hucksters on the high roads to accept it in payment. But this could not go on long, for the paper did not pass current amongst the civilian population. We spoke about the state of foreign relations. He admitted that the old distrust of foreigners still existed; the foreign representatives were regarded as a necessary evil, to be endured, but not to be embraced. Nothing pleased the Mikado's government so much as to see the diplomatists living at Yokohama, and the idea of asking their advice upon any matter was never entertained for a moment. In fact the representatives were looked upon much in the same light as the agents (*rusui*) of the *daimiôs*, *i.e.* persons sent to Japan by their respective governments to receive the Mikado's orders, whenever occasion might arise. The representatives were themselves partly to blame for this state of things. Fine houses, comfortable living and whole skins at Yokohama were doubtless preferable to makeshifts and dangers at Yedo, but for all they knew or could learn of pending international questions they might just as well be resident at Hongkong.

Another day was spent with the mayor of Kanasugi and three or four retainers at the classical theatre Kongo-daiyu in Iigura-chô, to see *Nô* and *Kiôgen*. Minami Torajirô was also among the audience. This was a young Aidzu *samurai*, who had come in the previous April to see me, with his countryman Hirozawa, when I had a great argument with the latter about Japanese politics and especially about the part our Legation had taken. It was the first time a foreigner had been present at this kind of theatrical performance. *Nô* is a sort of tragedy or historical play, *Kiôgen* is low comedy. There is no scenery and the costumes are all in an ancient style. The stage is about 24 feet square, and a long passage on the left connects it with the greenroom from which the actors make their appearance. There are 200 *Nô*, and printed books of the text, known as *utai*, could be bought for a trifling cost. They are delivered in slow recitative to the accompaniment of the music, or rather dissonance, of the fife and small drum. The orchestra, likewise dressed in antique fashion, were seated on campstools at the back of the stage. The *Kiôgen*, which pleased me most, were *Suyéhirogari*, in which a sort of Moses Primrose is sent to Kiôto to buy a fan, and is cheated by the merchant into paying 500 *riô* for an umbrella, and *Oba ga saké*, in which a fellow having tried in vain to persuade his aunt, a rich old curmudgeon, to give him some *saké*, puts on a devil's mask and frightens her into submission, while he goes to get drunk at the store room where the liquor is kept. He threatens to eat her if she looks his way; her cries, "Oh fearful to behold; spare your retainer's life"; her anger on discovering in the drunken and sleepy demon her rascally nephew, were infinitely diverting. The *Nô* I could not understand until I borrowed the book from a Japanese lady in the next box, and was enabled to follow the text. This was *Hachi no ki*. Sano Genzayémon, who has been deprived of his feudal estate, entertains a Buddhist priest at night. Having no food to offer him nor fuel to warm the room, he cuts down his own favourite dwarf plum, cherry and pine trees, and makes a fire of the branches. In return for this the holy man persuades the Lord of Kamakura to restore to him his forfeited lands. There were at that time three other companies of *nô–yaku-sha*; Kanzé-daiyu, Kôshô-daiyu and Kompara-daiyu. The audience consisted entirely of the *samurai* class.

The two Aidzu princes were brought to the suburb of Senji on December 15. Matsudaira Higo (now, like all other rebels, shorn of his title of *Kami*) was placed in the charge of Inshiû, and Wakasa in that of Chikuzen. Ninnaji no Miya, the commander-in-chief of the imperialist forces engaged in Echigo and Oshiû, was expected to arrive in Yedo on the 17th. And on or about the 16th the foreign representatives were officially notified of the restoration of peace. The guns and stores of H.M.S. "Rattler" which had perforce to be left behind at Sôya when the "Dupleix" brought us away, had been offered to the Mikado's government and accepted by them. This was the news heard from Okubo and Yoshii, whom I met at Nakai's on the 16th.

As a measure of protection for British and French subjects at Hakodaté the "Satellite" and "Vénus" were despatched thither on the 14th, the former conveying our secretary of legation Adams. His *History of Japan*, vol. II., gives an account of what he saw and did there. Up to the 5th of December however that place had not been threatened with an attack from the fugitive Tokugawa navy.

My old writing master Tédzuka, who came to call, gave me the following statistics about his clan. The chief's name was Sengoku Sanuki no Kami, and he ruled over territories assessed at 30,000 *koku*. The actual yield to the *daimiô* was 16,000 *koku* of rice; of this 8,000 *koku* were accounted for by fiefs held by retainers; 4,000 *koku* were required for the maintenance of the *daimiô's* personal establishment, and an equal quantity went in expenses of administration. The latter included official salaries, cost of journeys to court at Yedo, of soldiers in the field, arms, etc. The clan numbered no more than 60 *samurai* families. Its constitution as regards the offices of *karô* and *yônin* was the same as in the case of other clans. In accordance with orders promulgated in No. 5 of the Kiôto Gazette the old practice of hereditary office-holding had been abolished, and a system of promotion by merit established in its stead. In order to carry out these new arrangements, the hereditary fiefs of the retainers ought he thought to be equalized.

When I went back to Yokohama on the 18th I found that news had been received of the capture, which I had anticipated, of Hakodaté by the runaway Tokugawa ships, and the flight of Shimidzu-dani with all his staff. The consul was, as one would expect, very seriously alarmed. And from the "Satellite's" expedition to the spot one could not look for any results of importance.

On December 21 a great conference was held at the legation in Yokohama of the chief with Daté, Higashi-Kuzé, Komatsu, Kido, Machida and Ikébé Goi (of Yanagawa in Kiûshiû). The first thing they wanted was that Sir Harry would arrange to give Yamaguchi Hanzô a passage on board an English man-of-war to Hakodaté, in order that he might open negotiations with the rebel leaders. The chief seemed to me to fear that this would involve him too much in the opinion of the public as a partizan of the imperial government, and he adviced them instead to despatch a common messenger across the strait from Awomori bearing written offers to treat. Seeing that they could not induce him to accede to their request, they acquiesced in his suggestion, but in such a half-hearted manner as to make one doubt whether they would follow his advice. A great discussion took place on the Christian question, in which the Japanese spoke very reasonably, and Sir Harry likewise, until he unfortunately lost his temper over the arguments used by Kido, and made use of very violent language such as I do not care to repeat. The result was that they promised to write Notes to the Foreign Representatives announcing the Mikado's intention of showing clemency to the converts. Next day Ikébé came to me to explain the theory of the imperial paper currency, but I did not understand much of what he said, and we wandered off into other subjects, especially Christianity. The old fellow professed to be not only an admirer of its doctrines, but also a believer. In the afternoon the chief and I went to return Daté's call at what had formerly been the governor's official residence at Tobé, a suburb of Yokohama. They had a long conversation, especially about the Christian question and the representative system, and Sir Harry tried to pump him about the future capital. Would it be at Kiôto, Ozaka or Yedo (Tôkei, Tôkiô), for we had of course read what Okubo Ichizô had written on the subject early in the year. The old prince gave him some very polite "digs in the ribs" about his violent language of the previous day, saying that when people became animated in conversation, spectators were apt to think that a dispute was going on, whereas instead of that being the case, it was merely that the speakers were in earnest; and naturally every man desired to express his own views. The chief replied that his animation was caused by the extreme regret he felt at seeing the Japanese do things that were prejudicial to themselves. On this Daté observed that it did them good now and then, to be got angry with (*hara wo tatté morau*). This set the chief "a-thynkynge," and as we were driving home he suddenly said: "I think they would never have spoken to the other representatives about Christianity, had it not been for the little piece of excitement I got up yesterday." I replied: "Well, it may be so but I think you hurt Kido's feelings; he shut up at once and preserved a marked silence." "Did you think so?" says P. "I am sorry to think he was offended." I then said: "If you will excuse my speaking freely, I believe that although that sort of thing may have a good effect in a particular case, it makes the Japanese dread interviews with you." Upon this the chief declared that he would have Kido to breakfast the next morning, and begged me to write him as polite a note of invitation as possible.

CHAPTER XXXV

1869—Audience of the Mikado at Yedo

On January 2 I went back to Yedo (as we long continued to call the Eastern capital, being, like most Englishmen, averse to innovation). The city had been opened to foreign trade and residence on the 1st, and dear old William Willis was installed as H.M. vice-consul. He and Adams had returned on December 29th, the one from caring for the wounded in Echigo and Aidzu, the other from Hakodaté.

On January 5 we had an audience of the Mikado. On this occasion Sir Harry asked a large number of naval and military officers, besides Captain Stanhope, R.N., of the "Ocean," and Colonel Norman, in command of the 2/ix. So the list of persons to be presented, fixed originally at twelve, was increased to double that figure. As usual the chief had mismanaged the business, because he insisted on doing it all himself instead of leaving details to his subordinates, and he did not even know the names of those who were to be presented. The Squadron furnished a guard of a hundred marines. The costumes worn were very various, especially those of the legation and consulate men. It was a terribly cold day, snow falling, which changed into sleet, and then into rain by the time we reached the castle, and what made things worse was that we had to ride on horseback instead of driving in carriages. The audience took place in the palace of the Nishi-no-Maru, just inside the Sakurada Gate. We were allowed to ride over the first bridge, past the usual *géba* or notice to alight, right up to the abutments of the second bridge, where we got down. Here we were met by Machida, who conducted us into the court-yard, from which we ascended at once into the ante-chamber. The Prince of Awa, Sanjô, Higashi-Kuzé, Nakayama Dainagon and Okubo came in and exchanged the usual compliments. Then we were ushered into a very dark room, where the Mikado was sitting under a canopy rather larger than that used at Ozaka. It was so dark that we could hardly distinguish his dress, but his face, which was whitened artifically, shone out brightly from the surrounding obscurity. The Prime Minister stood below on the right and after H.M. had uttered a few words of inquiry about the Queen's health, and congratulated the chief on continuing at Yedo as minister, read the Mikado's speech. To this Sir Harry replied very neatly. After the audience, which took up no more than five minutes, was over we cantered back to the old Legation building in Takanawa, now converted into a branch of the Japanese Foreign Office, where we had great feasting beginning by an entertainment in Japanese style, very good of its kind, followed by a late luncheon supplied from the hotel. Awa and Higashi-Kuzé presided in our room. The American Minister and the North German Chargé d'Affaires were also present. Higashi-Kuzé proposed the health of the Queen, the President and the King of Prussia *en bloc*, after which we drank to the health of the Mikado.

Katsu had come back to Yedo, and early in January was to start again for Sumpu, to lay a foundation for negotiation with the Tokugawa runaway ships at Hakodaté. On the 8th a review of the English troops in garrison at Yokohama was held for the entertain-ment of the prince of Awa, as our particular friend, and a party of young Court nobles. These were not men of political importance, and I do not think we ever heard of them again. The rapidity of the fire from the Snider rifles was a surprise to all the spectators.

On the 9th the chief and I having ridden up to Yedo in the morning, he had an important interview at Hama-goten, the sea-side palace of the Shôguns, with Iwakura. Kido, Higashi-Kuzé and Machida were also present. Many compliments were

offered to Sir Harry, and assurances of the gratitude which the
Mikado's government felt for the hearty recognition they had
received from Great Britain. To this succeeded some confidential
conversation. It was intended that the Mikado should return
to Kiôto to be married, and also for the performance of certain
funeral rites in honour of his late father. When these ceremonies
were completed he would come again to his Eastern Capital to
hold a great council of the empire. The date of this was not yet
fixed; it might be in the first month of the Japanese calendar,
perhaps in the third. Sir Harry advised Iwakura to notify this to
all the Foreign Representatives. The question of foreign neutrality and the situation at Hakodaté were then discussed. Iwakura
denounced very eloquently those of the ministers who, while
recognising the Mikado as sovereign, granted the status of bel-
ligerents to the Hakodaté pirates. Sir Harry declared for himself
and the French Minister, Outrey, that no neutrality existed, and
that they did not recognize Enomoto and his associates as bellig-
erents; nor did von Polsbroek. To this Iwakura responded: "Why
does the American Minister still allege a declaration of neutrality
as the ground of his refusal to hand over the 'Stonewall Jackson'
to the lawful government?" Sir Harry replied that the declaration in question had been of very great service to the Mikado's
government, that but for its existence Enomoto would now be in
possession of the iron-clad ram, and that he himself had been
mainly instrumental in procuring the signature of that document.
This was quite true. An excellent lunch was served from the hotel,
and we parted from our hosts just at sundown, both parties well
satisfied with each other.

I went on the 10th January to visit Siddall at his hospital on the
other side of the city; there I found Willis, who on the way there
from Tsukiji, the foreign Settlement, had been threatened by a
swash-buckler. We discussed together the means by which the
Japanese government might be induced to apply for the services of
Willis for a year in order to assist them in establishing their general hospital. So we told Ishigami that Siddall was to be recalled

to the Legation, and that Higashi-Kuzé must ask for Willis. The Mikado had presented Willis with seven rolls of beautiful gold brocade, and Higashi-Kuzé wrote a nice letter thanking the dear old fellow for his services to the Japanese wounded warriors.

On January 12 we heard that the "Kaiyô-maru" had sailed from Hakodaté, with her rudder lashed to her stern; her destination was supposed to be Esashi, where fighting was going on. It was believed that the pirates were running short of money and rice. The Ainos were reported to have joined the people of Matsumae in resisting the pirates.

I had some interesting conversation with Ikébé Goi, whom I went to see on the 13th. At his lodgings I met a young man named Yoshida Magoichirô, a councillor of the Yanagawa clan. We talked about Christianity, and Ikébé cited the Sermon on the Mount as a composition that pleased him more than anything written by Buddhist or Confucian Sages. I remarked that the Christian religion reversed the Chinese saying: "Do not unto others as ye would not that others should do unto you"; upon which he quoted the command to turn the other cheek to be smitten. After a little he began to talk about my chief's violence in conference, and said: "Now in his case, when he gets in a rage, so far from offering the other cheek, I feel inclined to kick him out of the room." Ikébé said that the Mikado would leave for Kiôto about the 17th or 18th January, and that a notification had been issued announcing his departure during the first decade of the 12th month, to return again in the spring.

On the morning of the 15th I was summoned by the chief to Yokohama in a great hurry to attend a conference between Iwakura and the foreign colleagues. I rode the 20 miles on my pony "Fushimi," in two hours and a half without drawing bridle, and arrived at the Legation to find the conference just assembling. Iwakura addressed to the colleagues pretty much the same arguments as he had made use of at Hama-goten on the 9th. They put a number of questions to him by way of reply, and at last said they could not give answer to so important a matter as he had laid before them without mature consideration. Iwakura then said that he would take the opportunity of saying a few words about the causes of the existing political situation. The present Mikado was the descendant of sovereigns who ruled the country more than 2,000 years back; the Shôgunate was an institution not more than 700 years old. Still, the power had been in its hands, and it was during the continuance of its authority that the Americans came to the country in 1853. The Shôgun's people were sharp enough to see the necessity and advantage of entering into relations with foreign countries, while the Mikado's Court, followed by the greater part of the nation, professed the anti-foreign policy. The country thus became disturbed, and the authority of the Shôgun could no longer be maintained. Then both the Mikado and the Shôgun died, and the latter's successor, a man of ability, was able to see the absolute indispensability of a government directed by the Mikado. Sincerely convinced of this, he surrendered the power into the hands of the Mikado, not as a mere gift, but because it was the only way of solving the political difficulties which existed. Thereupon the Mikado's government changed its policy with regard to foreigners, and did what never could have been done under the late sovereign, that is, entered into relations with the Treaty Powers. Hitherto our relations had been merely commercial, but the government hoped that they would improve and become something like those which existed among European and other civilized nations. The foreign ministers replied that they would consult together, and send him a reply without delay.

Sir Harry came up on the 19th from Yokohama to tell Iwakura the result of yesterday's conference of colleagues on the subject of neutrality. We were to have met him at Hama-goten, but when we got there we found the gates shut, and since no orders had been received to admit us, we came away. As we were returning to the Legation Mori came after us in a great hurry, and begged the chief to turn back, but he refused, and said Iwakura might come to see him. This message was misunderstood by Mori, and there was more delay, but at last everything was arranged, and

Iwakura came at half-past seven to the Legation, accompanied by Higashi-Kuzé. Iwakura had sent through Mori to ask me to come to Yedo, in order that he might speak to me personally, but I took no notice of this request, treating it merely as an invitation to the chief, or rather as a request to me to be present on the 19th in order to perform interpretation. He asked Sir Harry what had been the result of the conference of foreign ministers, and all he could say was that it had been adjourned. It appeared that the colleagues were willing to make a declaration that the war was over, but were not willing to give up the "Stonewall Jackson"; and that in order to justify her retention they would not withdraw their notifications of neutrality. To us this appeared highly illogical. The chief, after Iwakura had repeated all his arguments and had added that so far from desiring to get hold of the "Stonewall" in order to attack Enomoto, the Mikado's government were determined to offer him lenient terms, declared that in his own opinion the war had ceased, and that the neutrality lapsed with it; and that he was ready to state this in writing. Iwakura said that the Mikado was very desirous of knowing the answers of the ministers, and had therefore ordered him to stop behind for five days in order to try to settle this question and to rejoin him at Shimidzu, a port on the Tôkaidô, that he would like to get Sir Harry's answer confidentially, so that the Mikado might have a pleasant souvenir to carry away with him. Another thing Iwakura said was that the Mikado's government had made a sufficient display of power by reducing the provinces of Oshiû and Déwa in six months, whereas in former wars twelve years had been nothing extraordinary; that their intention was to adopt a humane line of conduct, and they had therefore ordered the two Tokugawas of Sumpu and Mito to proceed against the remaining rebels, and if they succeeded in arranging matters Keiki would be pardoned and restored to favour. He had himself seen Katsu, who believed that the offer of lenient terms would induce submission. The Mikado's government would not however consider any capitulation satisfactory that was not accompanied by a complete surrender of arms and ships of war. If the rebels proved obstinate they must be reduced by force. This frank statement drew out a favourable reply from Sir Harry. Iwakura also appeared to be alarmed about the attitude of Russia, and asked whether she might not possibly enter into an alliance with Enomoto. The chief thought this unlikely. The interview lasted three hours, and ended with many thanks from Iwakura and apologies for having kept Sir Harry waiting at the gate of Hama-goten. The chief on his side undertook to do everything possible to bring his colleagues round to his view and to induce them to send in their answer by the 25th, and he engaged to publish his own reply in the *Japan Herald* of the same day; that would be as decisive a manifestation of his policy as he could possibly give. I was greatly pleased myself to find that he had now made up his mind to "go the whole hog."

The Mikado passed through Takanawa about eight o'clock the following morning, on his way back to Kiôto. His train appeared to be smaller than on the occasion of his entry. News arrived from Hakodaté on January 21 that the "Kaiyô-maru" had got on the rocks near Esashi and was expected to stick there; her guns had been thrown overboard and buoyed.

The sentences on Aidzu and Sendai were promulgated on the 21st, with the penalties inflicted on other *daimiôs* of the northern provinces, and a few more who had held out to the last. The Aidzu princes were let off with their lives, but the whole of their territo-ries were confiscated. Sendai was reduced from 625,000 to 280,000 *koku*. The reigning prince was made to retire into private life, and was succeeded by a son of our old friend, the Daté of Uwajima.

On the 22nd a further conference of the ministers was held with reference to the question of withdrawing the declarations of neutral-ity, and the little Italian minister, who came up to Yedo on the 23rd, assured us that only Sir Harry and Polsbroek were willing to consent, the others having refused. Letters however arrived from Sir Harry showing that all the colleagues had agreed to write a *note identique* acknowledging that the war was over, but demanding a short delay in order to concert measures for the simultaneous withdrawal of their notifications. Also a note from him instructing me to arrange an interview with Iwakura for Adams and Montebello (Secretary of the French Legation) in order that they might hand to him the petition which the Tokugawa rebels at Hakodaté had asked M. Outrey and Sir Harry to forward to the Mikado. The translation of this document was made and sent off at once. Then, after learning from Higashi-Kuzé that 2 o'clock was fixed for the interview, Mitford and I went off to Kido, to whom I gave a copy of the *note identique* about neutrality. He at once pitched on the 'short delay' clause as unsatisfactory, but I could only give him my opinion that this was inserted as a sort of compromise; it was better, I said, for the Mikado's government that all the ministers should agree to recognise that the war was over, even with this slight drawback, than that only two of them should have recognied the fact and the other four have continued to declare themselves neutral. A memorandum reached us from Adams stating the nature of the final arrangement, and suggesting that the government should make it generally known by publishing the correspondence in their official Gazette. Then I went off to Higashi-Kuzé's place, to meet Adams, Montebello and Dubousquet,* who arrived there about a quarter past two. Proceedings began by Montebello handing in Outrey's copy of the *note identique*; Iwakura at once pointed out the sentence in the letters of the English and French ministers which spoke of 'a short delay,' and asked what was its meaning. Both Adams and Montebello replied that they had no authority to say anything on this point, but they undertook at his request to write to their chiefs, and obtain if possible a definite date. I also whispered to Yamaguchi Hanzo to tell Iwakura afterwards that Kido already knew all about the compromise. The business of handing over the petition of the Tokugawa rebels was then proceeded with. Iwakura was told that in delivering this document the ministers did not offer any opinion on its contents, and they renounced for themselves any idea of acting as

---

* An officer ot the French Military Mission who devoted himself to the study of the Japanese lauguage, and ultimately became interpreter to the French Legation.

mediators; but that as the Japanese Foreign Minister had expressed to both of them his desire to learn if possible the feelings and intentions of the fugitives, they were very glad to have this opportunity of complying with his request.

Iwakura replied that these men had now been declared to be rebels, and the two clans of Mito and Sumpu had been ordered out against them. That the proper course to adopt in presenting the petition which he had just read was to send it through the chiefs of those two clans. From the hasty glance he had cast over the document he could not profess to judge of its merits, but he was glad to see that the petitioners had some desire, however slight, of returning to their allegiance. (But if he had been aware of the extreme bumptiousness of the letter to Parkes and Outrey in which the petitions were forwarded, he would hardly have thought so.) Still, while thanking the ministers, and appreciating the disinterestedness of their motives, he could not consent to receive the petition through such a channel. Would the ministers mind forwarding it through the Tokugawa clan?

Adams and Montebello declined to have any business relations with the clan, and after some urging from the French side, Iwakura said he would accept the petition temporarily and give his answer to-morrow. We then returned home and Adams despatched a report to the chief. Next day (the 25th) in the afternoon came fresh instructions. Adams was to go to Iwakura, inform him of the surprise felt by both ministers at the refusal to accept the petition, and state that the expression 'a short delay' in the *note identique* respecting neutrality meant what it said. After consultation with Montebello, it was decided to ask for an interview with Iwakura at ten o'clock on the morning of the 26th, and a letter to that effect was sent off to Higashi-Kuzé. Before an answer could be received at the Legations there came a letter from Yamaguchi Hanzô written by Iwakura's order, refusing to accept the petition, and saying that as he was going down to Yokohama next day to see the representatives on the subject of neutrality, he would take the opportunity of speaking to the two ministers about the other matter as well. However Higashi-Kuzé's reply to our letter soon arrived to say that Iwakura's departure was postponed for a day, and that he would see the two secretaries as proposed by them.

On the 26th, as I was unwell, Mitford went in my stead to interpret for Adams. Iwakura receded from his previous attitude, and declared himself ready to receive the petition from the two ministers, but that he intended to return it to the Tokugawa fugitives without taking any notice of its contents. Further, that he was determined to demand from the ministers the meaning of the words 'a short delay.' He also addressed a letter to the two ministers thanking them for the trouble they had taken about the petition, which he characterized as impertinent; it would therefore have to be returned direct. This was a slap in the face for our two chiefs, who ought never to have presented the petition, considering the covering letters received by them, which threatened to throw down the gauntlet to the Mikado's government if it did not leave them in quiet possession of Yezo. But Sir Harry was drawn on by the fear that Outrey would manage to get the petition accepted, and thereby win prestige; but if so, Outrey's little game was frustrated by Iwakura's good luck or perspicacity.

The following day I had to rush down to Yokohama for Iwakura's meeting with the Foreign Representatives. He asked what they meant by 'a short time.' They appeared to him to have had time enough already. When issuing their original notifications of neutrality they had acted immediately on receiving the communication of the Mikado's government, and why hesitate now? The colleagues fenced a little with the question and then retired into another room to consider their answer. When they emerged they announced their readiness to issue proclamations in fourteen days' time at the furthest. With this Iwakura was forced to be content. But our chief had gained the battle, and was correspondingly

---

* Originally the flagship of Captain Sherard Osborn, when in command of the Chinese flotilla brought out by H. N. Lay, and afterwards bought by Satsuma.

rejoiced. Iwakura left the same afternoon in the "Keangsoo"* for the port of Toba in Shima. Higashi-Kuzé informed the ministers that Yedo was to be the capital of the country, after the Mikado's return there next Japanese New-Year, but this decision was not at present to be made public. He displayed a map of the city and offered them the whole waterside from the Kanasugi Bridge to the Hotel, except the Owari *yashiki*, where the Foreign Office was to be, for sites on which to build Legations. All but Sir Harry declared their unwillingness to accept sites; I remarked to myself that he was gradually getting out of the bad habit of believing all the Japanese told him to be lies.

CHAPTER XXXVI

Last Days in Tokio and
Departure for Home

A week before this Iwakura had sent me a present of a beautiful lacquered cabinet by way of thanks for the trouble he
said I had taken in interpreting for him on various occasions, and
on January 28th when I returned to Yedo I found a letter from
Saméshima Seizô with presents from the Prince of Satsuma,
Okubo, Yoshii and himself. The letter said: "Prince Satsuma
wishes me to give you his thanks for your kindness and the trouble
you have hitherto taken for his sake. He presents you the two
boxes, and the rest, though a little, Okubo, Ioxy and myself present you merely to thank you for your kindness. We hope you will
always keep them as our memorial." The prince's present consisted
of a silver boat in the form of a peacock (called *Takara-buné*, or
Ship of Treasures) and the lacquered stand, besides two rolls of
white silk; Yoshii sent two pieces of Kiyomidzu porcelain, and
each of the others two pieces of white satin brocade. The spelling
Ioxy, which is in accordance with ancient Portuguese orthography
of Japanese names, shows that this letter came in English.

My translation of the sentences of the northern *daimiôs* was
published in the *Japan Herald* of January 30. This state paper completed the discomfiture of the *som-bak-ka* diplomats, the term
invented by the Japanese for application to the foreign ministers

who supported the cause of the Shôgunate as far as was possible for them.

February 11 was the Japanese New Year's Day, which I passed at Yedo. Rice-cakes (*mochi*) had been prepared and decorated in proper fashion with a Seville orange and fern, and dried fronds had also been hung up in the alcove (*toko-no-ma*) of my study. Silk cushions had been provided for a guest and myself to sit on as we ate our *zôni*. This is a soup in which pieces of fried *mochi* are soaked; on the first day of the year one is eaten, on the second two, on the third three. A New Year's drink called *toso* was also provided; this is a sweet *saké* mingled with spices; it is drunk from porcelain cups of gradually decreasing size, placed on a stand. Every member of the household came in turn to wish me a happy new year, and to thank me for the *O Sébo*, or presents given to them at the end of the year, proportioned to the respective merits of the different servants. Next evening I gave an entertainment to my Japanese escort, to which the Legation writer Ono Seigorô, Mitford's teacher Nagazawa and my household were also invited. Mitford and I sat on white brocade cushions at the head of the room, with a big lacquered brazier between us; the Japanese guests were ranged along both sides of the room and at the end. I had to apologize by way of form for sitting on a cushion, which as host I ought not to have done, under the pretence that it made my knees sore to squat on the mats. There was a great deal of stiff conversation at first, until the *saké* was brought, and the waiting women from the restaurant that supplied the dinner, the *geishas*, Noguchi's wife and a very clever girl from Yokohama made their appearance. We had comic dances, charades, songs and the Manzai new year's dance. An immense quantity of *saké* was drunk, and every one departed well pleased by twelve o'clock.

Alexander Siebold, who had been in France with Mimbu Taiyu, had at last arrived back in Japan, releasing me from the duties that had kept me two years longer than provided by the existing rules about leave of absence. On February 14 he and I went to call on Katsu, who had been such a valuable source of political information ever since the downfall of the Shôgunate. Katsu thought the Tokugawa rebels at Hakodaté would give in their submission. At parting he gave me his *wakizashi* (short sword), and we separated with many mutual expressions of regret. He was quartered in an out-house at the Kishiû *yashiki*, where old Takénouchi, a Kishiû retainer who had been our purveyor of news and papers current among the *daimiô yashikis*, was also living; we had to go into his rooms and drink a cup of tea; there I found the secretary of Daté Gorô, a distinguished Kishiû official, to whom I sent my farewell compliments. We got back to my house just in time to rush off again, to a dinner at the hotel, given by Higashi-Kuzé in honour of my departure. Besides Mitford, Siebold and myself, the other guests were the Prince of Bizen, the Court Noble Ohara Jijiû, Kido, Machida, Mori (afterwards known as Mori Arinori), Kanda Kôhei a professor at the School of Languages and editor of one of the recently established Yedo newspapers, and Tsudzuki Shôzô of Uwajima. It was a very pleasant party. Little Bizen greeted me very politely, said he had heard a great deal about me, but had not had a previous opportunity of meeting me, so had taken advantage of this farewell entertainment to make my acquaintance. I had the post of honour at the left of Higashi-Kuzé. After dinner they drank my health in bumpers of champagne and wished me a pleasant voyage. Every one had some commission to give me. The Japanese government wanted six expensive gold watches and chains. Tsudzuki Shôzô, who presented me with a farewell letter written in the name of old Daté, asked for a copy of Hertslet's Treaties. Besides parting gifts from the Prince of Satsuma, Okubo, Yoshii and Saméshima, I received presents from Machida, my Japanese escort men, and a host of other people, including Kido. The latter spoke to me confidentially after dinner about the advantages which would result to Japan from opening a port in Corea; not so much material as moral, by teaching the Coreans to look abroad outside their own country. Both he and Mori talked about the native Christians and asked my advice. I counselled moderate measures, and long Notes to the Foreign Ministers now and then to keep them quiet. I acknowledged the difficulty of instilling the idea of toleration into the minds of the whole Japanese people by Act of Parliament, and told them of the disabilities under which Protestants had lain in Spain until recently, but I did not see the advantage of Mori's suggestion of allotting lands in Yezo to the Christians with the free exercise of their religion. Tsudzuki confided to me as a great secret the intended visit to England of a young Bizen *karô* named Tokura. Altogether we spent a very satisfactory evening, in spite of the long distance we had to go for our dinner.

Next day I left Yedo for good. As I passed the entrance to the barracks of the Legation mounted escort of London policemen, Inspector Peacock and the men came out to wish me a pleasant journey. Noguchi, Mitford's teacher Nagazawa and four of my Japanese guard came down the road as far as Mmé-yashiki, where we had a parting cup. Higashi-Kuzé sent me a complimentary letter, regretting my departure, and presenting me with a big lacquered cabinet as a mark of the Mikado's appreciation of all I had done to smooth diplomatic relations. Kido also wrote, asking me to communicate to him any information about Japanese affairs that I might pick up in Europe, promising to answer any letters I might send him, wishing me a fine voyage and a happy arrival in England.

On the 24th February I sailed from Yokohama in the P. and O. steamer "Ottawa," 814 tons, master Edmond. Lady Parkes also was on board on her way to England, and the English community paid her the compliment of sending out a band, which played "Home, sweet home" as the anchor was weighed. I felt the tears come into my eyes. It would be hard to say whether they were caused by the emotion that a much-loved piece of music always produces, or by regret at leaving a country where I had lived so happily for six years and a half. With me I had my faithful Aidzu *samurai*, Noguchi Tomizô.

Glossary

akéni, a wicker trunk for luggage.

anata, you.

arimasu, is, there is.

ashigaru, common soldier in the service of a baron.

awabi, rocksucker, a species of univalve shell-fish, *haliotis japonicus*, which furnishes also mother-of-pearl.

bai-shin, arrière vassal.

baku-fu, 'military power,' term applied to the *de facto* government by its adversaries, see p. 187.

betté, a member of the corps of guards enrolled for the protection of the foreign legations.

betté-gumi, the corps of guards, see betté.

bugiô, governor, commissioner.

cha-dai, present made to an innkeeper, which takes the place of tips to waiters and chambermaids.

cha-no-yu, tea-drinking with an elaborate ceremonial.

chô-téki, rebel against the sovereign.

daimiô, baron, see p. 23.

denka, Highness.

doma, the pit in a theatre.

dôshin, constable.

fudai, lesser barons, vassals of the Tokugawa family, see p. 23.

gai-koku bugiô, commissioners for foreign affairs, corresponding to our Under-Secretaries of State.

gai-koku-gata, official of the department of foreign affairs.

gaimushô, ministry of foreign affairs.

Gautama, family name of the founder of Buddhism.

géba, notice to alight from horseback.

gei-sha, a female musician, employed at dinner-parties.

gijô, head of an administrative department, see p. 321 n.

gisô, a councillor acting as intermediary between the Mikado and the Tycoon, q.v.

go-ké-nin, an ordinary retainer of the Tokugawa family.

gorôjiû, the Shogun's council, see p. 61.

goten, the palace of a *daimiô* or baron, as distinguished from his castle.

gun-kan, army-inspector.

hakama, a pair of wide trousers.

haori, a mantle.

harakiri, self-immolation by disembowelment, described at p. 377.

hatago, charge for entertainment at an inn.

hatamoto, name of lesser vassals of the Tokugawa family, see p. 23.

heika, Majesty.

hikido kago, a palanquin with sliding doors, see p. 215.

hiraketa, civilized.

homma da, it is true.

hommaru, keep of a castle.

honjin, literally 'headquarters,' mostly used for the official inn at a posting town.

hôren, phoenix-chariot, name given to the Mikado's state palanquin.

ichibu, a silver coin, value varying from 10d to 1s 8d, according to the rate of exchange.

in-kio, applied to the retired head of a family, whether noble or commoner, see p. 181.

jimbaori, war-surcoat.

jingasa, war-hat.

jinketsu, a man of mark, cleverest man.

jinrikisha, vulgo 'rickshaw,' a light carriage for one person, drawn by a man.

jin-shin fu-ori-ai, unsettlement of the popular mind.

jô-dan, elevated floor.

jô-i, expulsion of barbarians.

jô-yaku, a chief clerk.

jû-bako, consisting of a pile of open boxes for holding food, the top one of which alone has a cover.

kago, a palanquin.

kaiseijo, government school for teaching European languages.

kai-shaku, 'best man' of one who is performing *harakiri*, q.v. p. 377.

kakké, dropsy of the lower limbs.

kaku-rô, unceremonious appellation of the Tycoon's Council, see p. 179.

kami, title corresponding to earl, baron, when following the name of a province, but after the name of a government department equivalent to minister.

kami, English 'sire.'

kami-shimo, costume consisting of hempen trousers and mantle, worn on occasions of ceremony.

kamon, a class of barons, see p. 22.

kan-tô, rebel, traitor.

kara-yô, the Chinese style of running-hand script.

kari-ginu, gala dress of a noble.

karô, the higher class of hereditary councillors of a baron.

katakana, a Japanese syllabary, corresponding to our Roman alphabet.

kenshi, an official inspector.

kerai, retainer of a baron.

kiki-yaku, agent for the sale of a baron's produce as rent paid in kind.

kin-ô, jô-i, honouring the sovereign and expelling barbarians.

kinsatsu, gold-note, paper-money so-called.

kinshin, voluntary self-confinement in expiation of an offence.

kiôgen, farce.

kiri-bô kago, a palanquin suspended from a pole of Paulownia wood.

kô-fuku, surrender.

koku, a measure, equal to about 5 bushels, used also as a measure of land assessment, see p. 23.

kokushi, a baron whose fief comprised one or more provinces.

kôtei, Emperor, the same as the Chinese term 'hwang-ti,' see p. 169.

ko-t'ou, Chinese expression meaning to knock the forehead on the floor.

kwambaku, Grand Vizier, see p. 187.

kwan-rei, administrator for the Shôgun, see p. 25.

kubô-sama, title applied by the people to the Shogun, and meaning 'civil ruler'; sama is the equivalent of the French 'monsieur,' see p. 179.

kumi-gashira, vice-governor.

kurô, trouble, used in the sense of 'thank you.'

mae-daré, apron.

machi-kata, municipal officer.

metsuké, an official with no administrative functions, whose duty was to report, if necessary, on the proceedings of others, variously translated, see pp. 8, 125, 260, 293.

mochi, a cake made of glutinous rice.

Mikado, the ancient title of the Japanese sovereign.

mikoshi, a god's litter carried in religious pageants.

mirin, a sweet liquor brewed from rice.

miso, a paste made from a bean called *ko-mamé*, and used chiefly in the preparation of soup.

mokusa-nuri, lacquered articles showing a sea-weed pattern.

naga-bô, long pole, used to denote a palanquin with an extra long pole.

nanko, name of a game, see p. 432.

nanushi, mayor.

Nippon, same as Nihon, the Japanese word which we have corrupted into Japan.

nôshi, a noble's court dress.

nô-yakusha, actor of the classical drama, see p. 439.

ôbiroma, hall of audience.

ohaguro, a dye composed of galls and sulphate of iron, used for staining the teeth.

ohiruyasumi, midday rest; *o* is an honorific prefix.

okoyasumi, a slight rest.

oku-go-yû-hitsu, an official private secretary.

ometsuké, see metsuké; *o* is the honorific prefix.

ô-metsuké, a chief *metsuké*, q.v.; *ô*, chief.

onna-gochisô, an entertainment at which women were employed to amuse the guests.

on-ye-riû, a Japanese style of running-hand script.

o-shiro-jô-in, a hall in the Tycoon's palace inside the castle.

o yasumi nasai, 'good-night,' literally 'be pleased to repose.'

peggi, corruption of a Malay word, used in Japan in the sense of 'go away.'

rambô-rôzéki, disturbance and violence, see p. 165.

rei-hei-shi, name of an envoy sent by the Mikado to worship at the tomb of Iyéyasu at Nikkô.

riô, a Japanese coin of account, formerly equivalent to about 1 1/3 Mexican dollar.

riô-gaké, a pair of wicker-trunks for luggage, suspended from the opposite ends of a pole carried on the shoulder.

rô-jiû, councillors of the Shôgun, see pp. 26 and 61.

rônin, a run-away retainer of a baron, see p. 72.

rusui, a person left in charge of an establishment during the absence of the owner or master.

sakana, food taken with liquor; as it chiefly consists of fish, it is often used in the sense of 'fish' as a food.

saké, a light liquor brewed from rice, mostly drunk mulled.

sakuron, 'a political discussion,' see p. 325.

samurai, a member of the military class, entitled to wear a pair of swords, a longer and a shorter one, the latter being an over-grown dirk.

sanyo, councillor, see p. 294.

sarampan, corruption of a Malay word used in Japan in the sense of 'break,' 'broken.'

sazai, a shell-fish named *Turbo cornutus*; the shell also furnishes mother-of-pearl.

sei-i-tai-Shôgun, the full title of the Tycoon or Shôgun, see p. 179.

seishi, herald, harbinger.

sengaré, a familiar word meaning son, and used only by the father in speaking of him.

sessha, a self-depreciatory word used for the pronoun of the 1st person.

shibori, a kind of crape resembling the Indian bandhanna.

shibukami, thick paper rendered tough by being soaked in the juice of the unripe persimmon fruit.

shinsen-gumi, a body of armed *samurai* or two-sworded men, recently raised.

shirabé-yaku, director in an administrative department.

shishinden, name of the Emperor's hall of audience.

shiro-in, private drawing-room.

shisetsu, literally 'purple snow,' a patent medicine.

shitaniro, down!

Shôgun, the *de facto* ruler of Japan when it was opened to foreign trade in 1859, see p. 19. By foreigners he was usually called 'the Tycoon,' which means 'great prince,' a title properly belonging to the sovereign. It seems to have been originally used in diplomatic correspondence with Korea; see also p. 169.

sô-kwai-sho, municipal office.

sôsai, chief minister, see p. 325.

shugo-shoku, office of the guardian of the Mikado's person, see p. 320.

shuku-yakunin, alderman of a posting-station.

shussei, administrator, minister.

tai, Serranus marginalis, sometimes called sea-bream.

taikomochi, a professional jester.

tatéba, a halfway tea-house between two posting-stations.

tengu-ren, 'goblin-band,' name assumed by a society of seditious men of the military class.

tenshi, the central tower rising from the keep of a castle.

tensô, an official whose duty it was to report to the Mikado the decisions of the Shôgun.

tobayé, caricature.

tokonoma, the shallow recess or alcove in a room, originally the bedplace; in front of it was the place of honour.

Tô-kai-dô, properly speaking the row of provinces along the coast between Ozaka and Yedo, but also applied to the high road from Kiôto to Yedo.

toso, a new-year's drink, see p. 456.

tozama, descendants of barons who had submitted to the supremacy of Iyéyasu, see p. 23.

tsutsushindé oru, used to express the retirement of a personage in order to signify his acknowledgment that he has committed an offence against his superior.

tycoon, see Shôgun.

utai, the classical drama of Japan.

wakizashi, the short sword or dirk worn alongside of the fighting sword by a member of the military class, and not laid aside within doors as the other is.

wasabi, *Eutrema wasabi*, root of a plant belonging to the same order as horse-radish.

yakata-buné, house-boat.

yaku-biô, official indisposition.

yakunin, official.

yamato-nishiki, cotton brocade.

yashiki, the hotel of a baron or lesser noble, also at trading centres the depôt for the sale of a baron's produce received as payment of rent or taxes in kind.

Yedo, the original name of Tôkiô, the seat of government.

yogi, large stuffed bed-gown, used as a coverlet.

yônin, hereditary councillor of a baron, of lower rank than *karô*, q.v.

yû-geki-tai, literally 'brave fighting-men,' see p. 324.

yukata, a cotton bathing-gown.

zoku-miô, the name borne by a male child until adolescence.

zôni, a soup eaten at New Year, see p. 456.

Index